UNSPORTSMANLIKE CONDUCT

Other *Pearls Before Swine* Collections

Because Sometimes You Just Gotta Draw a Cover with Your Left Hand
Larry in Wonderland
When Pigs Fly
50,000,000 Pearls Fans Can't Be Wrong
The Saturday Evening Pearls
Macho Macho Animals
The Sopratos
Da Brudderhood of Zeeba Zeeba Eata
The Ratvolution Will Not Be Televised
Nighthogs
This Little Piggy Stayed Home
BLTs Taste So Darn Good

Treasuries

Pearls Freaks the #%# Out*
Pearls Blows Up
Pearls Sells Out
The Crass Menagerie
Lions and Tigers and Crocs, Oh My!
Sgt. Piggy's Lonely Hearts Club Comic

Gift Books

Friends Should Know When They're Not Wanted
Da Crockydile Book o' Frendsheep

UNSPORTSMANLIKE CONDUCT

A *Pearls Before Swine* Collection

by Stephan Pastis

Andrews McMeel
Publishing, LLC
Kansas City • Sydney • London

Pearls Before Swine is distributed internationally by Universal Uclick.

Unsportsmanlike Conduct copyright © 2013 by Stephan Pastis. All rights reserved. Printed in the United States of America. No part of this book may be used or reproduced in any manner whatsoever without written permission except in the case of reprints in the context of reviews.

Andrews McMeel Publishing, LLC
an Andrews McMeel Universal company
1130 Walnut Street, Kansas City, Missouri 64106

www.andrewsmcmeel.com

13 14 15 16 17 RR2 10 9 8 7 6 5 4 3 2 1

ISBN: 978-1-4494-2774-0

Library of Congress Control Number: 2012949302

Pearls Before Swine can be viewed on the Internet at
www.pearlscomic.com

These strips appeared in newspapers from February 28, 2011, to December 4, 2011.

To my wife, Staci, who upon seeing this cover said,
"That seems inappropriate."

And to my kids, Thomas and Julia, who laughed.

Introduction

It had been a long few months.

Every day I checked my email, and every day I found the same thing.

No furious readers.

Not an angry email to me. Not a whiny email to an editor.

It was a drought of immense proportion.

So I checked another usually reliable source, Google News. There, I could enter "Pearls Before Swine" in the search field and always be sure to see a complaint.

And what did I find?

Nothing.

Something was dreadfully wrong.

For years, I have prided myself on being an edgy cartoonist. (Well, edgy for the newspaper comics page. Which is to say boring for anywhere else.)

So I racked my tiny cartoonist brain for at least five minutes, which is the longest I can think about any one subject.

All to figure out one thing.

What had happened?

Had I gone soft? Had I lost my edge? Was my work now as easy on the hearts and minds of newspaper readers as *Hi and Lois* and *Ziggy*?

I had no time to spare.

So I rushed to the drawing table.

First, I knew I had to draw a Sunday strip. Being edgy on a Sunday always gets more complaints.

But what would the strip be about?

Violence.

Someone getting their butt kicked. That always ticks people off. Especially on a Sunday.

Better yet, a violent act on the part of a character most people usually love. (That works like gold, because readers feel a strong attachment to the character, and don't want to see him be mean.)

But that wasn't enough. It had to have swearing. In fact, I needed to suggest the "F" word in an unmistakable context where it could not be mistaken for any other word.

But that *still* wasn't enough. So I did what any edgy cartoonist would do in that situation.

I threw in a church.

Surely, this was enough.

But no.

I could not chance it.

So I added one more finishing touch:

Confusion.

You see, your average Sunday funnies reader hates to be confused. Because being confused makes people feel dumb. And when people feel dumb, they complain.

So I ripped apart the panels of the strip. And rearranged them in a new order.

The reader would now have to put the panels in the right sequence *in order to even read the stupid thing*. Something even *I* had trouble doing after I finished the strip.

Oooh, this was good.

And the result was this:

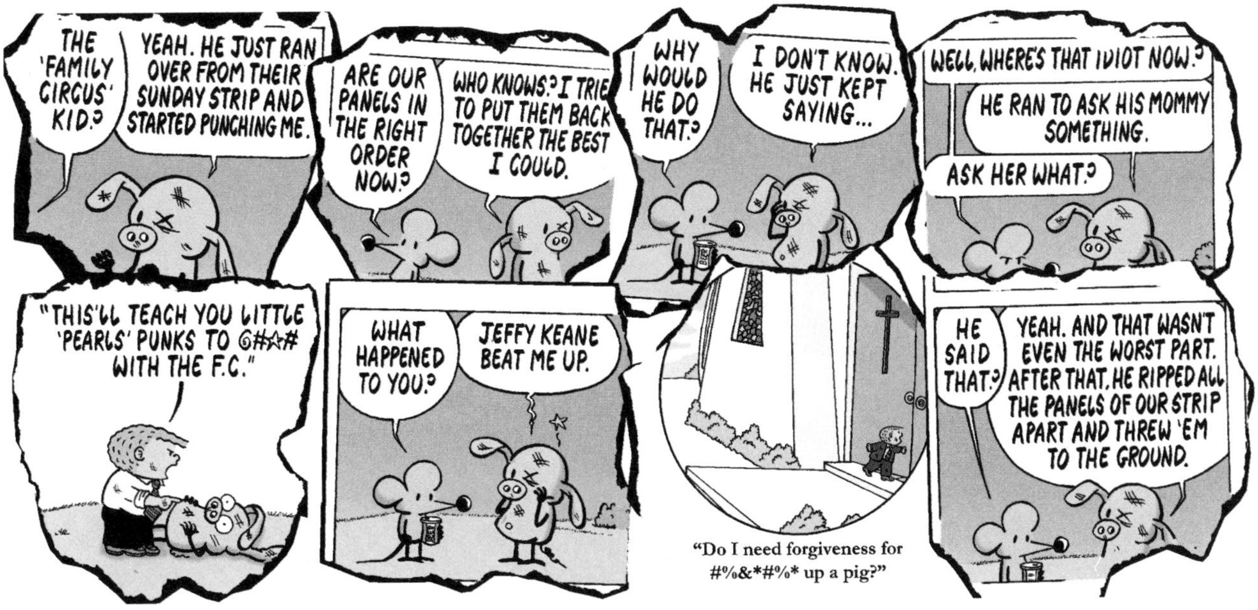
THE 'FAMILY CIRCUS' KID?
YEAH. HE JUST RAN OVER FROM THEIR SUNDAY STRIP AND STARTED PUNCHING ME.
ARE OUR PANELS IN THE RIGHT ORDER NOW?
WHO KNOWS? I TRIE TO PUT THEM BACK TOGETHER THE BEST I COULD.
WHY WOULD HE DO THAT?
I DON'T KNOW. HE JUST KEPT SAYING...
WELL, WHERE'S THAT IDIOT NOW?
HE RAN TO ASK HIS MOMMY SOMETHING.
ASK HER WHAT?
"THIS'LL TEACH YOU LITTLE 'PEARLS' PUNKS TO @#☆# WITH THE F.C."
WHAT HAPPENED TO YOU?
JEFFY KEANE BEAT ME UP.
"Do I need forgiveness for #%&*#%* up a pig?"
HE SAID THAT?
YEAH. AND THAT WASN'T EVEN THE WORST PART. AFTER THAT, HE RIPPED ALL THE PANELS OF OUR STRIP APART AND THREW 'EM TO THE GROUND.

And on the day it ran in newspapers, I rushed to my email in-box.

And waited. And waited.

And waited.

And then, like pennies from heaven, it came.

From: (ADDRESS DELETED)
To: pearlscomic@gmail.com

Mr. Pastis:

I want to tell you how shocked and offended I am by today's Pearls Before Swine comic strip. Not only do you depict a beloved Family Circus child as a horrible bully, you also clearly telegraphed the most offensive word in the English language, not once, but twice, and in one of these instances, this child is yelling this word into a church. This is not the kind of material I want to read when I eat my grapefruit and oatmeal for breakfast.

Sincerely yours,
(NAME DELETED)

I was so excited, I stood. And with my arms raised, I cheered.

I had not only generated a complaint.

I had ruined someone's grapefruit.

At last.

The drought was over.

Stephan Pastis
February 2013

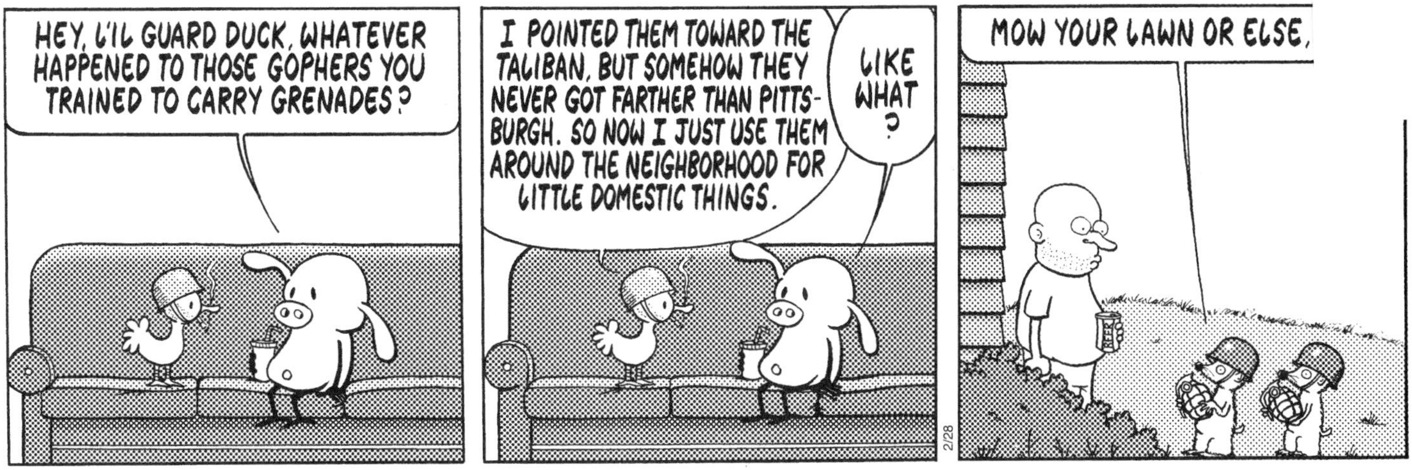
HEY, LI'L GUARD DUCK, WHATEVER HAPPENED TO THOSE GOPHERS YOU TRAINED TO CARRY GRENADES?
I POINTED THEM TOWARD THE TALIBAN, BUT SOMEHOW THEY NEVER GOT FARTHER THAN PITTSBURGH. SO NOW I JUST USE THEM AROUND THE NEIGHBORHOOD FOR LITTLE DOMESTIC THINGS.
LIKE WHAT?
MOW YOUR LAWN OR ELSE.
2/28

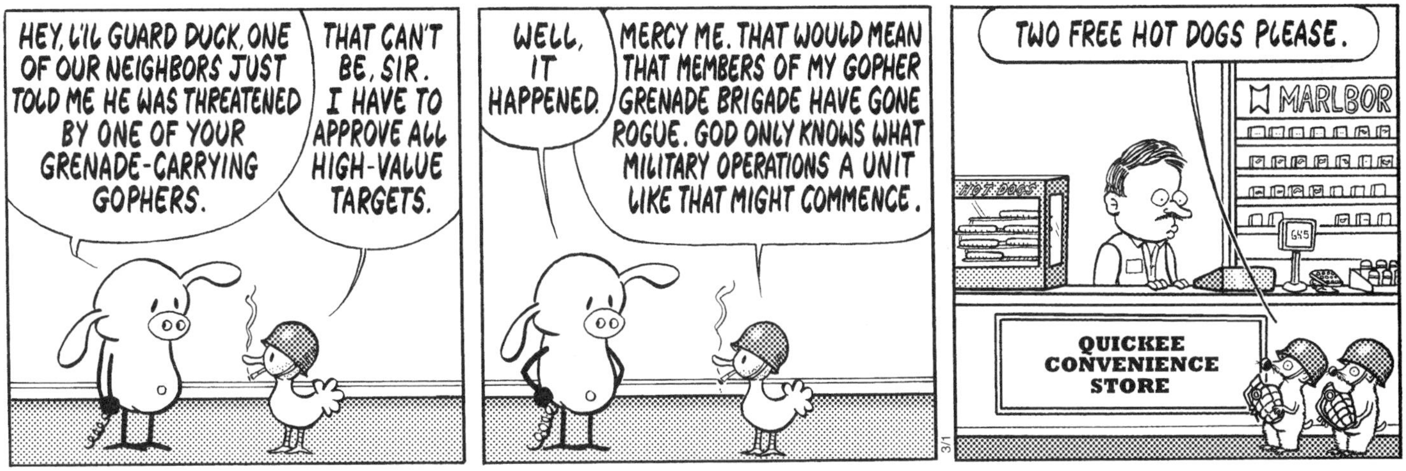
HEY, LI'L GUARD DUCK, ONE OF OUR NEIGHBORS JUST TOLD ME HE WAS THREATENED BY ONE OF YOUR GRENADE-CARRYING GOPHERS.
THAT CAN'T BE, SIR. I HAVE TO APPROVE ALL HIGH-VALUE TARGETS.
WELL, IT HAPPENED.
MERCY ME. THAT WOULD MEAN THAT MEMBERS OF MY GOPHER GRENADE BRIGADE HAVE GONE ROGUE. GOD ONLY KNOWS WHAT MILITARY OPERATIONS A UNIT LIKE THAT MIGHT COMMENCE.
TWO FREE HOT DOGS PLEASE.
MARLBOR
HOT DOGS
QUICKEE CONVENIENCE STORE
3/1

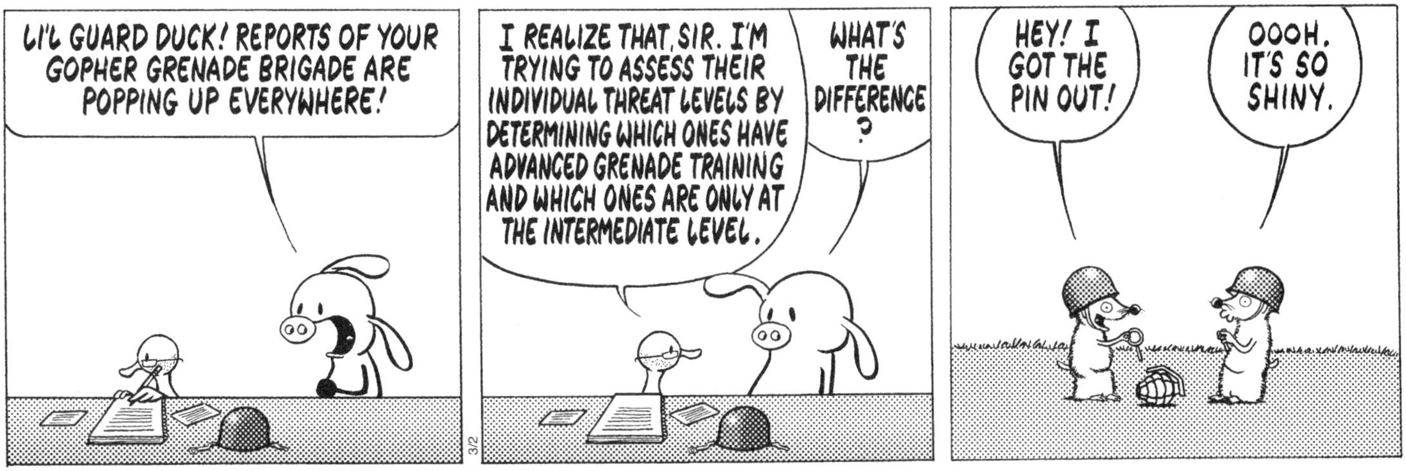
LI'L GUARD DUCK! REPORTS OF YOUR GOPHER GRENADE BRIGADE ARE POPPING UP EVERYWHERE!
I REALIZE THAT, SIR. I'M TRYING TO ASSESS THEIR INDIVIDUAL THREAT LEVELS BY DETERMINING WHICH ONES HAVE ADVANCED GRENADE TRAINING AND WHICH ONES ARE ONLY AT THE INTERMEDIATE LEVEL.
WHAT'S THE DIFFERENCE?
HEY! I GOT THE PIN OUT!
OOOH. IT'S SO SHINY.
3/2

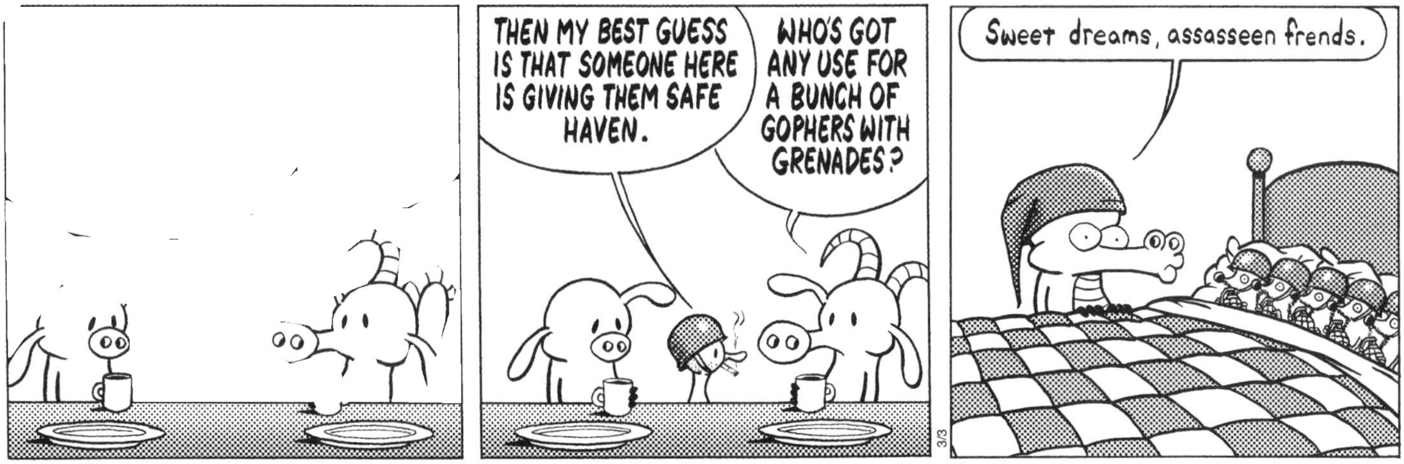
THEN MY BEST GUESS IS THAT SOMEONE HERE IS GIVING THEM SAFE HAVEN.
WHO'S GOT ANY USE FOR A BUNCH OF GOPHERS WITH GRENADES?
3/3
Sweet dreams, assasseen frends.

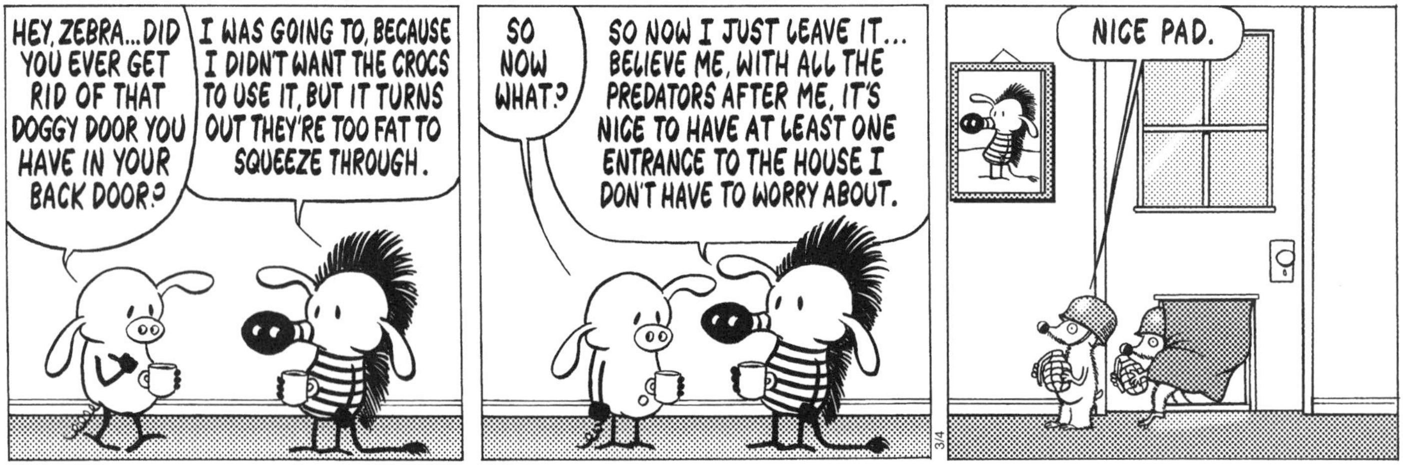
HEY, ZEBRA...DID YOU EVER GET RID OF THAT DOGGY DOOR YOU HAVE IN YOUR BACK DOOR?
I WAS GOING TO, BECAUSE I DIDN'T WANT THE CROCS TO USE IT, BUT IT TURNS OUT THEY'RE TOO FAT TO SQUEEZE THROUGH.
SO NOW WHAT?
SO NOW I JUST LEAVE IT... BELIEVE ME, WITH ALL THE PREDATORS AFTER ME, IT'S NICE TO HAVE AT LEAST ONE ENTRANCE TO THE HOUSE I DON'T HAVE TO WORRY ABOUT.
3/4
NICE PAD.

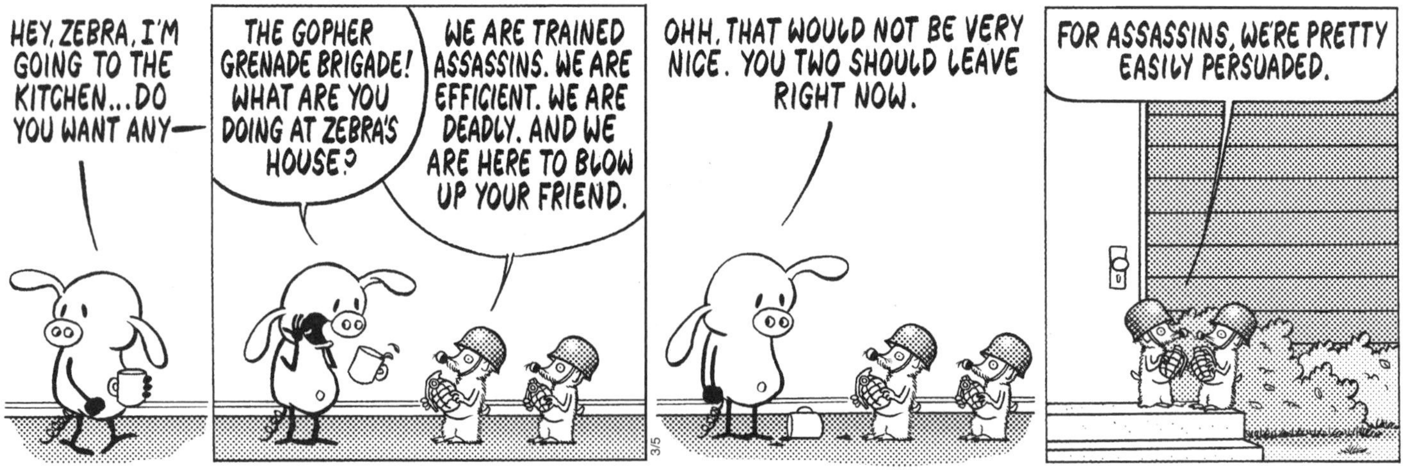
HEY, ZEBRA, I'M GOING TO THE KITCHEN...DO YOU WANT ANY—
THE GOPHER GRENADE BRIGADE! WHAT ARE YOU DOING AT ZEBRA'S HOUSE?
WE ARE TRAINED ASSASSINS. WE ARE EFFICIENT. WE ARE DEADLY. AND WE ARE HERE TO BLOW UP YOUR FRIEND.
3/5
OHH. THAT WOULD NOT BE VERY NICE. YOU TWO SHOULD LEAVE RIGHT NOW.
FOR ASSASSINS, WE'RE PRETTY EASILY PERSUADED.

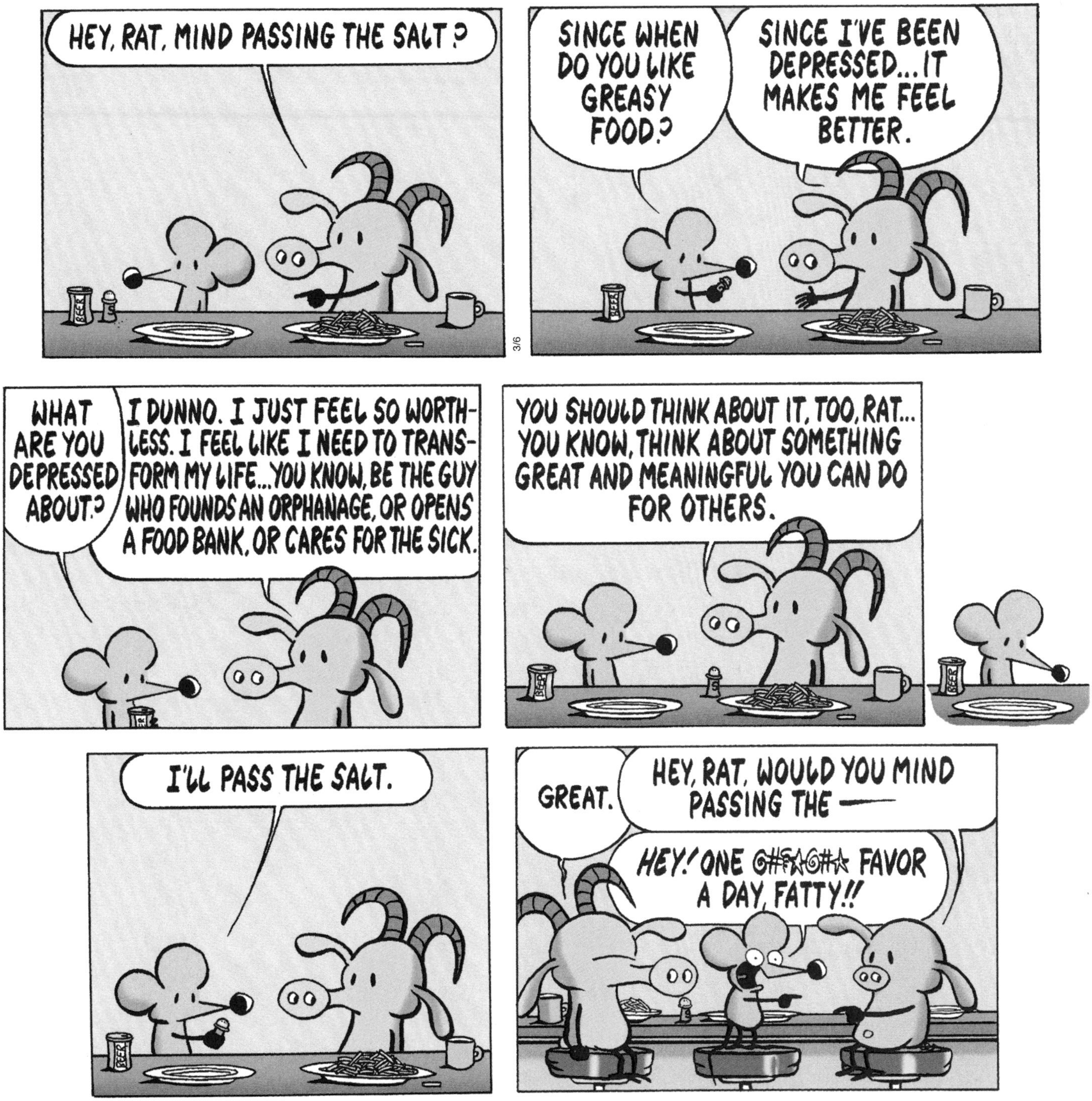
HEY, RAT, MIND PASSING THE SALT?
3/6
SINCE WHEN DO YOU LIKE GREASY FOOD?
SINCE I'VE BEEN DEPRESSED... IT MAKES ME FEEL BETTER.
WHAT ARE YOU DEPRESSED ABOUT?
I DUNNO. I JUST FEEL SO WORTHLESS. I FEEL LIKE I NEED TO TRANSFORM MY LIFE...YOU KNOW, BE THE GUY WHO FOUNDS AN ORPHANAGE, OR OPENS A FOOD BANK, OR CARES FOR THE SICK.
YOU SHOULD THINK ABOUT IT, TOO, RAT... YOU KNOW, THINK ABOUT SOMETHING GREAT AND MEANINGFUL YOU CAN DO FOR OTHERS.
I'LL PASS THE SALT.
GREAT.
HEY, RAT, WOULD YOU MIND PASSING THE —
HEY! ONE @#☆@#☆ FAVOR A DAY, FATTY!!

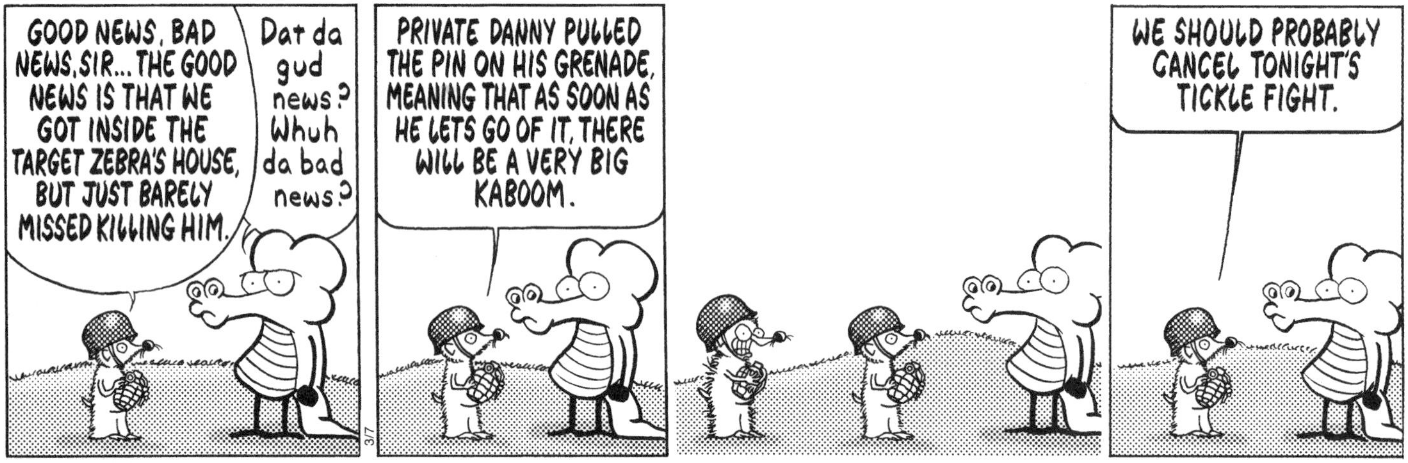
GOOD NEWS, BAD NEWS, SIR... THE GOOD NEWS IS THAT WE GOT INSIDE THE TARGET ZEBRA'S HOUSE, BUT JUST BARELY MISSED KILLING HIM.
Dat da gud news? Whuh da bad news?
3/7
PRIVATE DANNY PULLED THE PIN ON HIS GRENADE, MEANING THAT AS SOON AS HE LETS GO OF IT, THERE WILL BE A VERY BIG KABOOM.
WE SHOULD PROBABLY CANCEL TONIGHT'S TICKLE FIGHT.

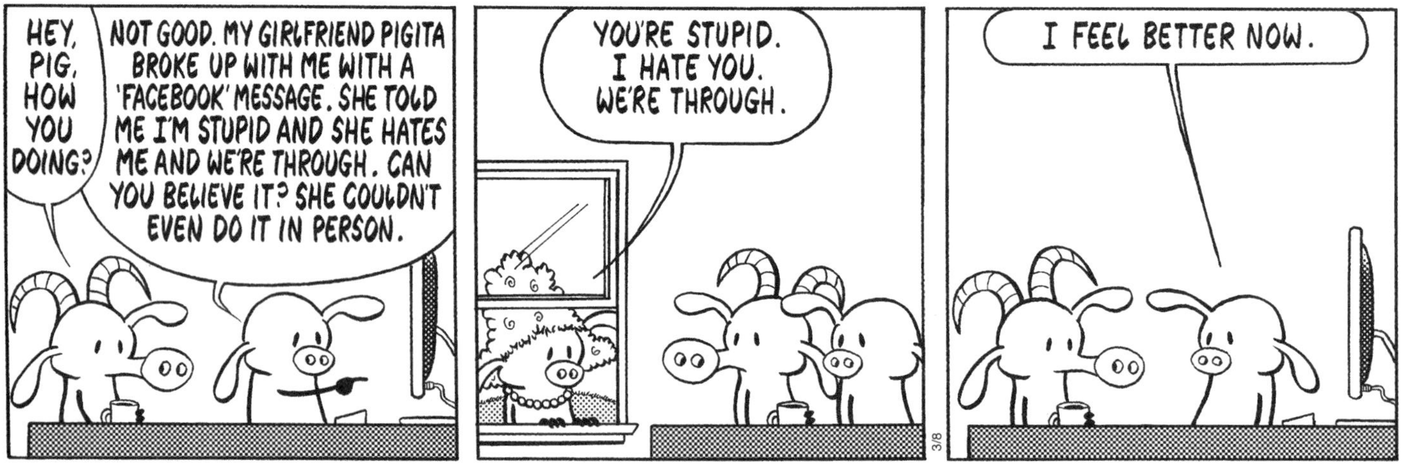
HEY, PIG, HOW YOU DOING?
NOT GOOD. MY GIRLFRIEND PIGITA BROKE UP WITH ME WITH A 'FACEBOOK' MESSAGE. SHE TOLD ME I'M STUPID AND SHE HATES ME AND WE'RE THROUGH. CAN YOU BELIEVE IT? SHE COULDN'T EVEN DO IT IN PERSON.
YOU'RE STUPID. I HATE YOU. WE'RE THROUGH.
3/8
I FEEL BETTER NOW.

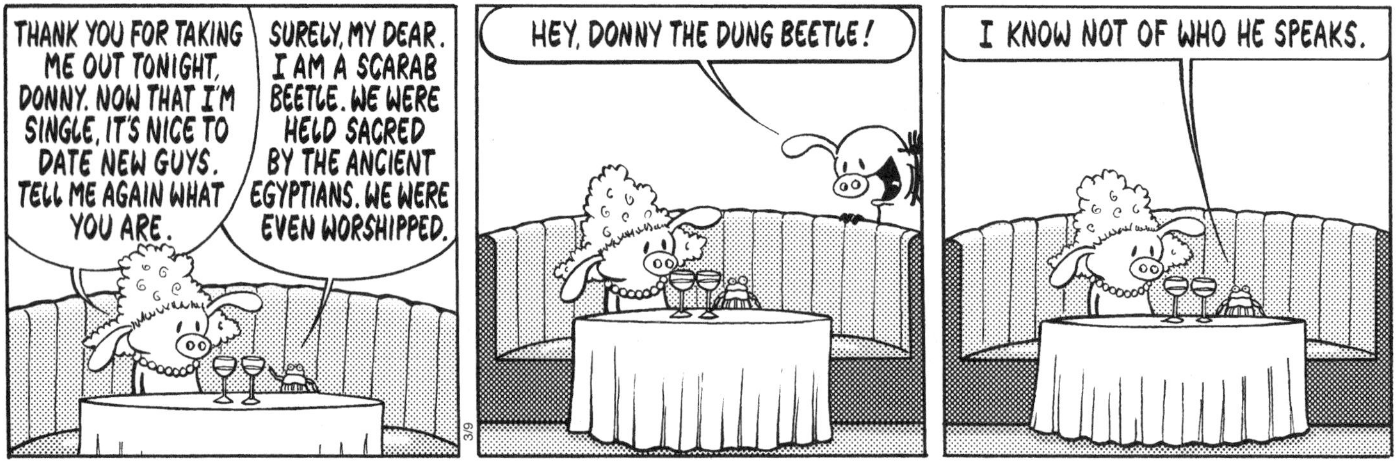
THANK YOU FOR TAKING ME OUT TONIGHT, DONNY. NOW THAT I'M SINGLE, IT'S NICE TO DATE NEW GUYS. TELL ME AGAIN WHAT YOU ARE.
SURELY, MY DEAR. I AM A SCARAB BEETLE. WE WERE HELD SACRED BY THE ANCIENT EGYPTIANS. WE WERE EVEN WORSHIPPED.
3/9
HEY, DONNY THE DUNG BEETLE!
I KNOW NOT OF WHO HE SPEAKS.

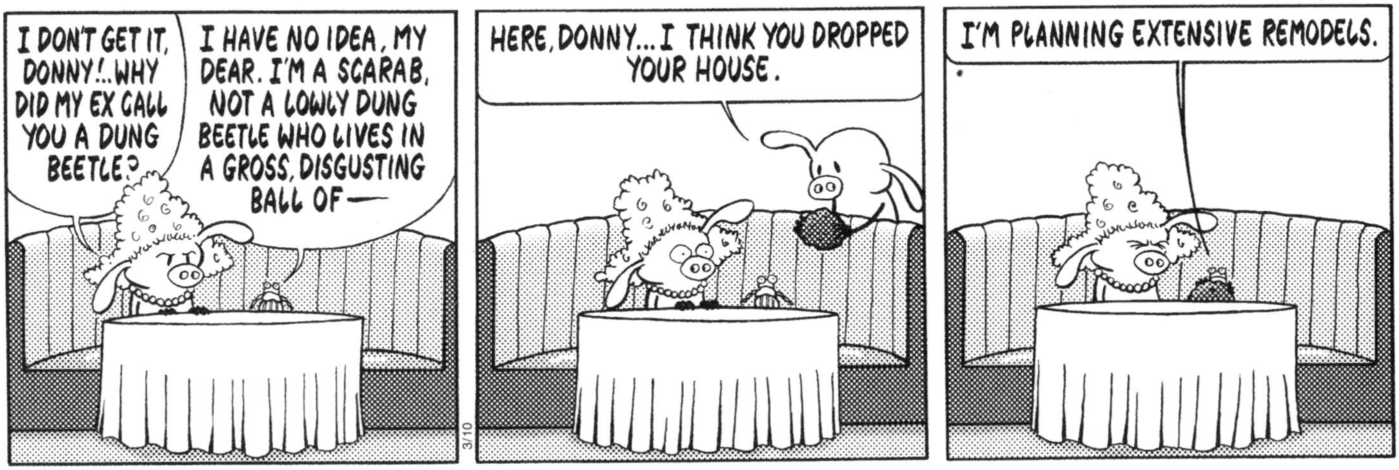
I DON'T GET IT, DONNY!..WHY DID MY EX CALL YOU A DUNG BEETLE?
I HAVE NO IDEA, MY DEAR. I'M A SCARAB, NOT A LOWLY DUNG BEETLE WHO LIVES IN A GROSS, DISGUSTING BALL OF—
3/10
HERE, DONNY... I THINK YOU DROPPED YOUR HOUSE.
I'M PLANNING EXTENSIVE REMODELS.

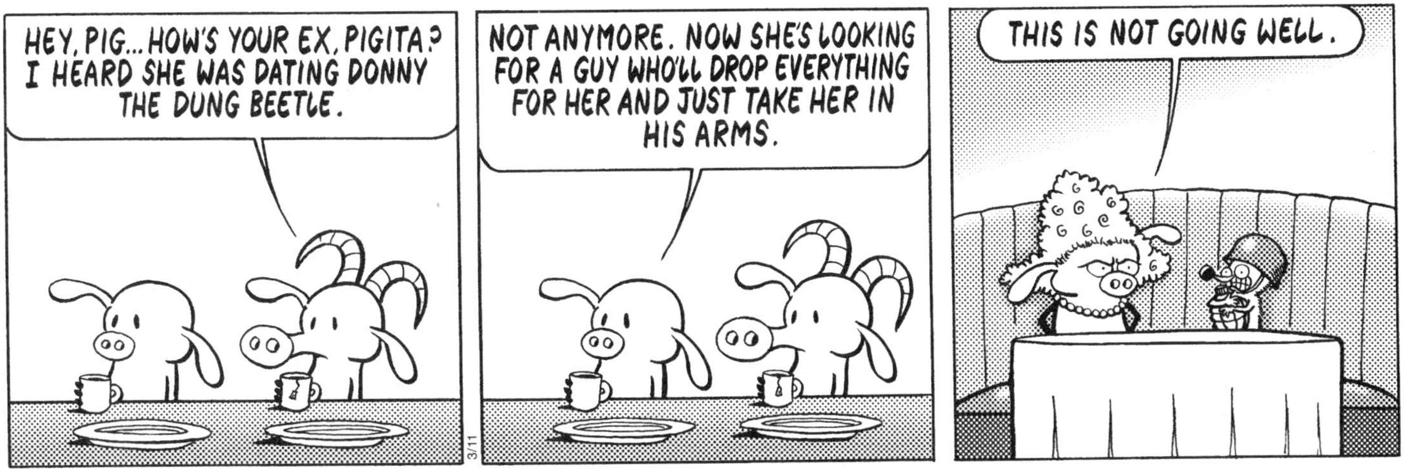
HEY, PIG... HOW'S YOUR EX, PIGITA? I HEARD SHE WAS DATING DONNY THE DUNG BEETLE.
3/11
NOT ANYMORE. NOW SHE'S LOOKING FOR A GUY WHO'LL DROP EVERYTHING FOR HER AND JUST TAKE HER IN HIS ARMS.
THIS IS NOT GOING WELL.

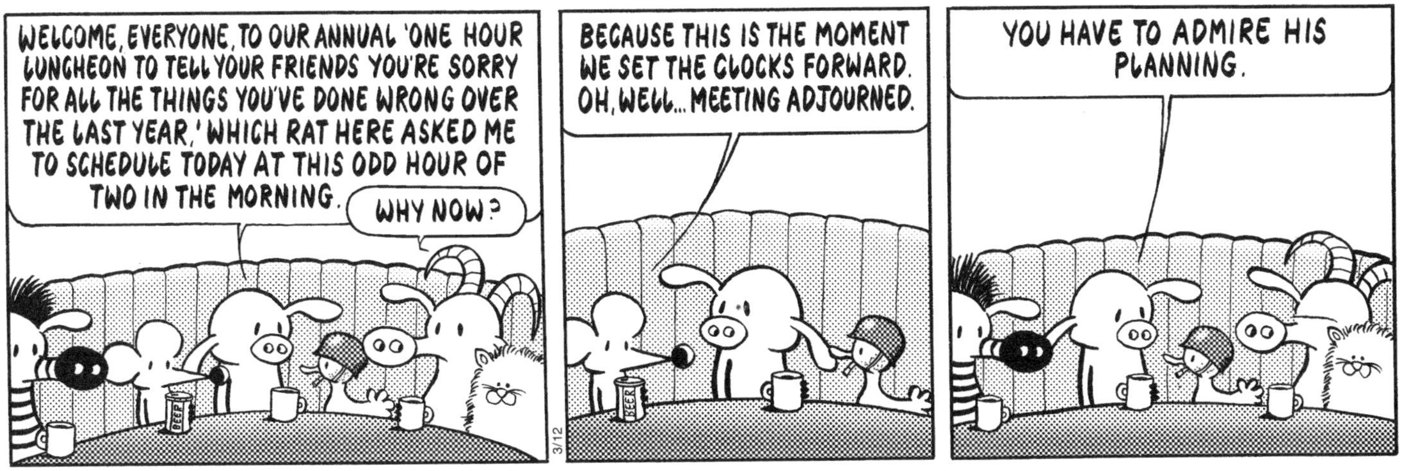
WELCOME, EVERYONE, TO OUR ANNUAL 'ONE HOUR LUNCHEON TO TELL YOUR FRIENDS YOU'RE SORRY FOR ALL THE THINGS YOU'VE DONE WRONG OVER THE LAST YEAR,' WHICH RAT HERE ASKED ME TO SCHEDULE TODAY AT THIS ODD HOUR OF TWO IN THE MORNING.
WHY NOW?
BEER
3/12
BECAUSE THIS IS THE MOMENT WE SET THE CLOCKS FORWARD. OH, WELL... MEETING ADJOURNED.
BEER
YOU HAVE TO ADMIRE HIS PLANNING.

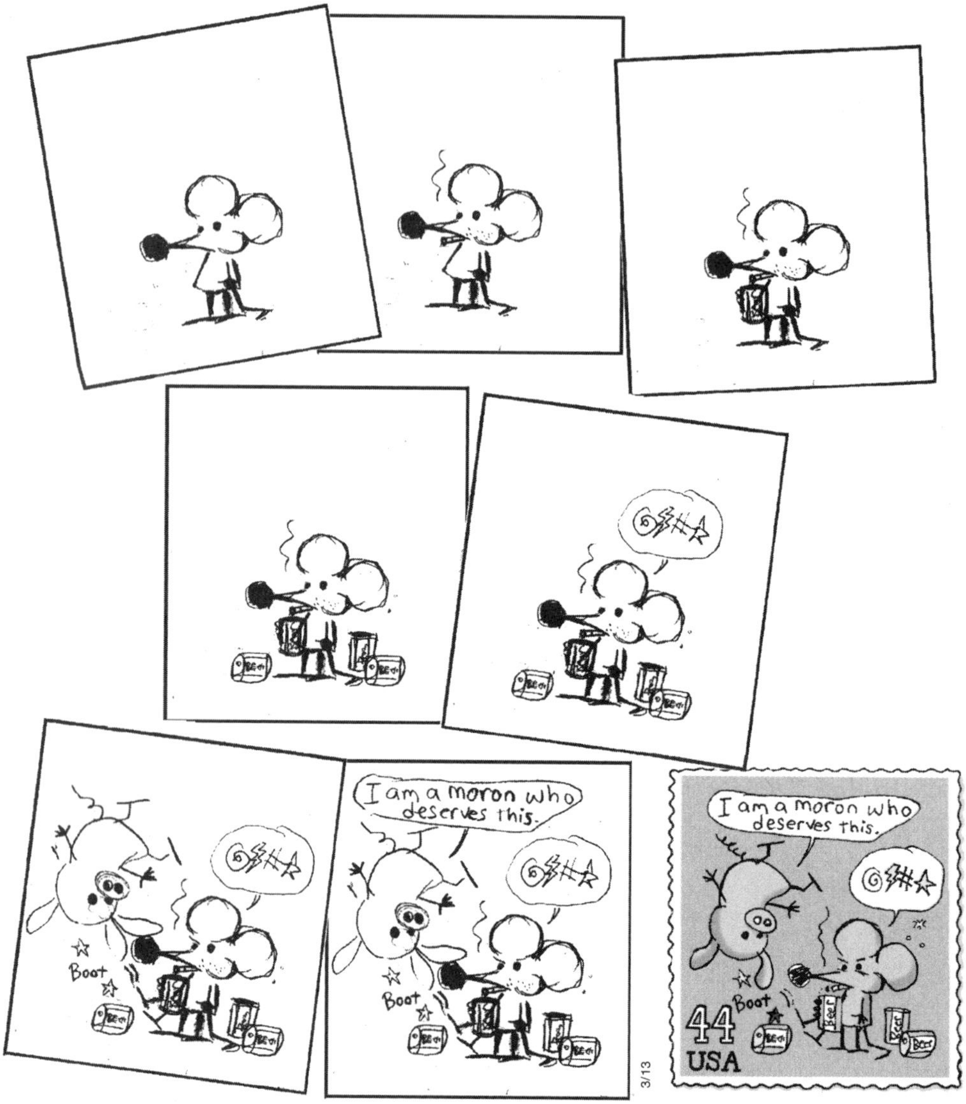

I am a moron who deserves this.
Boot
I am a moron who deserves this.
Boot
3/13
I am a moron who deserves this.
Boot
44
USA

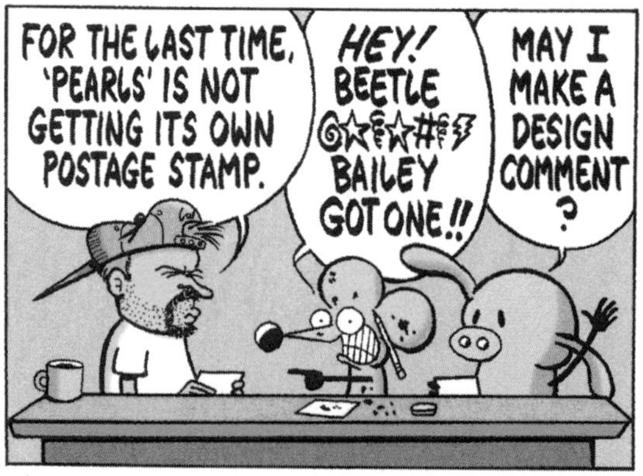

FOR THE LAST TIME, 'PEARLS' IS NOT GETTING ITS OWN POSTAGE STAMP.
HEY! BEETLE BAILEY GOT ONE!!
MAY I MAKE A DESIGN COMMENT ?

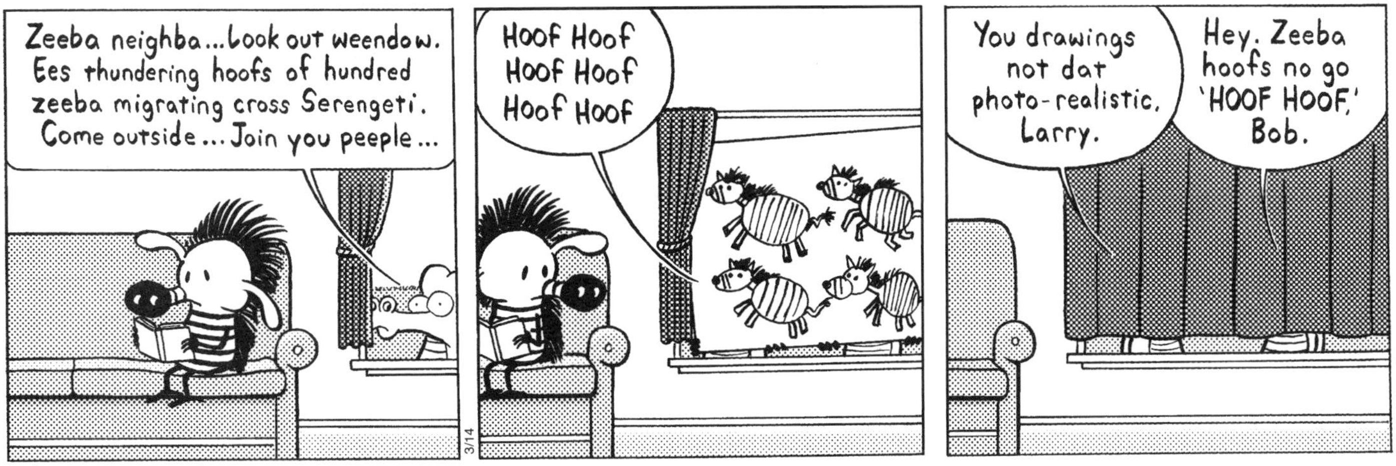
Zeeba neighba...Look out weendow. Ees thundering hoofs of hundred zeeba migrating cross Serengeti. Come outside...Join you peeple...
Hoof Hoof Hoof Hoof Hoof Hoof
You drawings not dat photo-realistic, Larry.
Hey. Zeeba hoofs no go 'HOOF HOOF,' Bob.

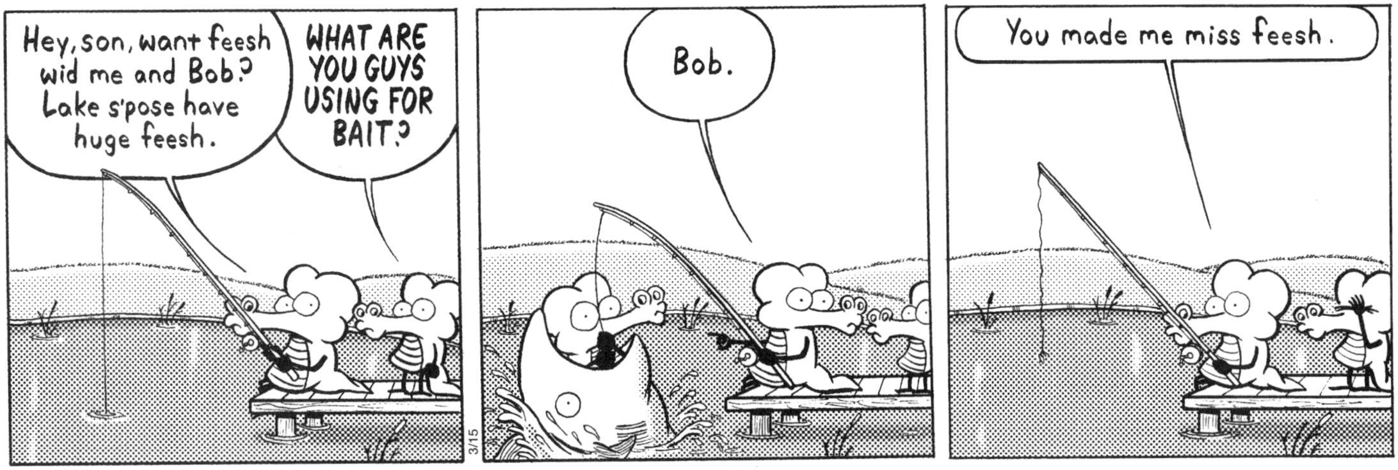
Hey, son, want feesh wid me and Bob? Lake s'pose have huge feesh.
WHAT ARE YOU GUYS USING FOR BAIT?
Bob.
You made me miss feesh.

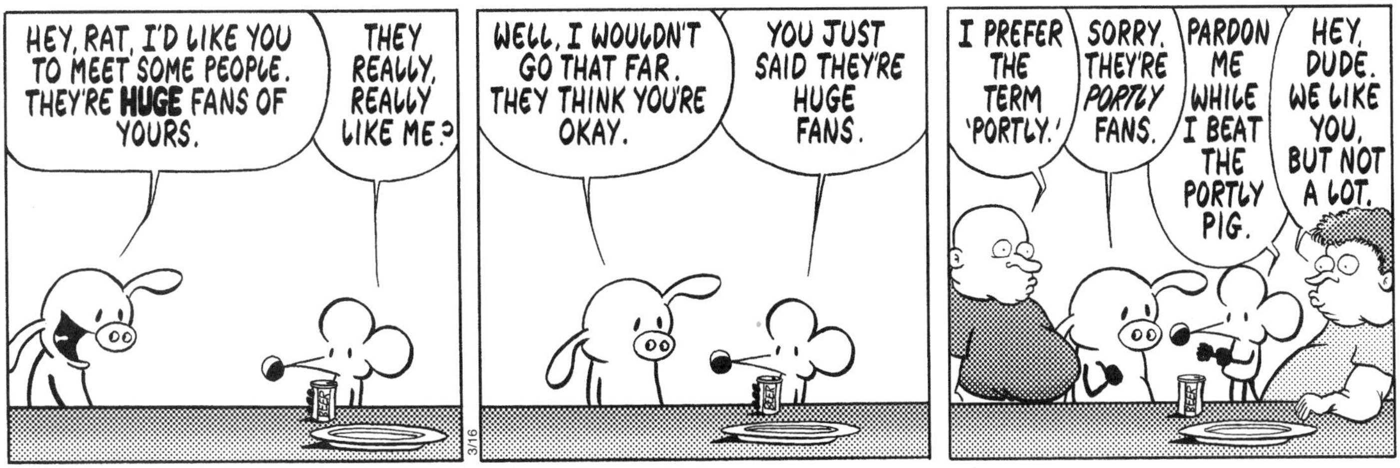
HEY, RAT, I'D LIKE YOU TO MEET SOME PEOPLE. THEY'RE HUGE FANS OF YOURS.
THEY REALLY, REALLY LIKE ME?
WELL, I WOULDN'T GO THAT FAR. THEY THINK YOU'RE OKAY.
YOU JUST SAID THEY'RE HUGE FANS.
I PREFER THE TERM 'PORTLY.'
SORRY. THEY'RE PORTLY FANS.
PARDON ME WHILE I BEAT THE PORTLY PIG.
HEY, DUDE. WE LIKE YOU, BUT NOT A LOT.

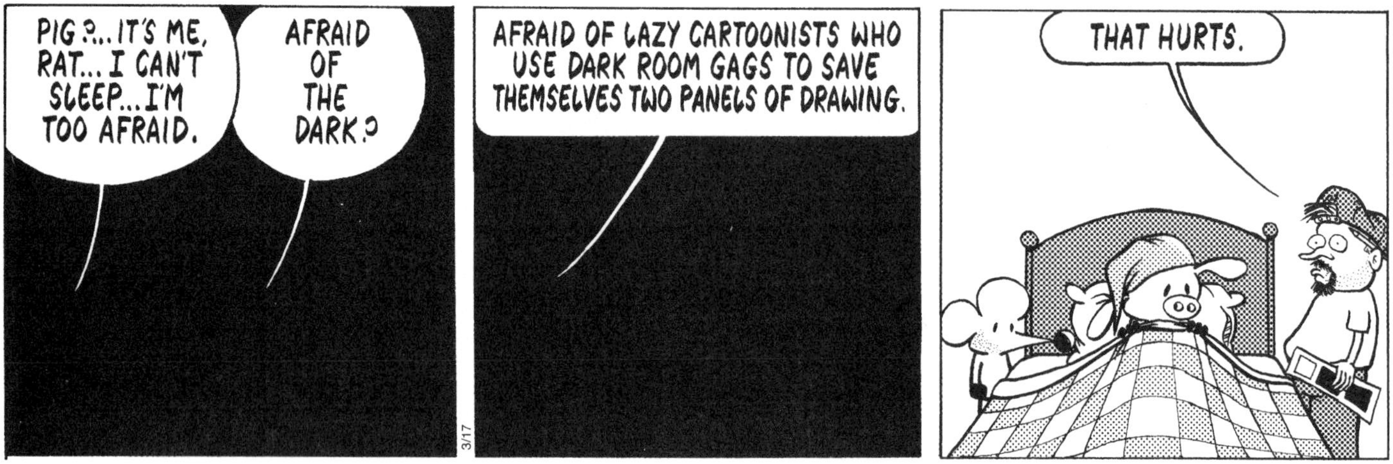
PIG?... IT'S ME, RAT... I CAN'T SLEEP... I'M TOO AFRAID.
AFRAID OF THE DARK?
3/17
AFRAID OF LAZY CARTOONISTS WHO USE DARK ROOM GAGS TO SAVE THEMSELVES TWO PANELS OF DRAWING.
THAT HURTS.

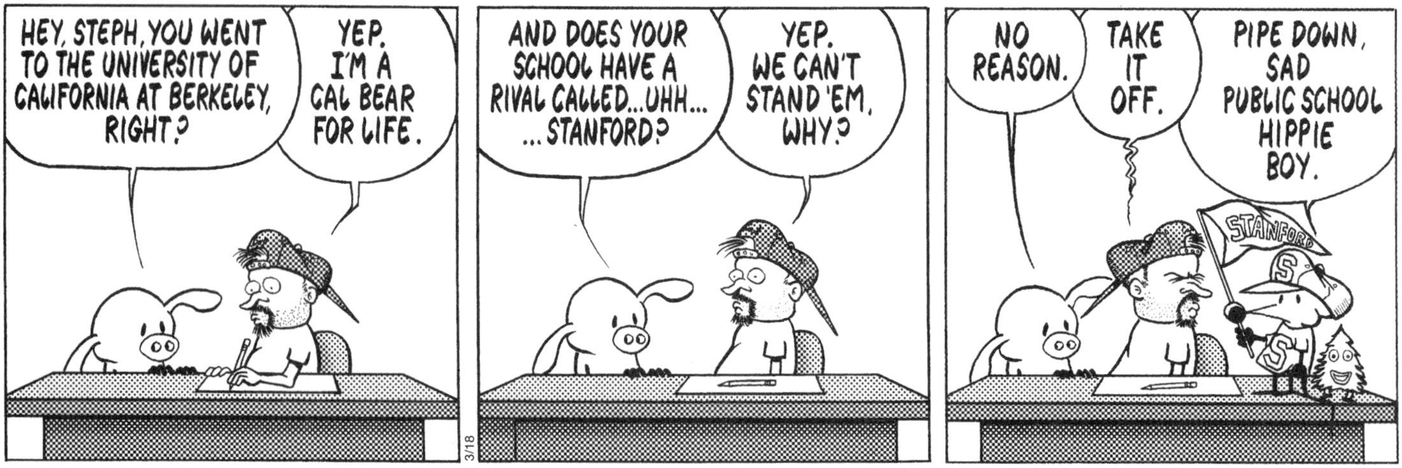
HEY, STEPH, YOU WENT TO THE UNIVERSITY OF CALIFORNIA AT BERKELEY, RIGHT?
YEP. I'M A CAL BEAR FOR LIFE.
3/18
AND DOES YOUR SCHOOL HAVE A RIVAL CALLED... UHH... ...STANFORD?
YEP. WE CAN'T STAND 'EM. WHY?
NO REASON.
TAKE IT OFF.
PIPE DOWN, SAD PUBLIC SCHOOL HIPPIE BOY.
STANFORD
S

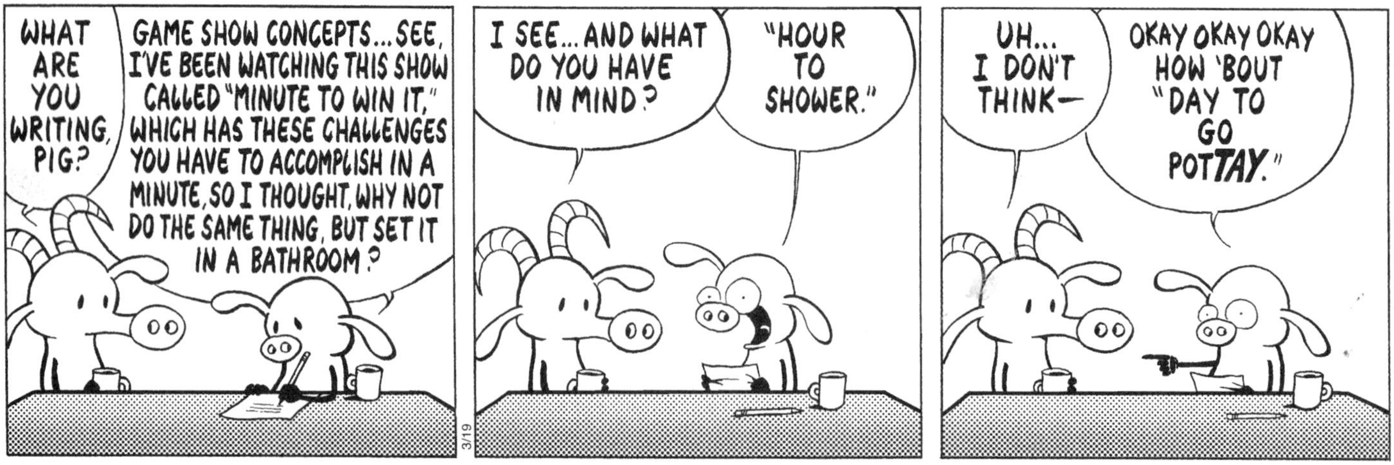
WHAT ARE YOU WRITING, PIG?
GAME SHOW CONCEPTS... SEE, I'VE BEEN WATCHING THIS SHOW CALLED "MINUTE TO WIN IT," WHICH HAS THESE CHALLENGES YOU HAVE TO ACCOMPLISH IN A MINUTE, SO I THOUGHT, WHY NOT DO THE SAME THING, BUT SET IT IN A BATHROOM?
3/19
I SEE... AND WHAT DO YOU HAVE IN MIND?
"HOUR TO SHOWER."
UH... I DON'T THINK—
OKAY OKAY OKAY HOW 'BOUT "DAY TO GO POTTAY."

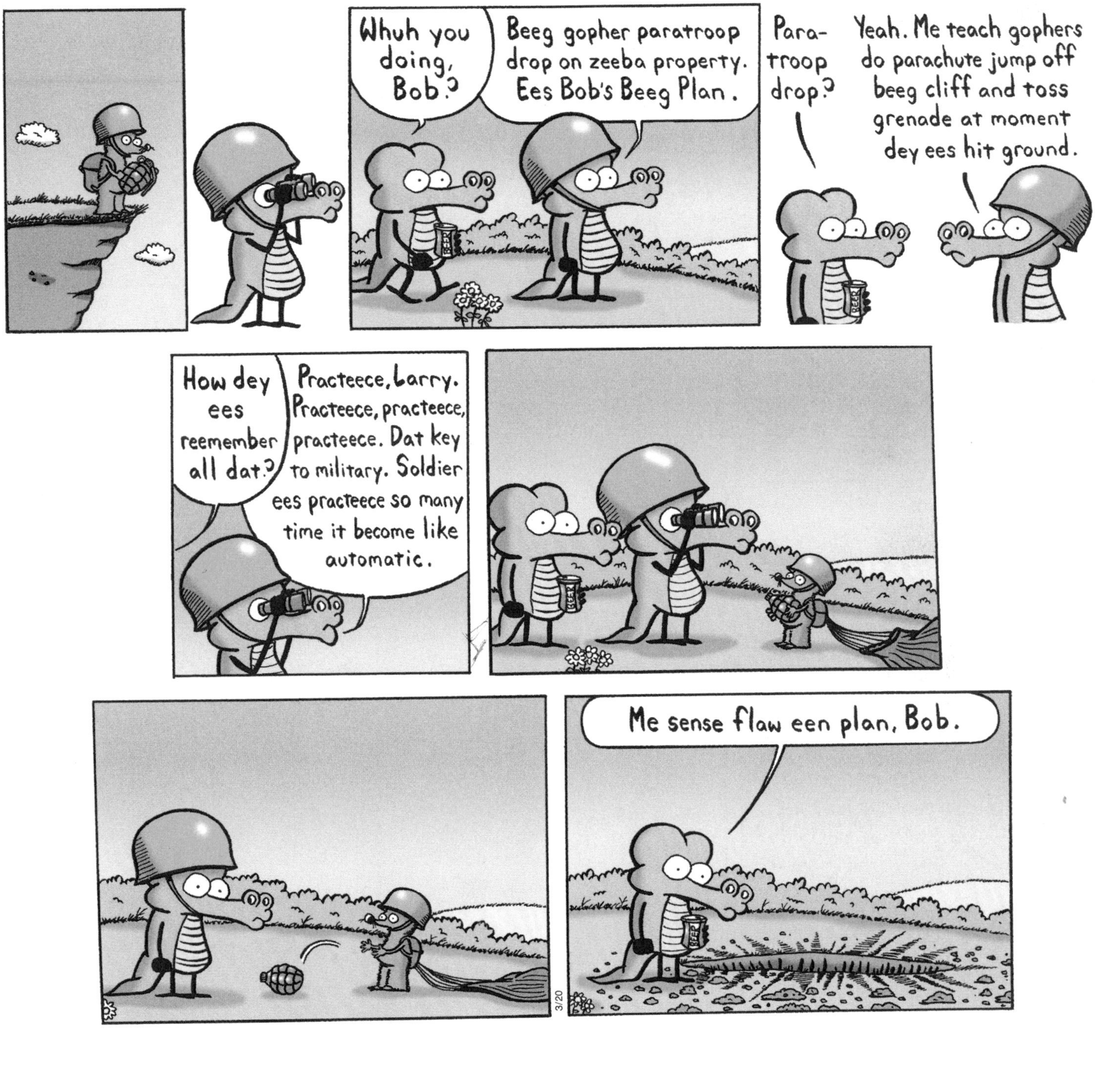

Whuh you doing, Bob?
Beeg gopher paratroop drop on zeeba property. Ees Bob's Beeg Plan.
Para-troop drop?
Yeah. Me teach gophers do parachute jump off beeg cliff and toss grenade at moment dey ees hit ground.
How dey ees reemember all dat?
Practeece, Larry. Practeece, practeece, practeece. Dat key to military. Soldier ees practeece so many time it become like automatic.
Me sense flaw een plan, Bob.

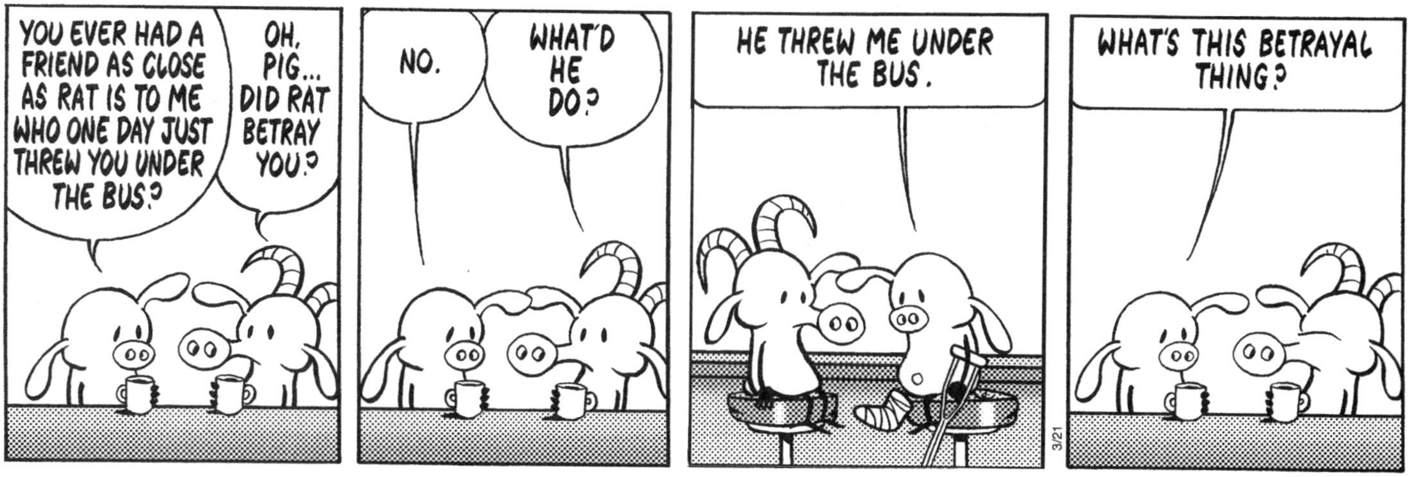
YOU EVER HAD A FRIEND AS CLOSE AS RAT IS TO ME WHO ONE DAY JUST THREW YOU UNDER THE BUS?
OH, PIG... DID RAT BETRAY YOU?
NO.
WHAT'D HE DO?
HE THREW ME UNDER THE BUS.
3/21
WHAT'S THIS BETRAYAL THING?

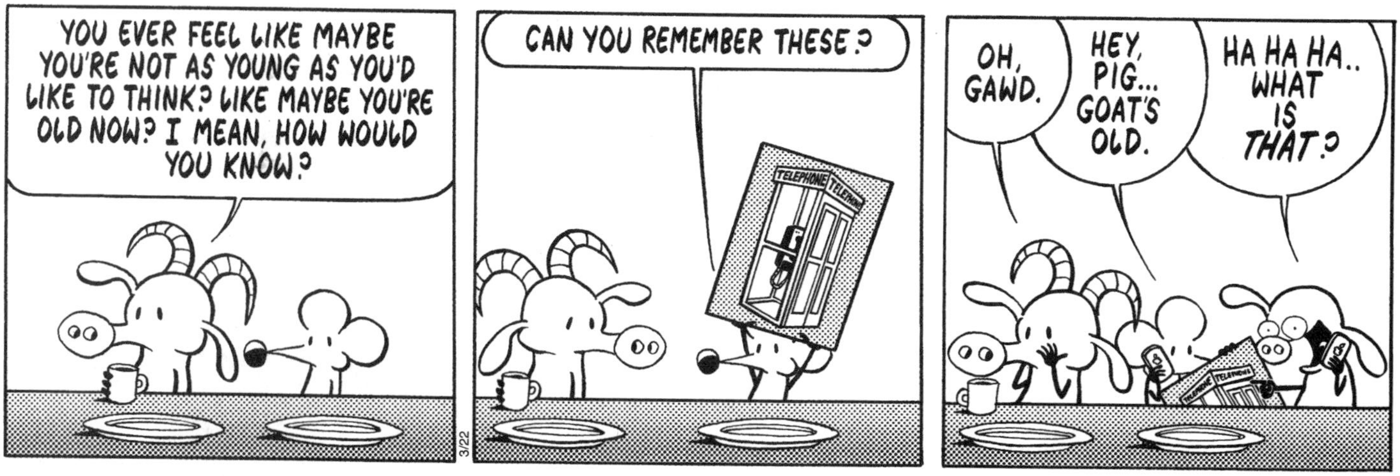
YOU EVER FEEL LIKE MAYBE YOU'RE NOT AS YOUNG AS YOU'D LIKE TO THINK? LIKE MAYBE YOU'RE OLD NOW? I MEAN, HOW WOULD YOU KNOW?
3/22
CAN YOU REMEMBER THESE?
TELEPHONE
OH, GAWD.
HEY, PIG... GOAT'S OLD.
HA HA HA.. WHAT IS *THAT*?

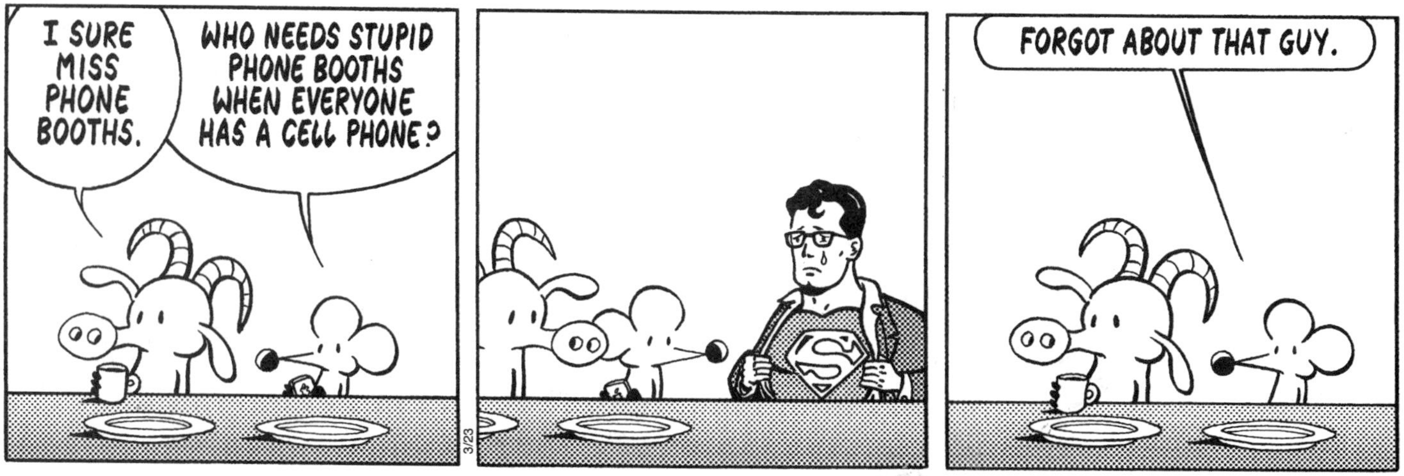
I SURE MISS PHONE BOOTHS.
WHO NEEDS STUPID PHONE BOOTHS WHEN EVERYONE HAS A CELL PHONE?
3/23
FORGOT ABOUT THAT GUY.

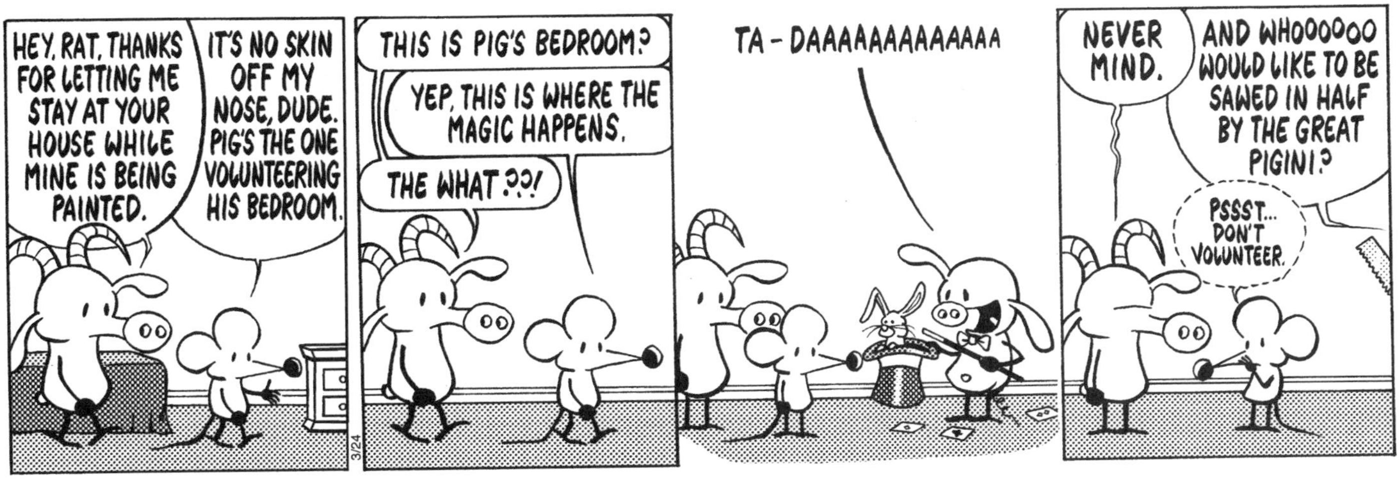
HEY, RAT, THANKS FOR LETTING ME STAY AT YOUR HOUSE WHILE MINE IS BEING PAINTED.
IT'S NO SKIN OFF MY NOSE, DUDE. PIG'S THE ONE VOLUNTEERING HIS BEDROOM.
3/24
THIS IS PIG'S BEDROOM?
YEP, THIS IS WHERE THE MAGIC HAPPENS.
THE WHAT ??!
TA - DAAAAAAAAAAAAA
NEVER MIND.
AND WHOOOOOO WOULD LIKE TO BE SAWED IN HALF BY THE GREAT PIGINI?
PSSST... DON'T VOLUNTEER.

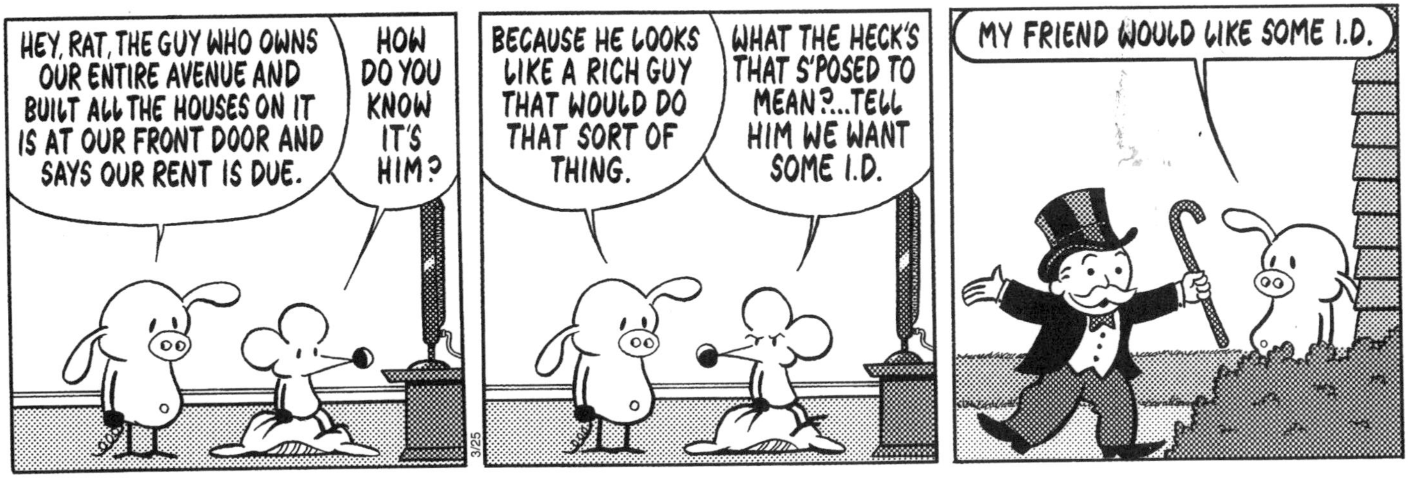
HEY, RAT, THE GUY WHO OWNS OUR ENTIRE AVENUE AND BUILT ALL THE HOUSES ON IT IS AT OUR FRONT DOOR AND SAYS OUR RENT IS DUE.
HOW DO YOU KNOW IT'S HIM?
3/25
BECAUSE HE LOOKS LIKE A RICH GUY THAT WOULD DO THAT SORT OF THING.
WHAT THE HECK'S THAT S'POSED TO MEAN?...TELL HIM WE WANT SOME I.D.
MY FRIEND WOULD LIKE SOME I.D.

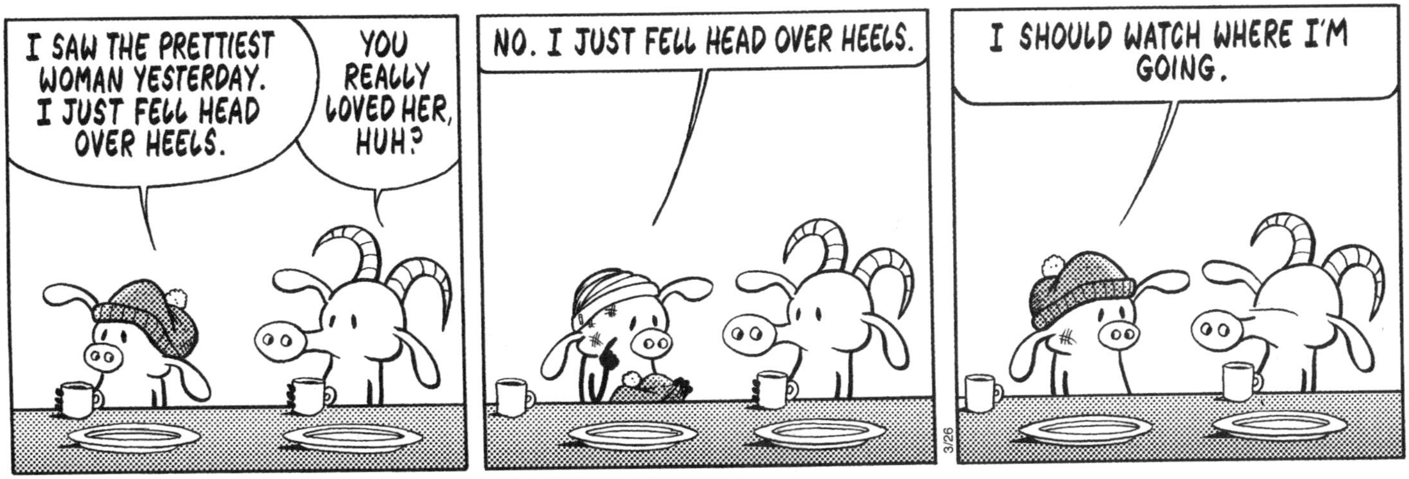
I SAW THE PRETTIEST WOMAN YESTERDAY. I JUST FELL HEAD OVER HEELS.
YOU REALLY LOVED HER, HUH?
NO. I JUST FELL HEAD OVER HEELS.
3/26
I SHOULD WATCH WHERE I'M GOING.

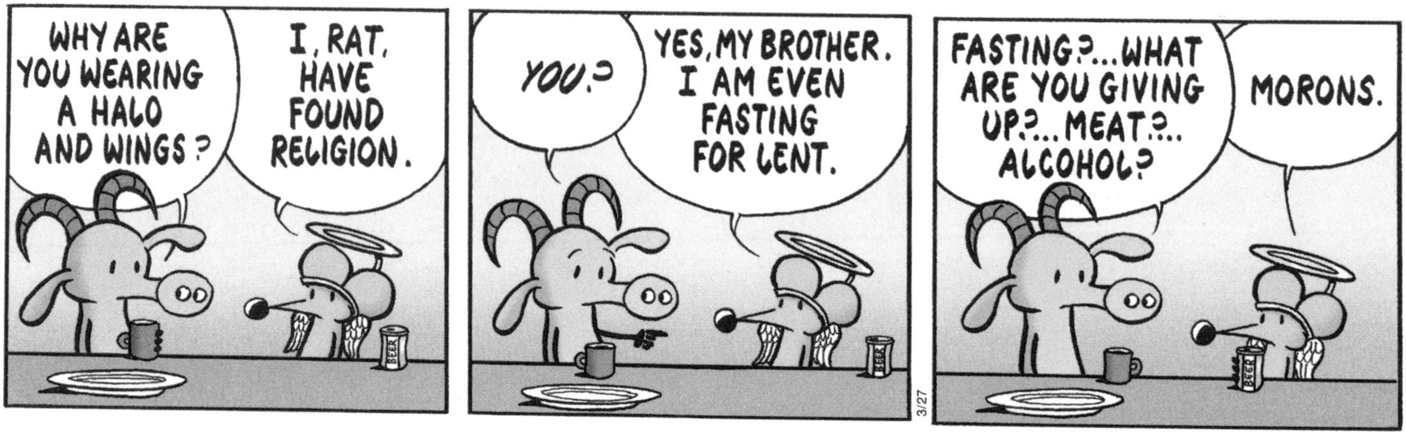
WHY ARE YOU WEARING A HALO AND WINGS?
I, RAT, HAVE FOUND RELIGION.
YOU?
YES, MY BROTHER. I AM EVEN FASTING FOR LENT.
BEER
3/27
FASTING?...WHAT ARE YOU GIVING UP?...MEAT?... ALCOHOL?
MORONS.

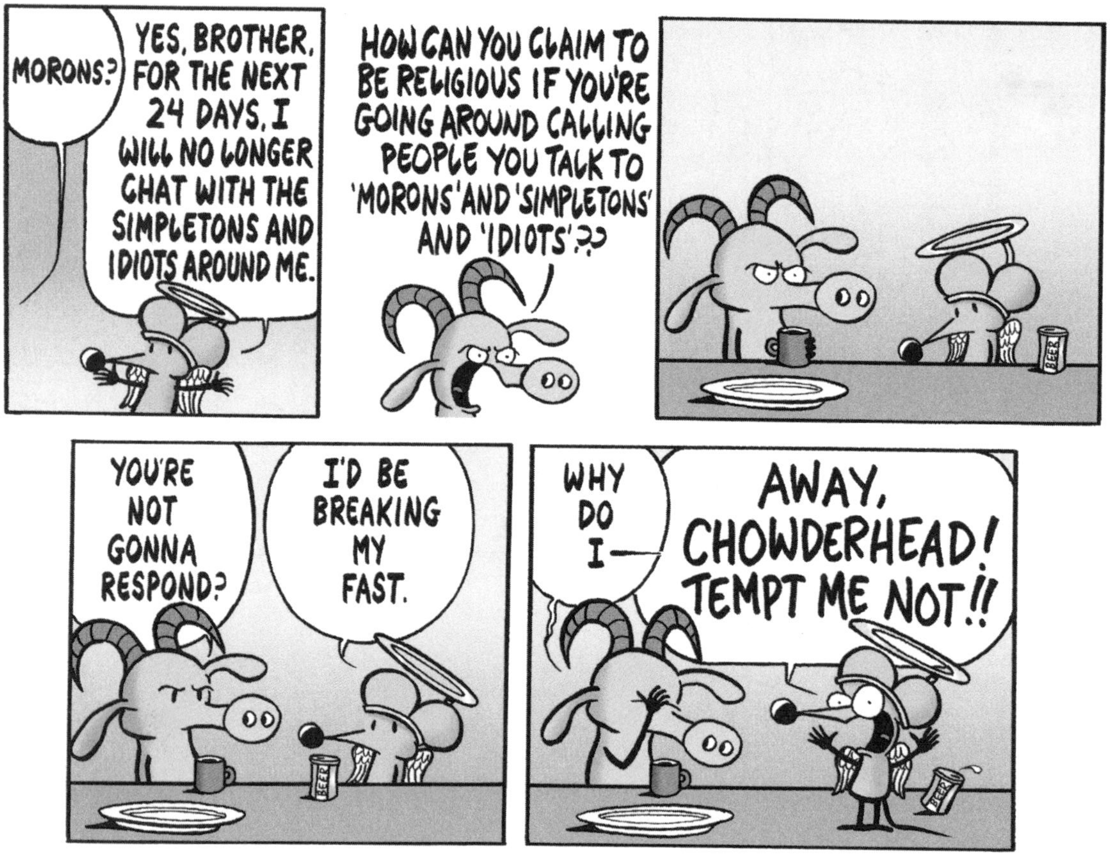
MORONS?
YES, BROTHER. FOR THE NEXT 24 DAYS, I WILL NO LONGER CHAT WITH THE SIMPLETONS AND IDIOTS AROUND ME.
HOW CAN YOU CLAIM TO BE RELIGIOUS IF YOU'RE GOING AROUND CALLING PEOPLE YOU TALK TO 'MORONS' AND 'SIMPLETONS' AND 'IDIOTS'??
BEER
YOU'RE NOT GONNA RESPOND?
I'D BE BREAKING MY FAST.
WHY DO I—
AWAY, CHOWDERHEAD! TEMPT ME NOT!!

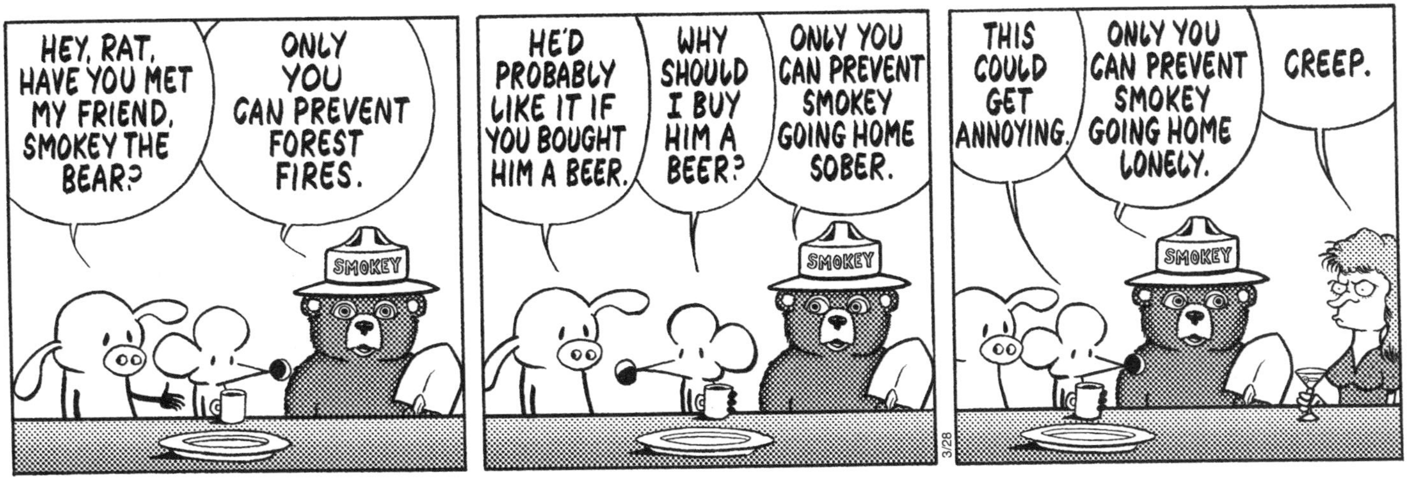
HEY, RAT, HAVE YOU MET MY FRIEND, SMOKEY THE BEAR?
ONLY YOU CAN PREVENT FOREST FIRES.
SMOKEY
HE'D PROBABLY LIKE IT IF YOU BOUGHT HIM A BEER.
WHY SHOULD I BUY HIM A BEER?
ONLY YOU CAN PREVENT SMOKEY GOING HOME SOBER.
SMOKEY
3/28
THIS COULD GET ANNOYING.
ONLY YOU CAN PREVENT SMOKEY GOING HOME LONELY.
CREEP.
SMOKEY

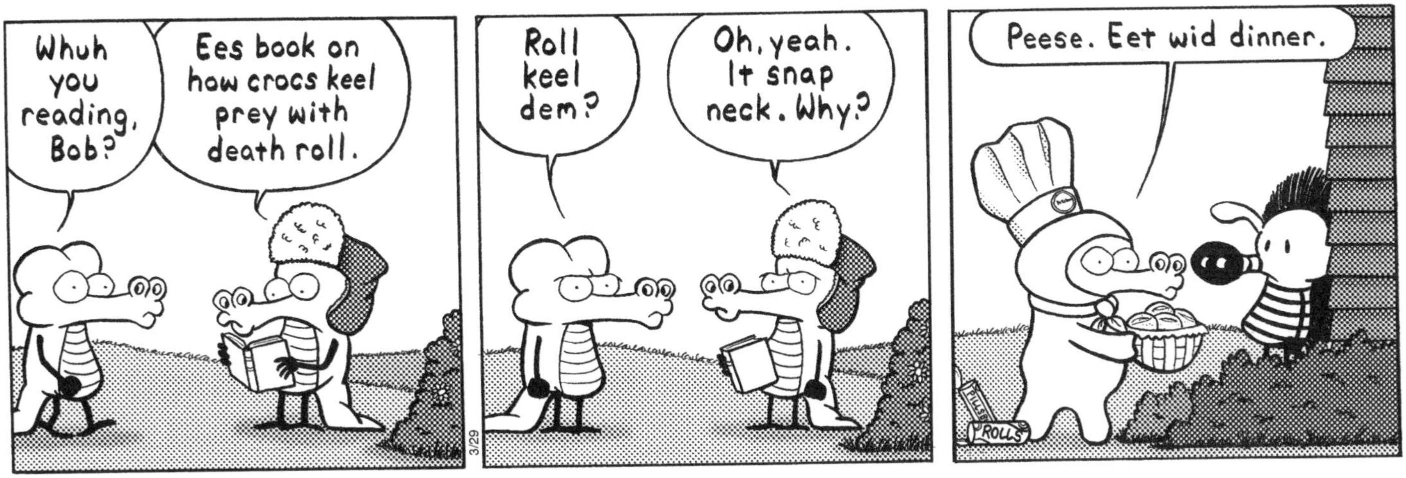
Whuh you reading, Bob?
Ees book on how crocs keel prey with death roll.
3/29
Roll keel dem?
Oh, yeah. It snap neck. Why?
Peese. Eet wid dinner.
ROLLS

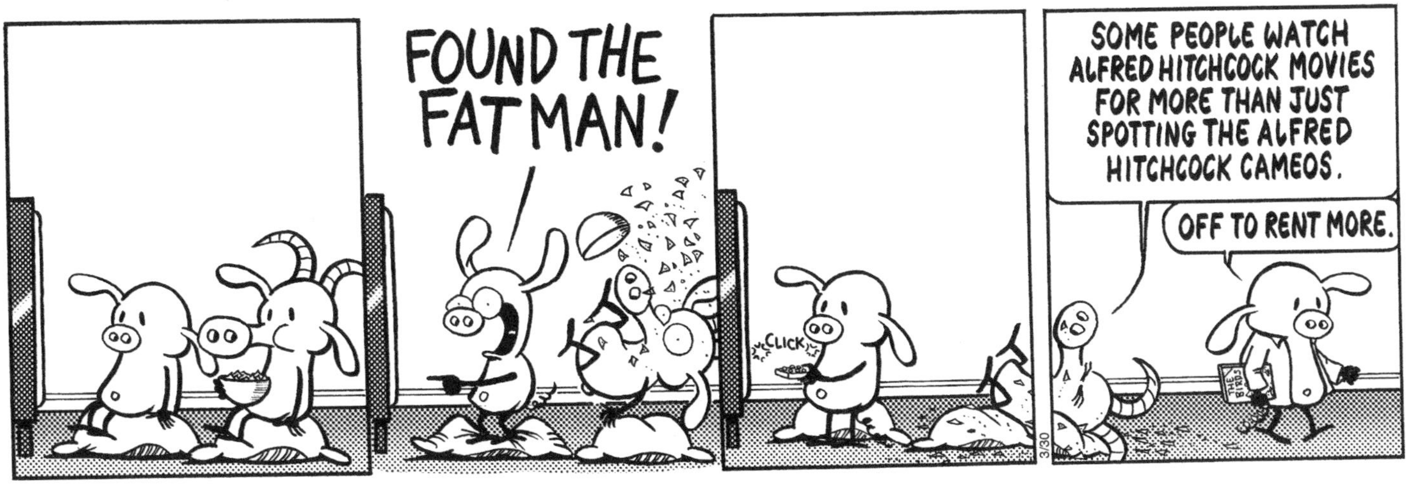
FOUND THE FAT MAN!
CLICK
3/30
SOME PEOPLE WATCH ALFRED HITCHCOCK MOVIES FOR MORE THAN JUST SPOTTING THE ALFRED HITCHCOCK CAMEOS.
OFF TO RENT MORE.

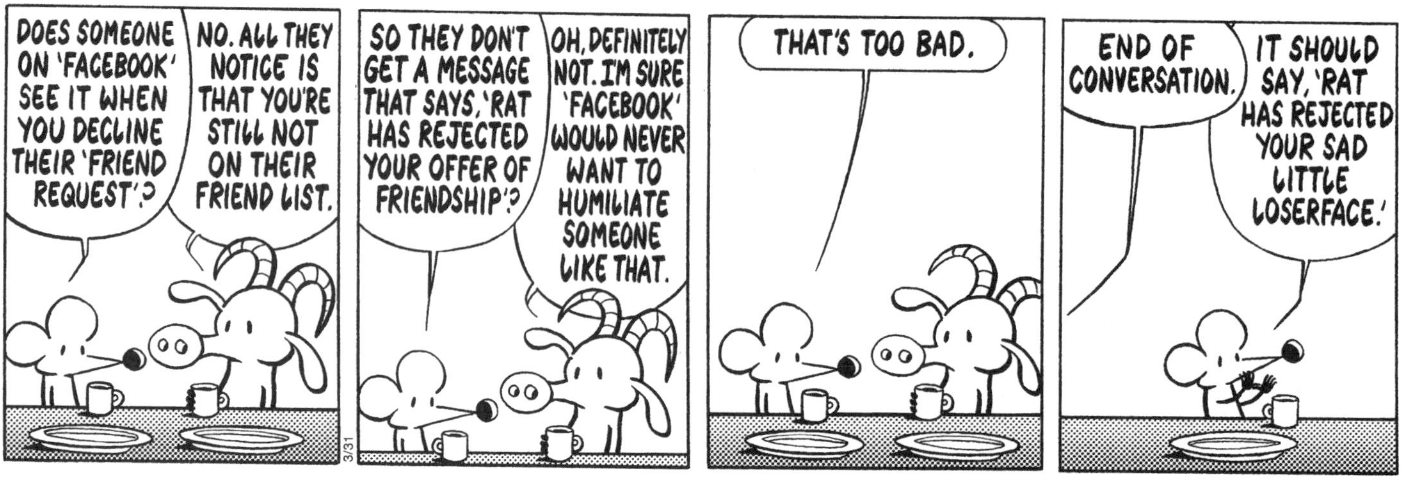
DOES SOMEONE ON 'FACEBOOK' SEE IT WHEN YOU DECLINE THEIR 'FRIEND REQUEST'?
NO. ALL THEY NOTICE IS THAT YOU'RE STILL NOT ON THEIR FRIEND LIST.
3/31
SO THEY DON'T GET A MESSAGE THAT SAYS, 'RAT HAS REJECTED YOUR OFFER OF FRIENDSHIP'?
OH, DEFINITELY NOT. I'M SURE 'FACEBOOK' WOULD NEVER WANT TO HUMILIATE SOMEONE LIKE THAT.
THAT'S TOO BAD.
END OF CONVERSATION.
IT SHOULD SAY, 'RAT HAS REJECTED YOUR SAD LITTLE LOSERFACE.'

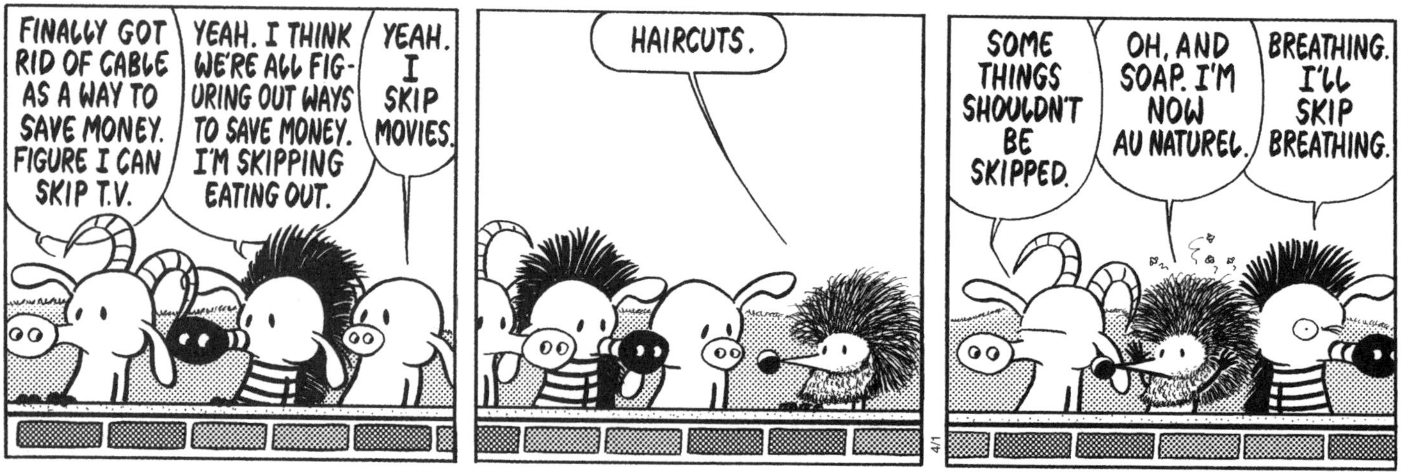
FINALLY GOT RID OF CABLE AS A WAY TO SAVE MONEY. FIGURE I CAN SKIP T.V.
YEAH. I THINK WE'RE ALL FIGURING OUT WAYS TO SAVE MONEY. I'M SKIPPING EATING OUT.
YEAH. I SKIP MOVIES.
HAIRCUTS.
4/1
SOME THINGS SHOULDN'T BE SKIPPED.
OH, AND SOAP. I'M NOW AU NATUREL.
BREATHING. I'LL SKIP BREATHING.

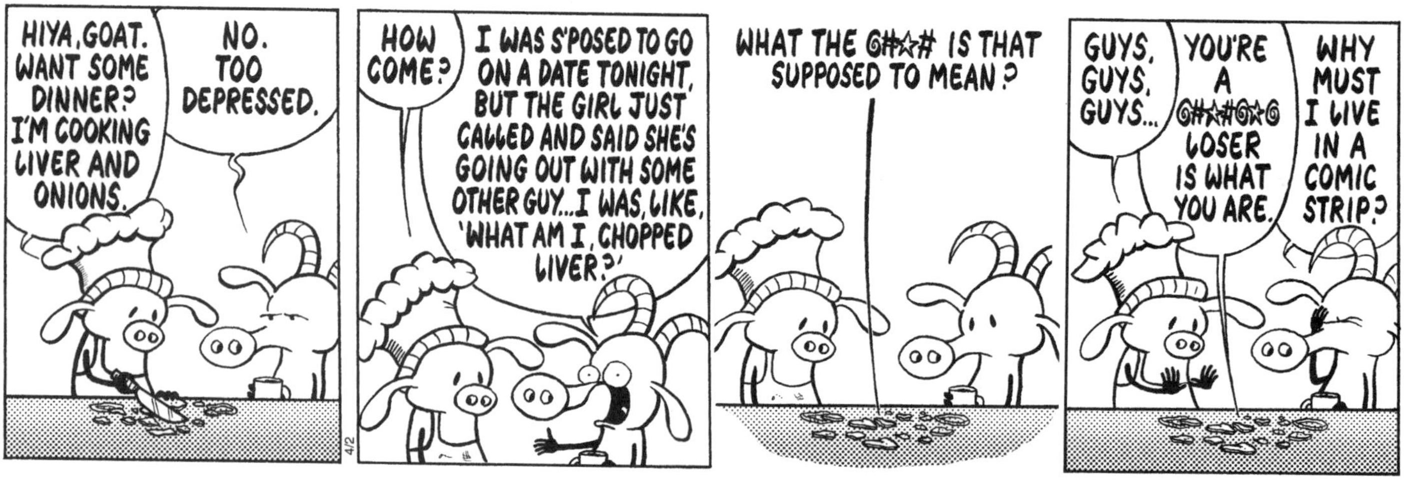
HIYA, GOAT. WANT SOME DINNER? I'M COOKING LIVER AND ONIONS.
NO. TOO DEPRESSED.
4/2
HOW COME?
I WAS S'POSED TO GO ON A DATE TONIGHT, BUT THE GIRL JUST CALLED AND SAID SHE'S GOING OUT WITH SOME OTHER GUY...I WAS, LIKE, 'WHAT AM I, CHOPPED LIVER?'
WHAT THE @#☆# IS THAT SUPPOSED TO MEAN?
GUYS, GUYS, GUYS...
YOU'RE A @#☆#@☆@ LOSER IS WHAT YOU ARE.
WHY MUST I LIVE IN A COMIC STRIP?

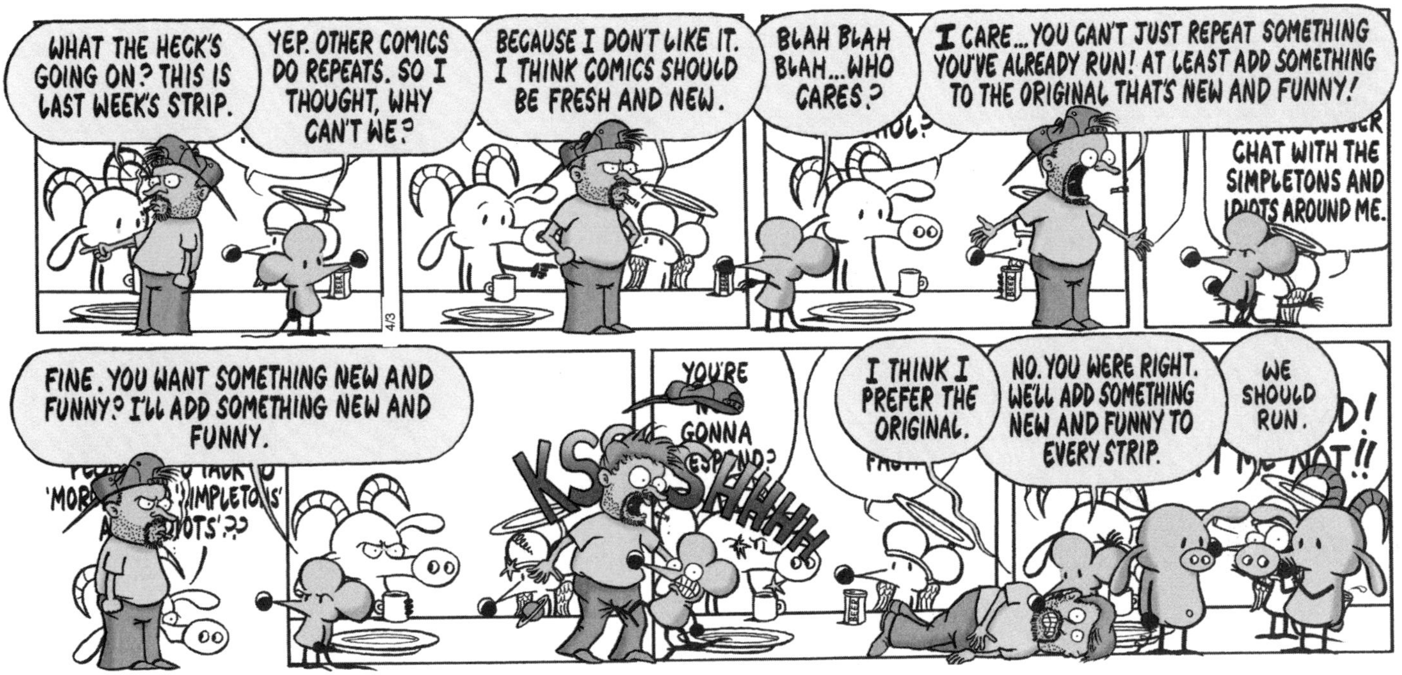
WHAT THE HECK'S GOING ON? THIS IS LAST WEEK'S STRIP.
YEP. OTHER COMICS DO REPEATS. SO I THOUGHT, WHY CAN'T WE?
BECAUSE I DON'T LIKE IT. I THINK COMICS SHOULD BE FRESH AND NEW.
BLAH BLAH BLAH... WHO CARES?
I CARE... YOU CAN'T JUST REPEAT SOMETHING YOU'VE ALREADY RUN! AT LEAST ADD SOMETHING TO THE ORIGINAL THAT'S NEW AND FUNNY!
CHAT WITH THE SIMPLETONS AND
FINE. YOU WANT SOMETHING NEW AND FUNNY? I'LL ADD SOMETHING NEW AND FUNNY.
I THINK I PREFER THE ORIGINAL.
NO. YOU WERE RIGHT. WE'LL ADD SOMETHING NEW AND FUNNY TO EVERY STRIP.
WE SHOULD RUN.

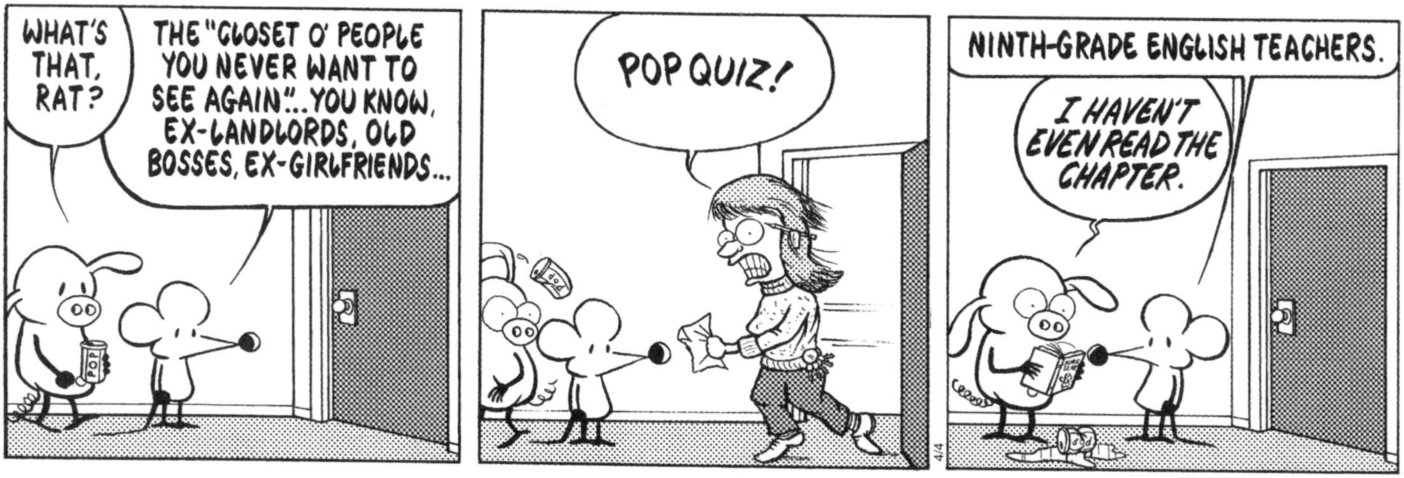
WHAT'S THAT, RAT?
THE "CLOSET O' PEOPLE YOU NEVER WANT TO SEE AGAIN"... YOU KNOW, EX-LANDLORDS, OLD BOSSES, EX-GIRLFRIENDS...
POP QUIZ!
NINTH-GRADE ENGLISH TEACHERS.
I HAVEN'T EVEN READ THE CHAPTER.
4/4

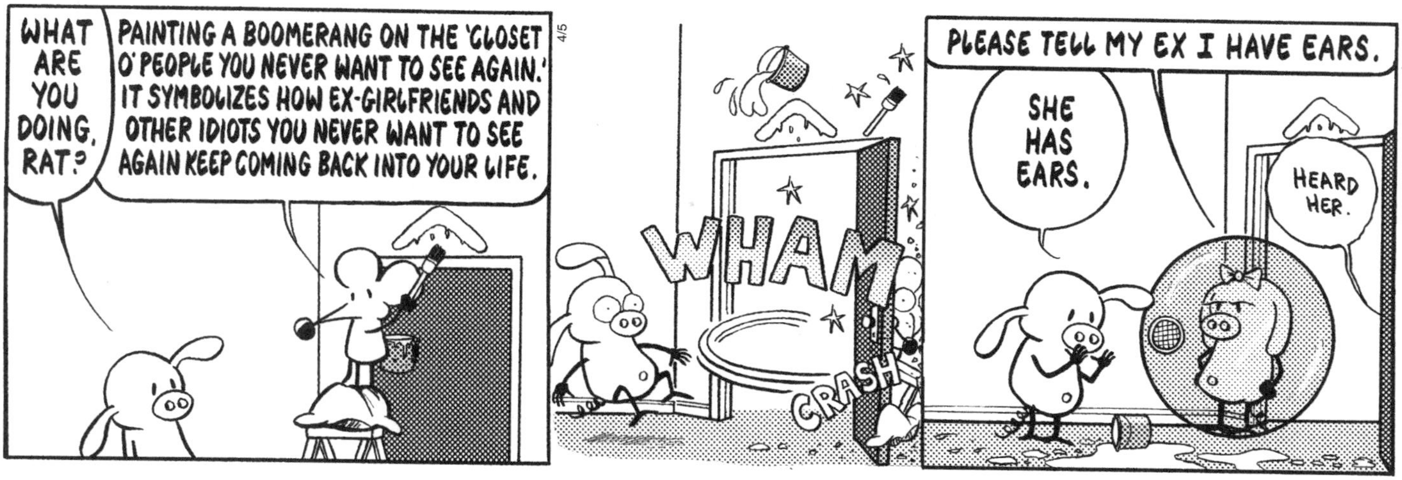
WHAT ARE YOU DOING, RAT?
PAINTING A BOOMERANG ON THE 'CLOSET O' PEOPLE YOU NEVER WANT TO SEE AGAIN.' IT SYMBOLIZES HOW EX-GIRLFRIENDS AND OTHER IDIOTS YOU NEVER WANT TO SEE AGAIN KEEP COMING BACK INTO YOUR LIFE.
4/5
WHAM
CRASH
PLEASE TELL MY EX I HAVE EARS.
SHE HAS EARS.
HEARD HER.

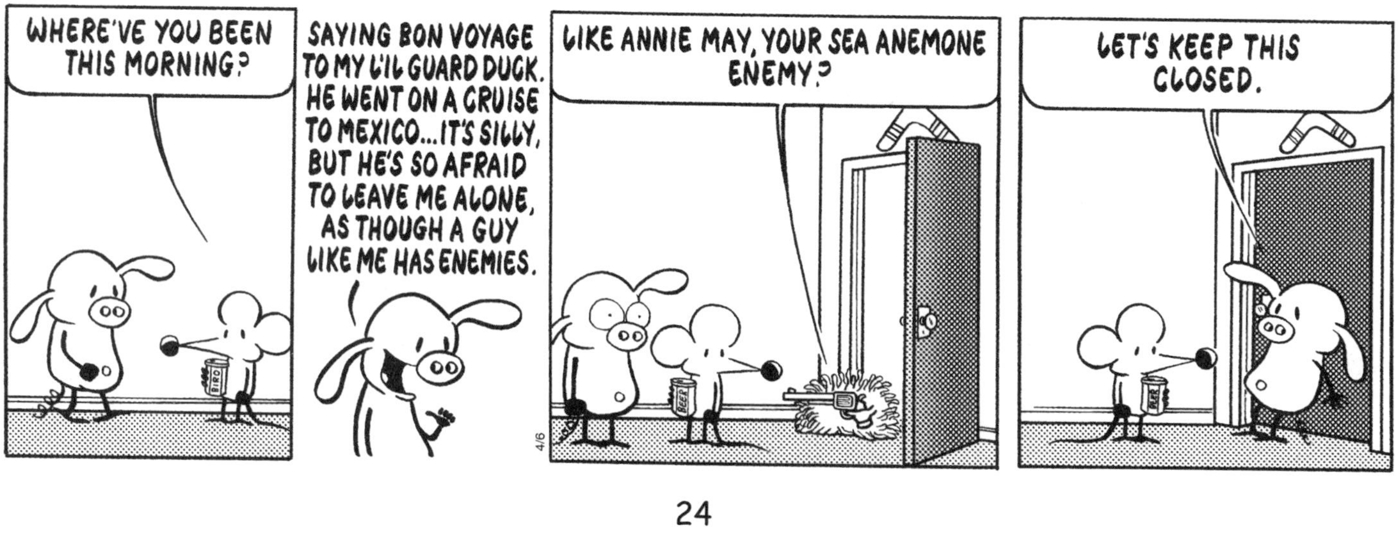
WHERE'VE YOU BEEN THIS MORNING?
SAYING BON VOYAGE TO MY LI'L GUARD DUCK. HE WENT ON A CRUISE TO MEXICO... IT'S SILLY, BUT HE'S SO AFRAID TO LEAVE ME ALONE, AS THOUGH A GUY LIKE ME HAS ENEMIES.
LIKE ANNIE MAY, YOUR SEA ANEMONE ENEMY?
4/6
LET'S KEEP THIS CLOSED.

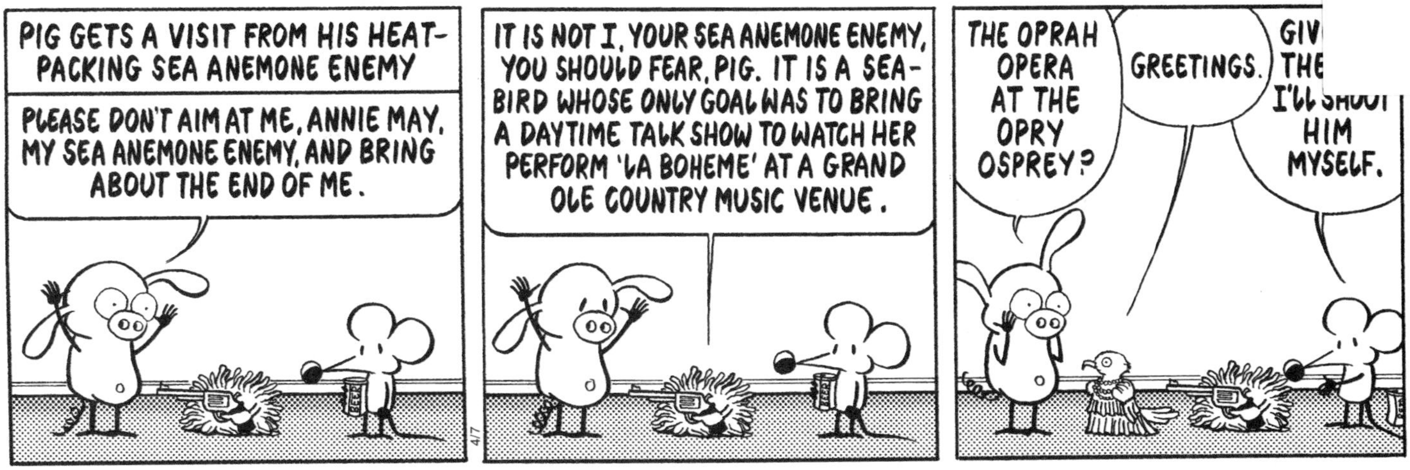
PIG GETS A VISIT FROM HIS HEAT-PACKING SEA ANEMONE ENEMY
PLEASE DON'T AIM AT ME, ANNIE MAY, MY SEA ANEMONE ENEMY, AND BRING ABOUT THE END OF ME.
4/7
IT IS NOT I, YOUR SEA ANEMONE ENEMY, YOU SHOULD FEAR, PIG. IT IS A SEA-BIRD WHOSE ONLY GOAL WAS TO BRING A DAYTIME TALK SHOW TO WATCH HER PERFORM 'LA BOHEME' AT A GRAND OLE COUNTRY MUSIC VENUE.
THE OPRAH OPERA AT THE OPRY OSPREY?
GREETINGS.
GIV THE I'LL
HIM MYSELF.

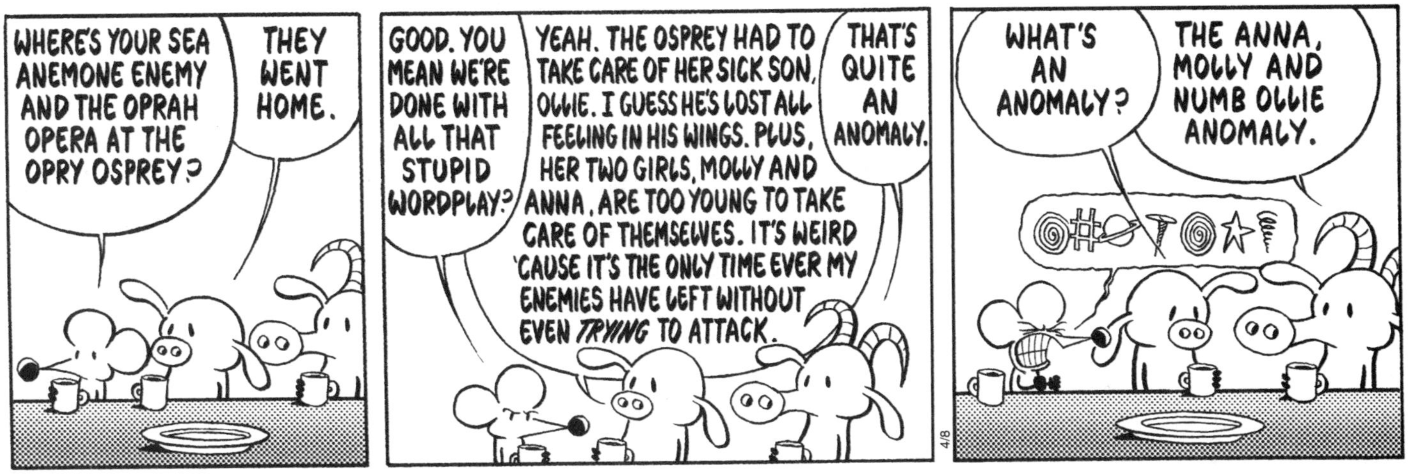
WHERE'S YOUR SEA ANEMONE ENEMY AND THE OPRAH OPERA AT THE OPRY OSPREY?
THEY WENT HOME.
GOOD. YOU MEAN WE'RE DONE WITH ALL THAT STUPID WORDPLAY?
YEAH. THE OSPREY HAD TO TAKE CARE OF HER SICK SON, OLLIE. I GUESS HE'S LOST ALL FEELING IN HIS WINGS. PLUS, HER TWO GIRLS, MOLLY AND ANNA, ARE TOO YOUNG TO TAKE CARE OF THEMSELVES. IT'S WEIRD 'CAUSE IT'S THE ONLY TIME EVER MY ENEMIES HAVE LEFT WITHOUT EVEN *TRYING* TO ATTACK.
THAT'S QUITE AN ANOMALY.
4/8
WHAT'S AN ANOMALY?
THE ANNA, MOLLY AND NUMB OLLIE ANOMALY.

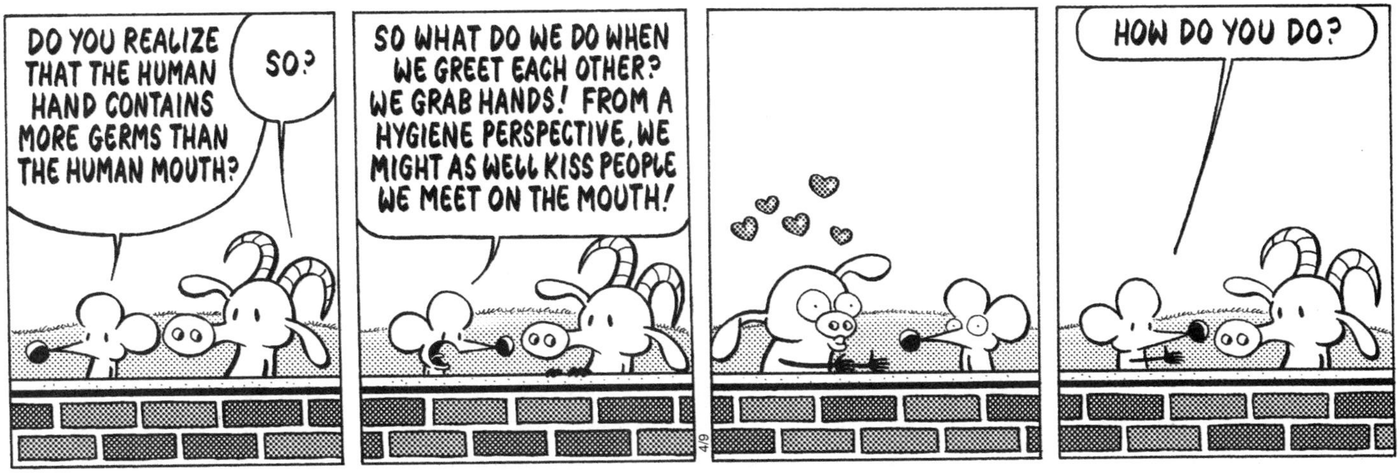
DO YOU REALIZE THAT THE HUMAN HAND CONTAINS MORE GERMS THAN THE HUMAN MOUTH?
SO?
SO WHAT DO WE DO WHEN WE GREET EACH OTHER? WE GRAB HANDS! FROM A HYGIENE PERSPECTIVE, WE MIGHT AS WELL KISS PEOPLE WE MEET ON THE MOUTH!
4/9
HOW DO YOU DO?

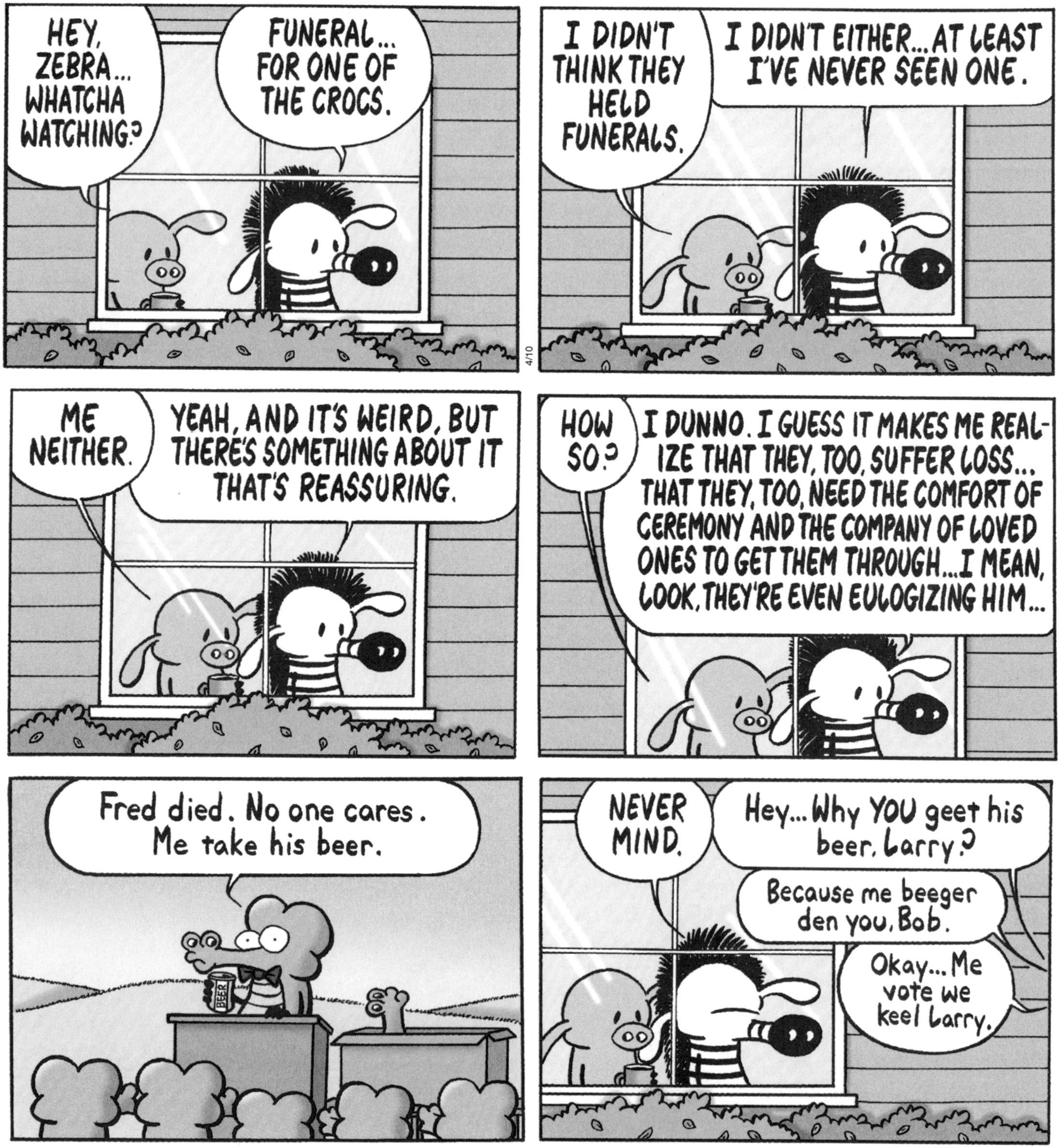
HEY, ZEBRA... WHATCHA WATCHING?
FUNERAL... FOR ONE OF THE CROCS.
4/10
I DIDN'T THINK THEY HELD FUNERALS.
I DIDN'T EITHER... AT LEAST I'VE NEVER SEEN ONE.
ME NEITHER.
YEAH, AND IT'S WEIRD, BUT THERE'S SOMETHING ABOUT IT THAT'S REASSURING.
HOW SO?
I DUNNO. I GUESS IT MAKES ME REALIZE THAT THEY, TOO, SUFFER LOSS... THAT THEY, TOO, NEED THE COMFORT OF CEREMONY AND THE COMPANY OF LOVED ONES TO GET THEM THROUGH... I MEAN, LOOK, THEY'RE EVEN EULOGIZING HIM...
Fred died. No one cares. Me take his beer.
BEER
NEVER MIND.
Hey... Why YOU geet his beer, Larry?
Because me beeger den you, Bob.
Okay... Me vote we keel Larry.

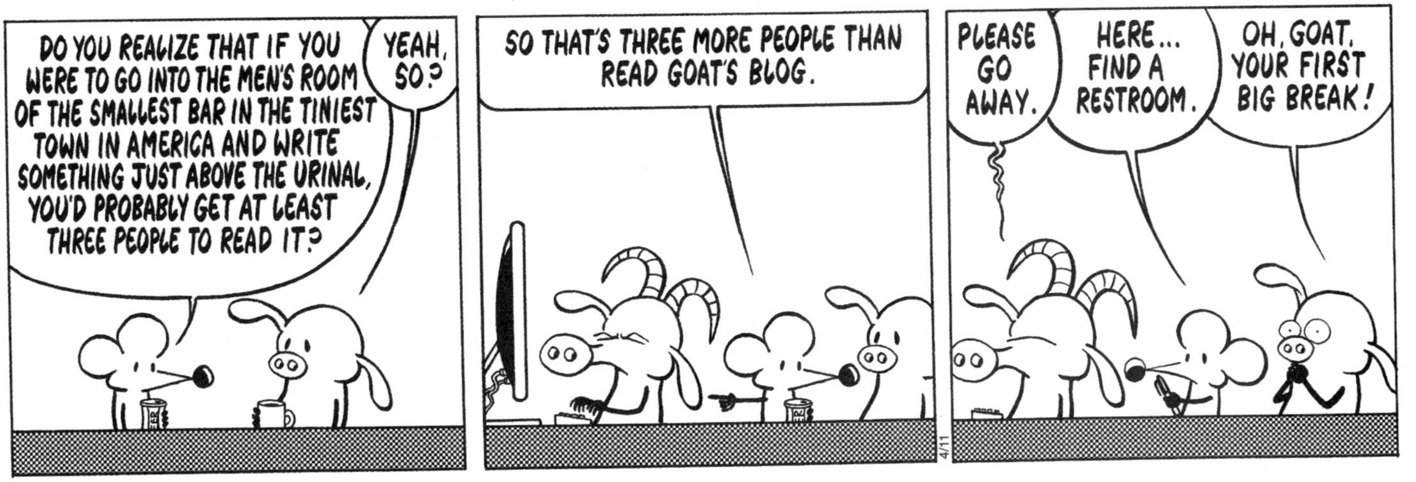
DO YOU REALIZE THAT IF YOU WERE TO GO INTO THE MEN'S ROOM OF THE SMALLEST BAR IN THE TINIEST TOWN IN AMERICA AND WRITE SOMETHING JUST ABOVE THE URINAL, YOU'D PROBABLY GET AT LEAST THREE PEOPLE TO READ IT?
YEAH, SO?
SO THAT'S THREE MORE PEOPLE THAN READ GOAT'S BLOG.
PLEASE GO AWAY.
HERE... FIND A RESTROOM.
OH, GOAT. YOUR FIRST BIG BREAK!
4/11

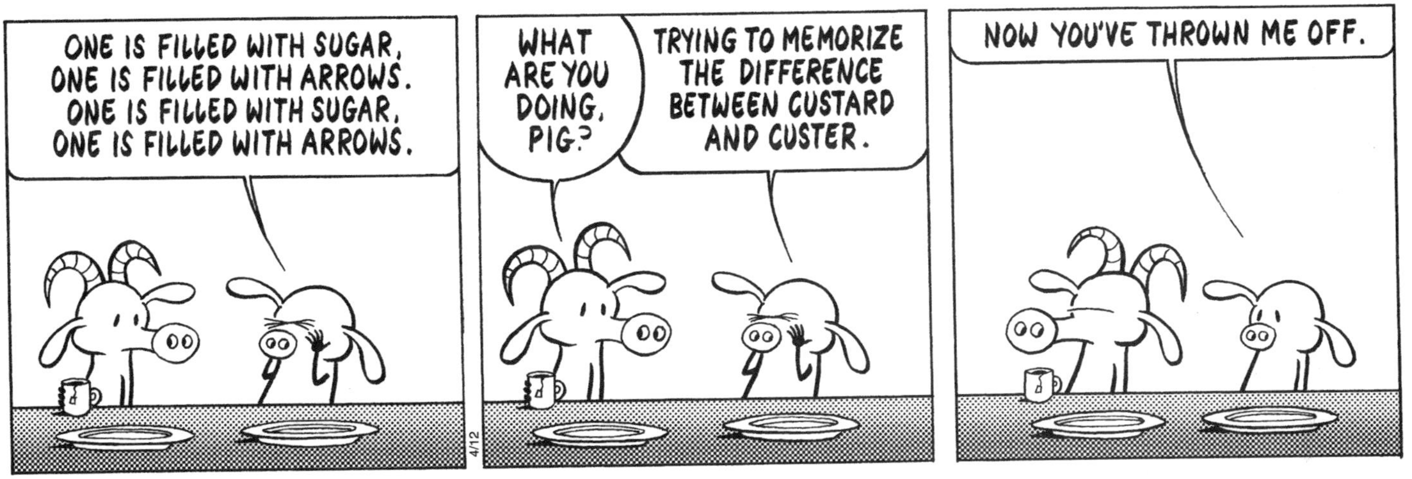
ONE IS FILLED WITH SUGAR, ONE IS FILLED WITH ARROWS. ONE IS FILLED WITH SUGAR, ONE IS FILLED WITH ARROWS.
4/12
WHAT ARE YOU DOING, PIG?
TRYING TO MEMORIZE THE DIFFERENCE BETWEEN CUSTARD AND CUSTER.
NOW YOU'VE THROWN ME OFF.

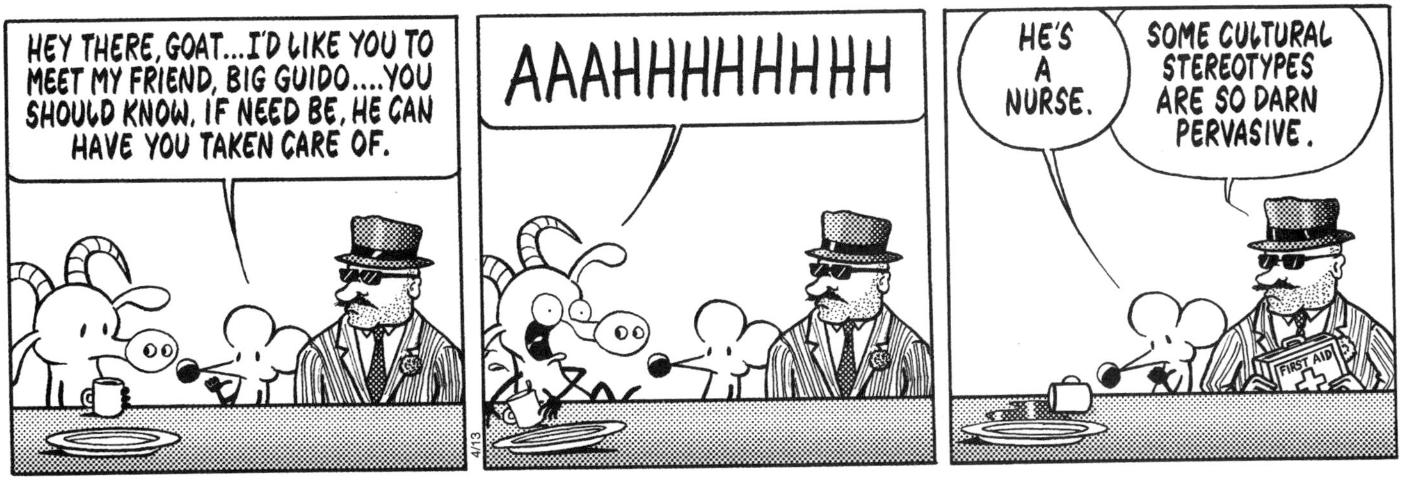
HEY THERE, GOAT...I'D LIKE YOU TO MEET MY FRIEND, BIG GUIDO....YOU SHOULD KNOW, IF NEED BE, HE CAN HAVE YOU TAKEN CARE OF.
4/13
AAAHHHHHHHH
HE'S A NURSE.
SOME CULTURAL STEREOTYPES ARE SO DARN PERVASIVE.
FIRST AID

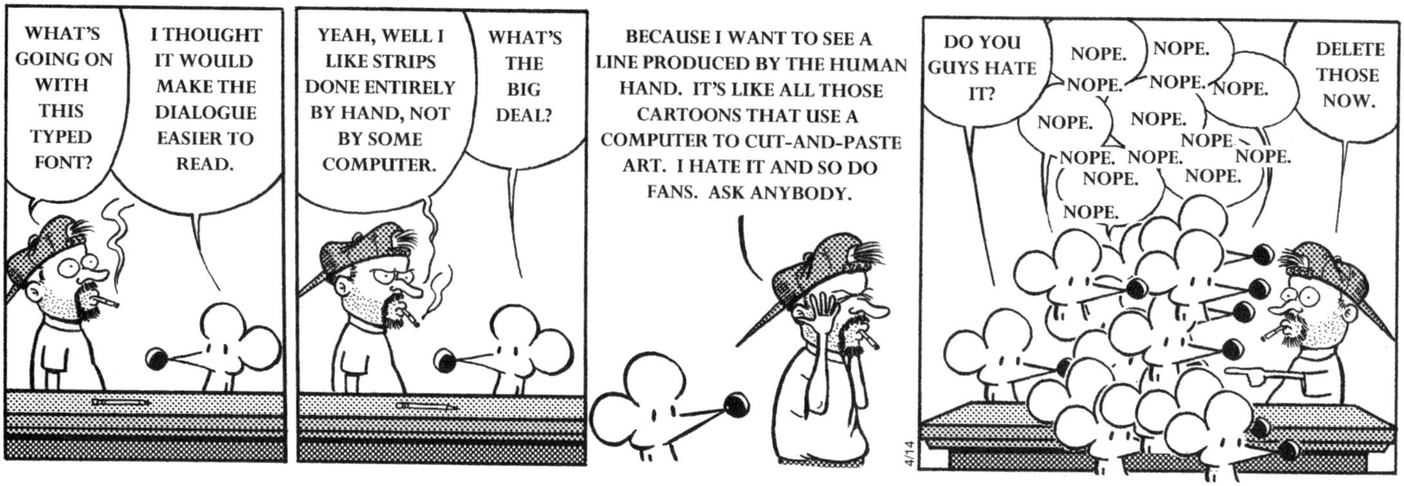
WHAT'S GOING ON WITH THIS TYPED FONT?
I THOUGHT IT WOULD MAKE THE DIALOGUE EASIER TO READ.
YEAH, WELL I LIKE STRIPS DONE ENTIRELY BY HAND, NOT BY SOME COMPUTER.
WHAT'S THE BIG DEAL?
BECAUSE I WANT TO SEE A LINE PRODUCED BY THE HUMAN HAND. IT'S LIKE ALL THOSE CARTOONS THAT USE A COMPUTER TO CUT-AND-PASTE ART. I HATE IT AND SO DO FANS. ASK ANYBODY.
DO YOU GUYS HATE IT?
NOPE.
NOPE.
NOPE.
NOPE.
NOPE.
NOPE.
NOPE.
NOPE
NOPE.
NOPE.
NOPE.
NOPE.
NOPE.
NOPE.
DELETE THOSE NOW.
4/14

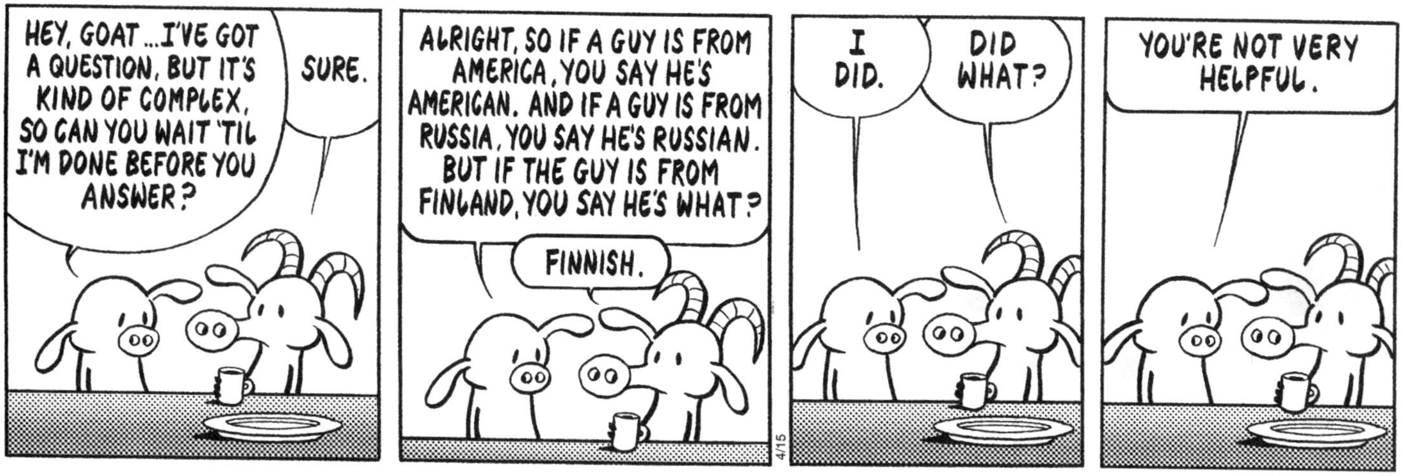
HEY, GOAT ... I'VE GOT A QUESTION, BUT IT'S KIND OF COMPLEX, SO CAN YOU WAIT 'TIL I'M DONE BEFORE YOU ANSWER?
SURE.
ALRIGHT, SO IF A GUY IS FROM AMERICA, YOU SAY HE'S AMERICAN. AND IF A GUY IS FROM RUSSIA, YOU SAY HE'S RUSSIAN. BUT IF THE GUY IS FROM FINLAND, YOU SAY HE'S WHAT?
FINNISH.
4/15
I DID.
DID WHAT?
YOU'RE NOT VERY HELPFUL.

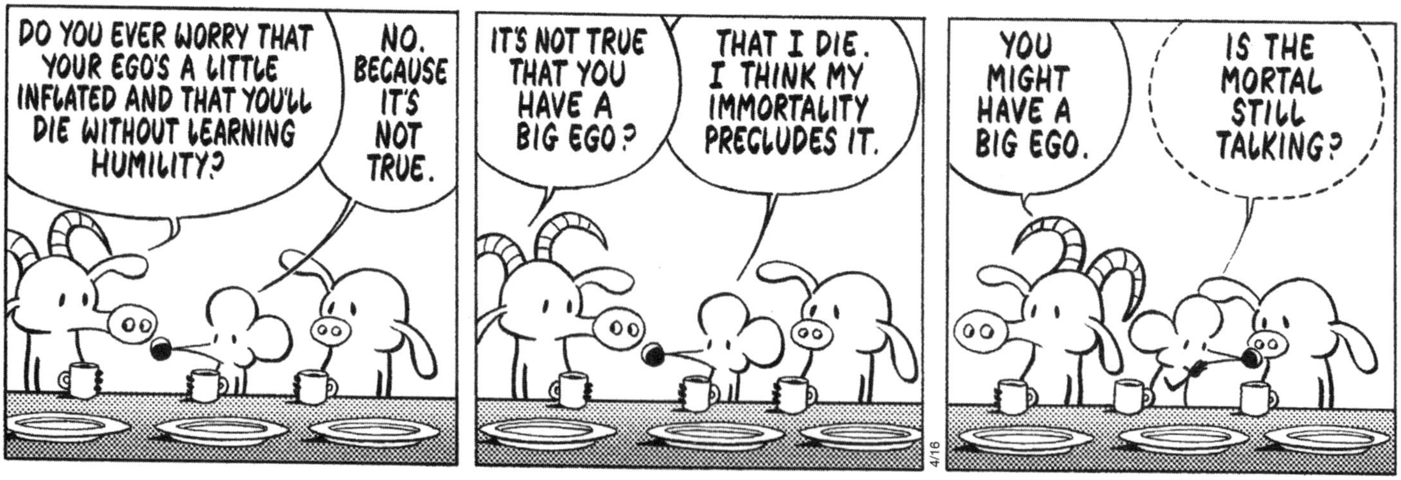
DO YOU EVER WORRY THAT YOUR EGO'S A LITTLE INFLATED AND THAT YOU'LL DIE WITHOUT LEARNING HUMILITY?
NO. BECAUSE IT'S NOT TRUE.
IT'S NOT TRUE THAT YOU HAVE A BIG EGO?
THAT I DIE. I THINK MY IMMORTALITY PRECLUDES IT.
4/16
YOU MIGHT HAVE A BIG EGO.
IS THE MORTAL STILL TALKING?

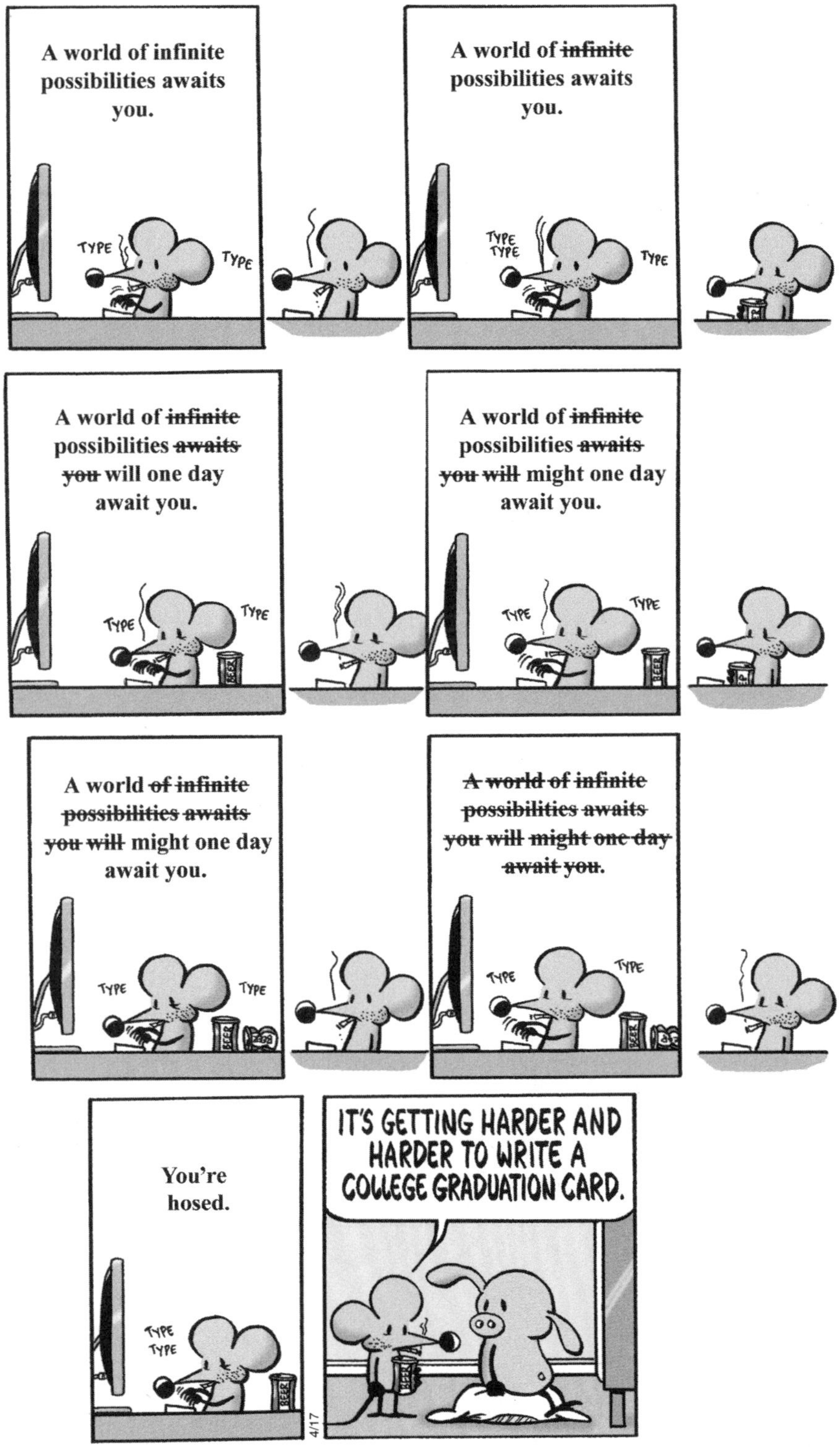
A world of infinite possibilities awaits you.
TYPE
TYPE
A world of ~~infinite~~ possibilities awaits you.
TYPE TYPE
TYPE
A world of ~~infinite~~ possibilities ~~awaits you~~ will one day await you.
TYPE
TYPE
A world of ~~infinite~~ possibilities ~~awaits you will~~ might one day await you.
TYPE
TYPE
A world ~~of infinite possibilities awaits you will~~ might one day await you.
TYPE
TYPE
~~A world of infinite possibilities awaits you will might one day await you~~.
TYPE
TYPE
You're hosed.
TYPE TYPE
IT'S GETTING HARDER AND HARDER TO WRITE A COLLEGE GRADUATION CARD.
4/17

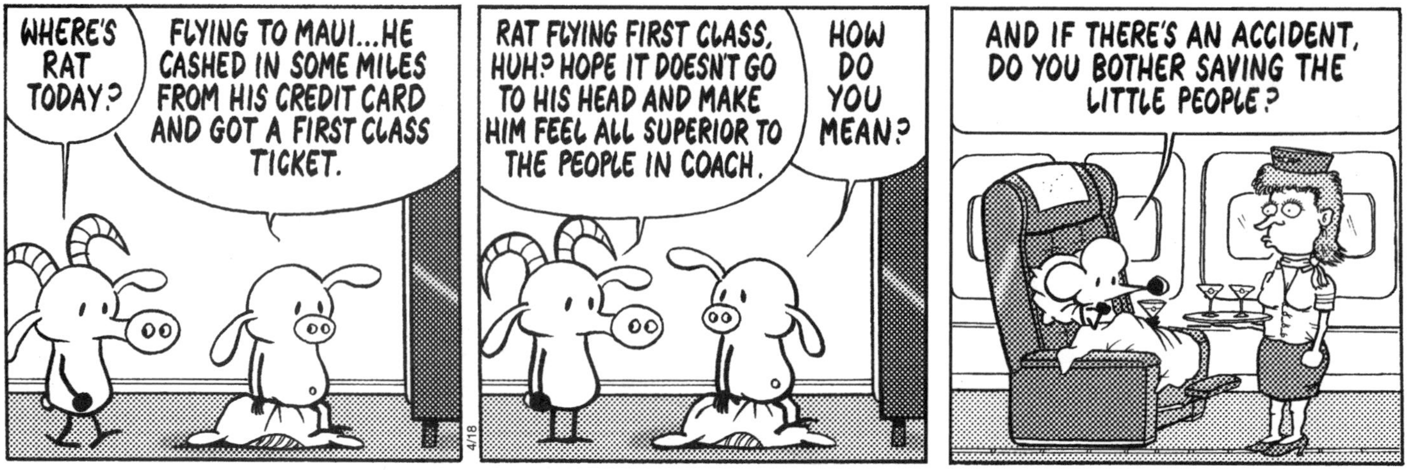
WHERE'S RAT TODAY?
FLYING TO MAUI...HE CASHED IN SOME MILES FROM HIS CREDIT CARD AND GOT A FIRST CLASS TICKET.
4/18
RAT FLYING FIRST CLASS, HUH? HOPE IT DOESN'T GO TO HIS HEAD AND MAKE HIM FEEL ALL SUPERIOR TO THE PEOPLE IN COACH.
HOW DO YOU MEAN?
AND IF THERE'S AN ACCIDENT, DO YOU BOTHER SAVING THE LITTLE PEOPLE?

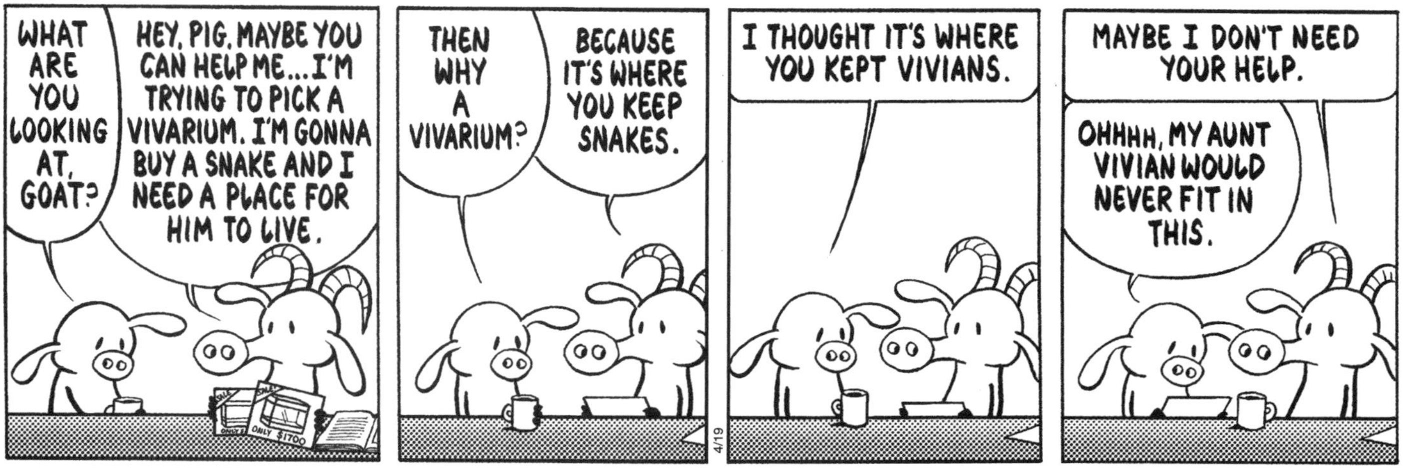
WHAT ARE YOU LOOKING AT, GOAT?
HEY, PIG, MAYBE YOU CAN HELP ME...I'M TRYING TO PICK A VIVARIUM. I'M GONNA BUY A SNAKE AND I NEED A PLACE FOR HIM TO LIVE.
ONLY $1700
THEN WHY A VIVARIUM?
BECAUSE IT'S WHERE YOU KEEP SNAKES.
4/19
I THOUGHT IT'S WHERE YOU KEPT VIVIANS.
MAYBE I DON'T NEED YOUR HELP.
OHHHH, MY AUNT VIVIAN WOULD NEVER FIT IN THIS.

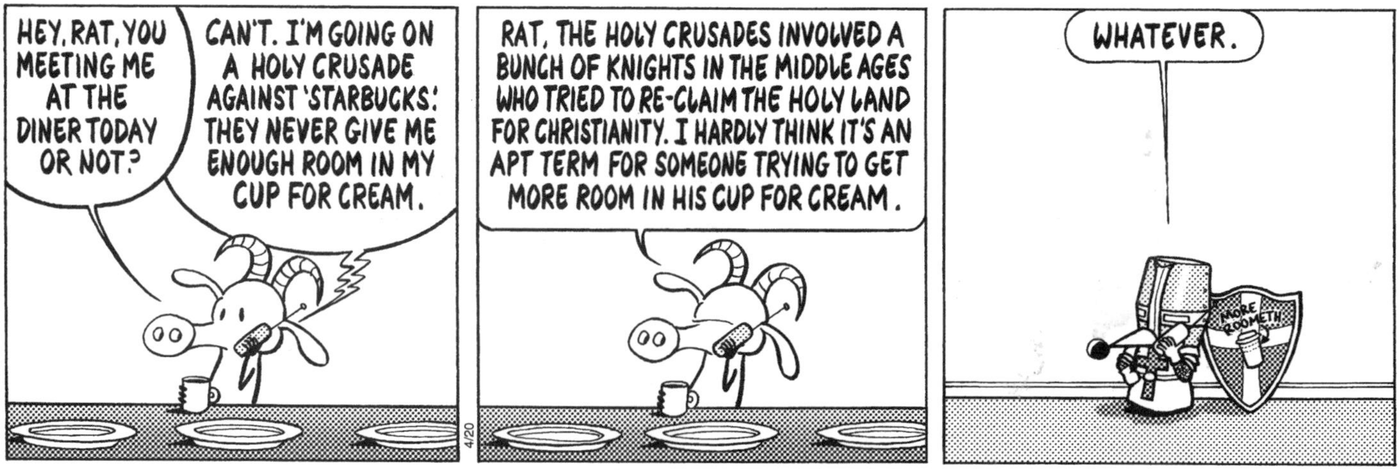
HEY, RAT, YOU MEETING ME AT THE DINER TODAY OR NOT?
CAN'T. I'M GOING ON A HOLY CRUSADE AGAINST 'STARBUCKS.' THEY NEVER GIVE ME ENOUGH ROOM IN MY CUP FOR CREAM.
4/20
RAT, THE HOLY CRUSADES INVOLVED A BUNCH OF KNIGHTS IN THE MIDDLE AGES WHO TRIED TO RE-CLAIM THE HOLY LAND FOR CHRISTIANITY. I HARDLY THINK IT'S AN APT TERM FOR SOMEONE TRYING TO GET MORE ROOM IN HIS CUP FOR CREAM.
WHATEVER.
MORE ROOMETH

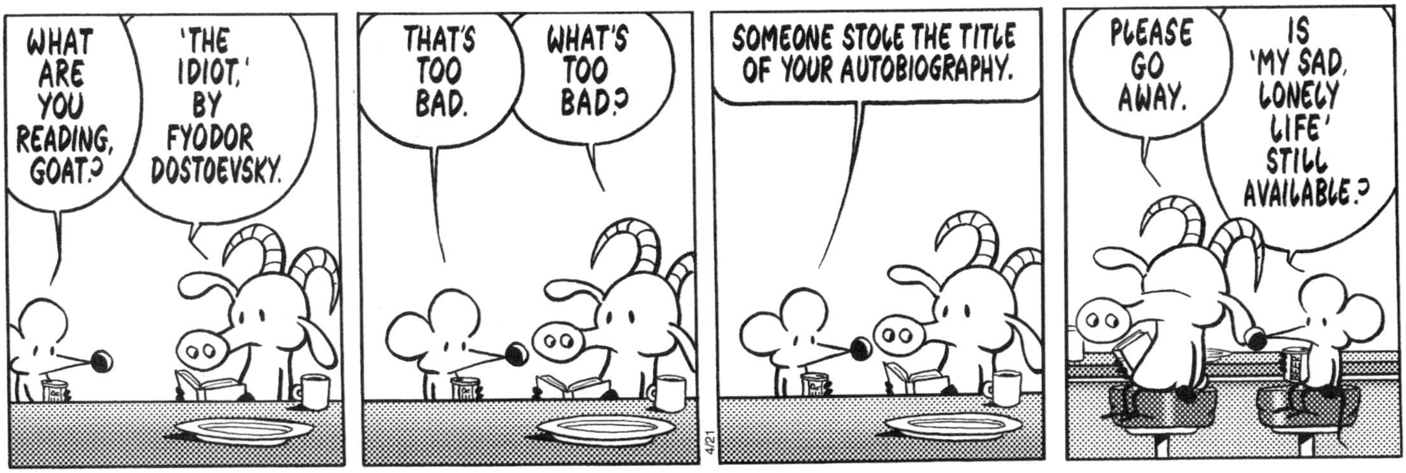
WHAT ARE YOU READING, GOAT?
'THE IDIOT,' BY FYODOR DOSTOEVSKY.
THAT'S TOO BAD.
WHAT'S TOO BAD?
SOMEONE STOLE THE TITLE OF YOUR AUTOBIOGRAPHY.
4/21
PLEASE GO AWAY.
IS 'MY SAD, LONELY LIFE' STILL AVAILABLE?

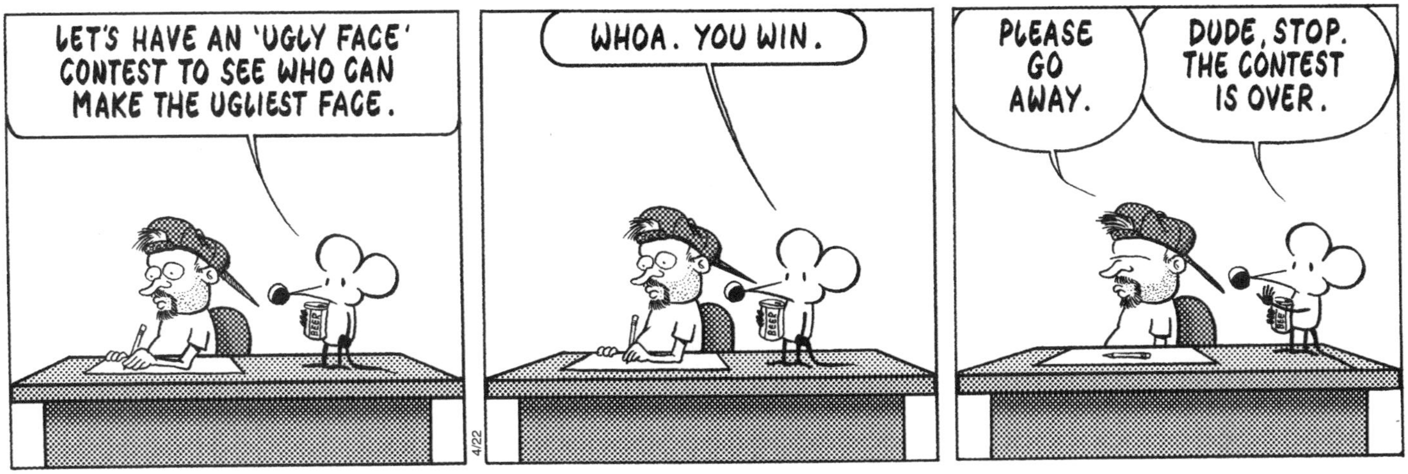
LET'S HAVE AN 'UGLY FACE' CONTEST TO SEE WHO CAN MAKE THE UGLIEST FACE.
4/22
WHOA. YOU WIN.
PLEASE GO AWAY.
DUDE, STOP. THE CONTEST IS OVER.

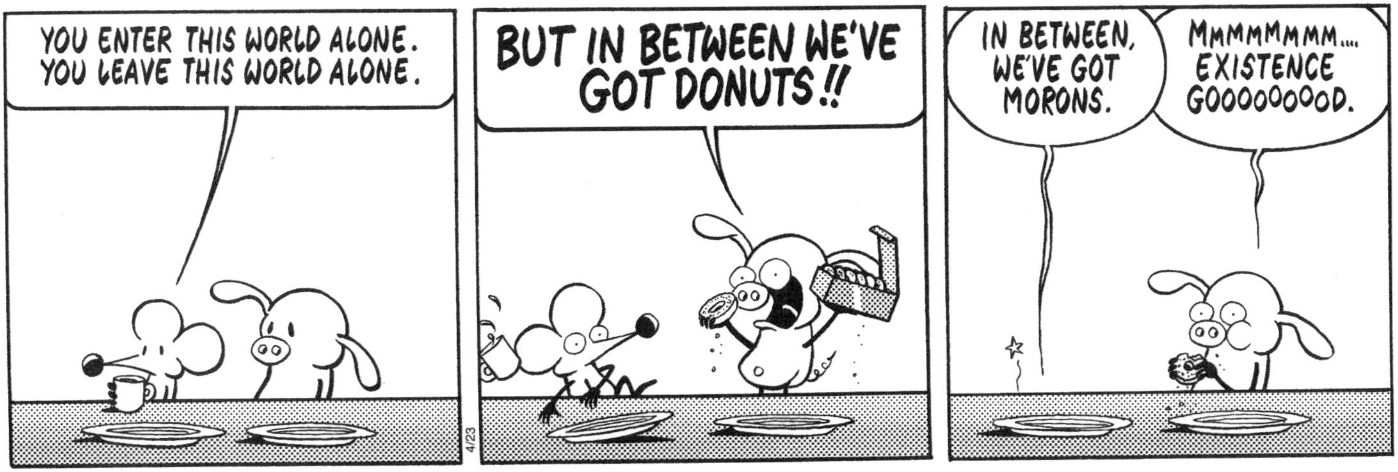
YOU ENTER THIS WORLD ALONE. YOU LEAVE THIS WORLD ALONE.
4/23
BUT IN BETWEEN WE'VE GOT DONUTS!!
IN BETWEEN, WE'VE GOT MORONS.
MMMMMMM.... EXISTENCE GOOOOOOOOD.

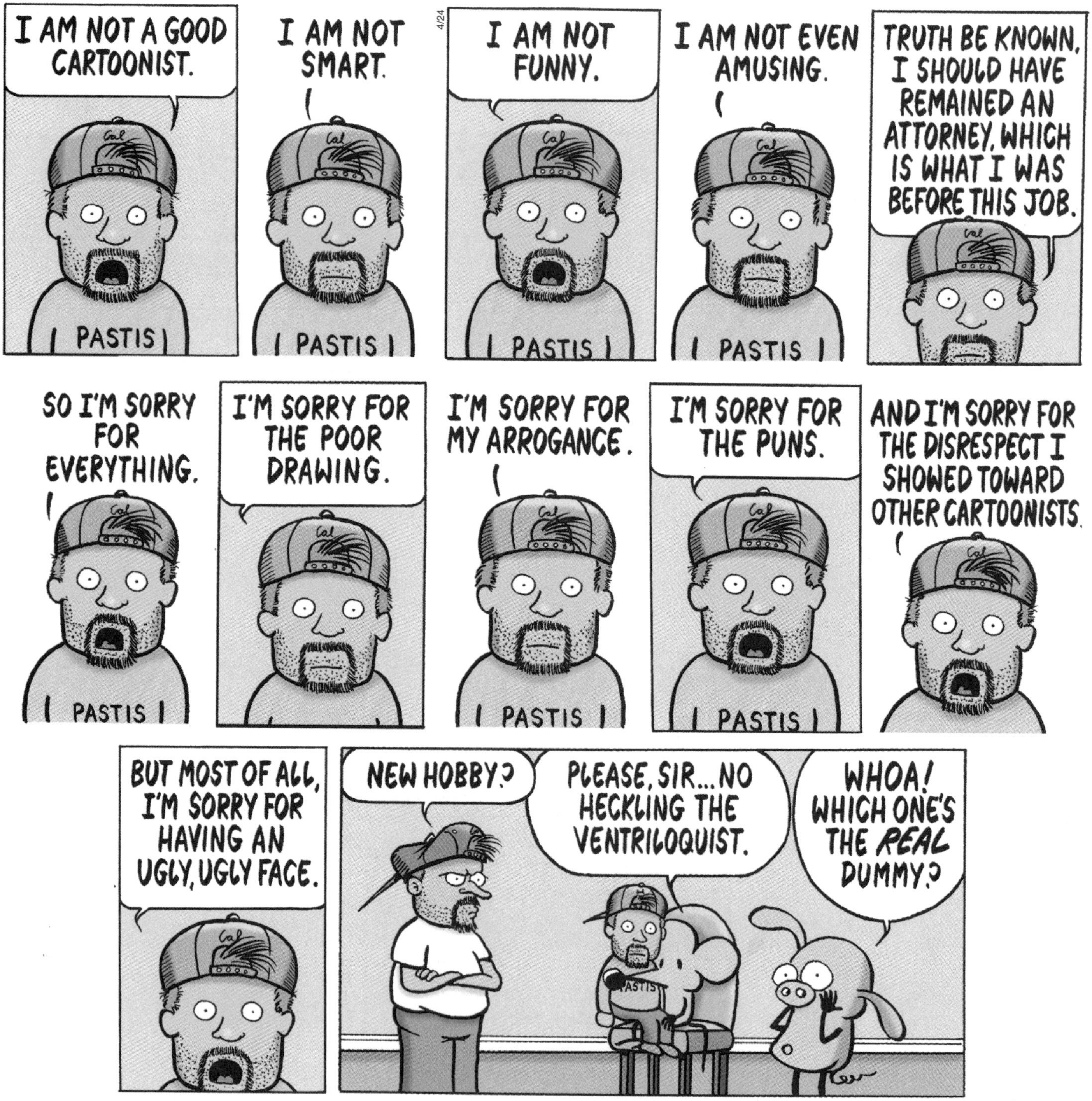

I AM NOT A GOOD CARTOONIST.
PASTIS
I AM NOT SMART.
PASTIS
4/24
I AM NOT FUNNY.
PASTIS
I AM NOT EVEN AMUSING.
PASTIS
TRUTH BE KNOWN, I SHOULD HAVE REMAINED AN ATTORNEY, WHICH IS WHAT I WAS BEFORE THIS JOB.
SO I'M SORRY FOR EVERYTHING.
PASTIS
I'M SORRY FOR THE POOR DRAWING.
I'M SORRY FOR MY ARROGANCE.
PASTIS
I'M SORRY FOR THE PUNS.
PASTIS
AND I'M SORRY FOR THE DISRESPECT I SHOWED TOWARD OTHER CARTOONISTS.
BUT MOST OF ALL, I'M SORRY FOR HAVING AN UGLY, UGLY FACE.
NEW HOBBY?
PLEASE, SIR... NO HECKLING THE VENTRILOQUIST.
WHOA! WHICH ONE'S THE *REAL* DUMMY?
PASTIS

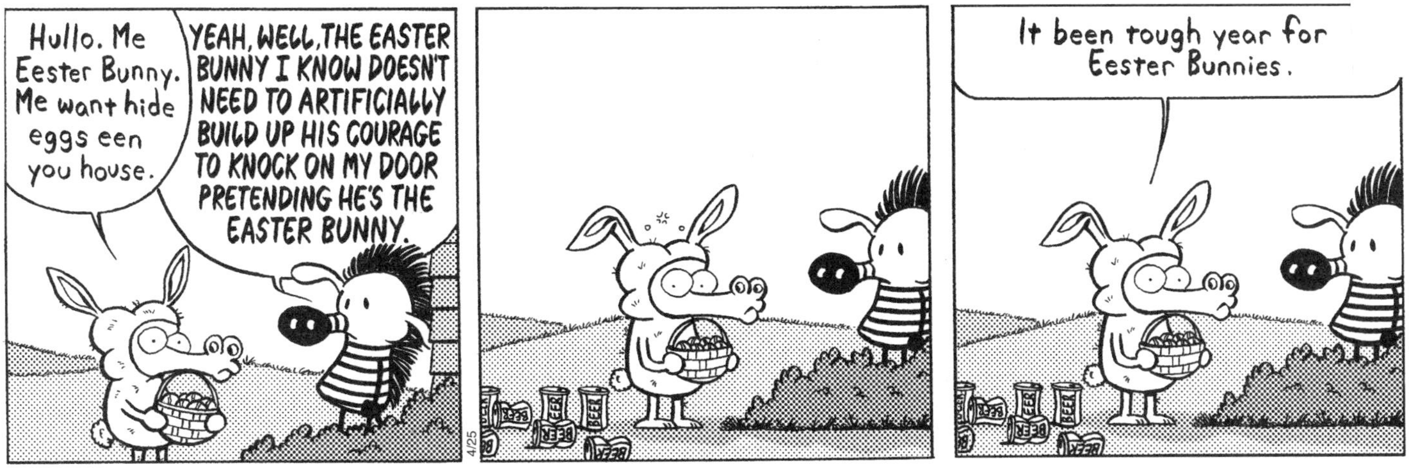
Hullo. Me Eester Bunny. Me want hide eggs een you house.
YEAH, WELL, THE EASTER BUNNY I KNOW DOESN'T NEED TO ARTIFICIALLY BUILD UP HIS COURAGE TO KNOCK ON MY DOOR PRETENDING HE'S THE EASTER BUNNY.
It been tough year for Eester Bunnies.

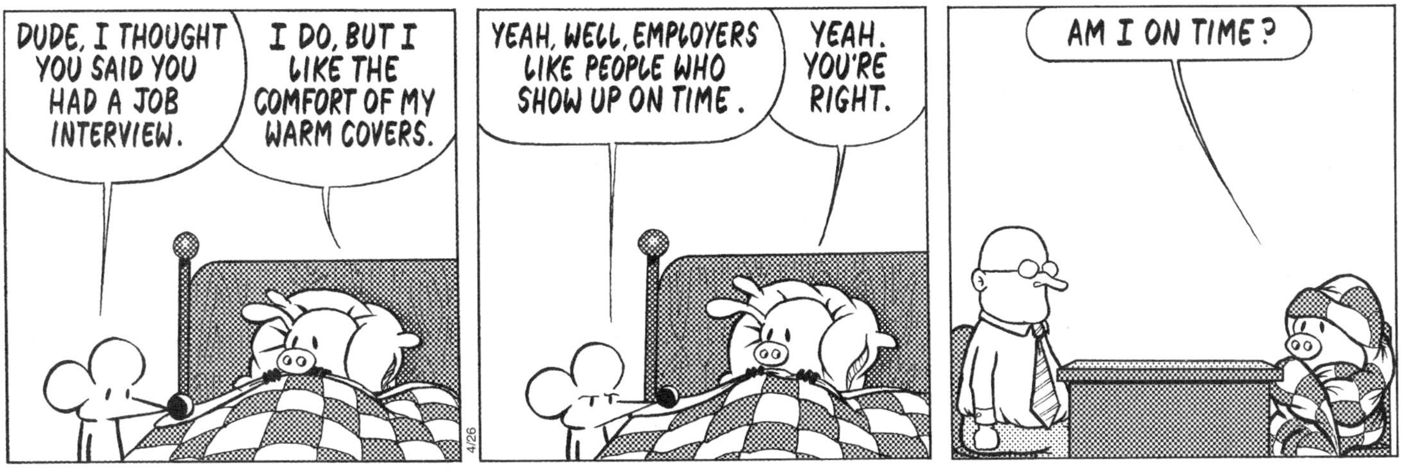
DUDE, I THOUGHT YOU SAID YOU HAD A JOB INTERVIEW.
I DO, BUT I LIKE THE COMFORT OF MY WARM COVERS.
YEAH, WELL, EMPLOYERS LIKE PEOPLE WHO SHOW UP ON TIME.
YEAH. YOU'RE RIGHT.
AM I ON TIME?

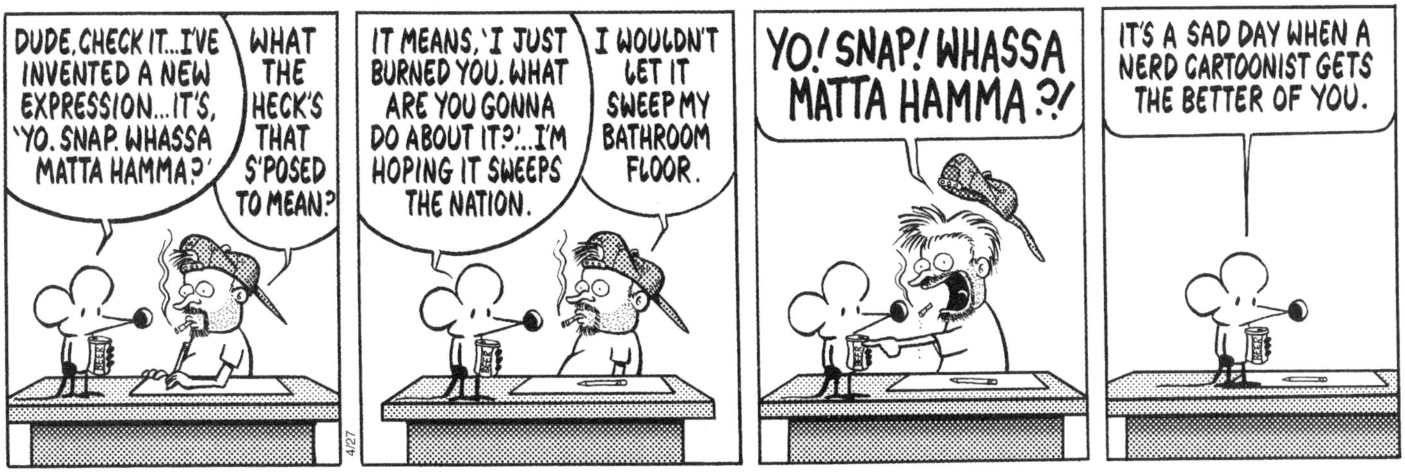
DUDE, CHECK IT...I'VE INVENTED A NEW EXPRESSION...IT'S, 'YO. SNAP. WHASSA MATTA HAMMA?'
WHAT THE HECK'S THAT S'POSED TO MEAN?
IT MEANS, 'I JUST BURNED YOU. WHAT ARE YOU GONNA DO ABOUT IT?'...I'M HOPING IT SWEEPS THE NATION.
I WOULDN'T LET IT SWEEP MY BATHROOM FLOOR.
YO! SNAP! WHASSA MATTA HAMMA?!
IT'S A SAD DAY WHEN A NERD CARTOONIST GETS THE BETTER OF YOU.

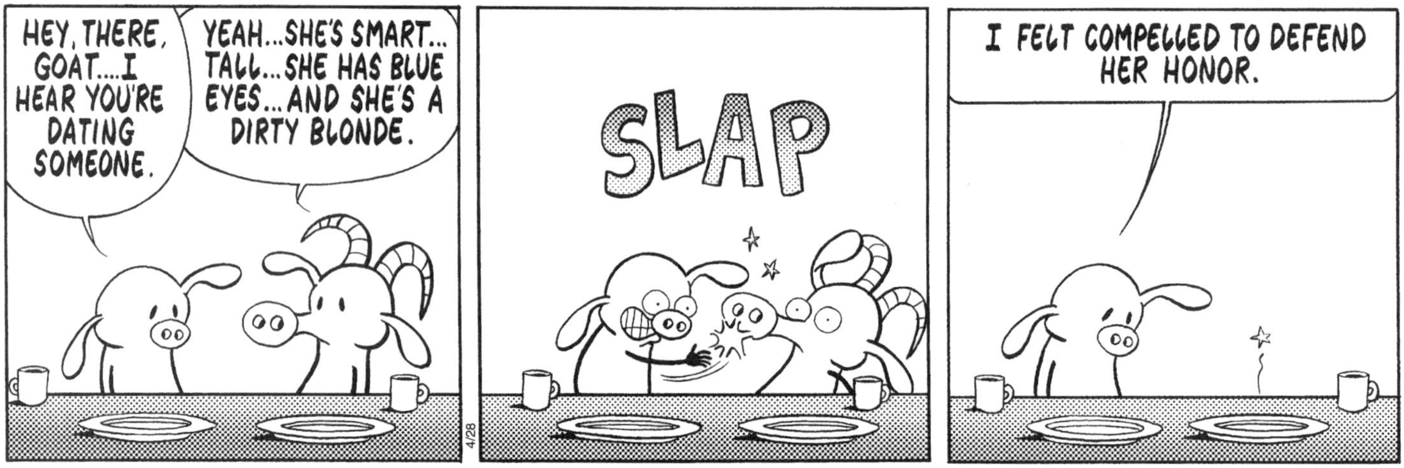
HEY, THERE, GOAT....I HEAR YOU'RE DATING SOMEONE.
YEAH...SHE'S SMART... TALL...SHE HAS BLUE EYES...AND SHE'S A DIRTY BLONDE.
SLAP
I FELT COMPELLED TO DEFEND HER HONOR.
4/28

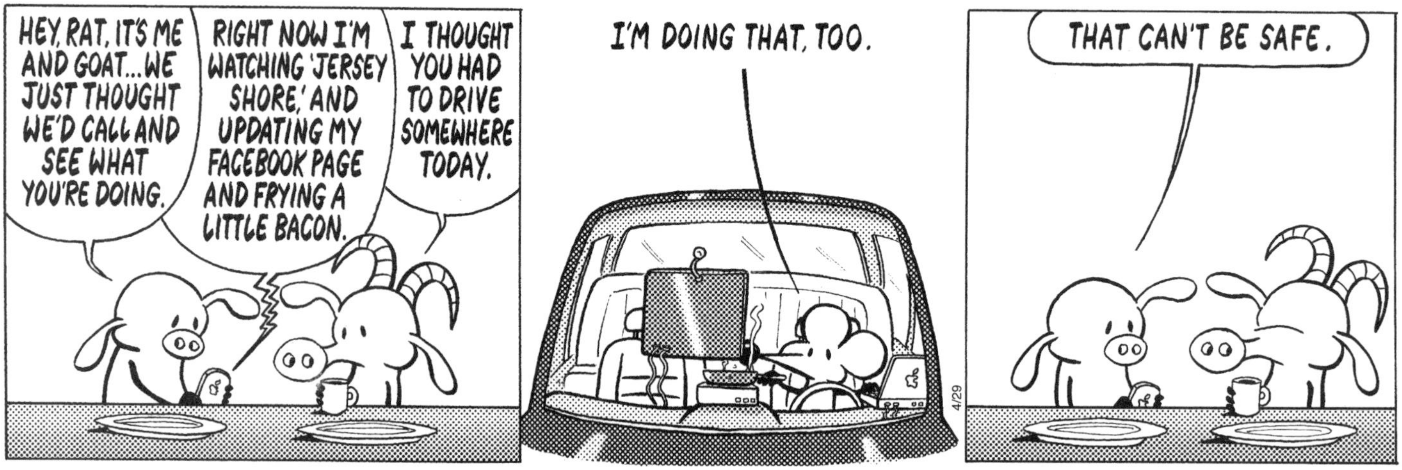
HEY, RAT, IT'S ME AND GOAT...WE JUST THOUGHT WE'D CALL AND SEE WHAT YOU'RE DOING.
RIGHT NOW I'M WATCHING 'JERSEY SHORE,' AND UPDATING MY FACEBOOK PAGE AND FRYING A LITTLE BACON.
I THOUGHT YOU HAD TO DRIVE SOMEWHERE TODAY.
I'M DOING THAT, TOO.
THAT CAN'T BE SAFE.
4/29

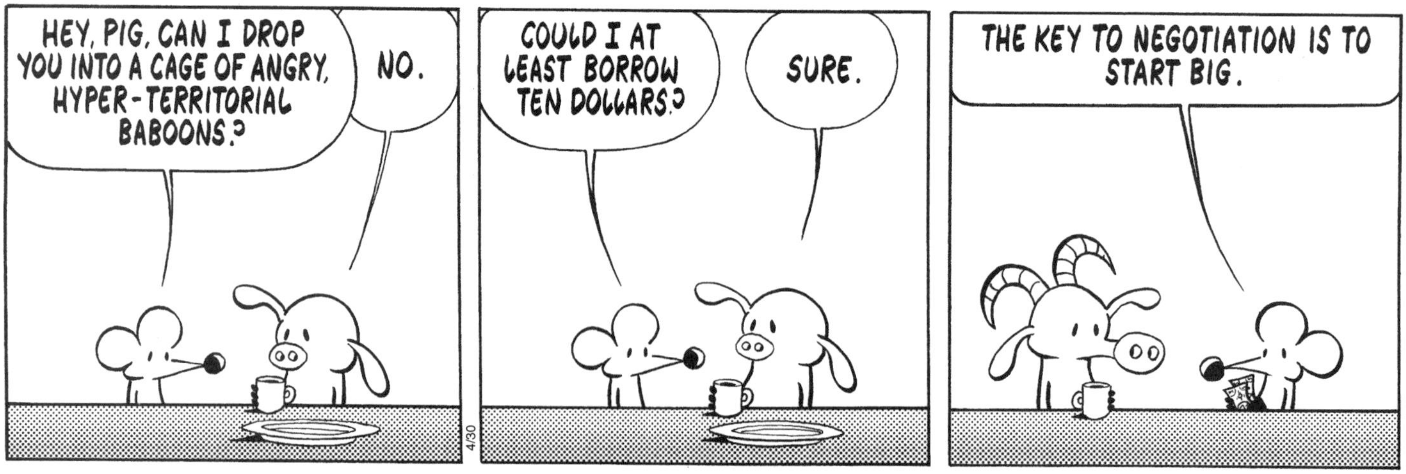
HEY, PIG, CAN I DROP YOU INTO A CAGE OF ANGRY, HYPER-TERRITORIAL BABOONS?
NO.
COULD I AT LEAST BORROW TEN DOLLARS?
SURE.
THE KEY TO NEGOTIATION IS TO START BIG.
4/30

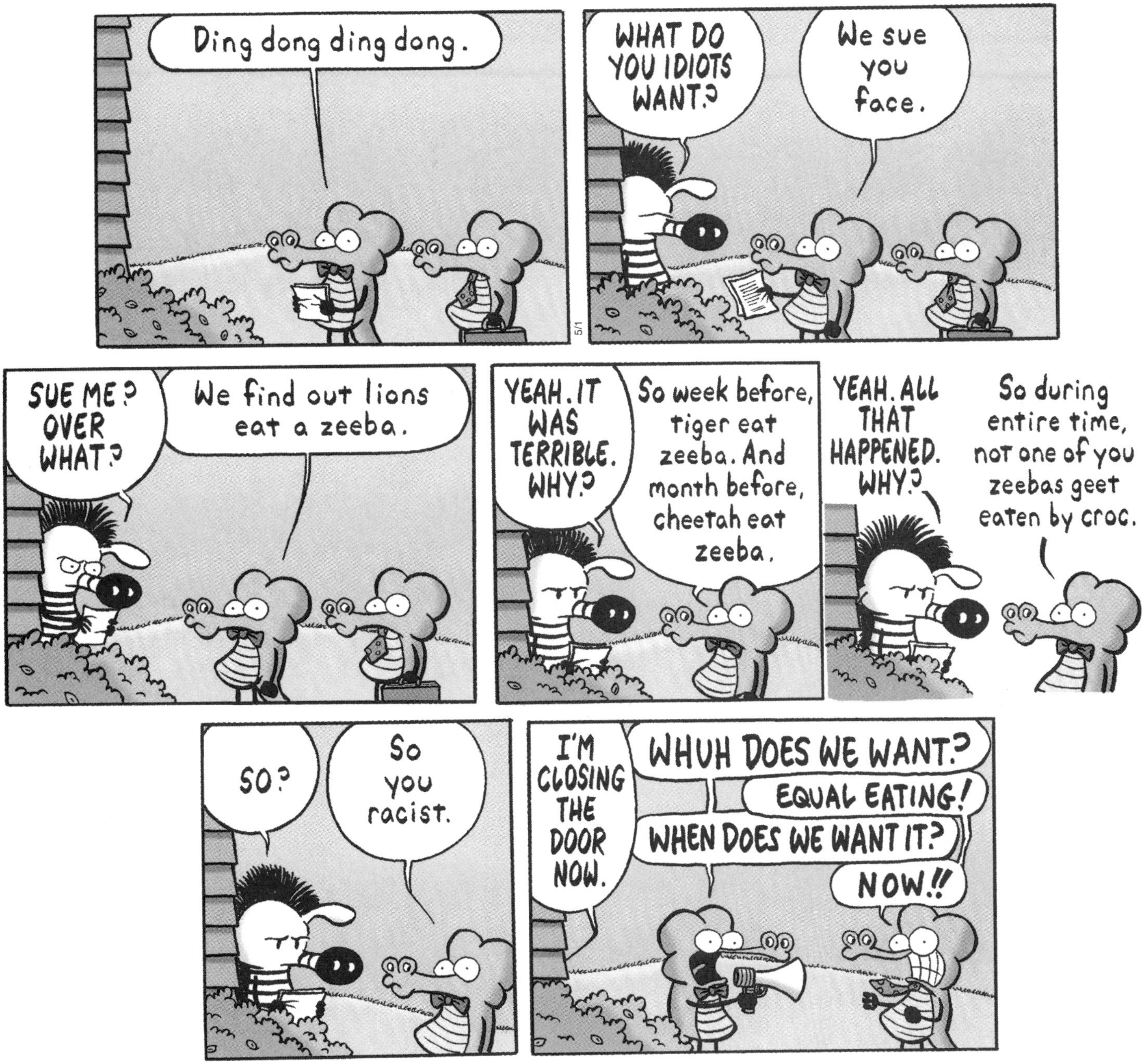
Ding dong ding dong.
5/1
WHAT DO YOU IDIOTS WANT?
We sue you face.
SUE ME? OVER WHAT?
We find out lions eat a zeeba.
YEAH. IT WAS TERRIBLE. WHY?
So week before, tiger eat zeeba. And month before, cheetah eat zeeba.
YEAH. ALL THAT HAPPENED. WHY?
So during entire time, not one of you zeebas geet eaten by croc.
SO?
So you racist.
I'M CLOSING THE DOOR NOW.
WHUH DOES WE WANT?
EQUAL EATING!
WHEN DOES WE WANT IT?
NOW!!

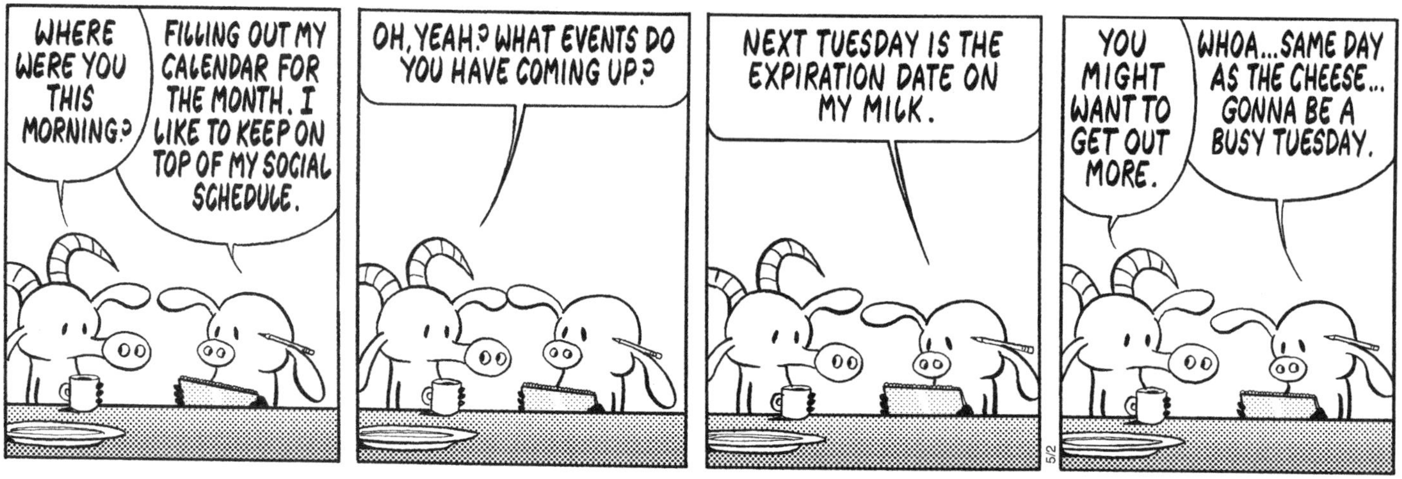

WHERE WERE YOU THIS MORNING?
FILLING OUT MY CALENDAR FOR THE MONTH. I LIKE TO KEEP ON TOP OF MY SOCIAL SCHEDULE.
OH, YEAH? WHAT EVENTS DO YOU HAVE COMING UP?
NEXT TUESDAY IS THE EXPIRATION DATE ON MY MILK.
YOU MIGHT WANT TO GET OUT MORE.
WHOA... SAME DAY AS THE CHEESE... GONNA BE A BUSY TUESDAY.
5/2

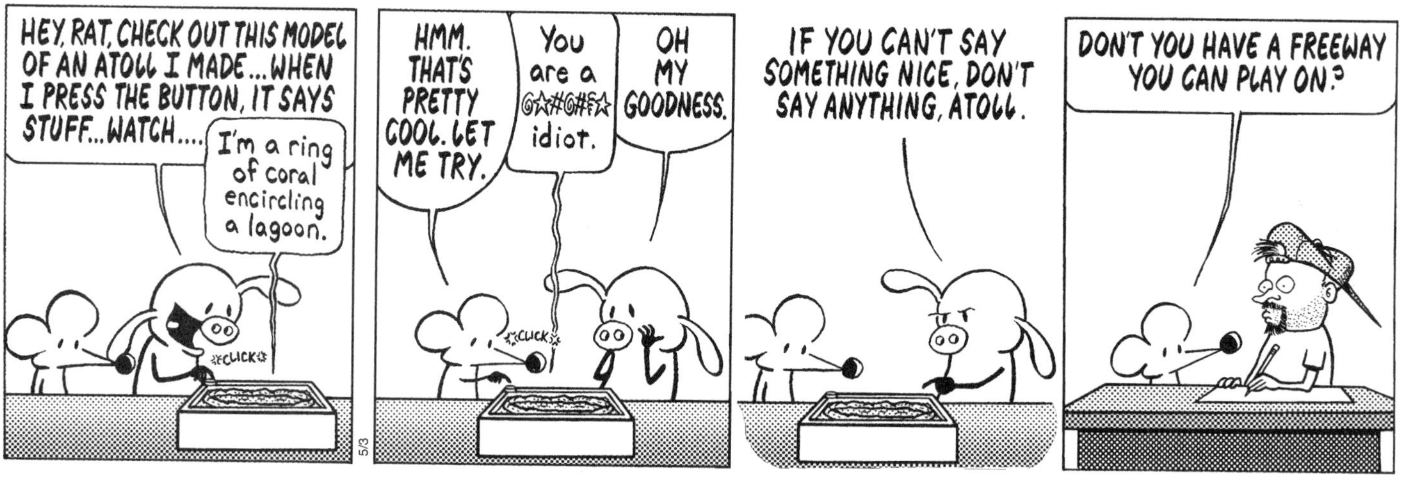

HEY, RAT, CHECK OUT THIS MODEL OF AN ATOLL I MADE... WHEN I PRESS THE BUTTON, IT SAYS STUFF... WATCH....
☆CLICK☆
I'm a ring of coral encircling a lagoon.
HMM. THAT'S PRETTY COOL. LET ME TRY.
☆CLICK☆
You are a @☆#@#$☆ idiot.
OH MY GOODNESS.
IF YOU CAN'T SAY SOMETHING NICE, DON'T SAY ANYTHING, ATOLL.
DON'T YOU HAVE A FREEWAY YOU CAN PLAY ON?
5/3

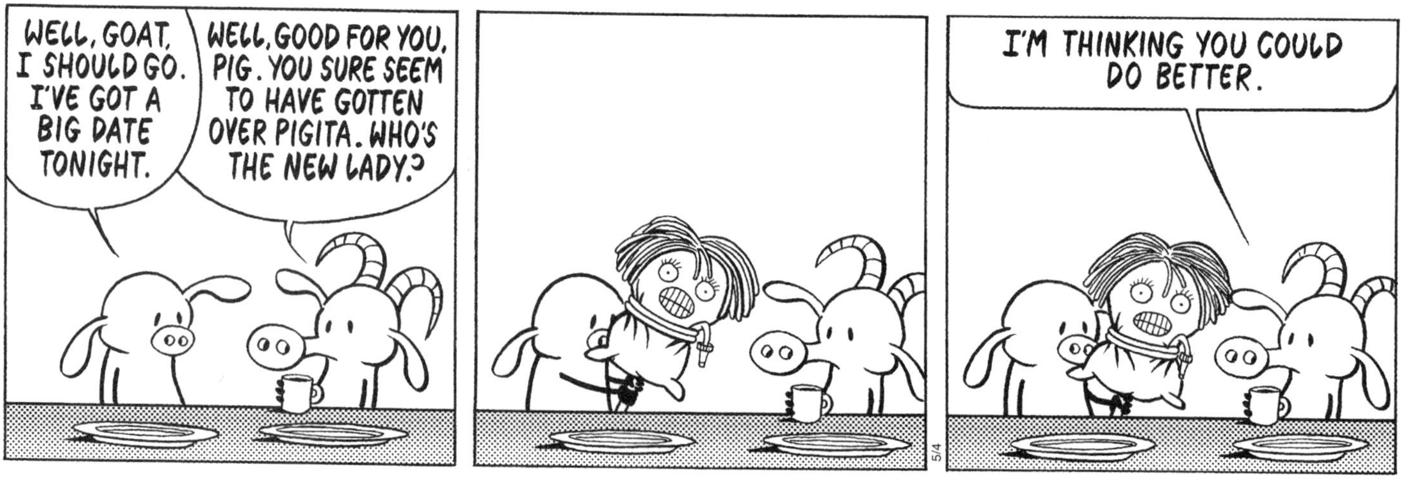

WELL, GOAT, I SHOULD GO. I'VE GOT A BIG DATE TONIGHT.
WELL, GOOD FOR YOU, PIG. YOU SURE SEEM TO HAVE GOTTEN OVER PIGITA. WHO'S THE NEW LADY?
I'M THINKING YOU COULD DO BETTER.
5/4

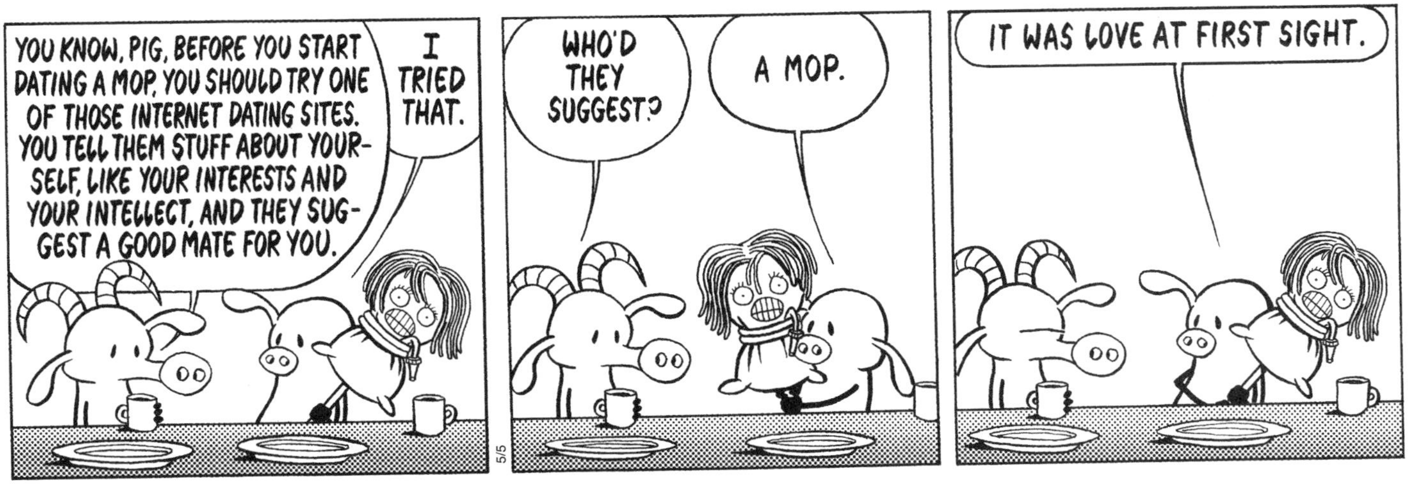
YOU KNOW, PIG, BEFORE YOU START DATING A MOP, YOU SHOULD TRY ONE OF THOSE INTERNET DATING SITES. YOU TELL THEM STUFF ABOUT YOURSELF, LIKE YOUR INTERESTS AND YOUR INTELLECT, AND THEY SUGGEST A GOOD MATE FOR YOU.
I TRIED THAT.
5/5
WHO'D THEY SUGGEST?
A MOP.
IT WAS LOVE AT FIRST SIGHT.

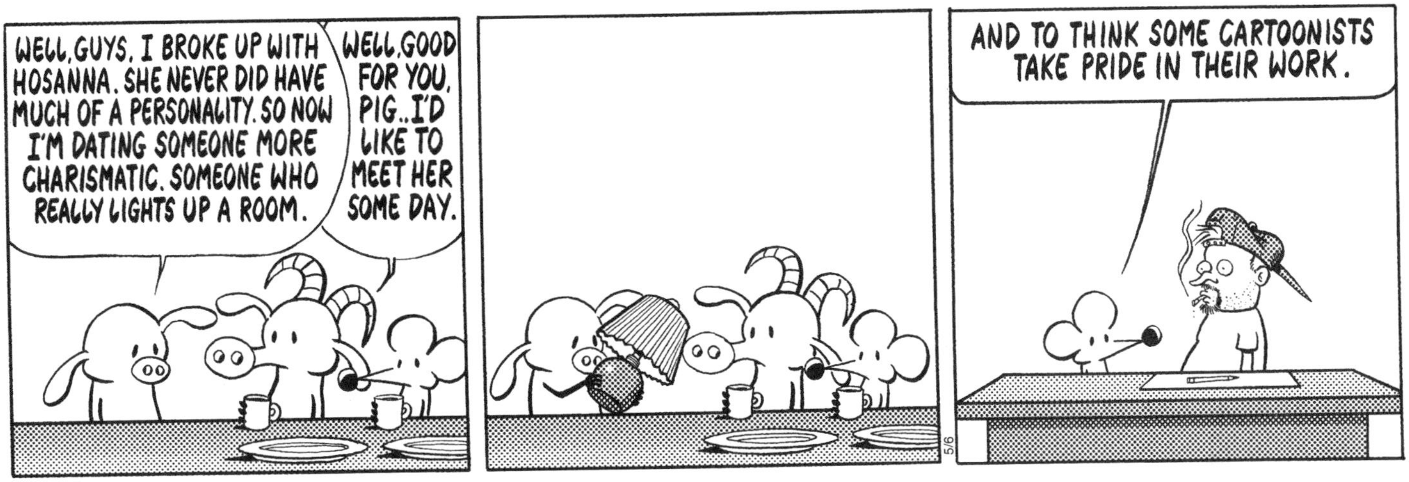
WELL, GUYS, I BROKE UP WITH HOSANNA. SHE NEVER DID HAVE MUCH OF A PERSONALITY. SO NOW I'M DATING SOMEONE MORE CHARISMATIC. SOMEONE WHO REALLY LIGHTS UP A ROOM.
WELL, GOOD FOR YOU, PIG.. I'D LIKE TO MEET HER SOME DAY.
5/6
AND TO THINK SOME CARTOONISTS TAKE PRIDE IN THEIR WORK.

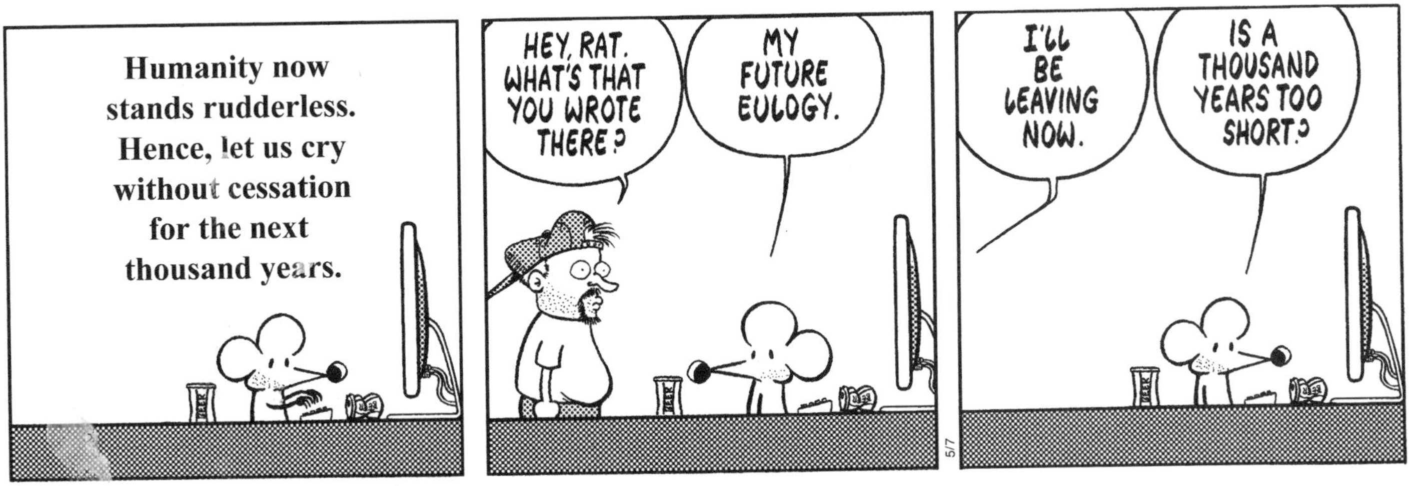
Humanity now stands rudderless. Hence, let us cry without cessation for the next thousand years.
HEY, RAT. WHAT'S THAT YOU WROTE THERE?
MY FUTURE EULOGY.
5/7
I'LL BE LEAVING NOW.
IS A THOUSAND YEARS TOO SHORT?

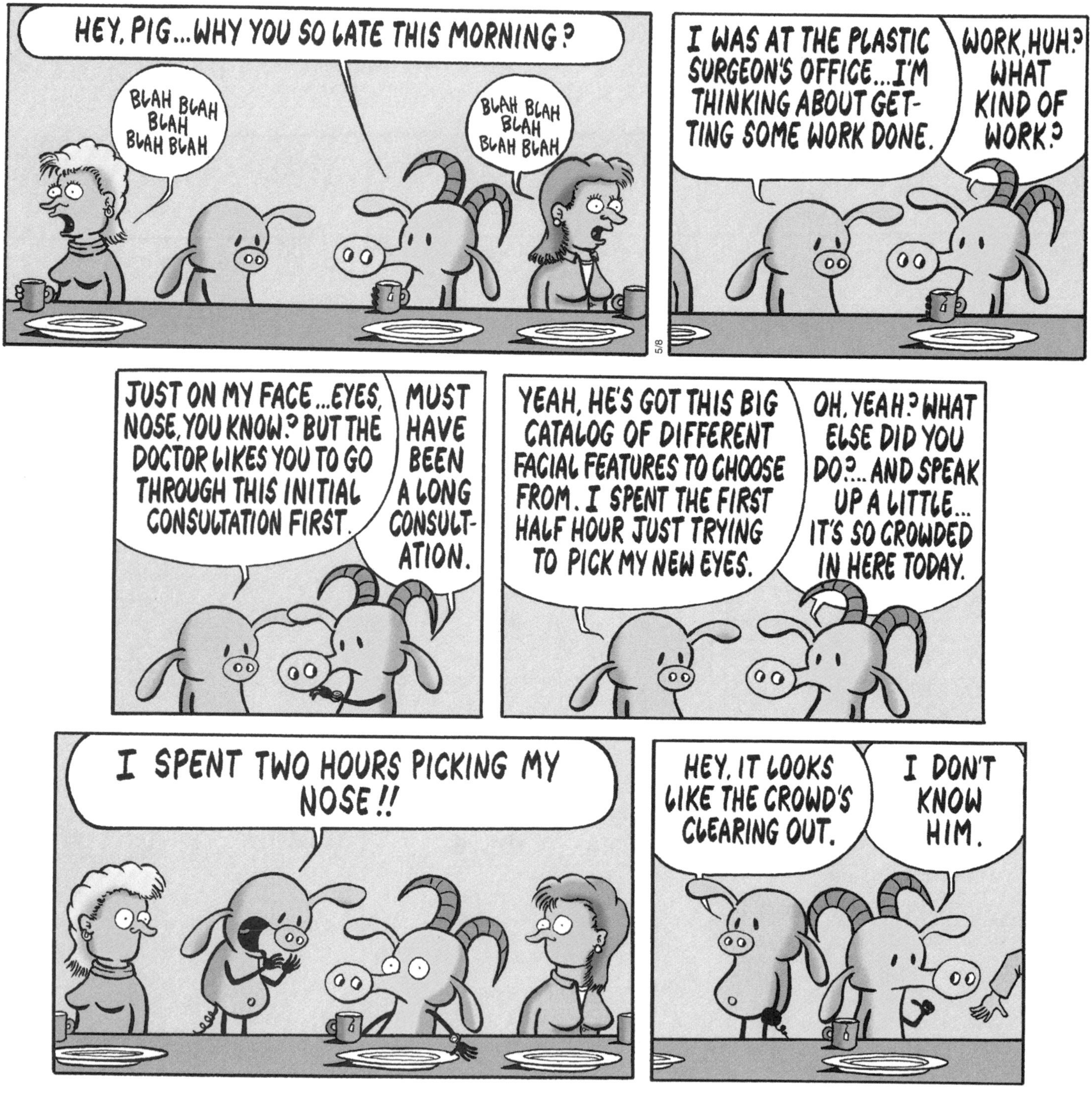

HEY, PIG...WHY YOU SO LATE THIS MORNING?
BLAH BLAH BLAH BLAH BLAH
BLAH BLAH BLAH BLAH BLAH
I WAS AT THE PLASTIC SURGEON'S OFFICE...I'M THINKING ABOUT GETTING SOME WORK DONE.
WORK, HUH? WHAT KIND OF WORK?
JUST ON MY FACE...EYES, NOSE, YOU KNOW? BUT THE DOCTOR LIKES YOU TO GO THROUGH THIS INITIAL CONSULTATION FIRST.
MUST HAVE BEEN A LONG CONSULT-ATION.
YEAH, HE'S GOT THIS BIG CATALOG OF DIFFERENT FACIAL FEATURES TO CHOOSE FROM. I SPENT THE FIRST HALF HOUR JUST TRYING TO PICK MY NEW EYES.
OH, YEAH? WHAT ELSE DID YOU DO?... AND SPEAK UP A LITTLE... IT'S SO CROWDED IN HERE TODAY.
I SPENT TWO HOURS PICKING MY NOSE!!
HEY, IT LOOKS LIKE THE CROWD'S CLEARING OUT.
I DON'T KNOW HIM.

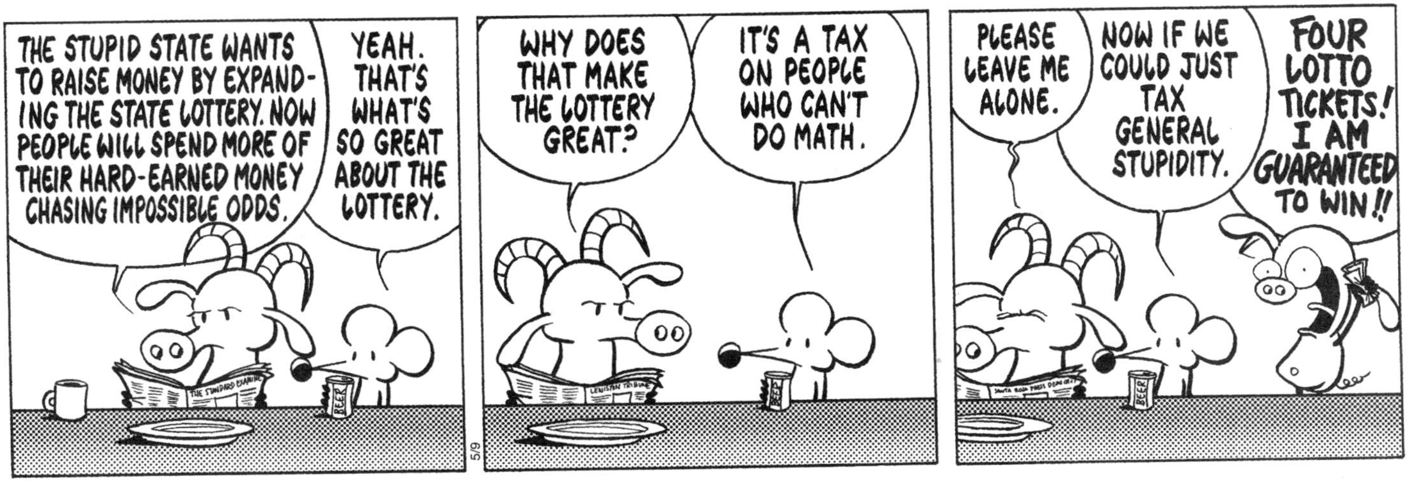
THE STUPID STATE WANTS TO RAISE MONEY BY EXPANDING THE STATE LOTTERY. NOW PEOPLE WILL SPEND MORE OF THEIR HARD-EARNED MONEY CHASING IMPOSSIBLE ODDS.
YEAH. THAT'S WHAT'S SO GREAT ABOUT THE LOTTERY.
WHY DOES THAT MAKE THE LOTTERY GREAT?
IT'S A TAX ON PEOPLE WHO CAN'T DO MATH.
PLEASE LEAVE ME ALONE.
NOW IF WE COULD JUST TAX GENERAL STUPIDITY.
FOUR LOTTO TICKETS! I AM GUARANTEED TO WIN!!

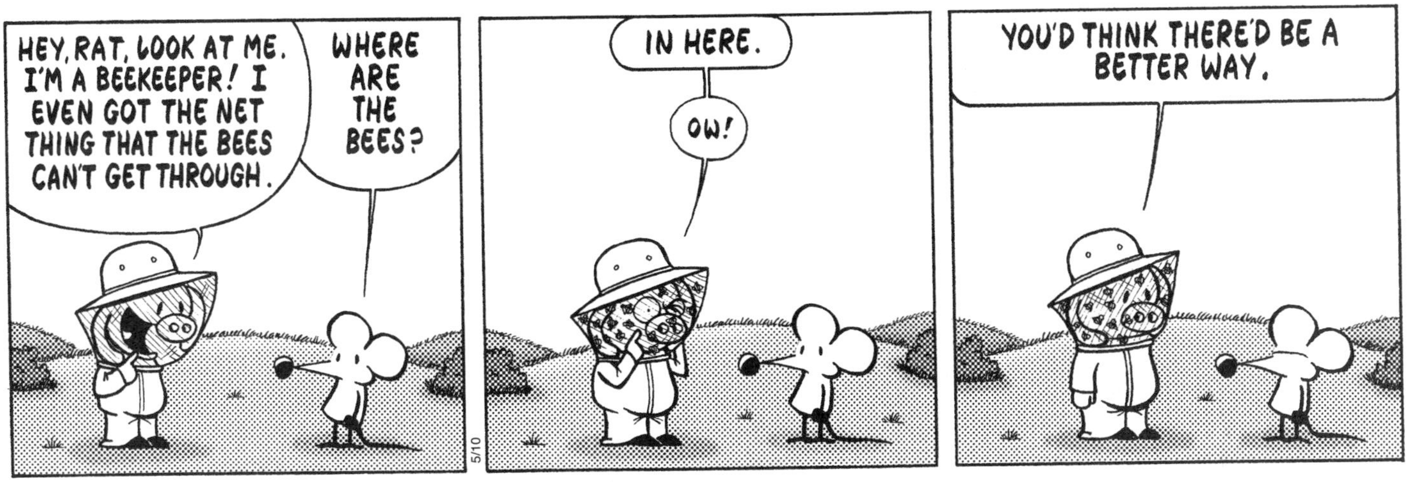
HEY, RAT, LOOK AT ME. I'M A BEEKEEPER! I EVEN GOT THE NET THING THAT THE BEES CAN'T GET THROUGH.
WHERE ARE THE BEES?
IN HERE.
OW!
YOU'D THINK THERE'D BE A BETTER WAY.

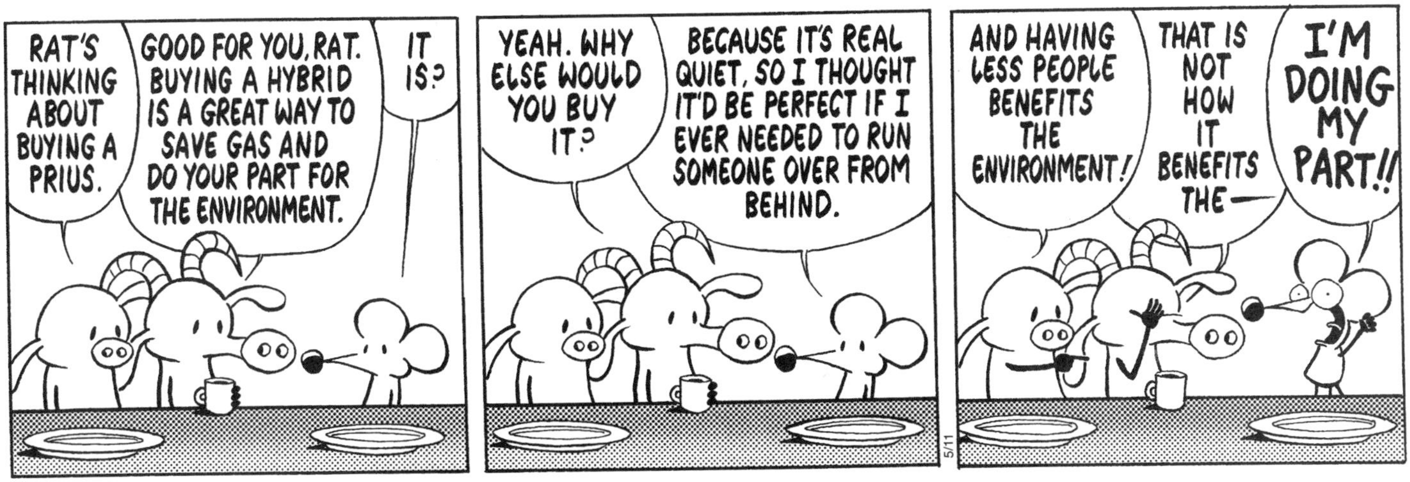
RAT'S THINKING ABOUT BUYING A PRIUS.
GOOD FOR YOU, RAT. BUYING A HYBRID IS A GREAT WAY TO SAVE GAS AND DO YOUR PART FOR THE ENVIRONMENT.
IT IS?
YEAH. WHY ELSE WOULD YOU BUY IT?
BECAUSE IT'S REAL QUIET, SO I THOUGHT IT'D BE PERFECT IF I EVER NEEDED TO RUN SOMEONE OVER FROM BEHIND.
AND HAVING LESS PEOPLE BENEFITS THE ENVIRONMENT!
THAT IS NOT HOW IT BENEFITS THE—
I'M DOING MY PART!!

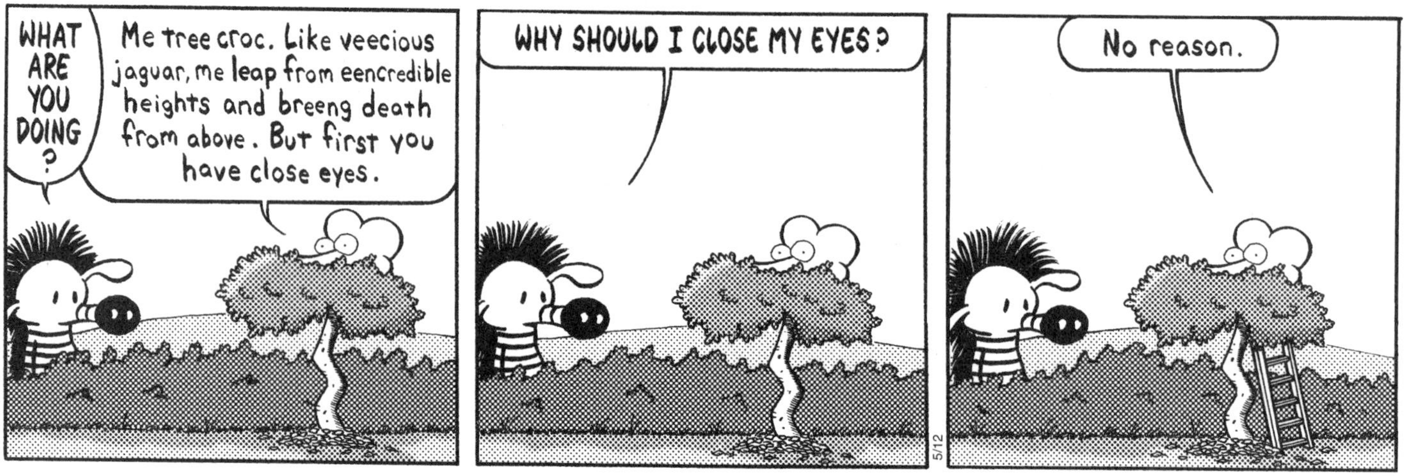
WHAT ARE YOU DOING?
Me tree croc. Like veecious jaguar, me leap from eencredible heights and breeng death from above. But first you have close eyes.
WHY SHOULD I CLOSE MY EYES?
No reason.
5/12

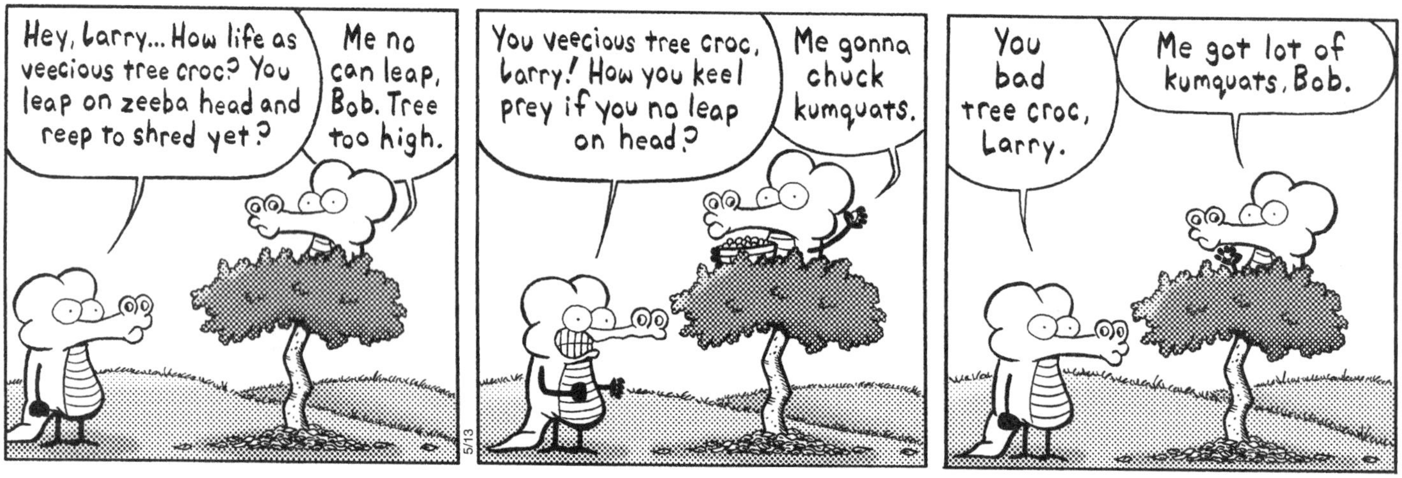
Hey, Larry... How life as veecious tree croc? You leap on zeeba head and reep to shred yet?
Me no can leap, Bob. Tree too high.
You veecious tree croc, Larry! How you keel prey if you no leap on head?
Me gonna chuck kumquats.
You bad tree croc, Larry.
Me got lot of kumquats, Bob.
5/13

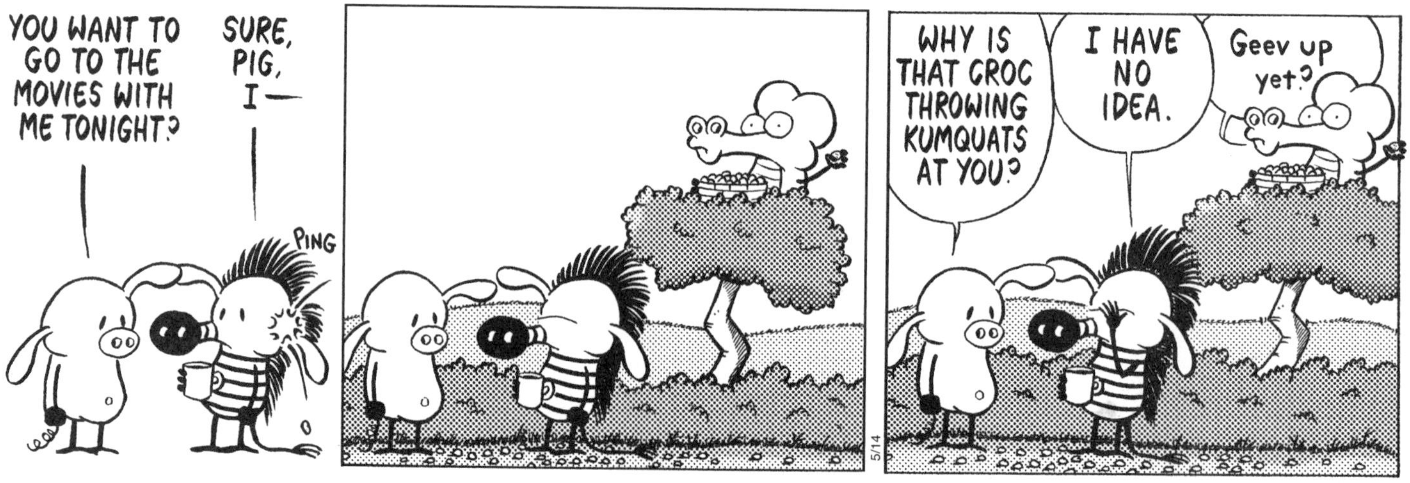
YOU WANT TO GO TO THE MOVIES WITH ME TONIGHT?
SURE, PIG, I—
PING
WHY IS THAT CROC THROWING KUMQUATS AT YOU?
I HAVE NO IDEA.
Geev up yet?
5/14

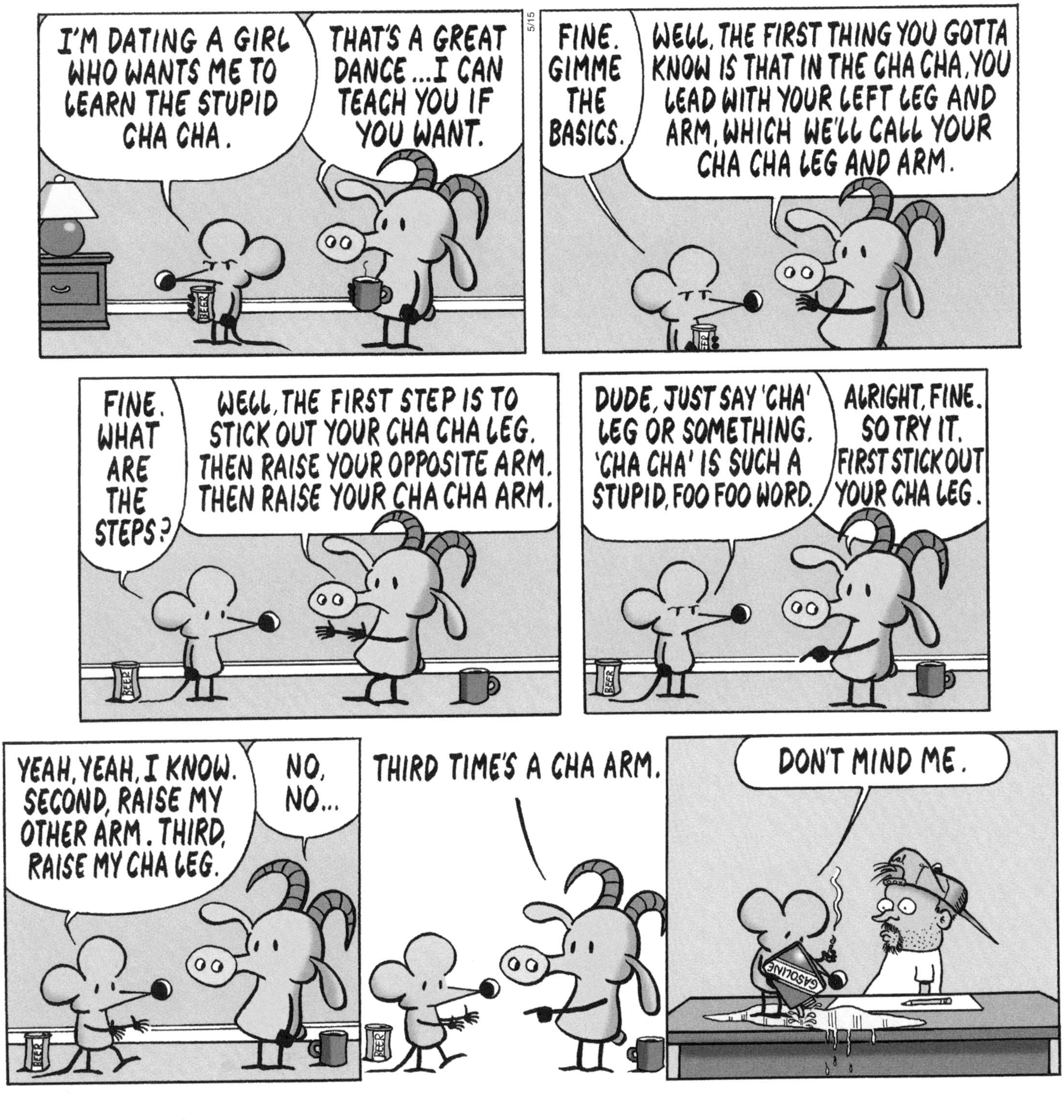
5/15
I'M DATING A GIRL WHO WANTS ME TO LEARN THE STUPID CHA CHA.
THAT'S A GREAT DANCE...I CAN TEACH YOU IF YOU WANT.
BEER
FINE. GIMME THE BASICS.
WELL, THE FIRST THING YOU GOTTA KNOW IS THAT IN THE CHA CHA, YOU LEAD WITH YOUR LEFT LEG AND ARM, WHICH WE'LL CALL YOUR CHA CHA LEG AND ARM.
FINE. WHAT ARE THE STEPS?
WELL, THE FIRST STEP IS TO STICK OUT YOUR CHA CHA LEG. THEN RAISE YOUR OPPOSITE ARM. THEN RAISE YOUR CHA CHA ARM.
BEER
DUDE, JUST SAY 'CHA' LEG OR SOMETHING. 'CHA CHA' IS SUCH A STUPID, FOO FOO WORD.
ALRIGHT, FINE. SO TRY IT. FIRST STICK OUT YOUR CHA LEG.
BEER
YEAH, YEAH, I KNOW. SECOND, RAISE MY OTHER ARM. THIRD, RAISE MY CHA LEG.
NO, NO...
BEER
THIRD TIME'S A CHA ARM.
BEER
DON'T MIND ME.
GASOLINE

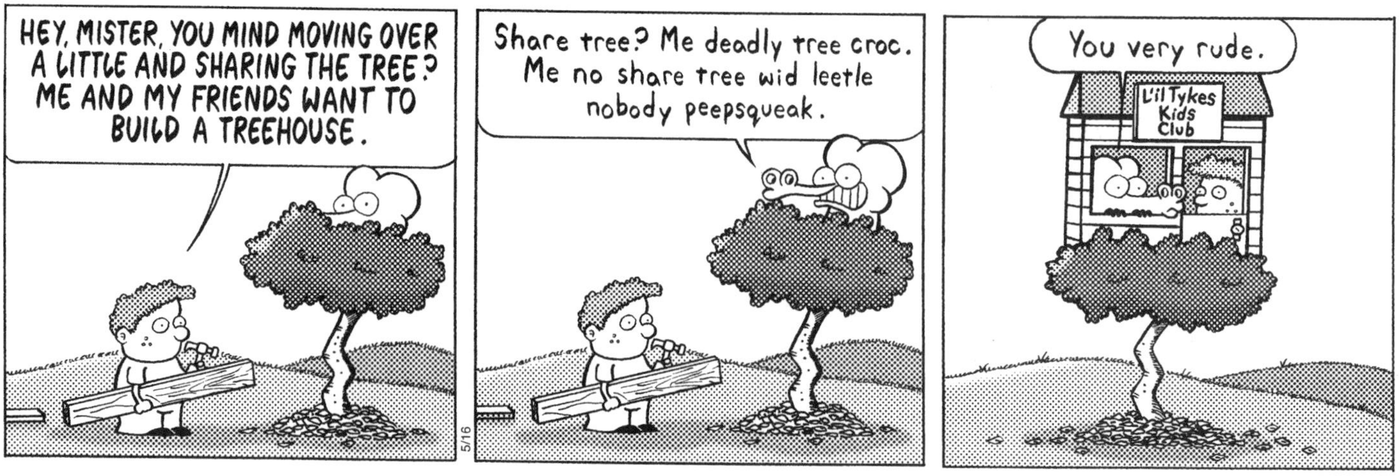
HEY, MISTER, YOU MIND MOVING OVER A LITTLE AND SHARING THE TREE? ME AND MY FRIENDS WANT TO BUILD A TREEHOUSE.
Share tree? Me deadly tree croc. Me no share tree wid leetle nobody peepsqueak.
5/16
You very rude.
L'il Tykes Kids Club

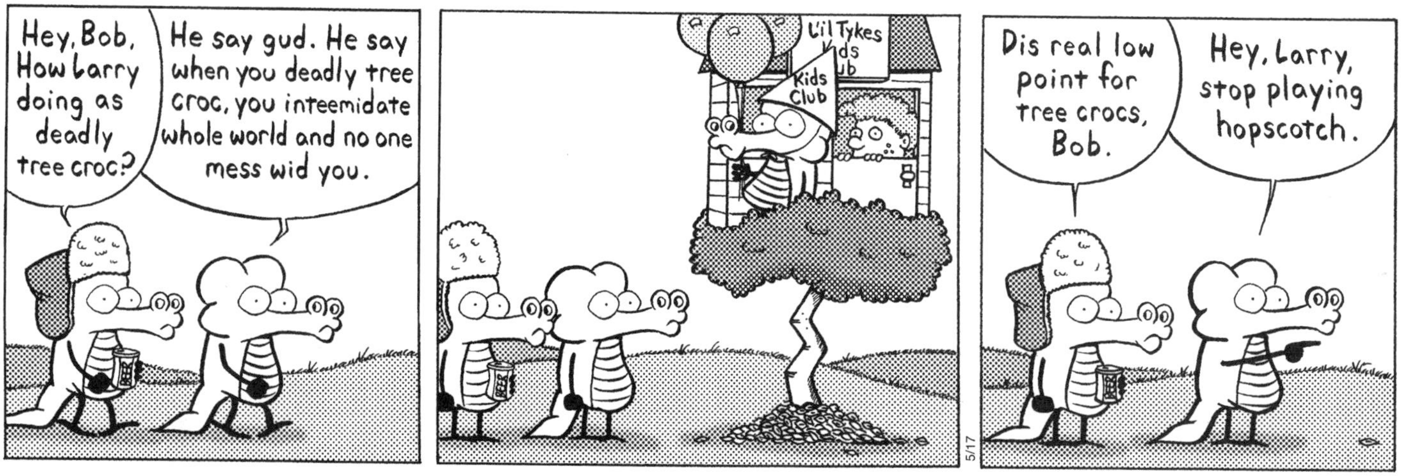
Hey, Bob, How Larry doing as deadly tree croc?
He say gud. He say when you deadly tree croc, you inteemidate whole world and no one mess wid you.
L'il Tykes Kids Club
Kids Club
Dis real low point for tree crocs, Bob.
Hey, Larry, stop playing hopscotch.
5/17

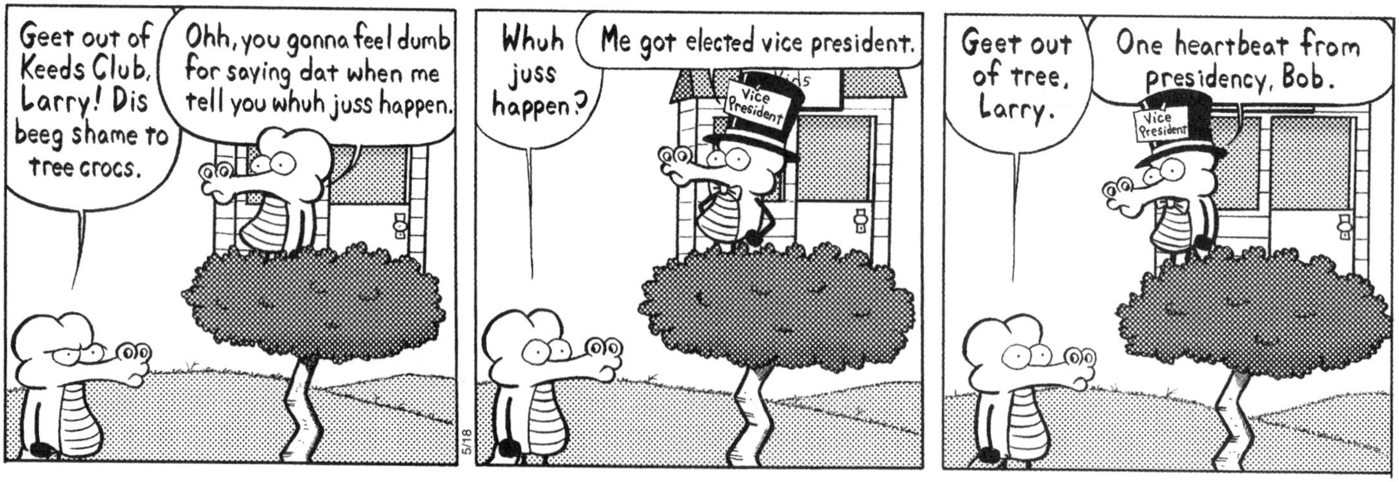
Geet out of Keeds Club, Larry! Dis beeg shame to tree crocs.
Ohh, you gonna feel dumb for saying dat when me tell you whuh juss happen.
5/18
Whuh juss happen?
Me got elected vice president.
Vice President
Geet out of tree, Larry.
One heartbeat from presidency, Bob.
Vice President

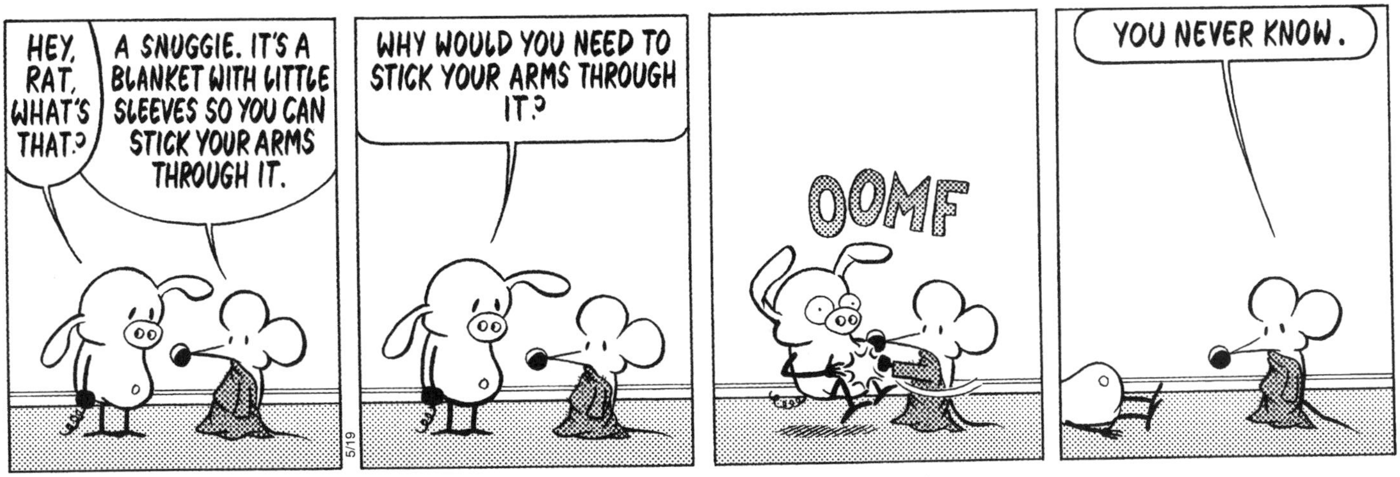
HEY, RAT, WHAT'S THAT?
A SNUGGIE. IT'S A BLANKET WITH LITTLE SLEEVES SO YOU CAN STICK YOUR ARMS THROUGH IT.
5/19
WHY WOULD YOU NEED TO STICK YOUR ARMS THROUGH IT?
OOMF
YOU NEVER KNOW.

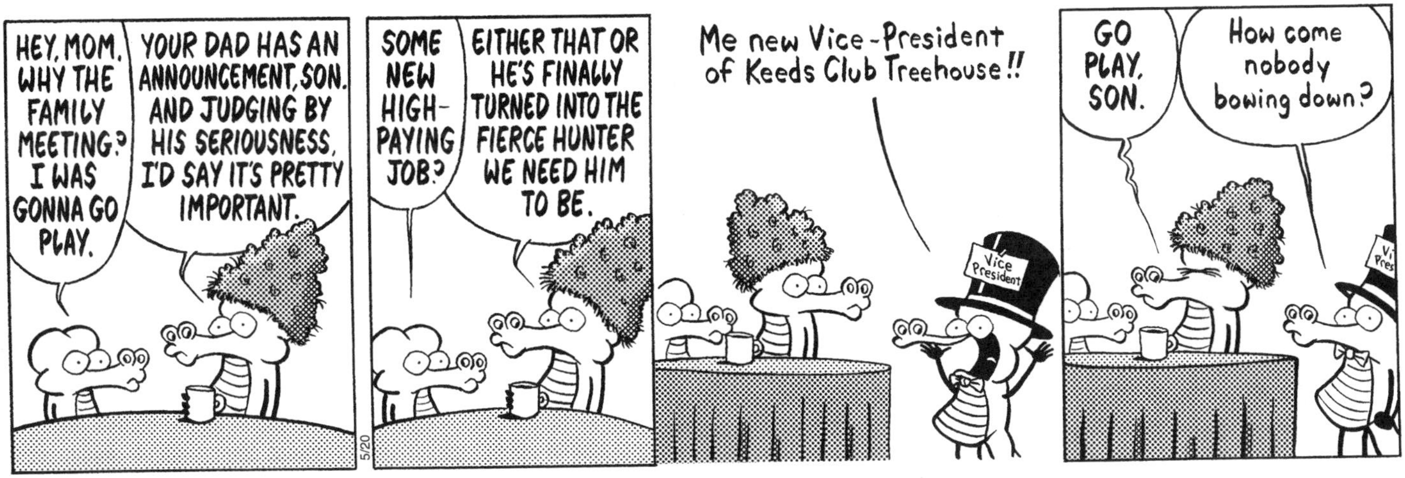
HEY, MOM. WHY THE FAMILY MEETING? I WAS GONNA GO PLAY.
YOUR DAD HAS AN ANNOUNCEMENT, SON. AND JUDGING BY HIS SERIOUSNESS, I'D SAY IT'S PRETTY IMPORTANT.
5/20
SOME NEW HIGH-PAYING JOB?
EITHER THAT OR HE'S FINALLY TURNED INTO THE FIERCE HUNTER WE NEED HIM TO BE.
Me new Vice-President of Keeds Club Treehouse!!
Vice President
GO PLAY, SON.
How come nobody bowing down?

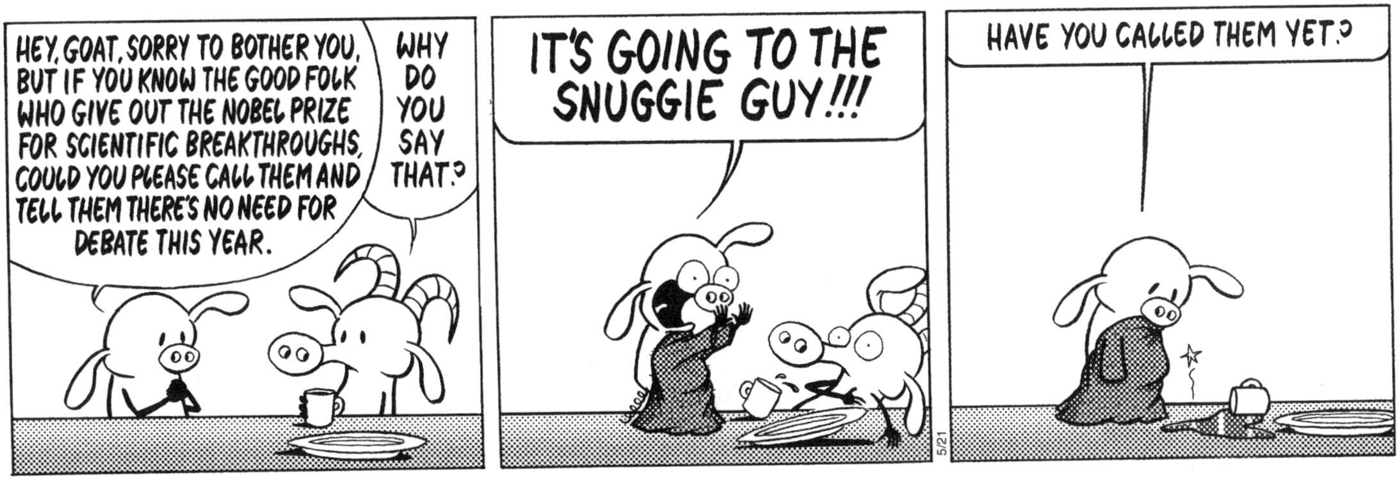
HEY, GOAT, SORRY TO BOTHER YOU, BUT IF YOU KNOW THE GOOD FOLK WHO GIVE OUT THE NOBEL PRIZE FOR SCIENTIFIC BREAKTHROUGHS, COULD YOU PLEASE CALL THEM AND TELL THEM THERE'S NO NEED FOR DEBATE THIS YEAR.
WHY DO YOU SAY THAT?
IT'S GOING TO THE SNUGGIE GUY!!!
5/21
HAVE YOU CALLED THEM YET?

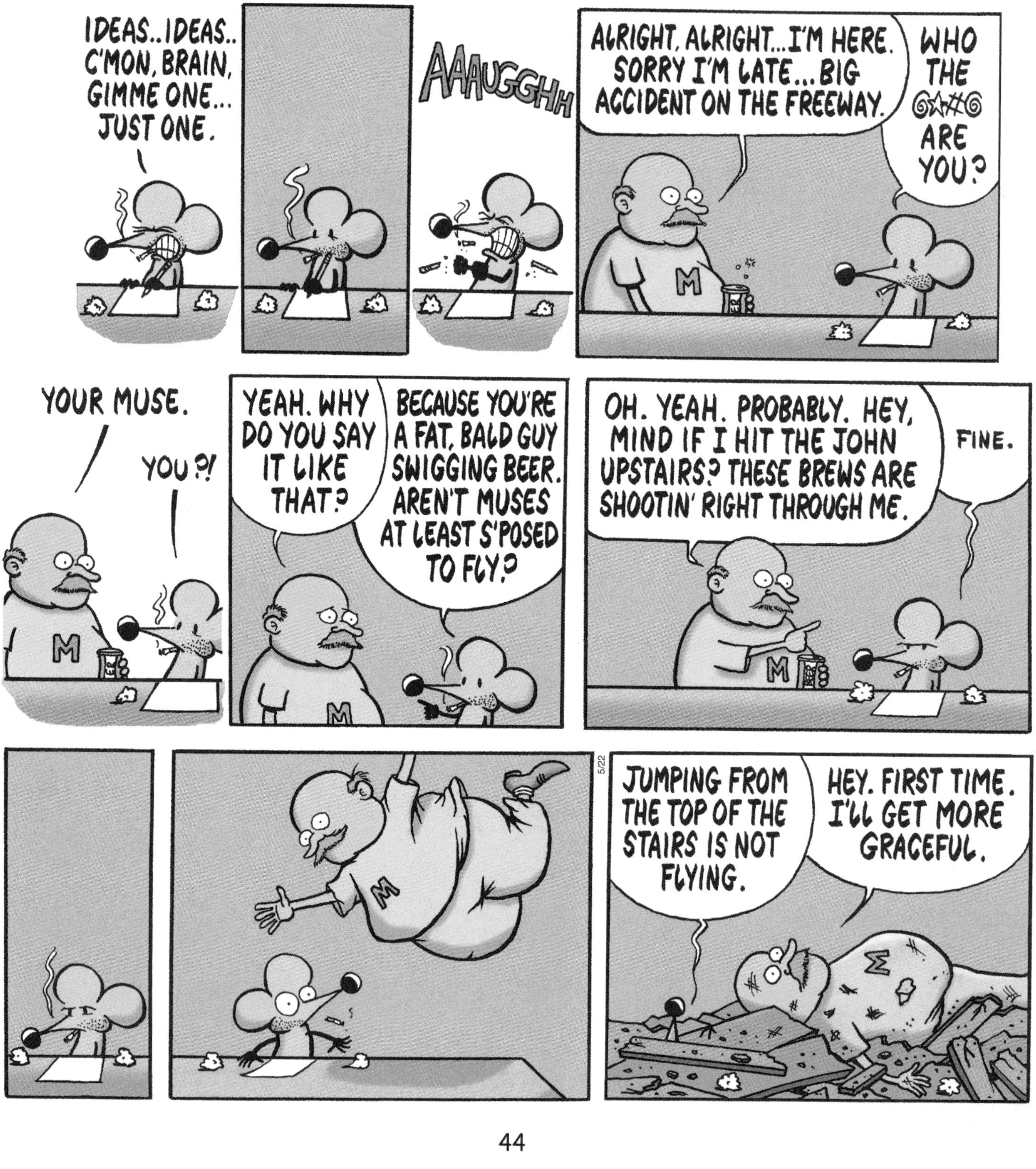
IDEAS..IDEAS..
C'MON, BRAIN,
GIMME ONE...
JUST ONE.
AAAUGGHH
ALRIGHT, ALRIGHT...I'M HERE.
SORRY I'M LATE...BIG
ACCIDENT ON THE FREEWAY.
WHO
THE
@☆#@
ARE
YOU?
YOUR MUSE.
YOU?!
YEAH. WHY
DO YOU SAY
IT LIKE
THAT?
BECAUSE YOU'RE
A FAT, BALD GUY
SWIGGING BEER.
AREN'T MUSES
AT LEAST S'POSED
TO FLY?
OH. YEAH. PROBABLY. HEY,
MIND IF I HIT THE JOHN
UPSTAIRS? THESE BREWS ARE
SHOOTIN' RIGHT THROUGH ME.
FINE.
5/22
JUMPING FROM
THE TOP OF THE
STAIRS IS NOT
FLYING.
HEY. FIRST TIME.
I'LL GET MORE
GRACEFUL.

Panel 1: INSIDE THE KIDS CLUB TREEHOUSE

HI... I'M TIMMY, OUR SECRETARY OF THE TREASURY. YOU MUST BE OUR NEW V.P.

Yeah. But you no has to bow. Me like keep tings eenformal.

Panel 2: OH, I'D HARDLY BOW. THE V.P. IS A MEANINGLESS FIGUREHEAD WITH NOTHING TO DO. BY THE WAY, WHAT'S THAT YOU WROTE ON YOUR NAMETAG?

'Meester Guy So Powerful It No Even Funny.'

Panel 3: YOU SEEM UNCLEAR ON THE CONCEPT.

Hey...Seence you secreetary, mebbe you geet Larry coffee?

Panel 4: HEY, PIG, WHAT ARE YOU DOING?

I'M WRITING A LETTER TO THE HOST OF THIS CABLE NEWS SHOW. HIS DISCUSSION OF AN ISSUE WAS SO UNFAIR.

Panel 5: GOOD FOR YOU, PIG...IT'S CRITICAL IN A DEMOCRACY THAT CITIZENS ENGAGE IN THE PROCESS BY DEBATING ISSUES THOUGHTFULLY WITH OTHERS. HERE, LET ME SEE WHAT YOU HAVE SO FAR.

Panel 6: Dear Poopyhead

Panel 7: PERHAPS I COULD BE THOUGHTFUL-ER.

Panel 8: WHY IS EVERYONE SO DOWN ON THE MORALS OF HOLLYWOOD? WHAT'S WRONG WITH PICKING THE STAR OF A MOVIE AS YOUR ROLE MODEL?

NOTHING, I GUESS. WHO WOULD YOU PICK?

Panel 9: JACK NICHOLSON IN 'THE SHINING.'

Panel 10: CHECK, PLEASE.

HEEEEEEERE'S RATTY...

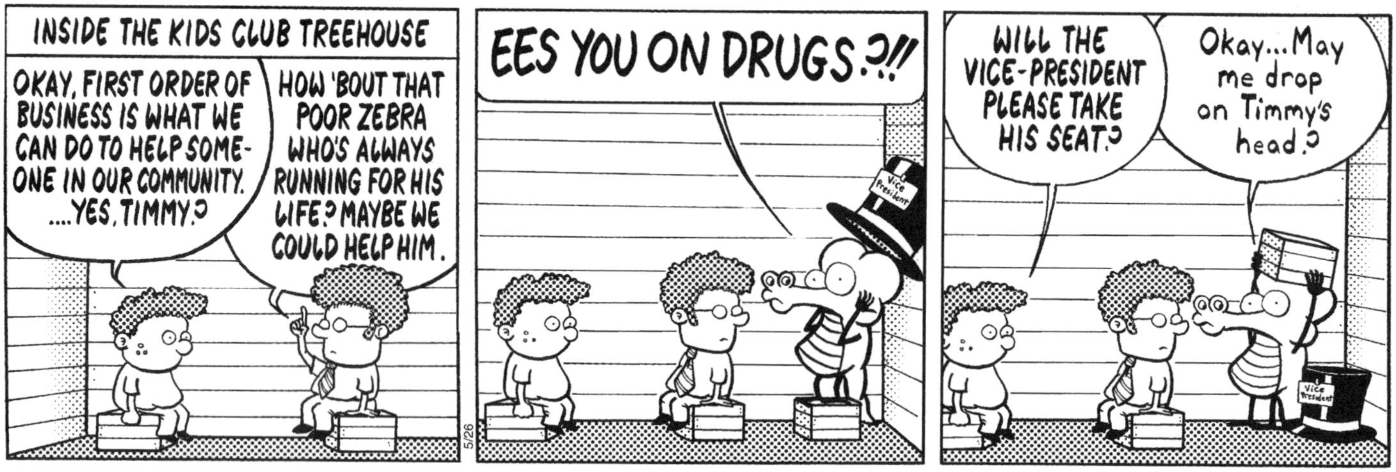
INSIDE THE KIDS CLUB TREEHOUSE
OKAY, FIRST ORDER OF BUSINESS IS WHAT WE CAN DO TO HELP SOMEONE IN OUR COMMUNITY. ....YES, TIMMY?
HOW 'BOUT THAT POOR ZEBRA WHO'S ALWAYS RUNNING FOR HIS LIFE? MAYBE WE COULD HELP HIM.
EES YOU ON DRUGS?!!
Vice President
5/26
WILL THE VICE-PRESIDENT PLEASE TAKE HIS SEAT?
Okay...May me drop on Timmy's head?
Vice President

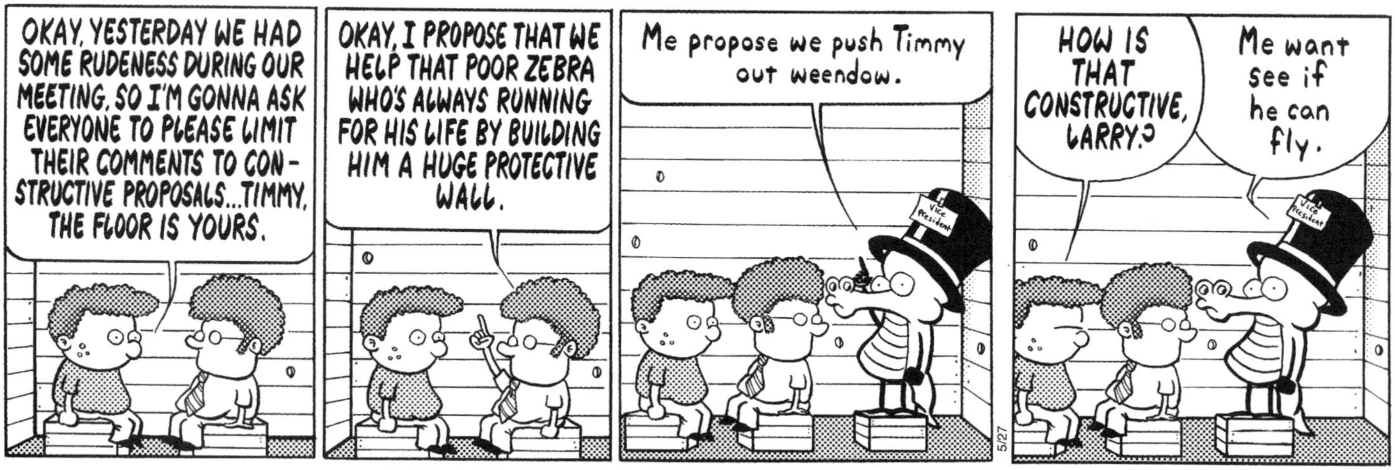
OKAY, YESTERDAY WE HAD SOME RUDENESS DURING OUR MEETING, SO I'M GONNA ASK EVERYONE TO PLEASE LIMIT THEIR COMMENTS TO CONSTRUCTIVE PROPOSALS...TIMMY, THE FLOOR IS YOURS.
OKAY, I PROPOSE THAT WE HELP THAT POOR ZEBRA WHO'S ALWAYS RUNNING FOR HIS LIFE BY BUILDING HIM A HUGE PROTECTIVE WALL.
Me propose we push Timmy out weendow.
Vice President
5/27
HOW IS THAT CONSTRUCTIVE, LARRY?
Me want see if he can fly.
Vice President

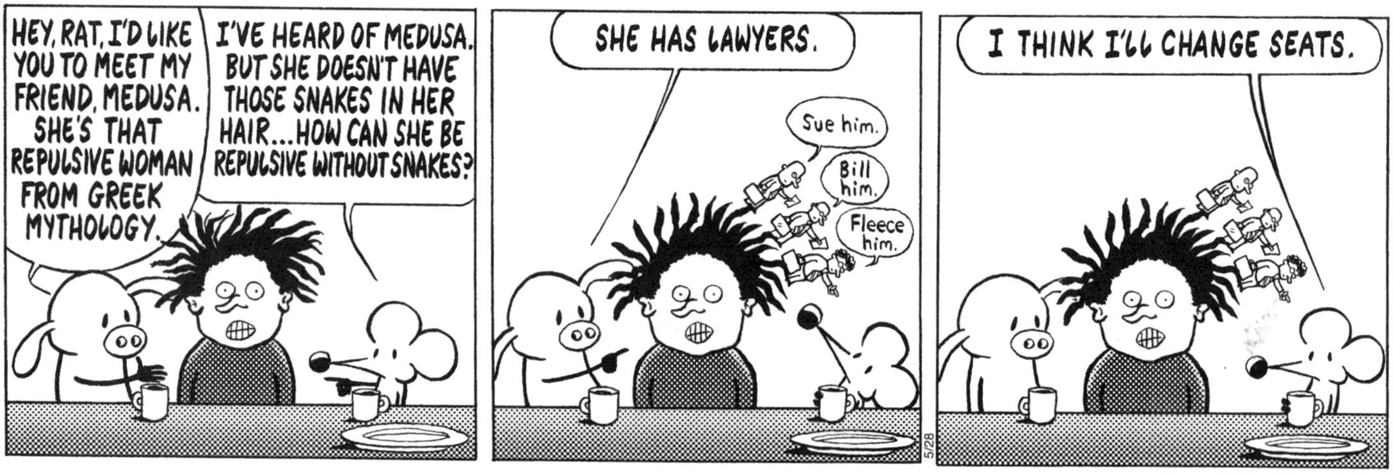
HEY, RAT, I'D LIKE YOU TO MEET MY FRIEND, MEDUSA. SHE'S THAT REPULSIVE WOMAN FROM GREEK MYTHOLOGY.
I'VE HEARD OF MEDUSA. BUT SHE DOESN'T HAVE THOSE SNAKES IN HER HAIR...HOW CAN SHE BE REPULSIVE WITHOUT SNAKES?
SHE HAS LAWYERS.
Sue him.
Bill him.
Fleece him.
5/28
I THINK I'LL CHANGE SEATS.

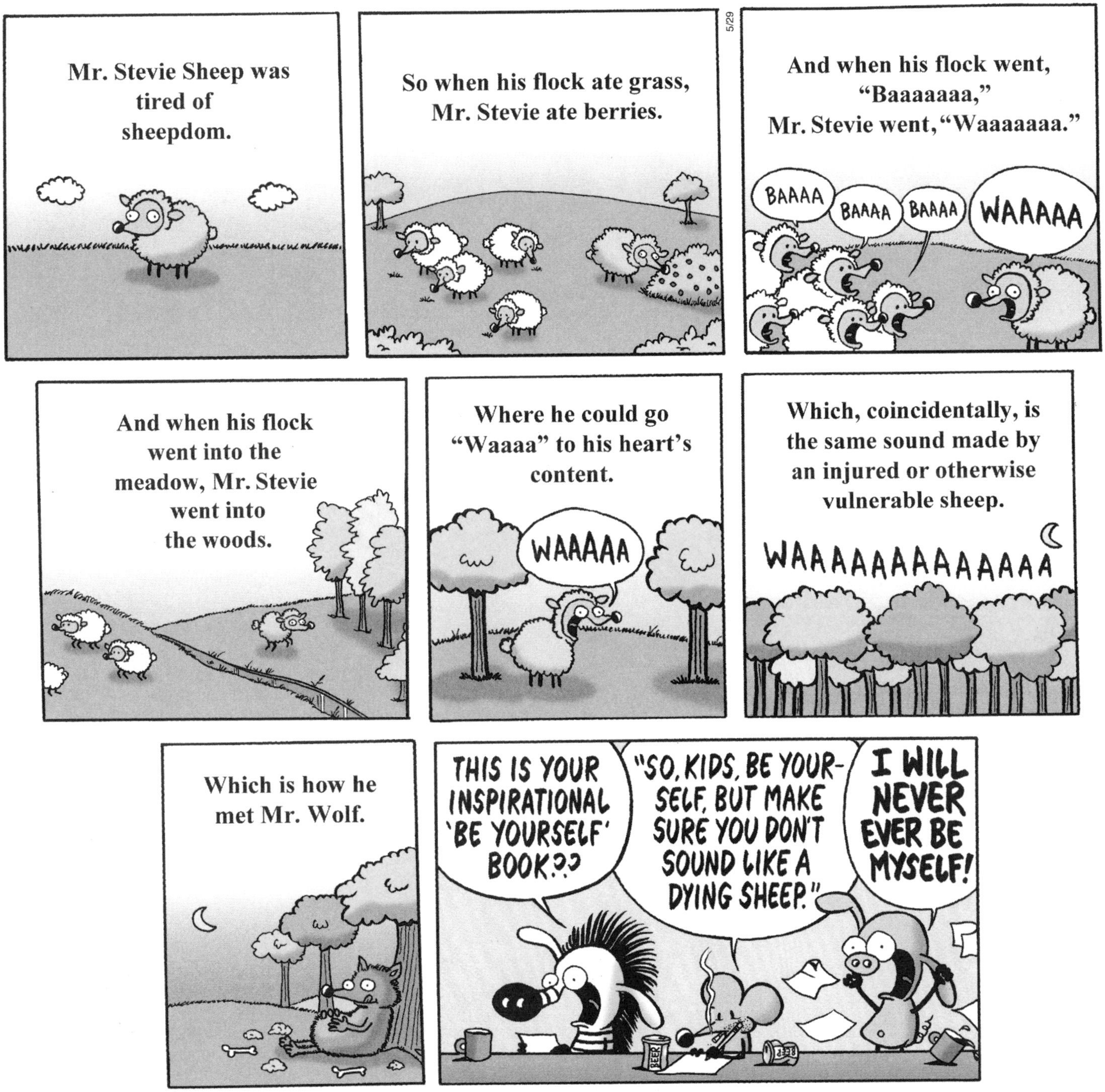
Mr. Stevie Sheep was tired of sheepdom.
So when his flock ate grass, Mr. Stevie ate berries.
5/29
And when his flock went, "Baaaaaaa," Mr. Stevie went, "Waaaaaaa."
BAAAA
BAAAA
BAAAA
WAAAAA
And when his flock went into the meadow, Mr. Stevie went into the woods.
Where he could go "Waaaa" to his heart's content.
WAAAAA
Which, coincidentally, is the same sound made by an injured or otherwise vulnerable sheep.
WAAAAAAAAAAAAA
Which is how he met Mr. Wolf.
THIS IS YOUR INSPIRATIONAL 'BE YOURSELF' BOOK?!?
"SO, KIDS, BE YOURSELF, BUT MAKE SURE YOU DON'T SOUND LIKE A DYING SHEEP."
I WILL NEVER EVER BE MYSELF!
BEER
BEER

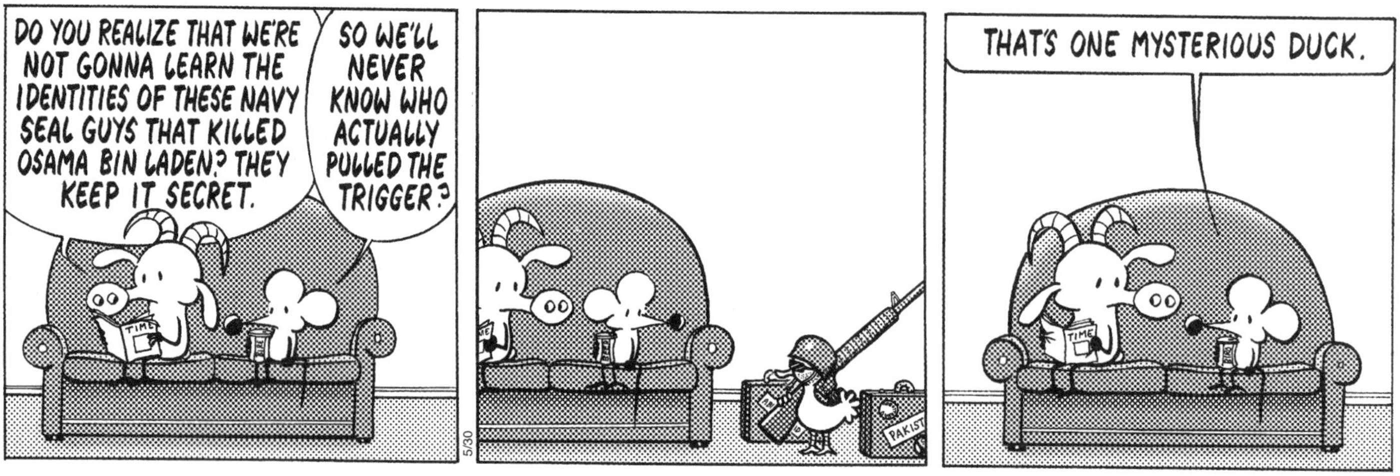
DO YOU REALIZE THAT WE'RE NOT GONNA LEARN THE IDENTITIES OF THESE NAVY SEAL GUYS THAT KILLED OSAMA BIN LADEN? THEY KEEP IT SECRET.
SO WE'LL NEVER KNOW WHO ACTUALLY PULLED THE TRIGGER?
5/30
THAT'S ONE MYSTERIOUS DUCK.

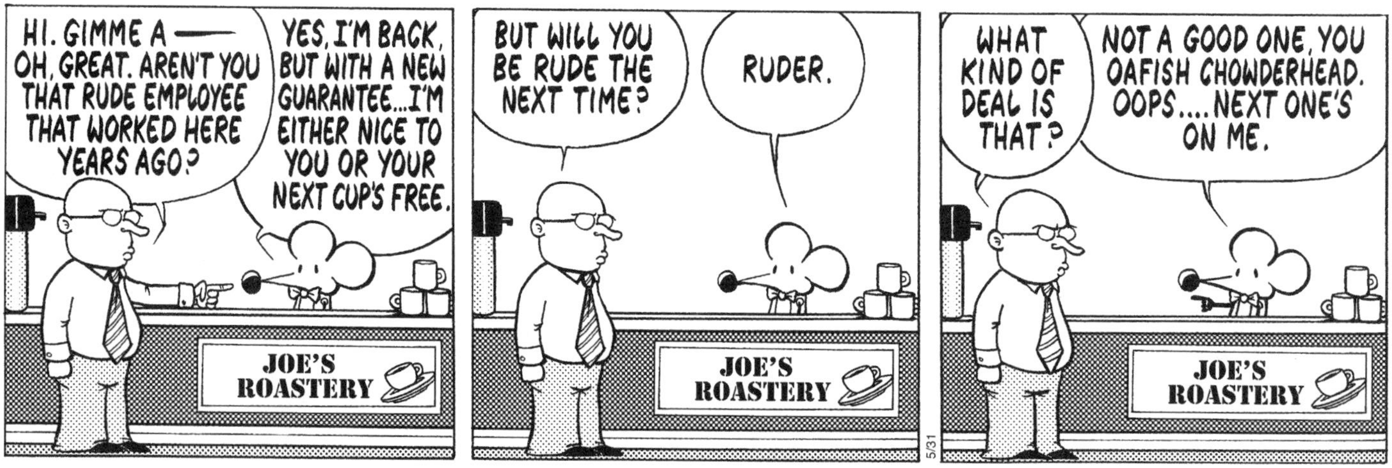
HI. GIMME A — OH, GREAT. AREN'T YOU THAT RUDE EMPLOYEE THAT WORKED HERE YEARS AGO?
YES, I'M BACK, BUT WITH A NEW GUARANTEE... I'M EITHER NICE TO YOU OR YOUR NEXT CUP'S FREE.
JOE'S ROASTERY
BUT WILL YOU BE RUDE THE NEXT TIME?
RUDER.
JOE'S ROASTERY
5/31
WHAT KIND OF DEAL IS THAT?
NOT A GOOD ONE, YOU OAFISH CHOWDERHEAD. OOPS.... NEXT ONE'S ON ME.
JOE'S ROASTERY

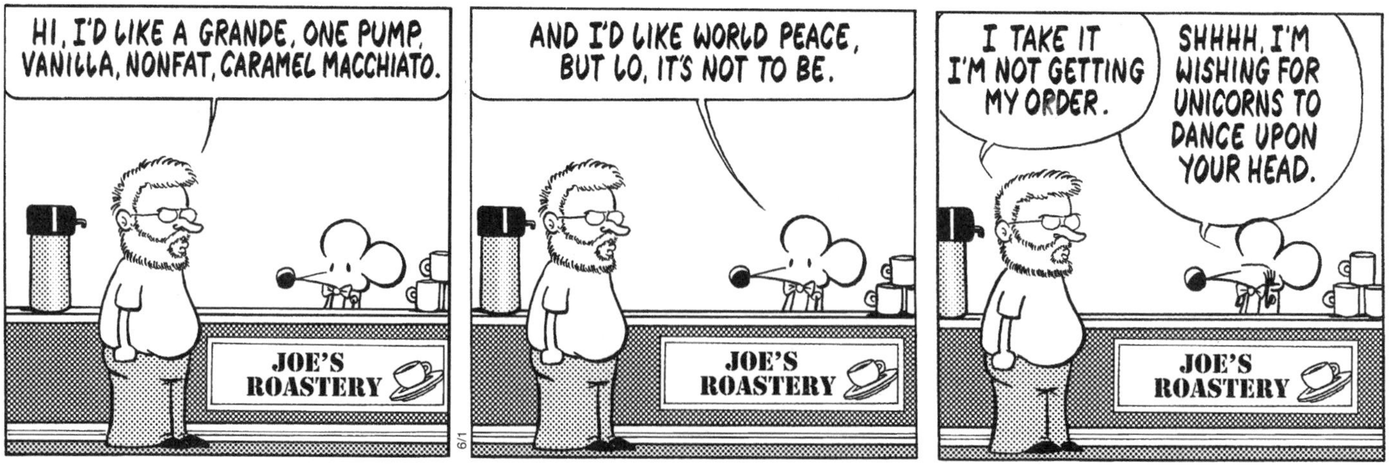
HI, I'D LIKE A GRANDE, ONE PUMP, VANILLA, NONFAT, CARAMEL MACCHIATO.
JOE'S ROASTERY
6/1
AND I'D LIKE WORLD PEACE, BUT LO, IT'S NOT TO BE.
JOE'S ROASTERY
I TAKE IT I'M NOT GETTING MY ORDER.
SHHHH, I'M WISHING FOR UNICORNS TO DANCE UPON YOUR HEAD.
JOE'S ROASTERY

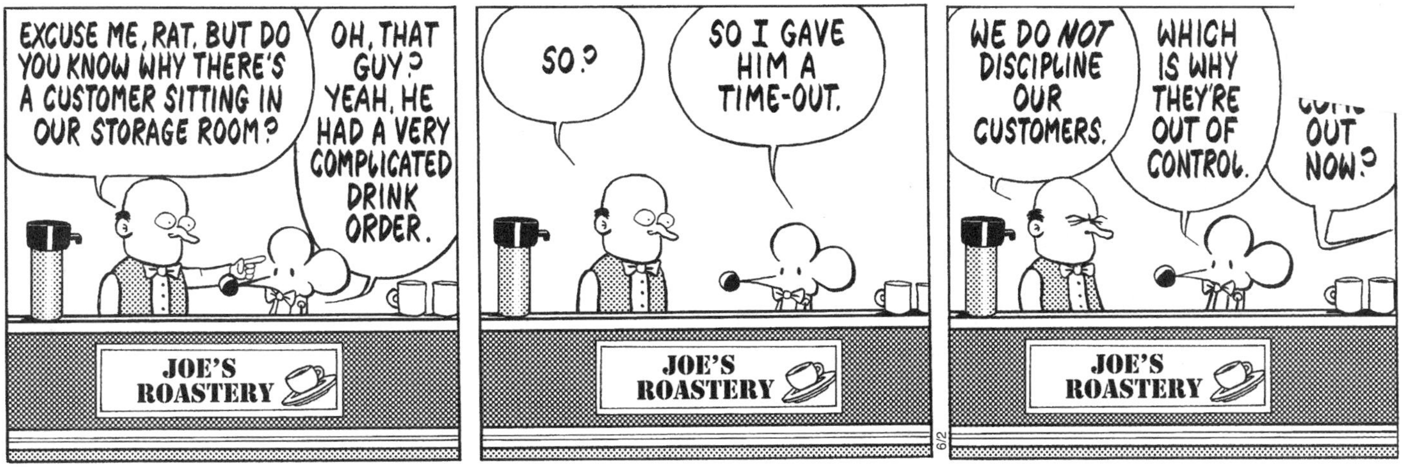
EXCUSE ME, RAT. BUT DO YOU KNOW WHY THERE'S A CUSTOMER SITTING IN OUR STORAGE ROOM?
OH, THAT GUY? YEAH, HE HAD A VERY COMPLICATED DRINK ORDER.
JOE'S ROASTERY
SO?
SO I GAVE HIM A TIME-OUT.
JOE'S ROASTERY
WE DO *NOT* DISCIPLINE OUR CUSTOMERS.
WHICH IS WHY THEY'RE OUT OF CONTROL.
OUT NOW?
JOE'S ROASTERY
6/2

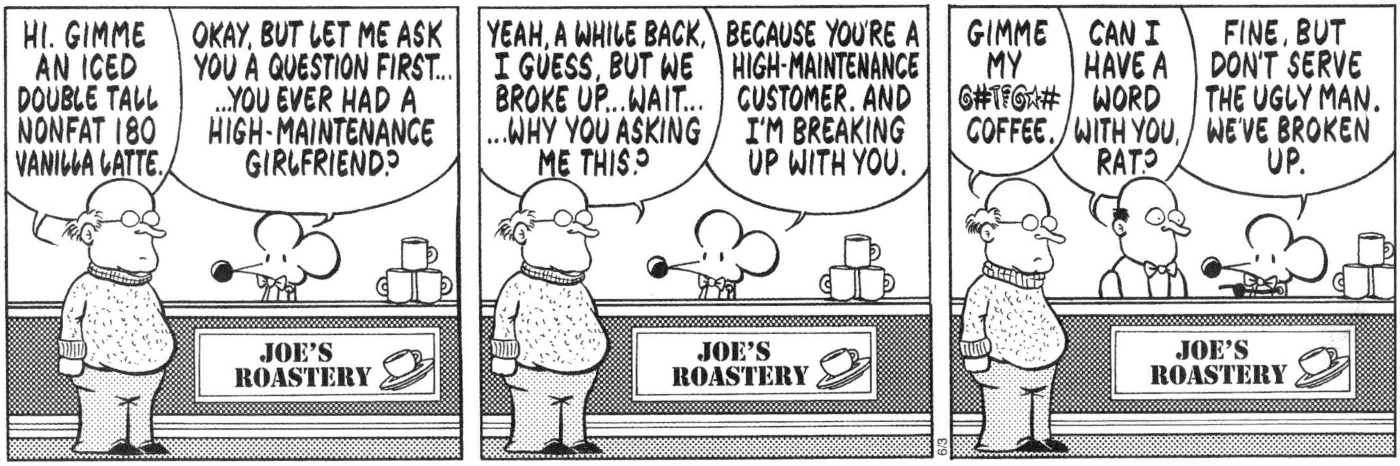
HI. GIMME AN ICED DOUBLE TALL NONFAT 180 VANILLA LATTE.
OKAY, BUT LET ME ASK YOU A QUESTION FIRST... ...YOU EVER HAD A HIGH-MAINTENANCE GIRLFRIEND?
JOE'S ROASTERY
YEAH, A WHILE BACK, I GUESS, BUT WE BROKE UP...WAIT... ...WHY YOU ASKING ME THIS?
BECAUSE YOU'RE A HIGH-MAINTENANCE CUSTOMER. AND I'M BREAKING UP WITH YOU.
JOE'S ROASTERY
GIMME MY @#T!@☆# COFFEE.
CAN I HAVE A WORD WITH YOU, RAT?
FINE, BUT DON'T SERVE THE UGLY MAN. WE'VE BROKEN UP.
JOE'S ROASTERY
6/3

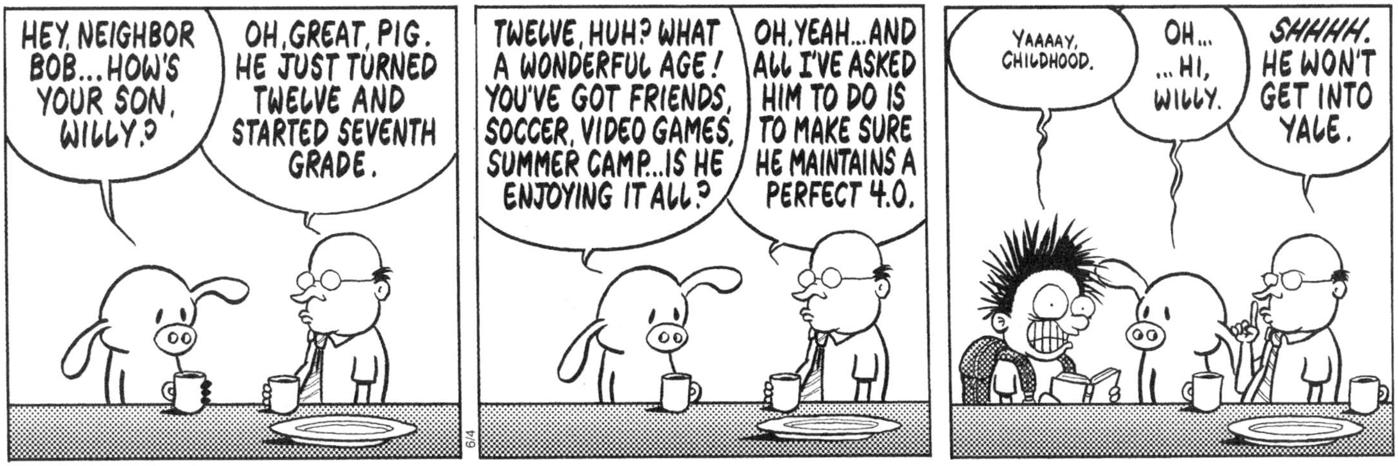
HEY, NEIGHBOR BOB...HOW'S YOUR SON, WILLY?
OH, GREAT, PIG. HE JUST TURNED TWELVE AND STARTED SEVENTH GRADE.
TWELVE, HUH? WHAT A WONDERFUL AGE! YOU'VE GOT FRIENDS, SOCCER, VIDEO GAMES, SUMMER CAMP...IS HE ENJOYING IT ALL?
OH, YEAH...AND ALL I'VE ASKED HIM TO DO IS TO MAKE SURE HE MAINTAINS A PERFECT 4.0.
YAAAAY, CHILDHOOD.
OH... ...HI, WILLY.
SHHHH. HE WON'T GET INTO YALE.
6/4

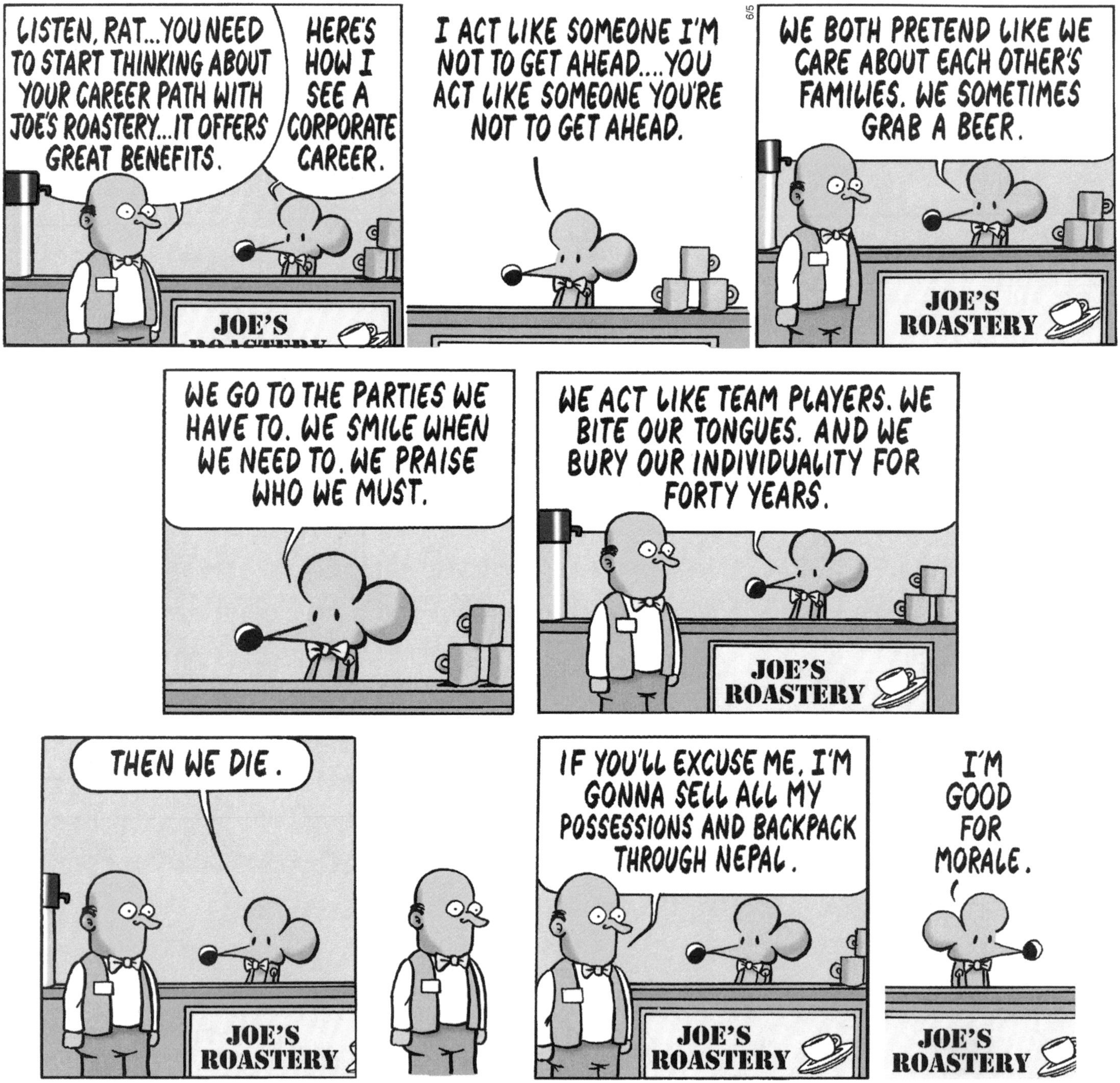
LISTEN, RAT...YOU NEED TO START THINKING ABOUT YOUR CAREER PATH WITH JOE'S ROASTERY...IT OFFERS GREAT BENEFITS.
HERE'S HOW I SEE A CORPORATE CAREER.
JOE'S
I ACT LIKE SOMEONE I'M NOT TO GET AHEAD.... YOU ACT LIKE SOMEONE YOU'RE NOT TO GET AHEAD.
6/5
WE BOTH PRETEND LIKE WE CARE ABOUT EACH OTHER'S FAMILIES. WE SOMETIMES GRAB A BEER.
JOE'S ROASTERY
WE GO TO THE PARTIES WE HAVE TO. WE SMILE WHEN WE NEED TO. WE PRAISE WHO WE MUST.
WE ACT LIKE TEAM PLAYERS. WE BITE OUR TONGUES. AND WE BURY OUR INDIVIDUALITY FOR FORTY YEARS.
JOE'S ROASTERY
THEN WE DIE.
JOE'S ROASTERY
IF YOU'LL EXCUSE ME, I'M GONNA SELL ALL MY POSSESSIONS AND BACKPACK THROUGH NEPAL.
JOE'S ROASTERY
I'M GOOD FOR MORALE.
JOE'S ROASTERY

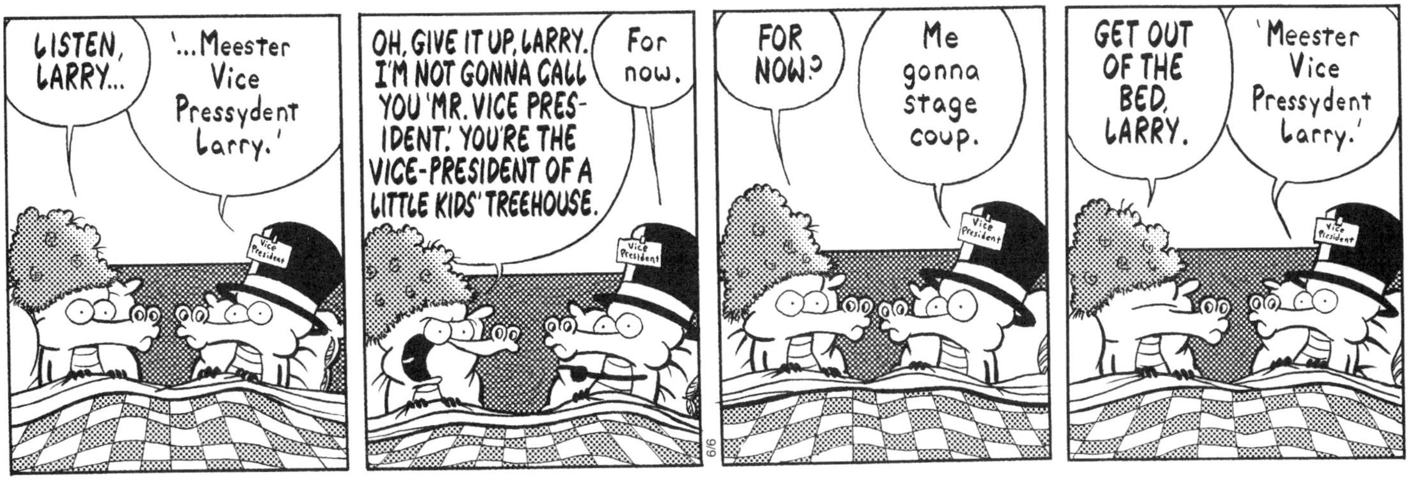
LISTEN, LARRY...
'...Meester Vice Pressydent Larry.'
OH, GIVE IT UP, LARRY. I'M NOT GONNA CALL YOU 'MR. VICE PRESIDENT.' YOU'RE THE VICE-PRESIDENT OF A LITTLE KIDS' TREEHOUSE.
For now.
Vice President
FOR NOW?
Me gonna stage coup.
GET OUT OF THE BED, LARRY.
'Meester Vice Pressydent Larry.'
6/6

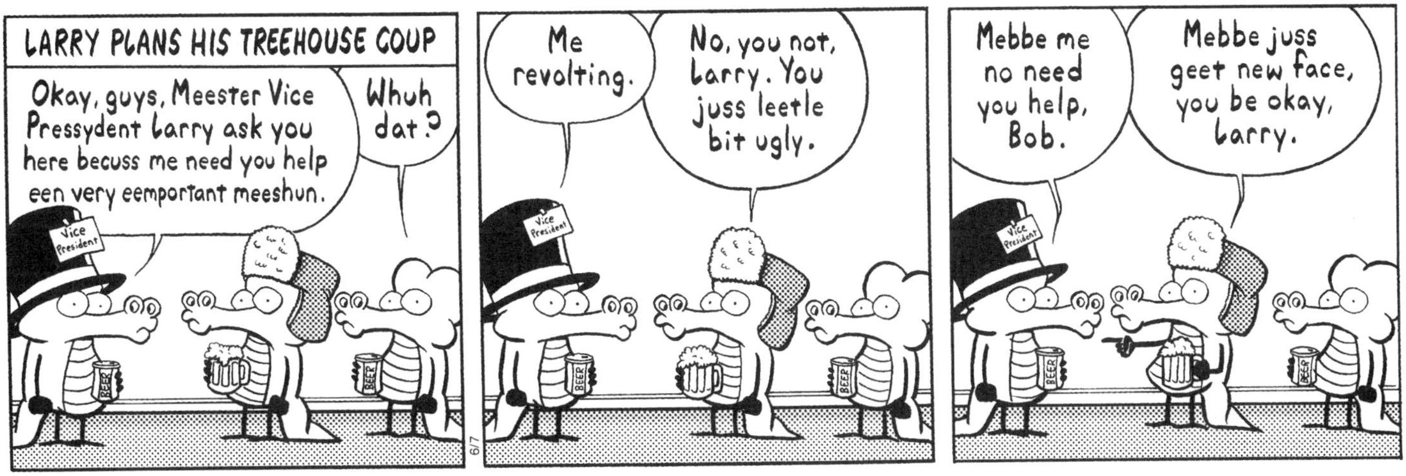
LARRY PLANS HIS TREEHOUSE COUP
Okay, guys, Meester Vice Pressydent Larry ask you here becuss me need you help een very eemportant meeshun.
Whuh dat?
Vice President
BEER
Me revolting.
No, you not, Larry. You juss leetle bit ugly.
Mebbe me no need you help, Bob.
Mebbe juss geet new face, you be okay, Larry.
6/7

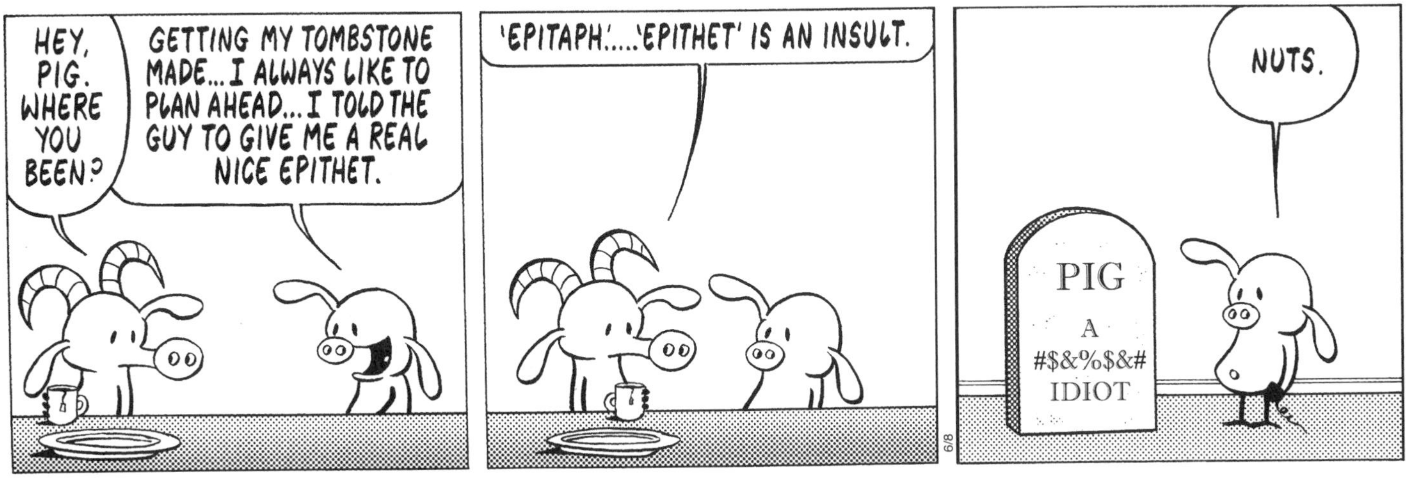
HEY, PIG. WHERE YOU BEEN?
GETTING MY TOMBSTONE MADE... I ALWAYS LIKE TO PLAN AHEAD... I TOLD THE GUY TO GIVE ME A REAL NICE EPITHET.
'EPITAPH.'....'EPITHET' IS AN INSULT.
PIG
A
#$&%$&#
IDIOT
NUTS.
6/8

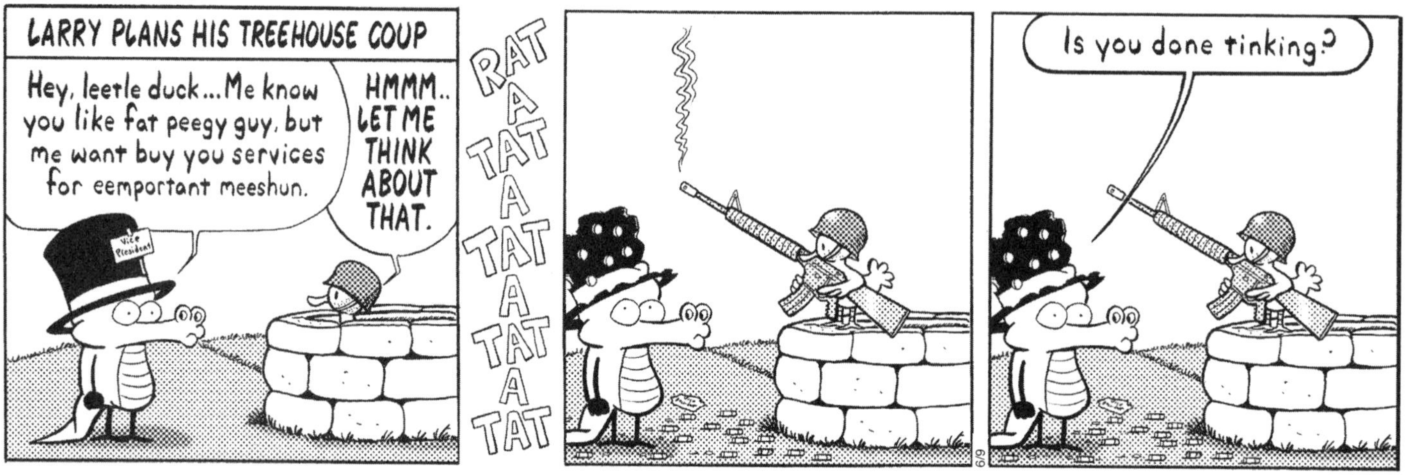
LARRY PLANS HIS TREEHOUSE COUP
Hey, leetle duck... Me know you like fat peegy guy, but me want buy you services for eemportant meeshun.
HMMM.. LET ME THINK ABOUT THAT.
RAT A TAT A TAT A TAT A TAT A TAT
Is you done tinking?
6/9

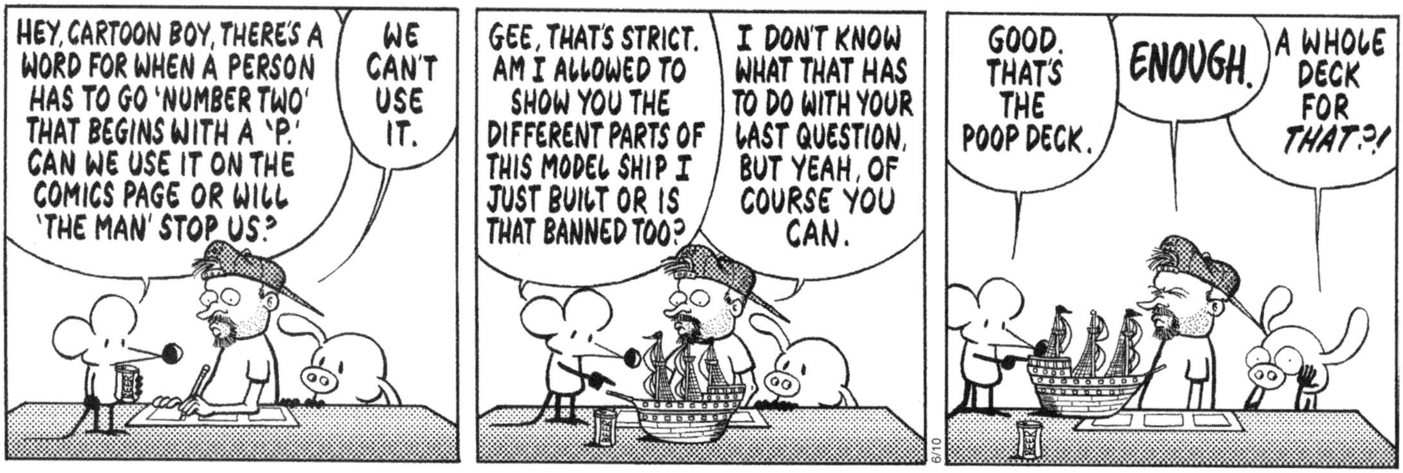
HEY, CARTOON BOY, THERE'S A WORD FOR WHEN A PERSON HAS TO GO 'NUMBER TWO' THAT BEGINS WITH A 'P.' CAN WE USE IT ON THE COMICS PAGE OR WILL 'THE MAN' STOP US?
WE CAN'T USE IT.
GEE, THAT'S STRICT. AM I ALLOWED TO SHOW YOU THE DIFFERENT PARTS OF THIS MODEL SHIP I JUST BUILT OR IS THAT BANNED TOO?
I DON'T KNOW WHAT THAT HAS TO DO WITH YOUR LAST QUESTION, BUT YEAH, OF COURSE YOU CAN.
GOOD. THAT'S THE POOP DECK.
ENOUGH.
A WHOLE DECK FOR THAT?!
6/10

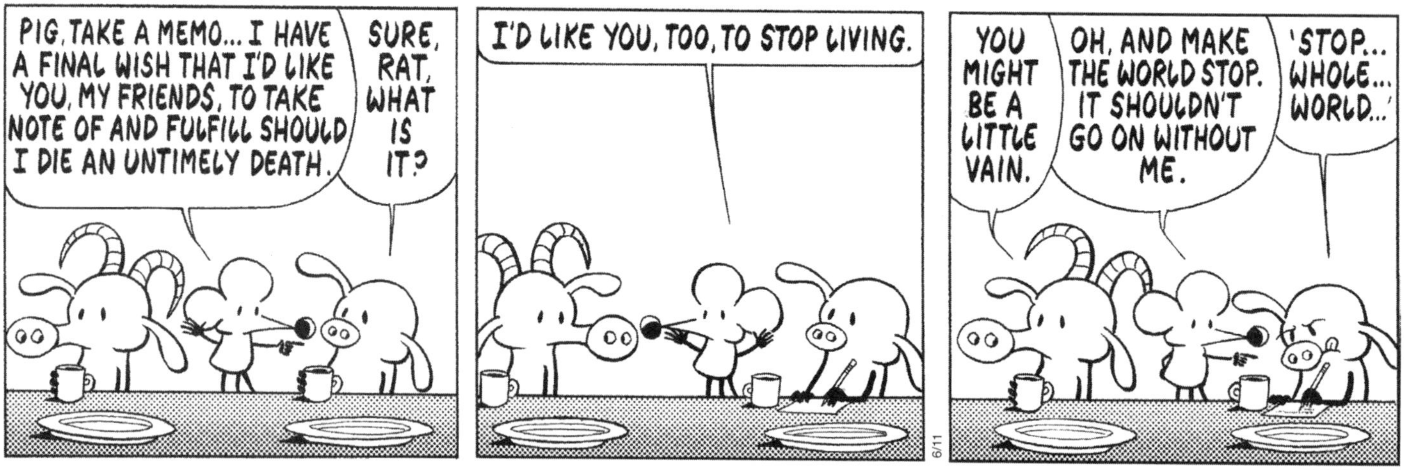
PIG, TAKE A MEMO... I HAVE A FINAL WISH THAT I'D LIKE YOU, MY FRIENDS, TO TAKE NOTE OF AND FULFILL SHOULD I DIE AN UNTIMELY DEATH.
SURE, RAT, WHAT IS IT?
I'D LIKE YOU, TOO, TO STOP LIVING.
YOU MIGHT BE A LITTLE VAIN.
OH, AND MAKE THE WORLD STOP. IT SHOULDN'T GO ON WITHOUT ME.
'STOP... WHOLE... WORLD...'
6/11

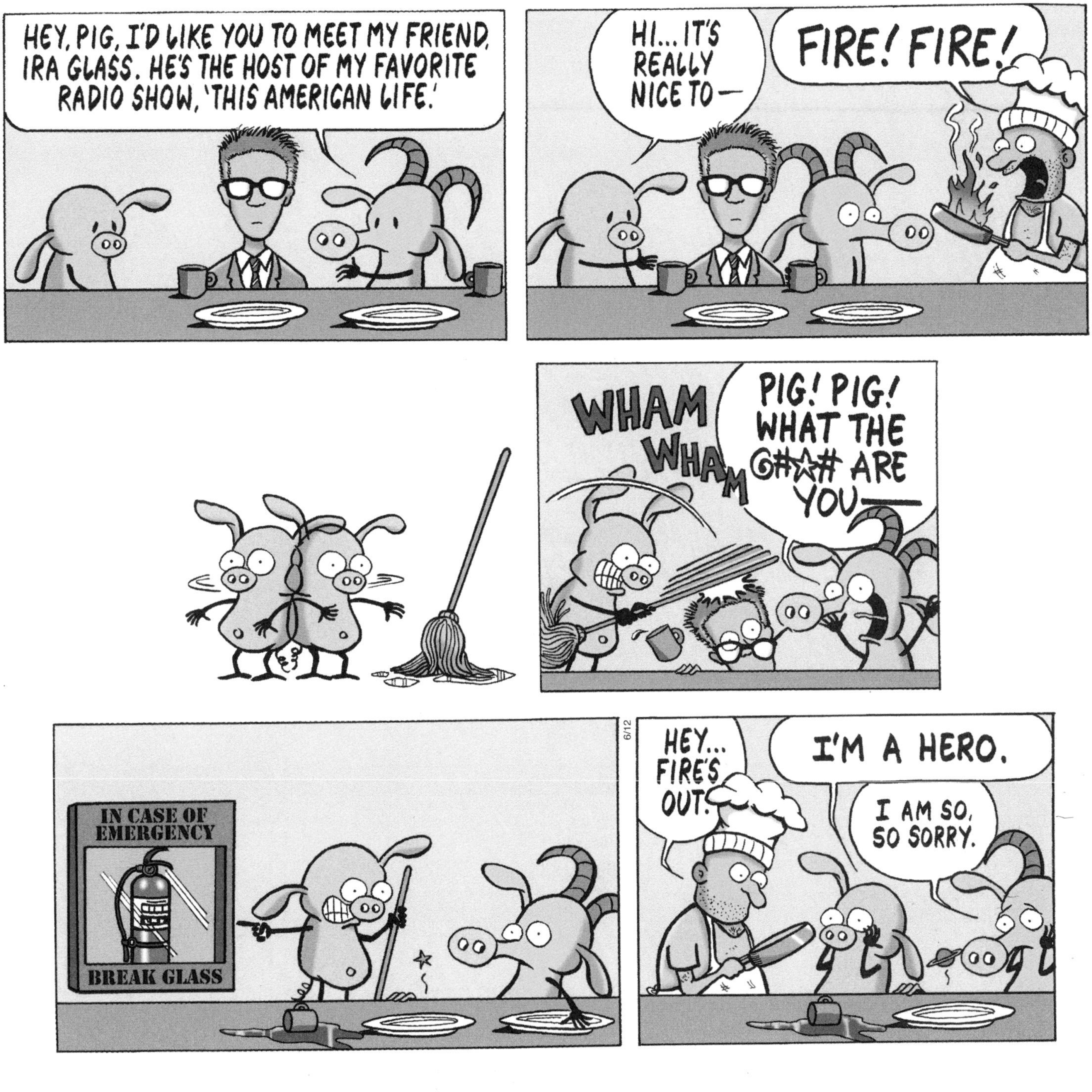
HEY, PIG, I'D LIKE YOU TO MEET MY FRIEND, IRA GLASS. HE'S THE HOST OF MY FAVORITE RADIO SHOW, 'THIS AMERICAN LIFE.'
HI... IT'S REALLY NICE TO—
FIRE! FIRE!
WHAM
WHAM
PIG! PIG! WHAT THE @#☆# ARE YOU—
IN CASE OF EMERGENCY
BREAK GLASS
6/12
HEY... FIRE'S OUT.
I'M A HERO.
I AM SO, SO SORRY.

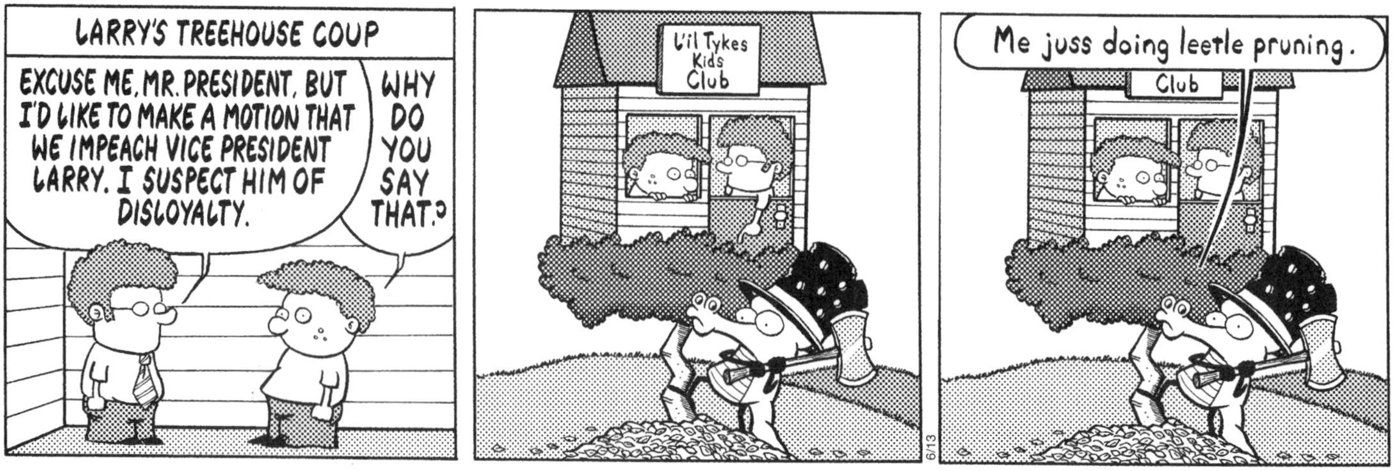
LARRY'S TREEHOUSE COUP
EXCUSE ME, MR. PRESIDENT, BUT I'D LIKE TO MAKE A MOTION THAT WE IMPEACH VICE PRESIDENT LARRY. I SUSPECT HIM OF DISLOYALTY.
WHY DO YOU SAY THAT?
L'il Tykes Kids Club
Me juss doing leetle pruning.
Club
6/13

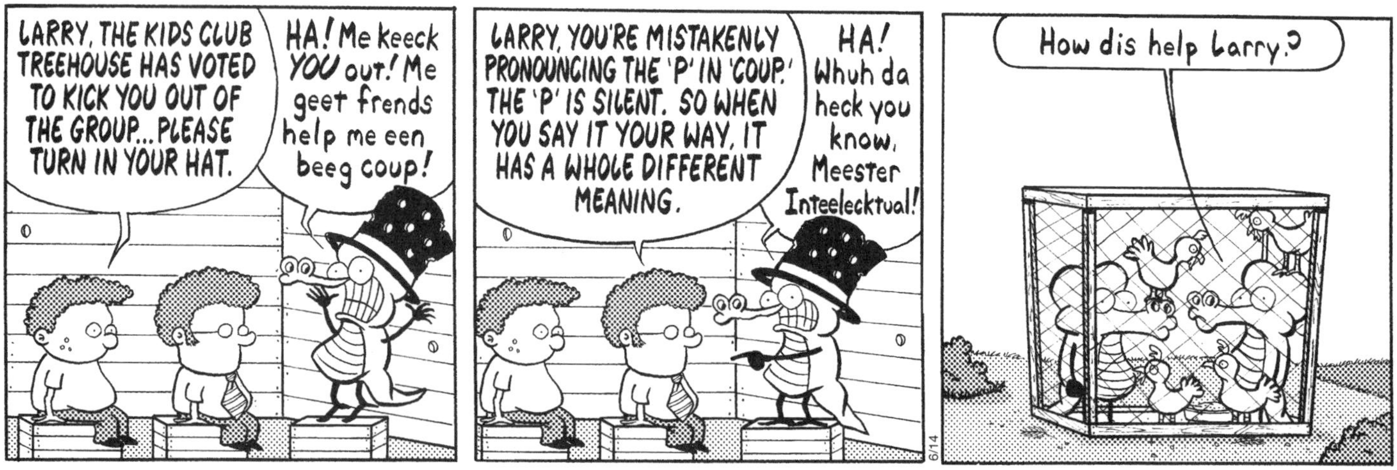
LARRY, THE KIDS CLUB TREEHOUSE HAS VOTED TO KICK YOU OUT OF THE GROUP... PLEASE TURN IN YOUR HAT.
HA! Me keeck YOU out! Me geet frends help me een beeg coup!
LARRY, YOU'RE MISTAKENLY PRONOUNCING THE 'P' IN 'COUP.' THE 'P' IS SILENT. SO WHEN YOU SAY IT YOUR WAY, IT HAS A WHOLE DIFFERENT MEANING.
HA! Whuh da heck you know, Meester Inteelecktual!
How dis help Larry?
6/14

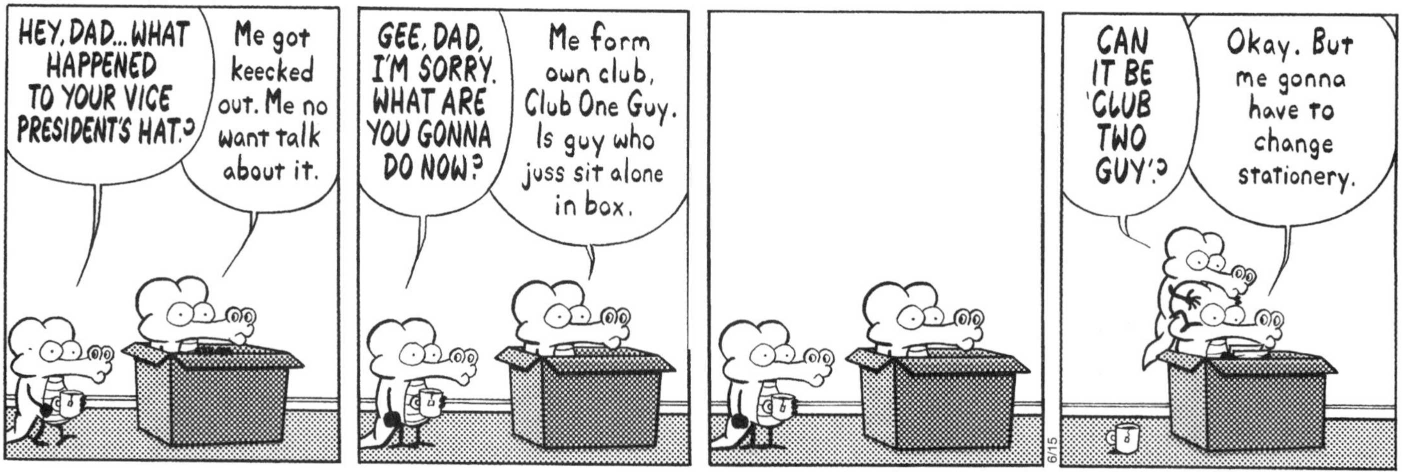
HEY, DAD... WHAT HAPPENED TO YOUR VICE PRESIDENT'S HAT?
Me got keecked out. Me no want talk about it.
GEE, DAD, I'M SORRY. WHAT ARE YOU GONNA DO NOW?
Me form own club, Club One Guy. Is guy who juss sit alone in box.
CAN IT BE 'CLUB TWO GUY'?
Okay. But me gonna have to change stationery.
6/15

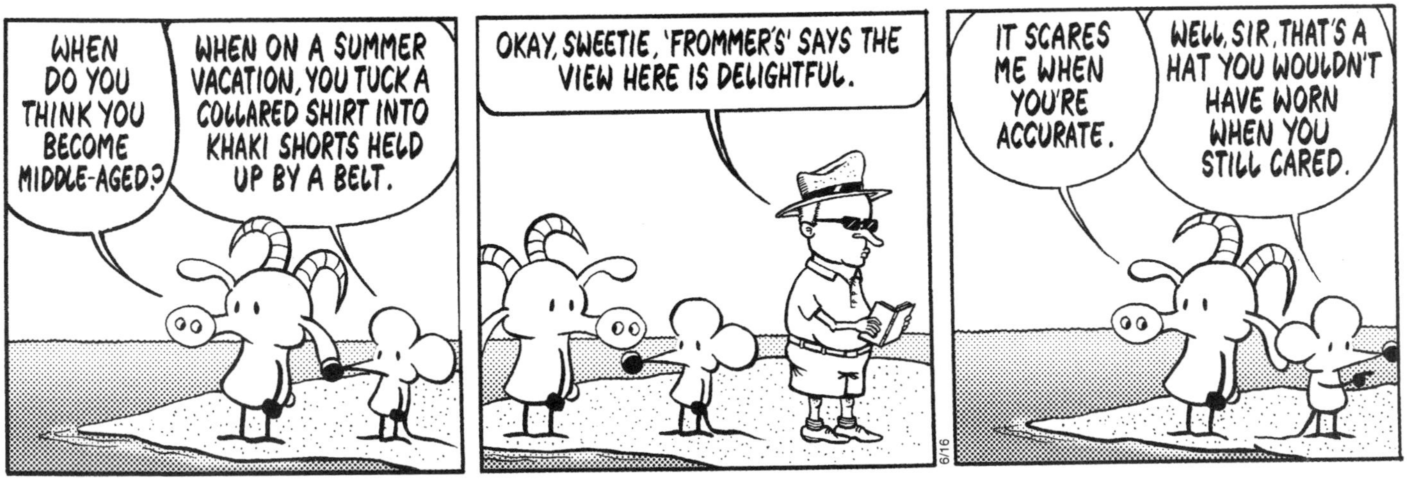
WHEN DO YOU THINK YOU BECOME MIDDLE-AGED?
WHEN ON A SUMMER VACATION, YOU TUCK A COLLARED SHIRT INTO KHAKI SHORTS HELD UP BY A BELT.
OKAY, SWEETIE, 'FROMMER'S' SAYS THE VIEW HERE IS DELIGHTFUL.
6/16
IT SCARES ME WHEN YOU'RE ACCURATE.
WELL, SIR, THAT'S A HAT YOU WOULDN'T HAVE WORN WHEN YOU STILL CARED.

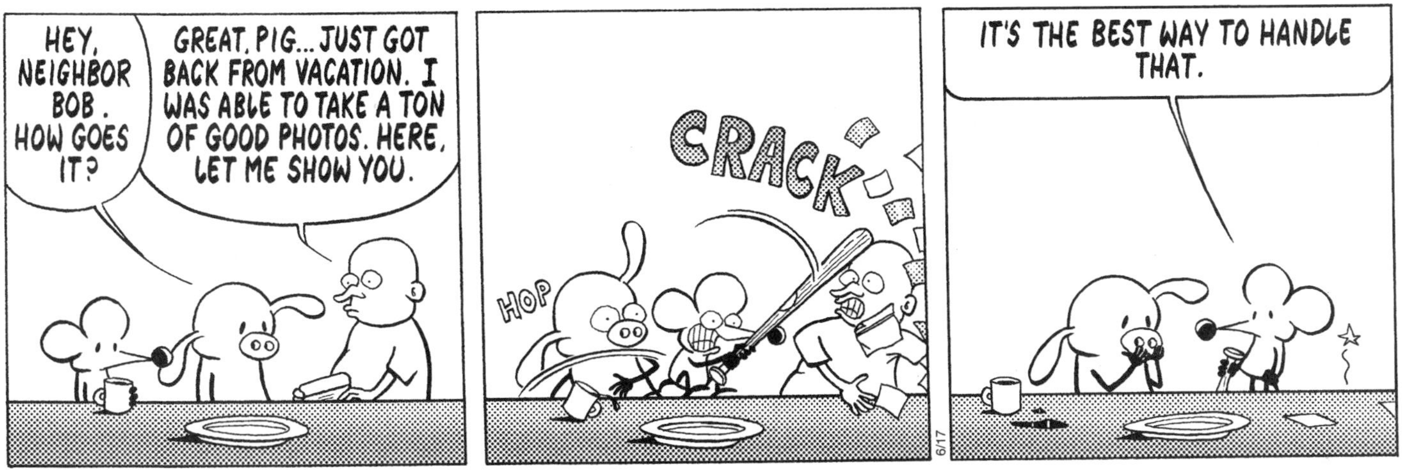
HEY, NEIGHBOR BOB. HOW GOES IT?
GREAT, PIG... JUST GOT BACK FROM VACATION. I WAS ABLE TO TAKE A TON OF GOOD PHOTOS. HERE, LET ME SHOW YOU.
CRACK
HOP
6/17
IT'S THE BEST WAY TO HANDLE THAT.

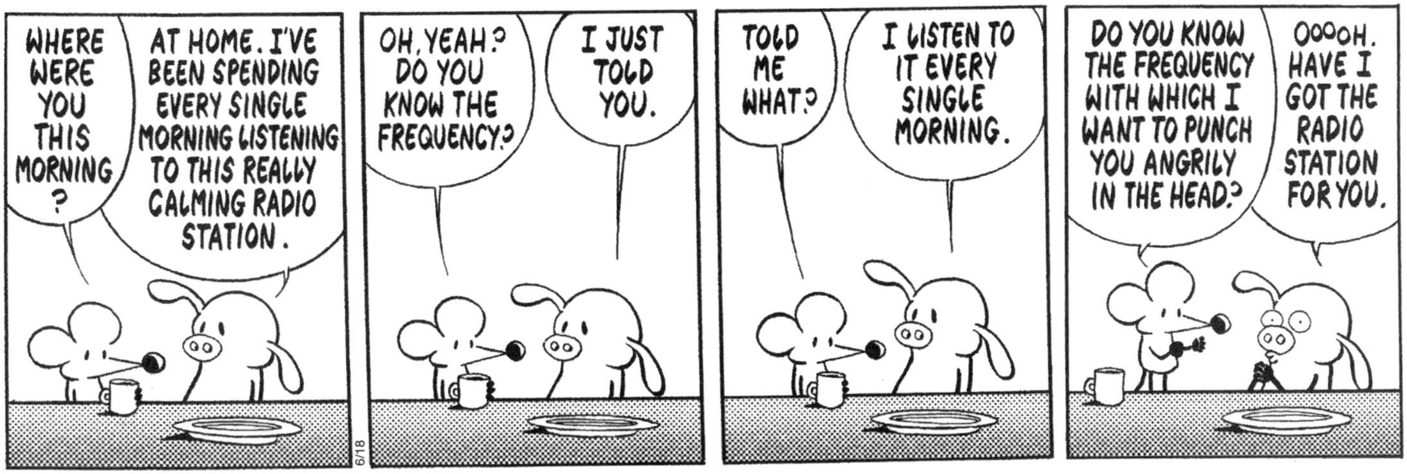
WHERE WERE YOU THIS MORNING?
AT HOME. I'VE BEEN SPENDING EVERY SINGLE MORNING LISTENING TO THIS REALLY CALMING RADIO STATION.
6/18
OH, YEAH? DO YOU KNOW THE FREQUENCY?
I JUST TOLD YOU.
TOLD ME WHAT?
I LISTEN TO IT EVERY SINGLE MORNING.
DO YOU KNOW THE FREQUENCY WITH WHICH I WANT TO PUNCH YOU ANGRILY IN THE HEAD?
OOOOH. HAVE I GOT THE RADIO STATION FOR YOU.

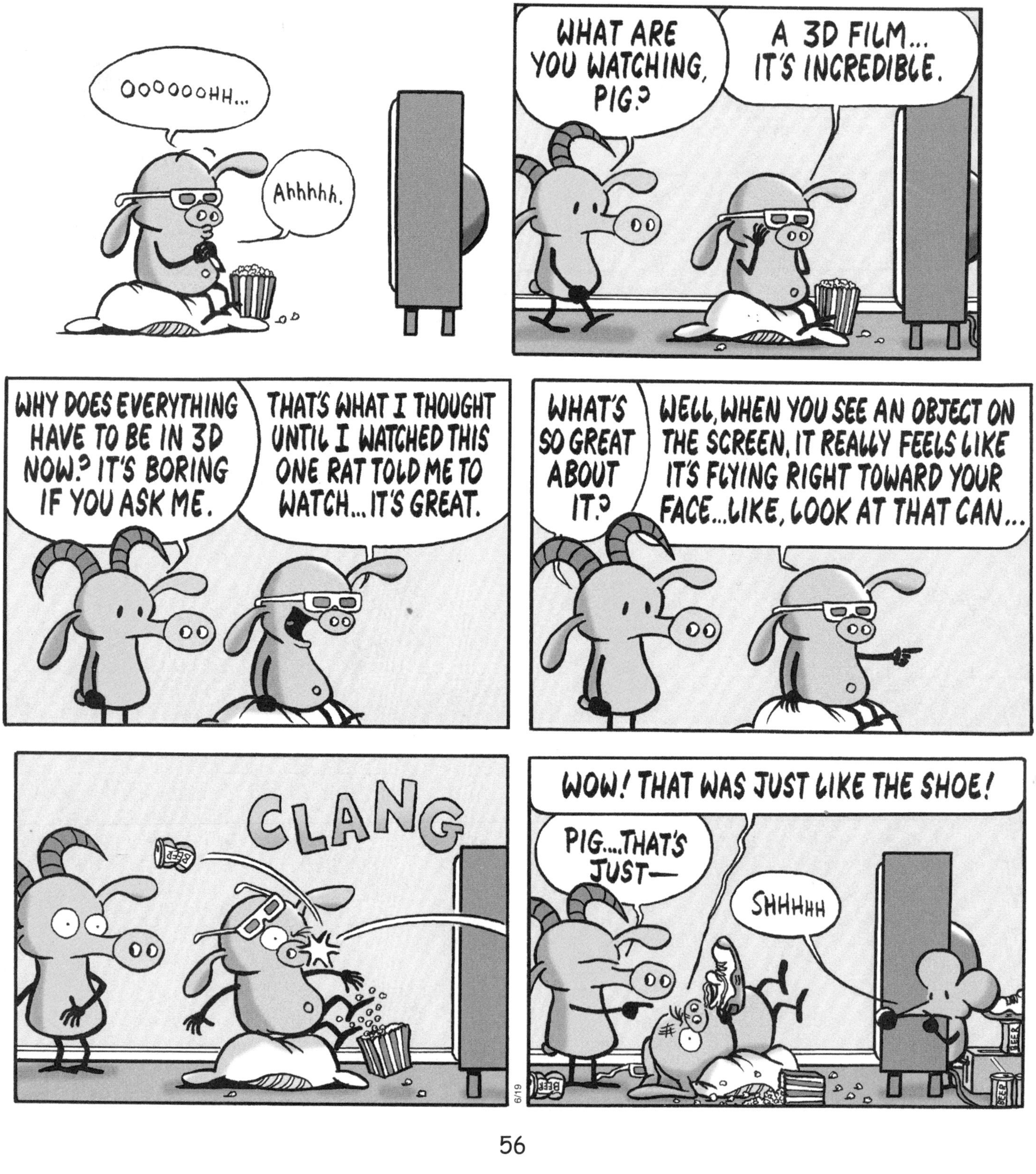
OOOOOOHH...
Ahhhhh.
WHAT ARE YOU WATCHING, PIG?
A 3D FILM... IT'S INCREDIBLE.
WHY DOES EVERYTHING HAVE TO BE IN 3D NOW? IT'S BORING IF YOU ASK ME.
THAT'S WHAT I THOUGHT UNTIL I WATCHED THIS ONE RAT TOLD ME TO WATCH... IT'S GREAT.
WHAT'S SO GREAT ABOUT IT?
WELL, WHEN YOU SEE AN OBJECT ON THE SCREEN, IT REALLY FEELS LIKE IT'S FLYING RIGHT TOWARD YOUR FACE... LIKE, LOOK AT THAT CAN...
CLANG
BEER
WOW! THAT WAS JUST LIKE THE SHOE!
PIG.... THAT'S JUST—
SHHHHH
6/19

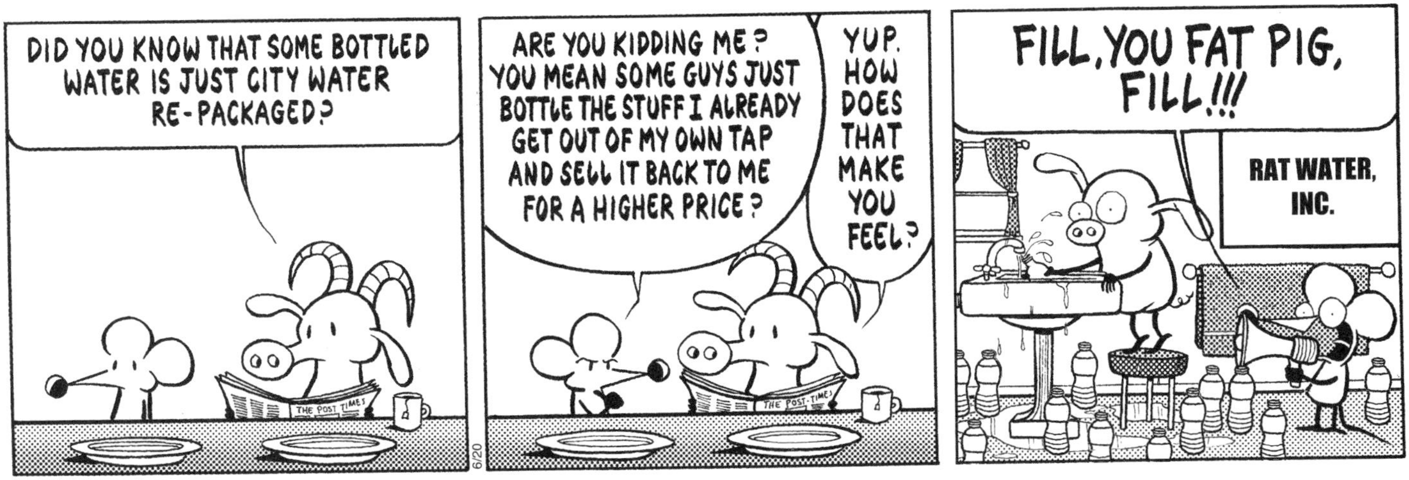
DID YOU KNOW THAT SOME BOTTLED WATER IS JUST CITY WATER RE-PACKAGED?
ARE YOU KIDDING ME? YOU MEAN SOME GUYS JUST BOTTLE THE STUFF I ALREADY GET OUT OF MY OWN TAP AND SELL IT BACK TO ME FOR A HIGHER PRICE?
YUP. HOW DOES THAT MAKE YOU FEEL?
FILL, YOU FAT PIG, FILL!!!
RAT WATER, INC.
6/20

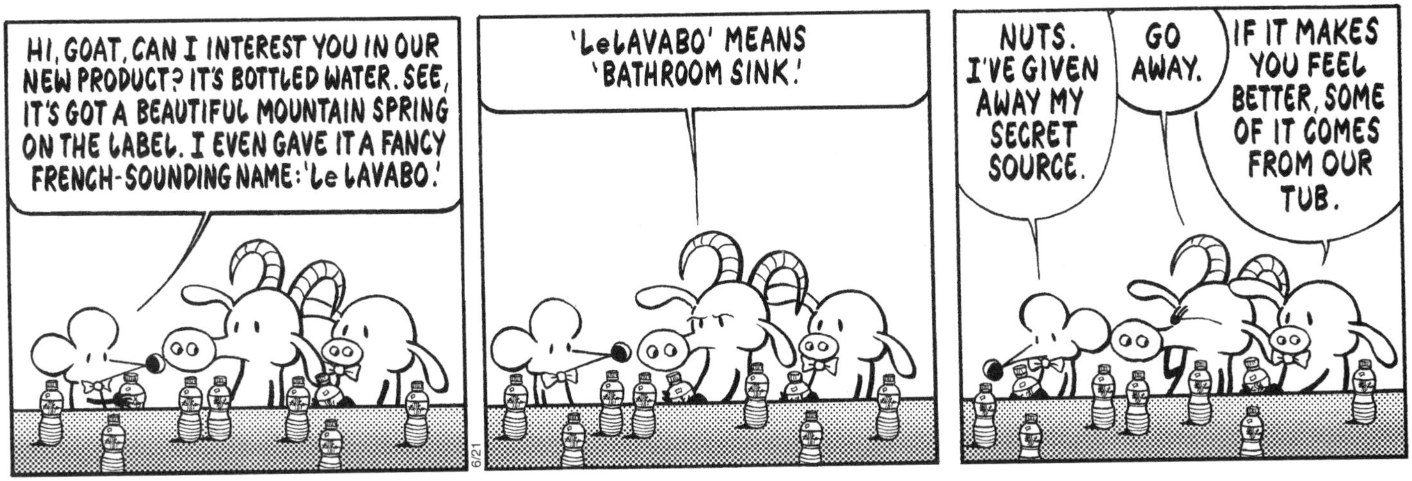
HI, GOAT, CAN I INTEREST YOU IN OUR NEW PRODUCT? IT'S BOTTLED WATER. SEE, IT'S GOT A BEAUTIFUL MOUNTAIN SPRING ON THE LABEL. I EVEN GAVE IT A FANCY FRENCH-SOUNDING NAME: 'Le LAVABO.'
'LeLAVABO' MEANS 'BATHROOM SINK.'
NUTS. I'VE GIVEN AWAY MY SECRET SOURCE.
GO AWAY.
IF IT MAKES YOU FEEL BETTER, SOME OF IT COMES FROM OUR TUB.
6/21

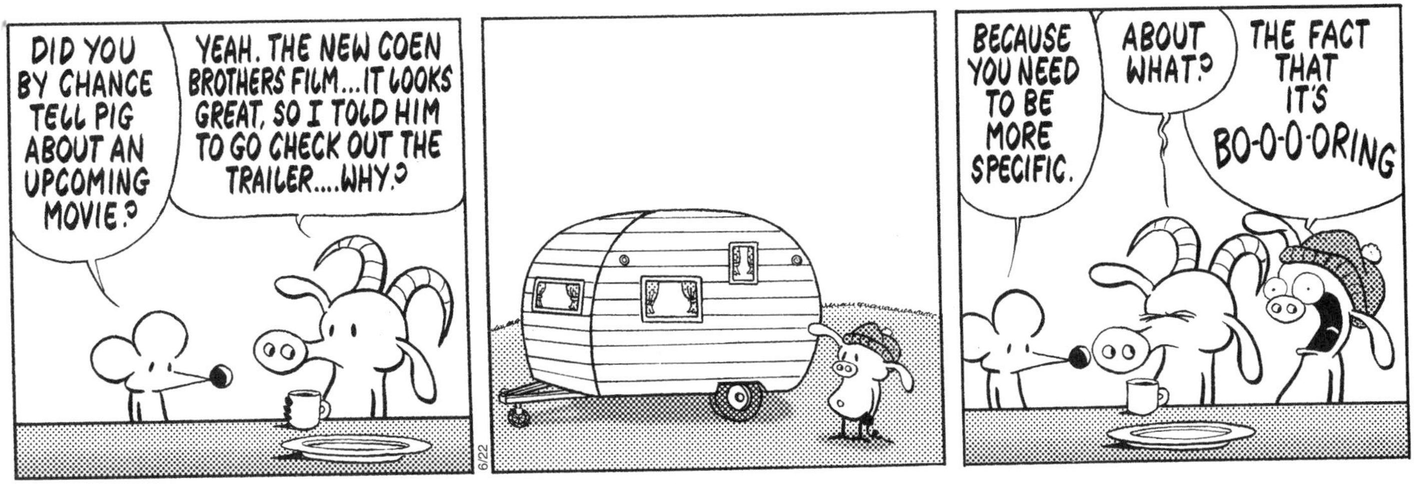
DID YOU BY CHANCE TELL PIG ABOUT AN UPCOMING MOVIE?
YEAH. THE NEW COEN BROTHERS FILM...IT LOOKS GREAT, SO I TOLD HIM TO GO CHECK OUT THE TRAILER....WHY?
BECAUSE YOU NEED TO BE MORE SPECIFIC.
ABOUT WHAT?
THE FACT THAT IT'S BO-O-O-ORING
6/22

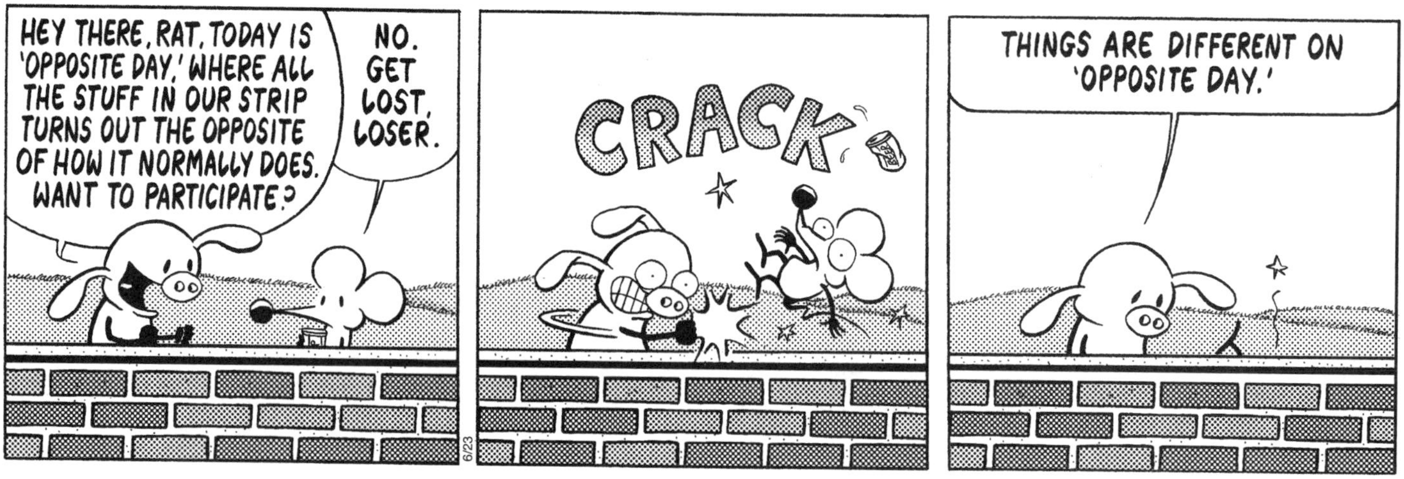
HEY THERE, RAT, TODAY IS 'OPPOSITE DAY,' WHERE ALL THE STUFF IN OUR STRIP TURNS OUT THE OPPOSITE OF HOW IT NORMALLY DOES. WANT TO PARTICIPATE?
NO. GET LOST, LOSER.
CRACK
THINGS ARE DIFFERENT ON 'OPPOSITE DAY.'
6/23

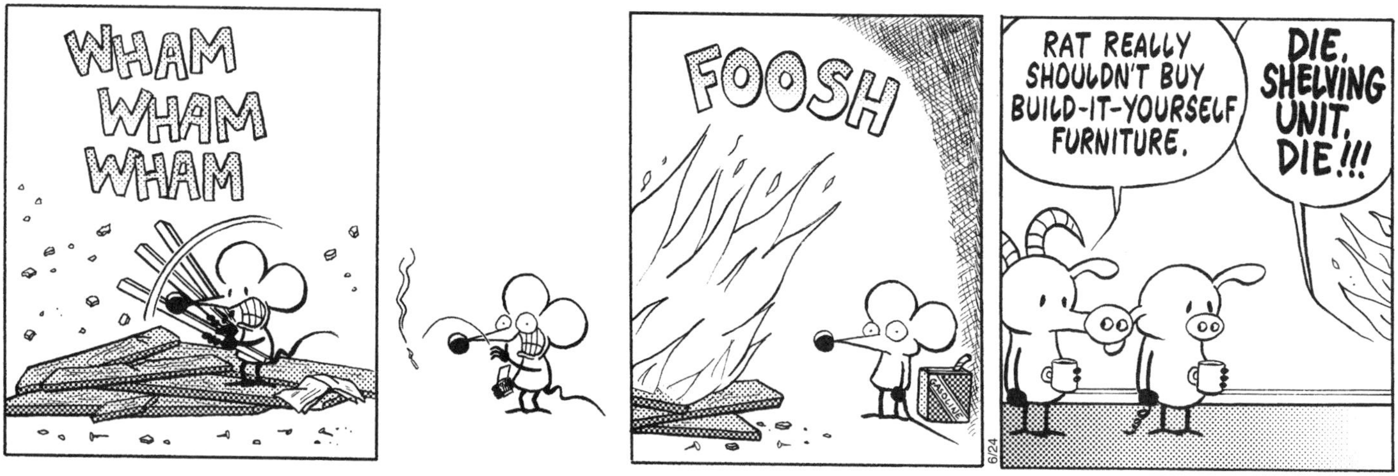
WHAM
WHAM
WHAM
FOOSH
RAT REALLY SHOULDN'T BUY BUILD-IT-YOURSELF FURNITURE.
DIE, SHELVING UNIT, DIE!!!
6/24

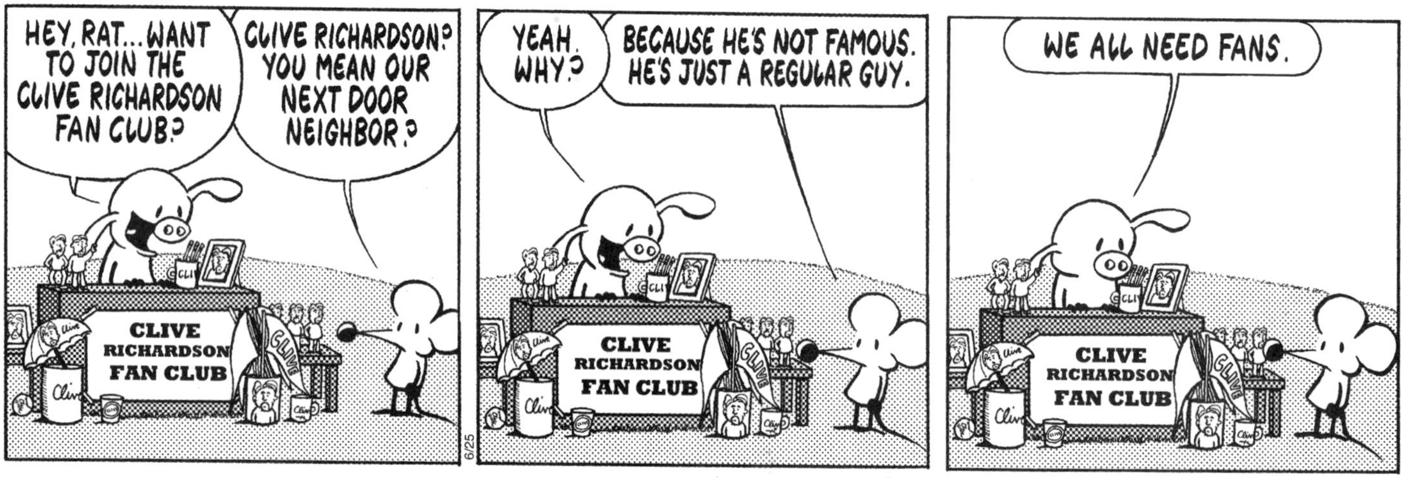
HEY, RAT... WANT TO JOIN THE CLIVE RICHARDSON FAN CLUB?
CLIVE RICHARDSON? YOU MEAN OUR NEXT DOOR NEIGHBOR?
CLIVE RICHARDSON FAN CLUB
YEAH. WHY?
BECAUSE HE'S NOT FAMOUS. HE'S JUST A REGULAR GUY.
CLIVE RICHARDSON FAN CLUB
WE ALL NEED FANS.
CLIVE RICHARDSON FAN CLUB
6/25

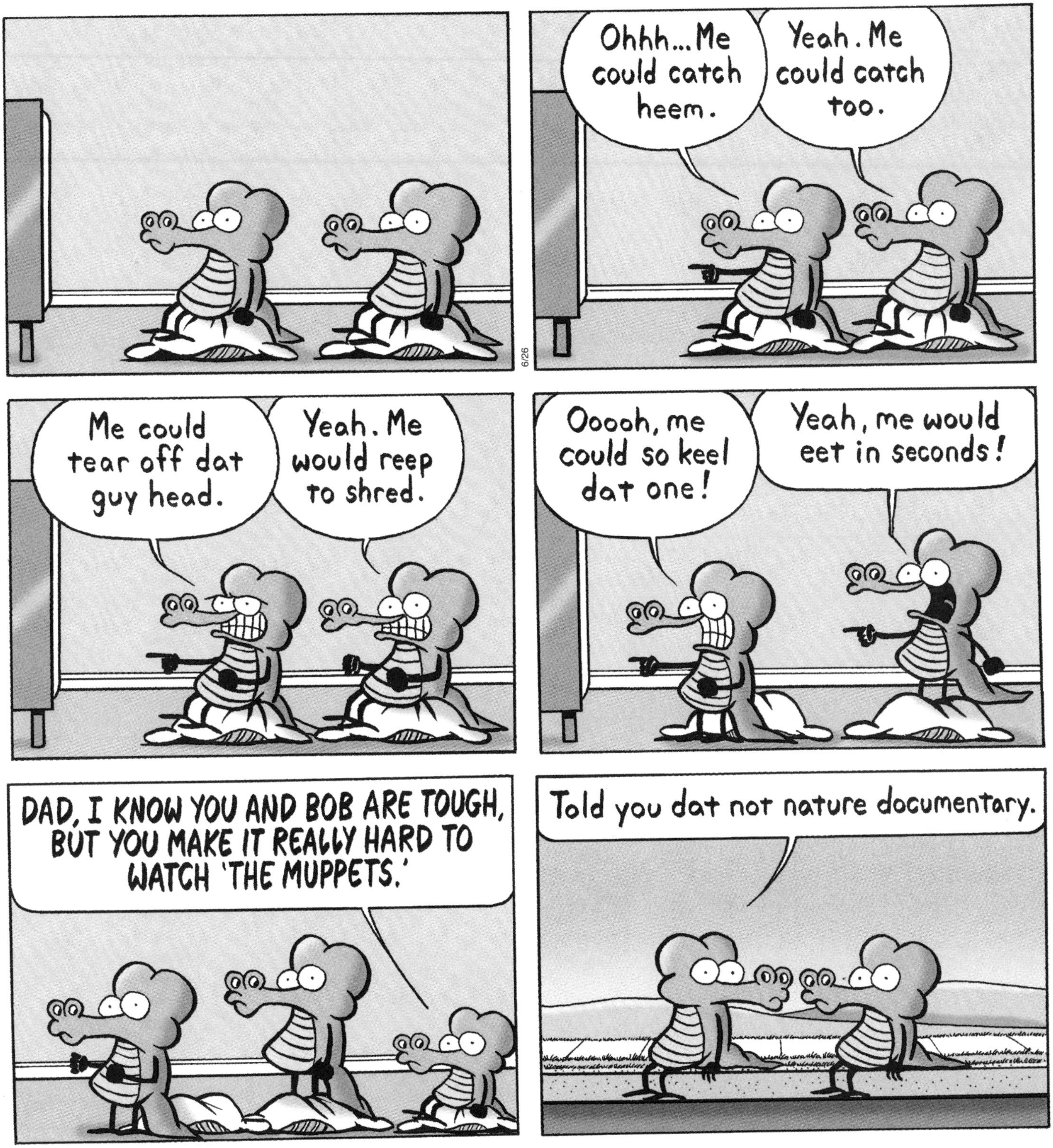
6/26
Ohhh...Me could catch heem.
Yeah. Me could catch too.
Me could tear off dat guy head.
Yeah. Me would reep to shred.
Ooooh, me could so keel dat one!
Yeah, me would eet in seconds!
DAD, I KNOW YOU AND BOB ARE TOUGH, BUT YOU MAKE IT REALLY HARD TO WATCH 'THE MUPPETS.'
Told you dat not nature documentary.

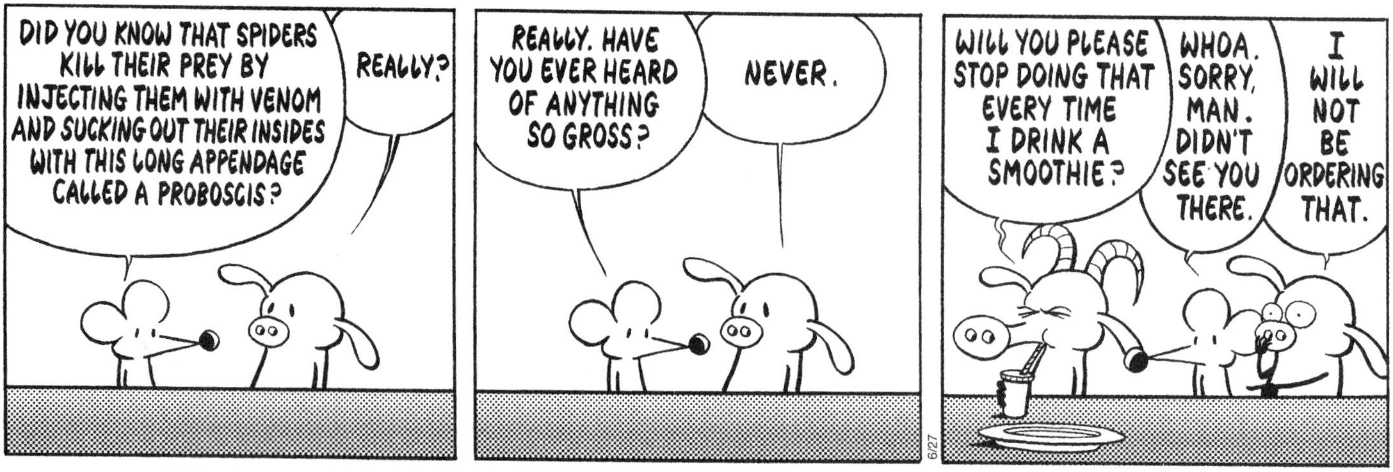
DID YOU KNOW THAT SPIDERS KILL THEIR PREY BY INJECTING THEM WITH VENOM AND SUCKING OUT THEIR INSIDES WITH THIS LONG APPENDAGE CALLED A PROBOSCIS?
REALLY?
REALLY. HAVE YOU EVER HEARD OF ANYTHING SO GROSS?
NEVER.
WILL YOU PLEASE STOP DOING THAT EVERY TIME I DRINK A SMOOTHIE?
WHOA. SORRY, MAN. DIDN'T SEE YOU THERE.
I WILL NOT BE ORDERING THAT.
6/27

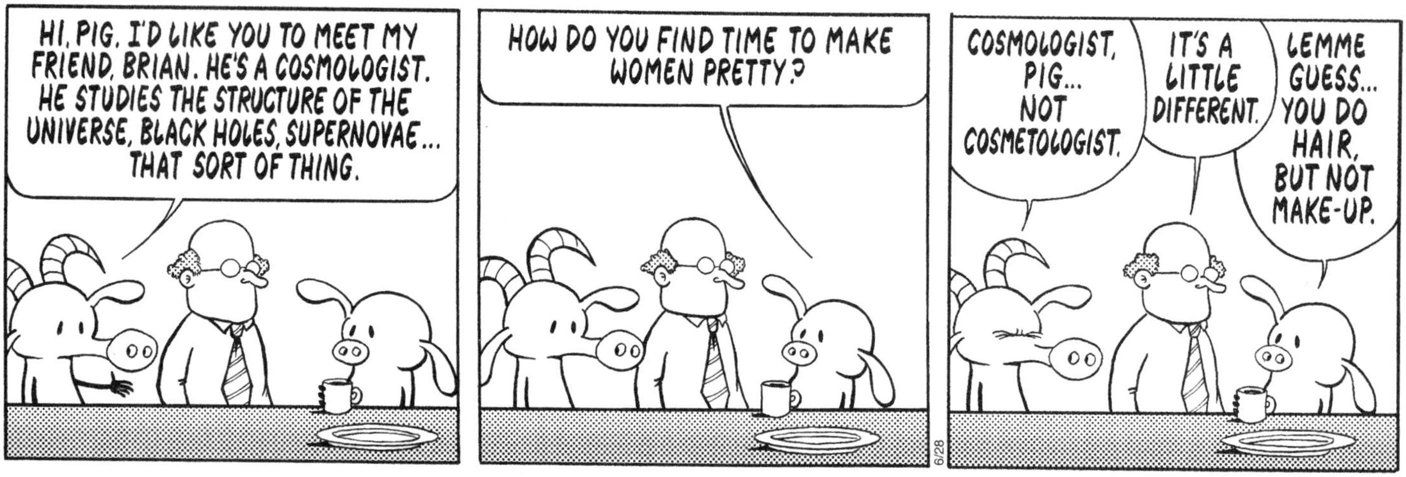
HI, PIG. I'D LIKE YOU TO MEET MY FRIEND, BRIAN. HE'S A COSMOLOGIST. HE STUDIES THE STRUCTURE OF THE UNIVERSE, BLACK HOLES, SUPERNOVAE... THAT SORT OF THING.
HOW DO YOU FIND TIME TO MAKE WOMEN PRETTY?
COSMOLOGIST, PIG... NOT COSMETOLOGIST.
IT'S A LITTLE DIFFERENT.
LEMME GUESS... YOU DO HAIR, BUT NOT MAKE-UP.
6/28

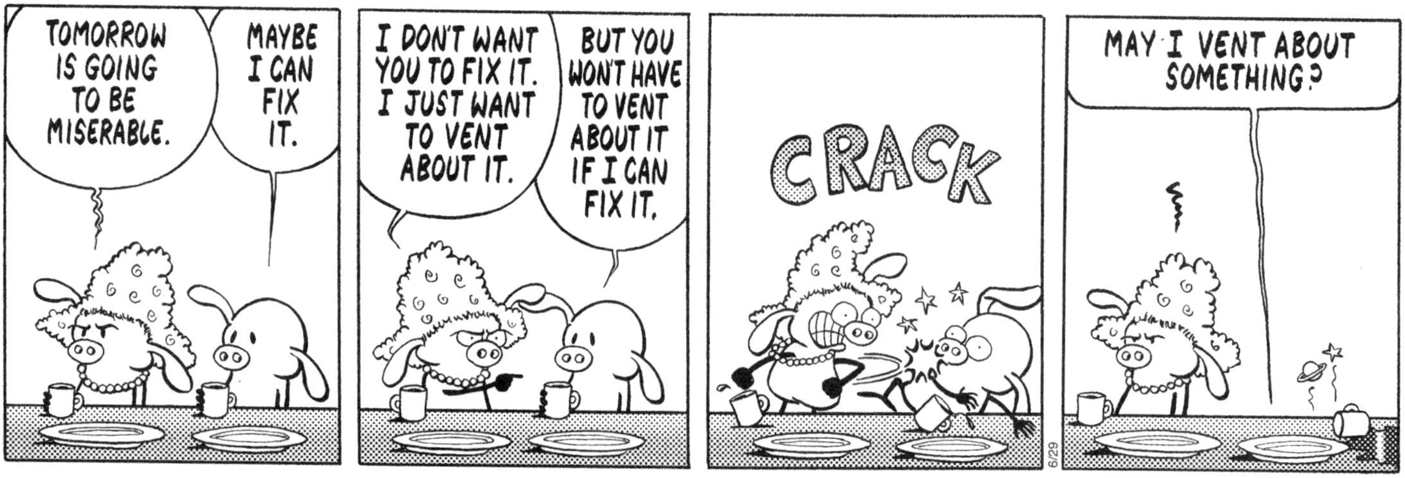
TOMORROW IS GOING TO BE MISERABLE.
MAYBE I CAN FIX IT.
I DON'T WANT YOU TO FIX IT. I JUST WANT TO VENT ABOUT IT.
BUT YOU WON'T HAVE TO VENT ABOUT IT IF I CAN FIX IT.
CRACK
MAY I VENT ABOUT SOMETHING?
6/29

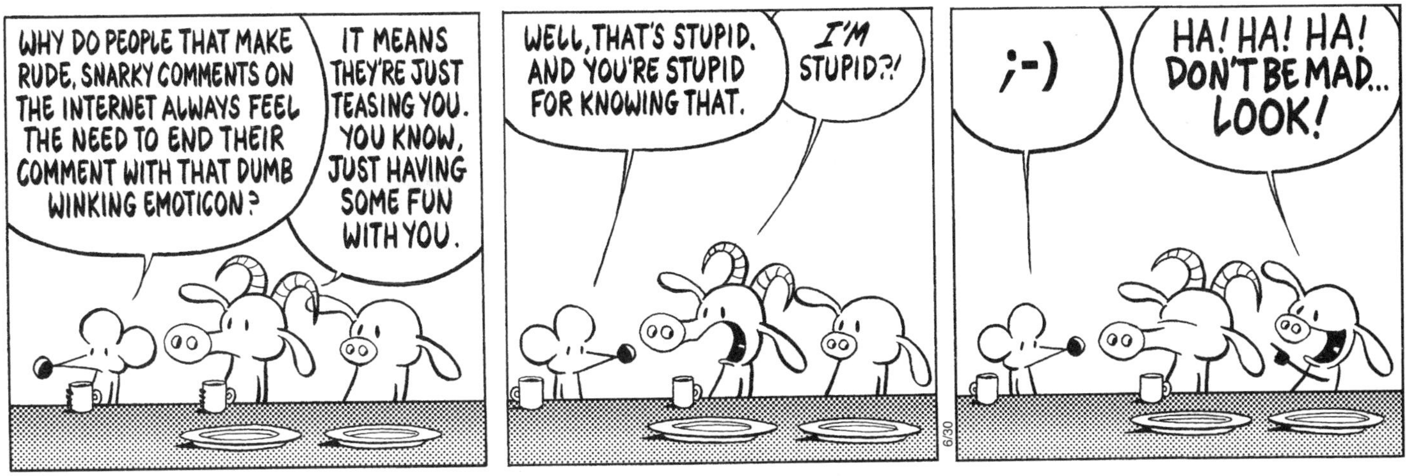
WHY DO PEOPLE THAT MAKE RUDE, SNARKY COMMENTS ON THE INTERNET ALWAYS FEEL THE NEED TO END THEIR COMMENT WITH THAT DUMB WINKING EMOTICON?
IT MEANS THEY'RE JUST TEASING YOU. YOU KNOW, JUST HAVING SOME FUN WITH YOU.
WELL, THAT'S STUPID. AND YOU'RE STUPID FOR KNOWING THAT.
I'M STUPID?!
;-)
HA! HA! HA! DON'T BE MAD... LOOK!
6/30

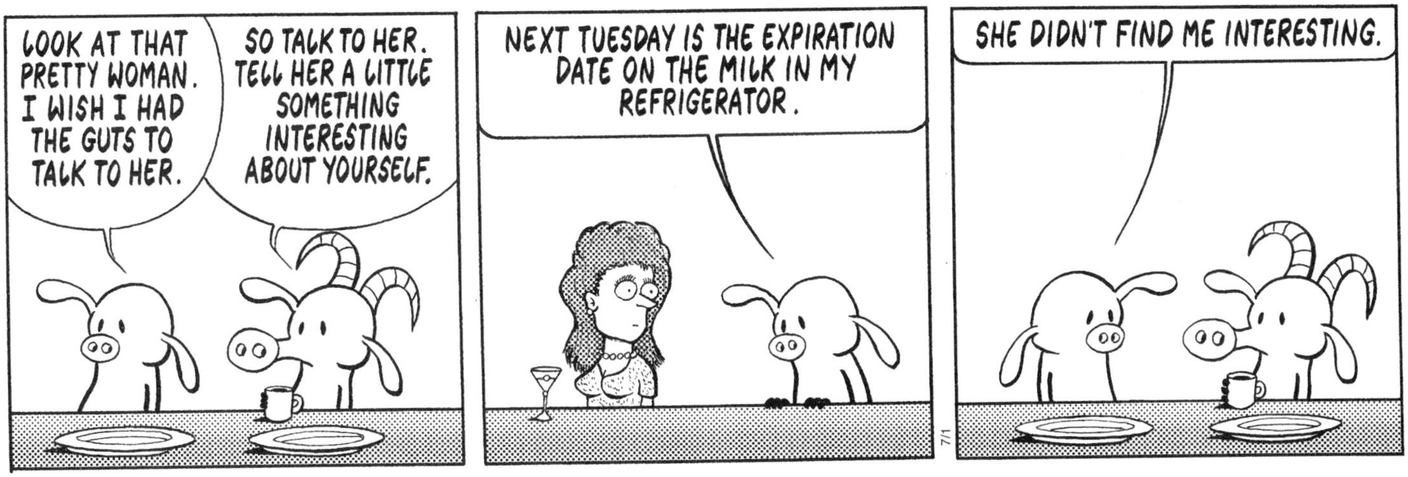
LOOK AT THAT PRETTY WOMAN. I WISH I HAD THE GUTS TO TALK TO HER.
SO TALK TO HER. TELL HER A LITTLE SOMETHING INTERESTING ABOUT YOURSELF.
NEXT TUESDAY IS THE EXPIRATION DATE ON THE MILK IN MY REFRIGERATOR.
SHE DIDN'T FIND ME INTERESTING.
7/1

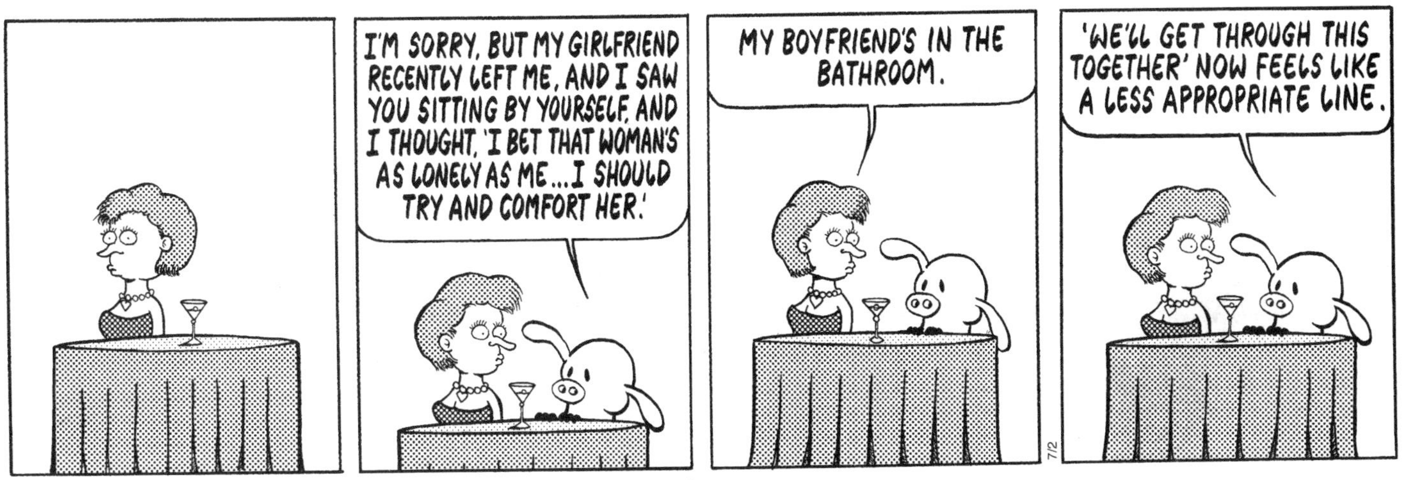
I'M SORRY, BUT MY GIRLFRIEND RECENTLY LEFT ME, AND I SAW YOU SITTING BY YOURSELF, AND I THOUGHT, 'I BET THAT WOMAN'S AS LONELY AS ME...I SHOULD TRY AND COMFORT HER.'
MY BOYFRIEND'S IN THE BATHROOM.
'WE'LL GET THROUGH THIS TOGETHER' NOW FEELS LIKE A LESS APPROPRIATE LINE.
7/2

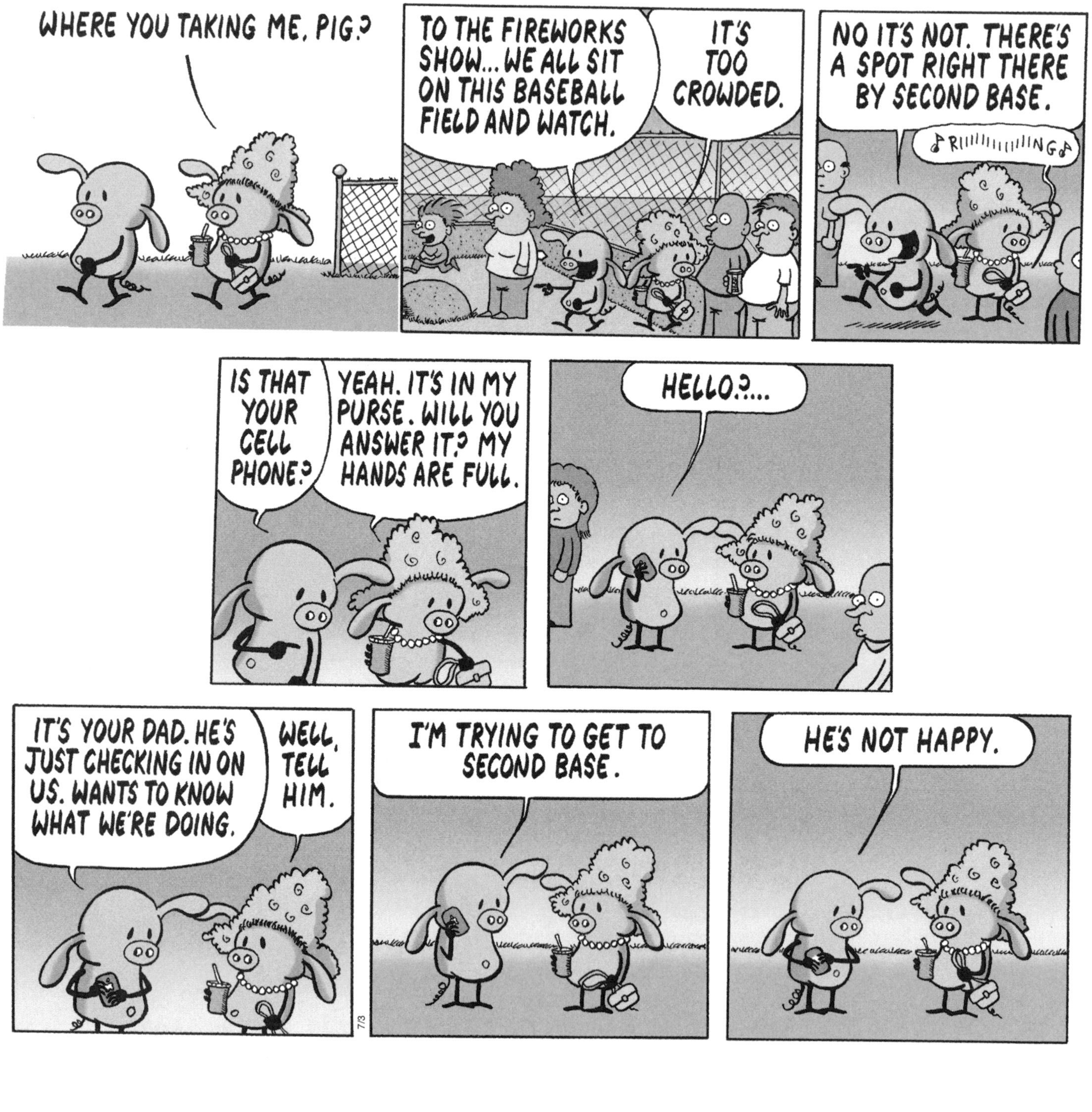
WHERE YOU TAKING ME, PIG?
TO THE FIREWORKS SHOW... WE ALL SIT ON THIS BASEBALL FIELD AND WATCH.
IT'S TOO CROWDED.
NO IT'S NOT. THERE'S A SPOT RIGHT THERE BY SECOND BASE.
RIIIIIIIIIIING
IS THAT YOUR CELL PHONE?
YEAH. IT'S IN MY PURSE. WILL YOU ANSWER IT? MY HANDS ARE FULL.
HELLO?...
IT'S YOUR DAD. HE'S JUST CHECKING IN ON US. WANTS TO KNOW WHAT WE'RE DOING.
WELL, TELL HIM.
7/3
I'M TRYING TO GET TO SECOND BASE.
HE'S NOT HAPPY.

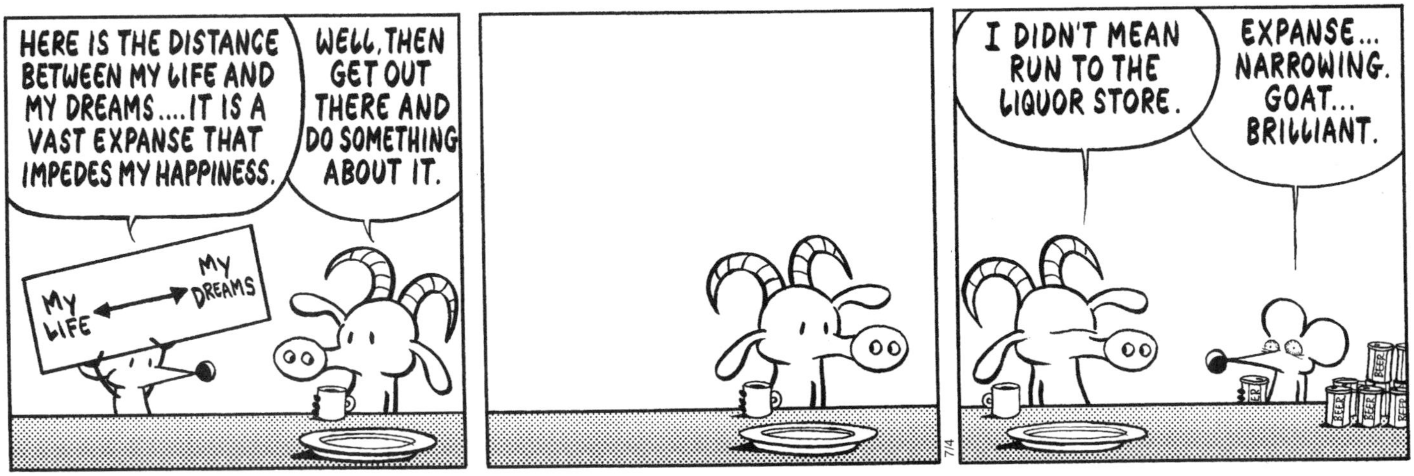
HERE IS THE DISTANCE BETWEEN MY LIFE AND MY DREAMS....IT IS A VAST EXPANSE THAT IMPEDES MY HAPPINESS.
MY LIFE
MY DREAMS
WELL, THEN GET OUT THERE AND DO SOMETHING ABOUT IT.
I DIDN'T MEAN RUN TO THE LIQUOR STORE.
EXPANSE... NARROWING. GOAT... BRILLIANT.
BEER
7/4

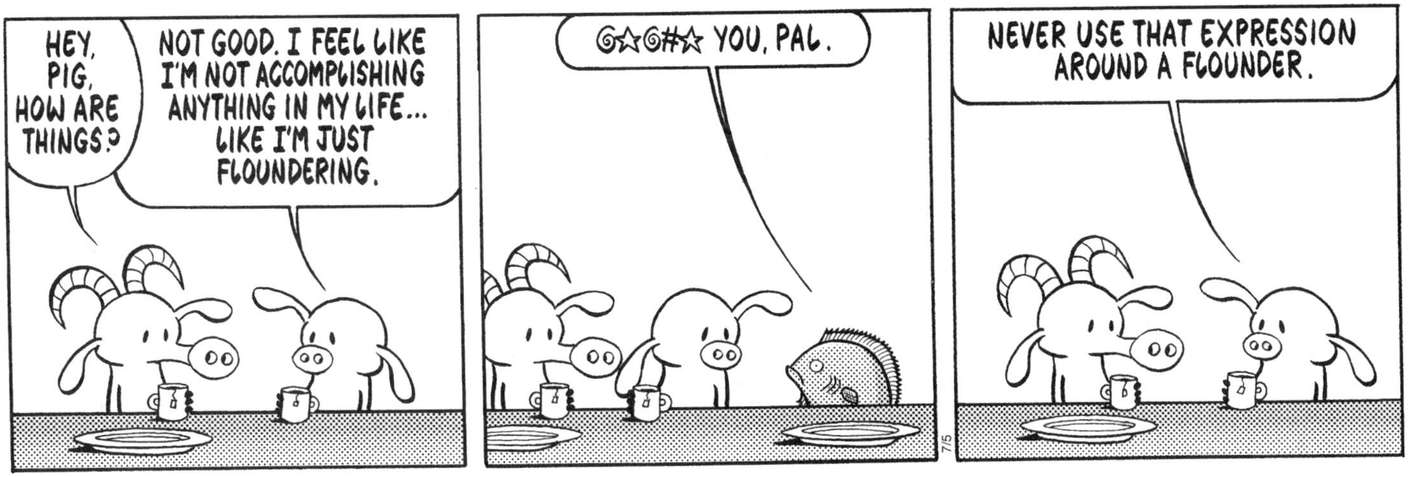
HEY, PIG, HOW ARE THINGS?
NOT GOOD. I FEEL LIKE I'M NOT ACCOMPLISHING ANYTHING IN MY LIFE... LIKE I'M JUST FLOUNDERING.
@☆@#☆ YOU, PAL.
NEVER USE THAT EXPRESSION AROUND A FLOUNDER.
7/5

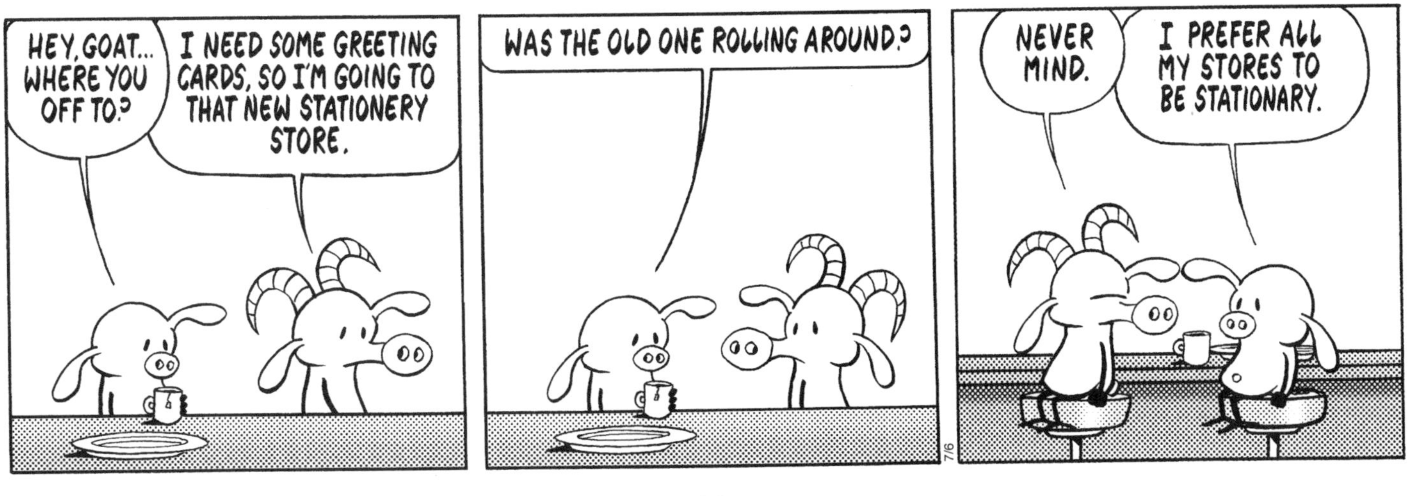
HEY, GOAT... WHERE YOU OFF TO?
I NEED SOME GREETING CARDS, SO I'M GOING TO THAT NEW STATIONERY STORE.
WAS THE OLD ONE ROLLING AROUND?
NEVER MIND.
I PREFER ALL MY STORES TO BE STATIONARY.
7/6

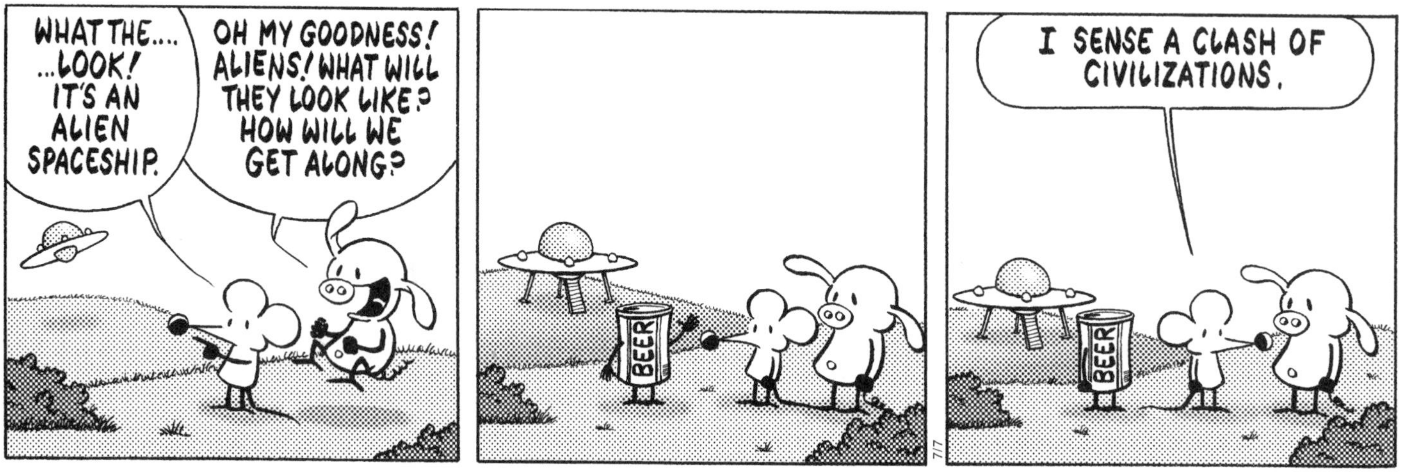
WHAT THE.... ...LOOK! IT'S AN ALIEN SPACESHIP.
OH MY GOODNESS! ALIENS! WHAT WILL THEY LOOK LIKE? HOW WILL WE GET ALONG?
BEER
7/7
I SENSE A CLASH OF CIVILIZATIONS.

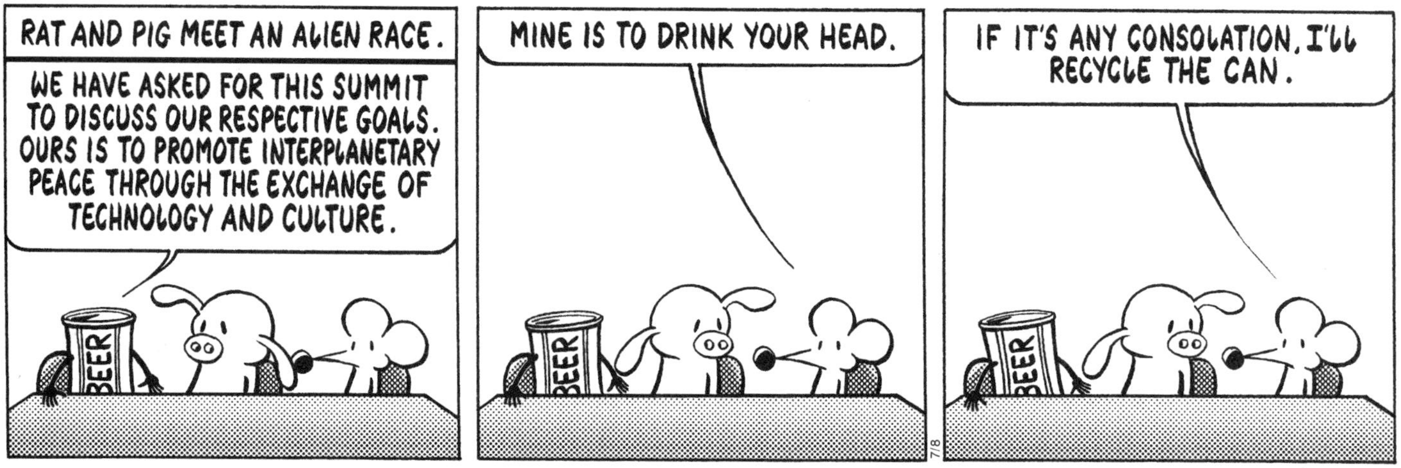
RAT AND PIG MEET AN ALIEN RACE.
WE HAVE ASKED FOR THIS SUMMIT TO DISCUSS OUR RESPECTIVE GOALS. OURS IS TO PROMOTE INTERPLANETARY PEACE THROUGH THE EXCHANGE OF TECHNOLOGY AND CULTURE.
BEER
MINE IS TO DRINK YOUR HEAD.
7/8
IF IT'S ANY CONSOLATION, I'LL RECYCLE THE CAN.

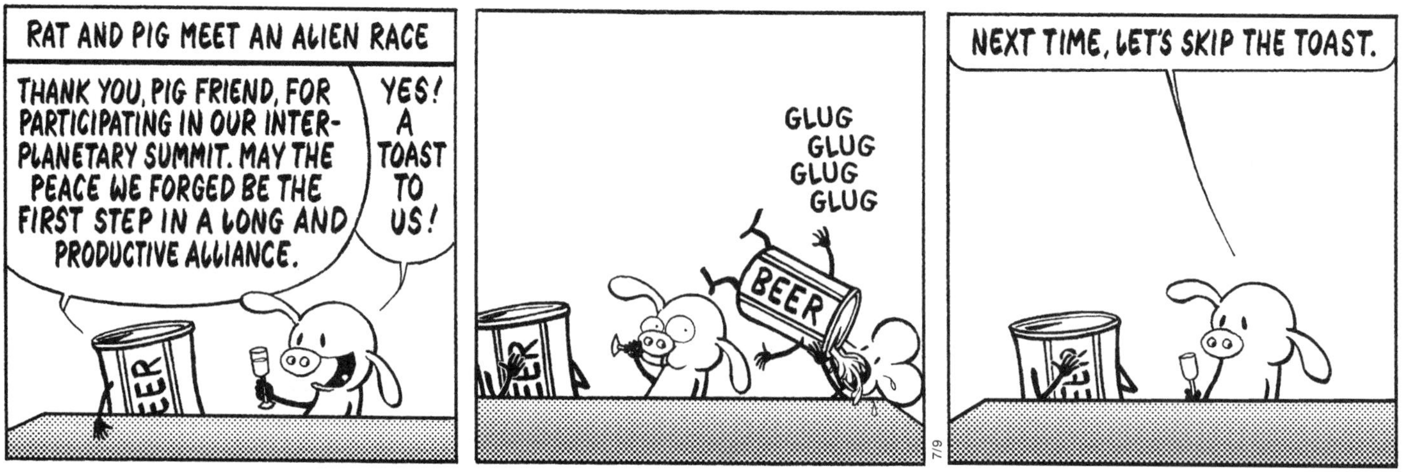
RAT AND PIG MEET AN ALIEN RACE
THANK YOU, PIG FRIEND, FOR PARTICIPATING IN OUR INTER-PLANETARY SUMMIT. MAY THE PEACE WE FORGED BE THE FIRST STEP IN A LONG AND PRODUCTIVE ALLIANCE.
YES! A TOAST TO US!
GLUG GLUG GLUG GLUG
BEER
7/9
NEXT TIME, LET'S SKIP THE TOAST.

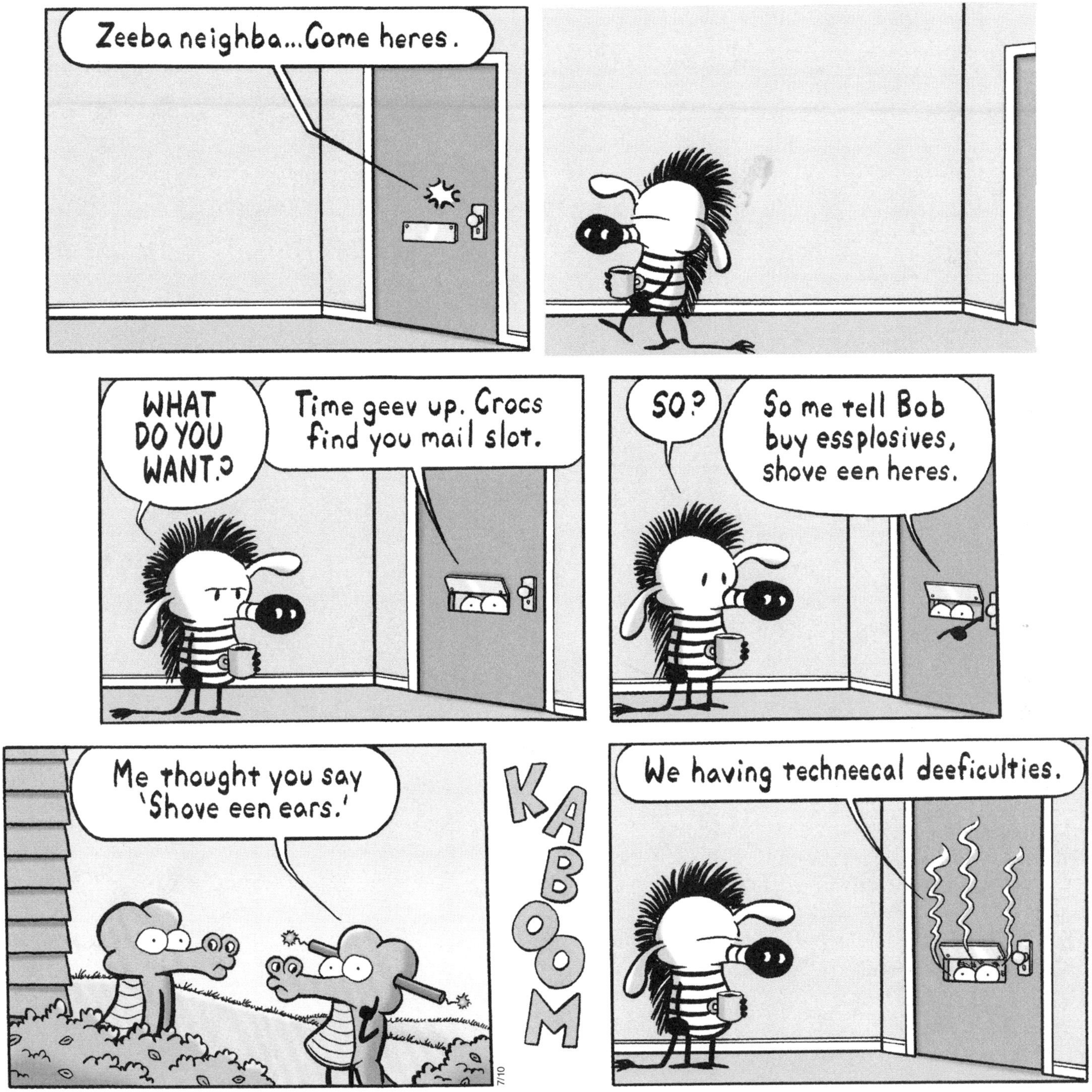

Zeeba neighba...Come heres.
WHAT DO YOU WANT?
Time geev up. Crocs find you mail slot.
SO?
So me tell Bob buy essplosives, shove een heres.
Me thought you say 'Shove een ears.'
KABOOM
We having techneecal deeficulties.
7/10

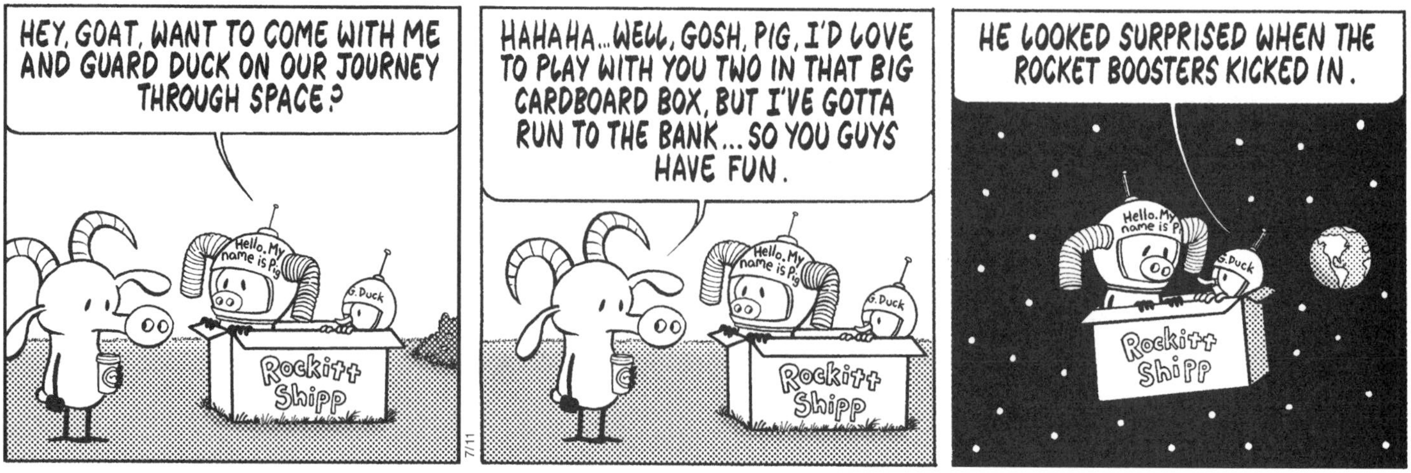
HEY, GOAT, WANT TO COME WITH ME AND GUARD DUCK ON OUR JOURNEY THROUGH SPACE?
Hello. My name is Pig
G. Duck
Rockitt Shipp
HAHAHA...WELL, GOSH, PIG, I'D LOVE TO PLAY WITH YOU TWO IN THAT BIG CARDBOARD BOX, BUT I'VE GOTTA RUN TO THE BANK... SO YOU GUYS HAVE FUN.
7/11
HE LOOKED SURPRISED WHEN THE ROCKET BOOSTERS KICKED IN.

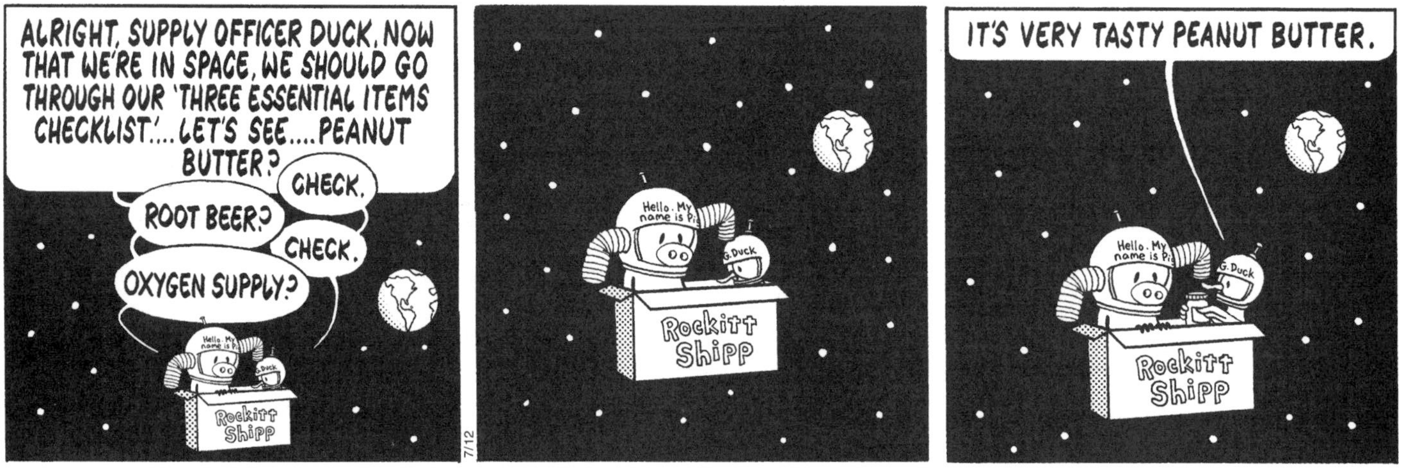
ALRIGHT, SUPPLY OFFICER DUCK, NOW THAT WE'RE IN SPACE, WE SHOULD GO THROUGH OUR 'THREE ESSENTIAL ITEMS CHECKLIST'.... LET'S SEE.... PEANUT BUTTER?
CHECK.
ROOT BEER?
CHECK.
OXYGEN SUPPLY?
7/12
IT'S VERY TASTY PEANUT BUTTER.

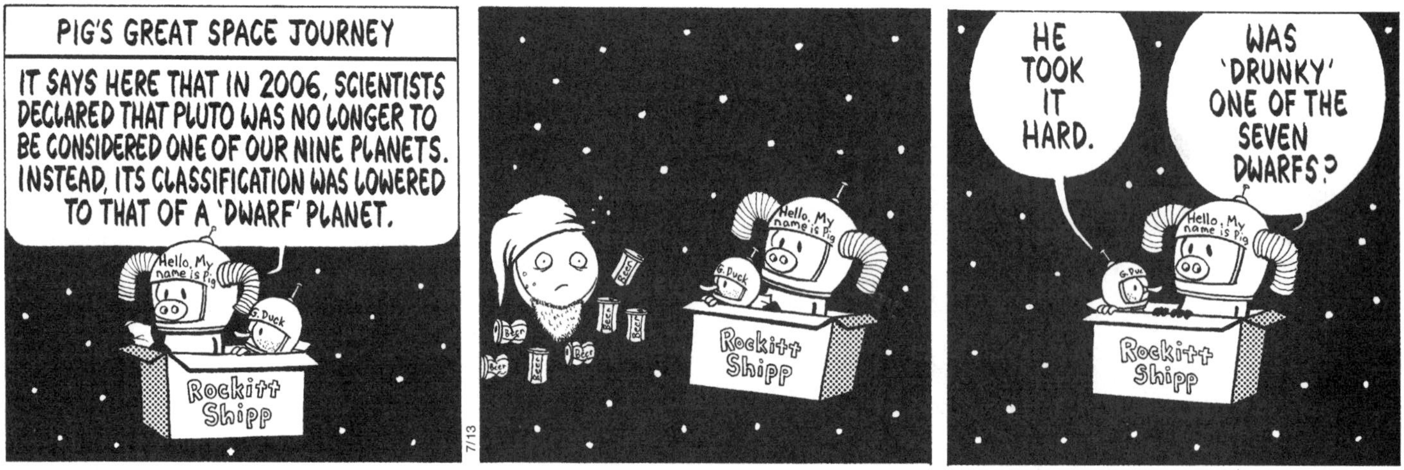
PIG'S GREAT SPACE JOURNEY
IT SAYS HERE THAT IN 2006, SCIENTISTS DECLARED THAT PLUTO WAS NO LONGER TO BE CONSIDERED ONE OF OUR NINE PLANETS. INSTEAD, ITS CLASSIFICATION WAS LOWERED TO THAT OF A 'DWARF' PLANET.
7/13
HE TOOK IT HARD.
WAS 'DRUNKY' ONE OF THE SEVEN DWARFS?

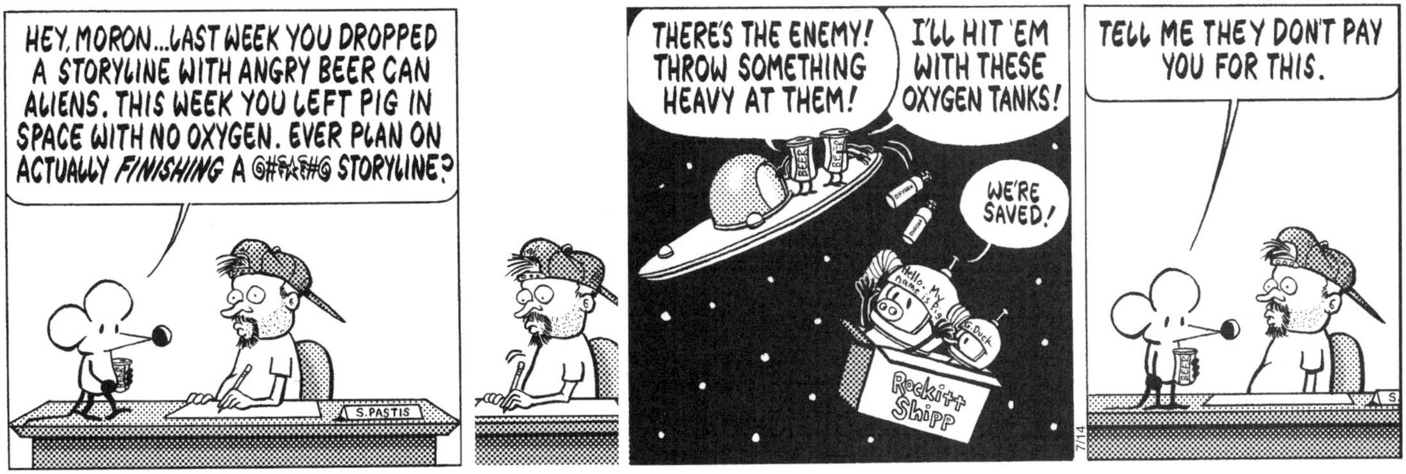
HEY, MORON...LAST WEEK YOU DROPPED A STORYLINE WITH ANGRY BEER CAN ALIENS. THIS WEEK YOU LEFT PIG IN SPACE WITH NO OXYGEN. EVER PLAN ON ACTUALLY *FINISHING* A @#%*#@ STORYLINE?
S. PASTIS
THERE'S THE ENEMY! THROW SOMETHING HEAVY AT THEM!
I'LL HIT 'EM WITH THESE OXYGEN TANKS!
BEER
BEER
WE'RE SAVED!
Hello, My name is Pig
G. Duck
Rockitt Shipp
7/14
TELL ME THEY DON'T PAY YOU FOR THIS.
BEER
S

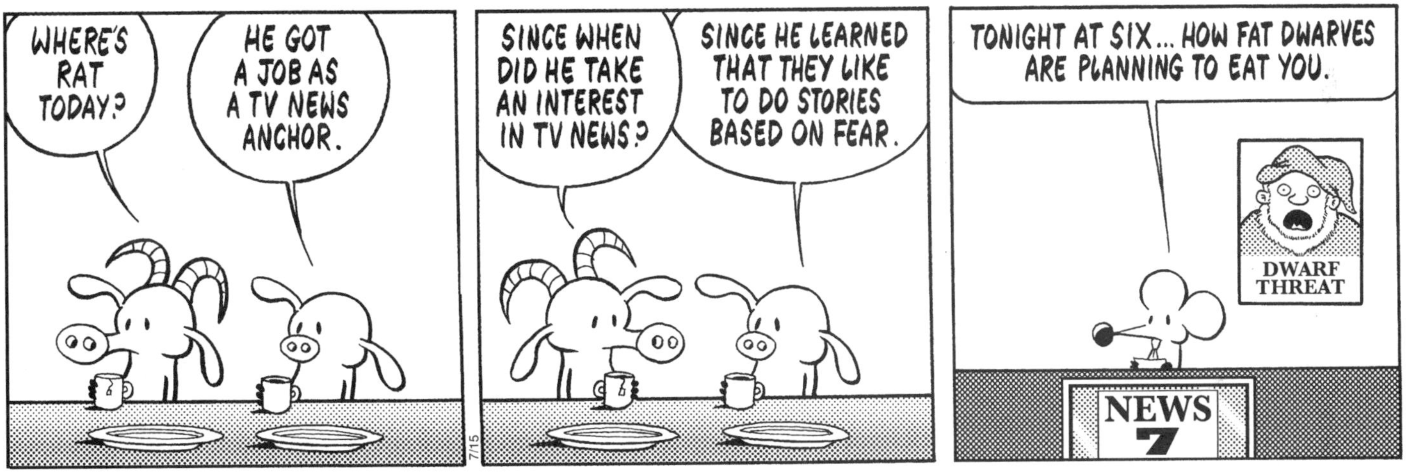
WHERE'S RAT TODAY?
HE GOT A JOB AS A TV NEWS ANCHOR.
7/15
SINCE WHEN DID HE TAKE AN INTEREST IN TV NEWS?
SINCE HE LEARNED THAT THEY LIKE TO DO STORIES BASED ON FEAR.
TONIGHT AT SIX... HOW FAT DWARVES ARE PLANNING TO EAT YOU.
DWARF THREAT
NEWS 7

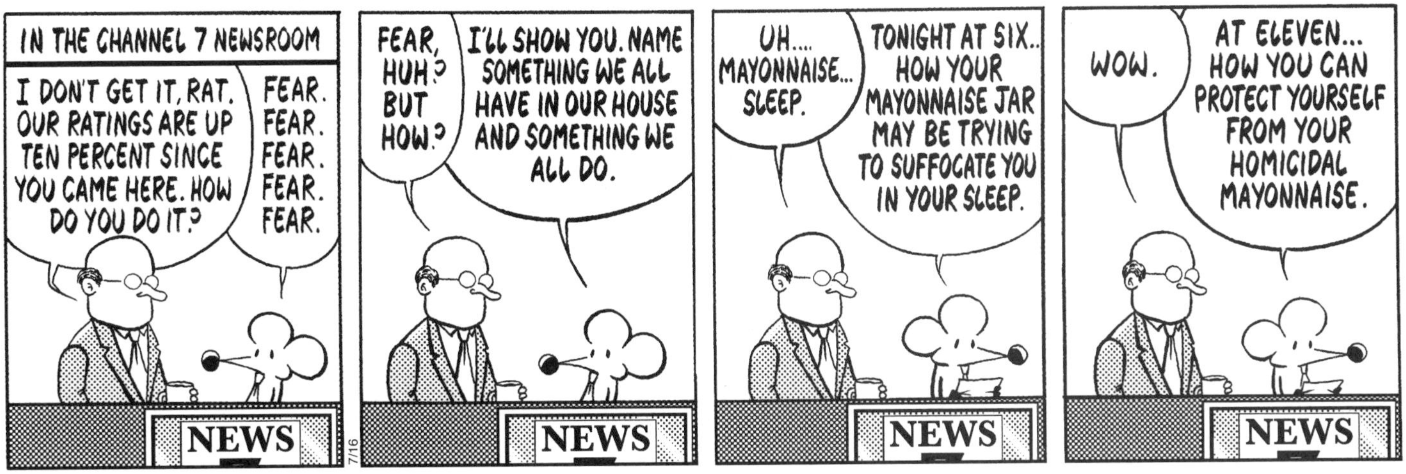
IN THE CHANNEL 7 NEWSROOM
I DON'T GET IT, RAT. OUR RATINGS ARE UP TEN PERCENT SINCE YOU CAME HERE. HOW DO YOU DO IT?
FEAR. FEAR. FEAR. FEAR. FEAR.
NEWS
7/16
FEAR, HUH? BUT HOW?
I'LL SHOW YOU. NAME SOMETHING WE ALL HAVE IN OUR HOUSE AND SOMETHING WE ALL DO.
NEWS
UH.... MAYONNAISE... SLEEP.
TONIGHT AT SIX.. HOW YOUR MAYONNAISE JAR MAY BE TRYING TO SUFFOCATE YOU IN YOUR SLEEP.
NEWS
WOW.
AT ELEVEN... HOW YOU CAN PROTECT YOURSELF FROM YOUR HOMICIDAL MAYONNAISE.
NEWS

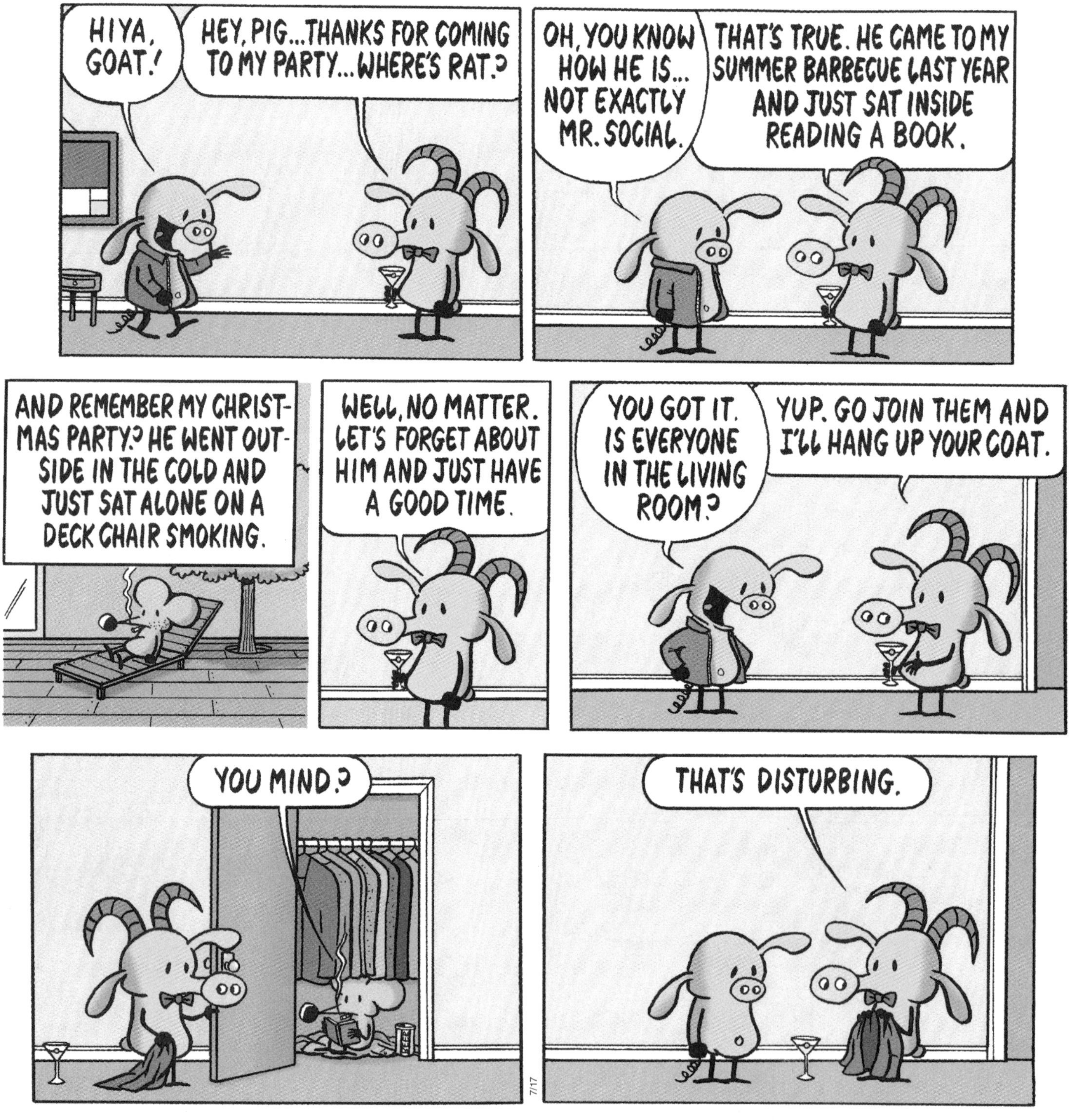
HIYA, GOAT!
HEY, PIG...THANKS FOR COMING TO MY PARTY...WHERE'S RAT?
OH, YOU KNOW HOW HE IS... NOT EXACTLY MR. SOCIAL.
THAT'S TRUE. HE CAME TO MY SUMMER BARBECUE LAST YEAR AND JUST SAT INSIDE READING A BOOK.
AND REMEMBER MY CHRISTMAS PARTY? HE WENT OUTSIDE IN THE COLD AND JUST SAT ALONE ON A DECK CHAIR SMOKING.
WELL, NO MATTER. LET'S FORGET ABOUT HIM AND JUST HAVE A GOOD TIME.
YOU GOT IT. IS EVERYONE IN THE LIVING ROOM?
YUP. GO JOIN THEM AND I'LL HANG UP YOUR COAT.
YOU MIND?
THAT'S DISTURBING.
7/17

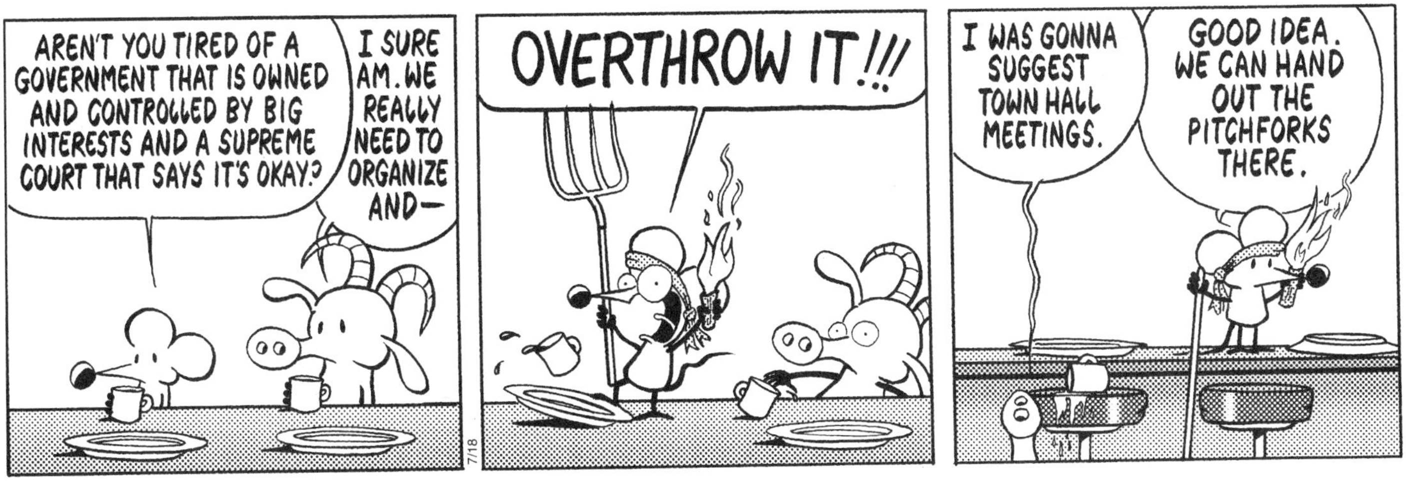
AREN'T YOU TIRED OF A GOVERNMENT THAT IS OWNED AND CONTROLLED BY BIG INTERESTS AND A SUPREME COURT THAT SAYS IT'S OKAY?
I SURE AM. WE REALLY NEED TO ORGANIZE AND—
7/18
OVERTHROW IT!!!
I WAS GONNA SUGGEST TOWN HALL MEETINGS.
GOOD IDEA. WE CAN HAND OUT THE PITCHFORKS THERE.

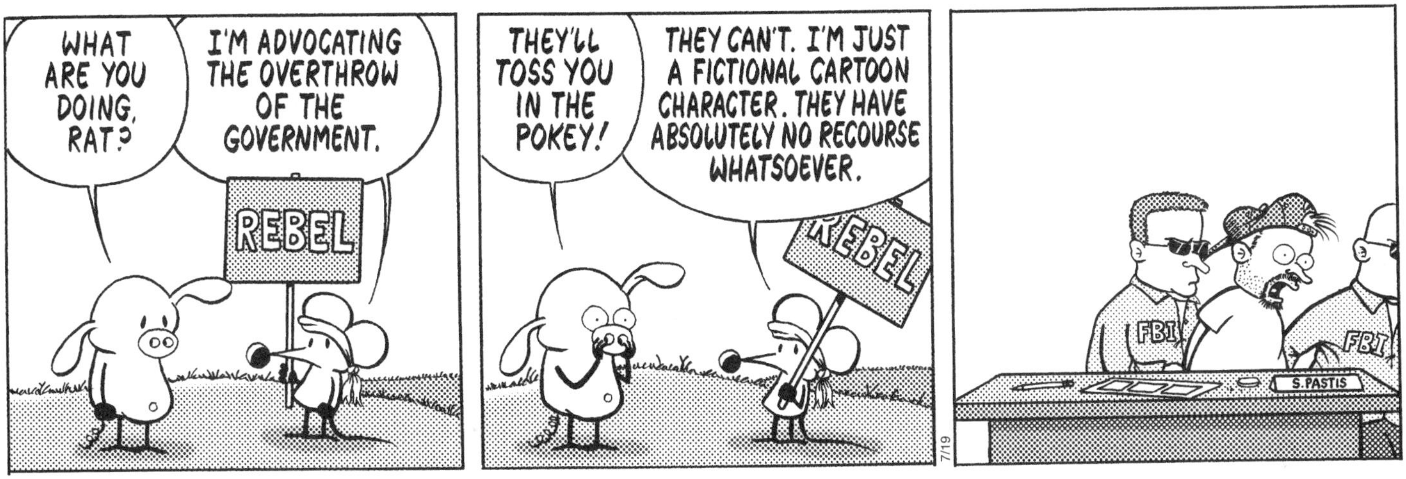
WHAT ARE YOU DOING, RAT?
I'M ADVOCATING THE OVERTHROW OF THE GOVERNMENT.
REBEL
THEY'LL TOSS YOU IN THE POKEY!
THEY CAN'T. I'M JUST A FICTIONAL CARTOON CHARACTER. THEY HAVE ABSOLUTELY NO RECOURSE WHATSOEVER.
REBEL
7/19
FBI
FBI
S. PASTIS

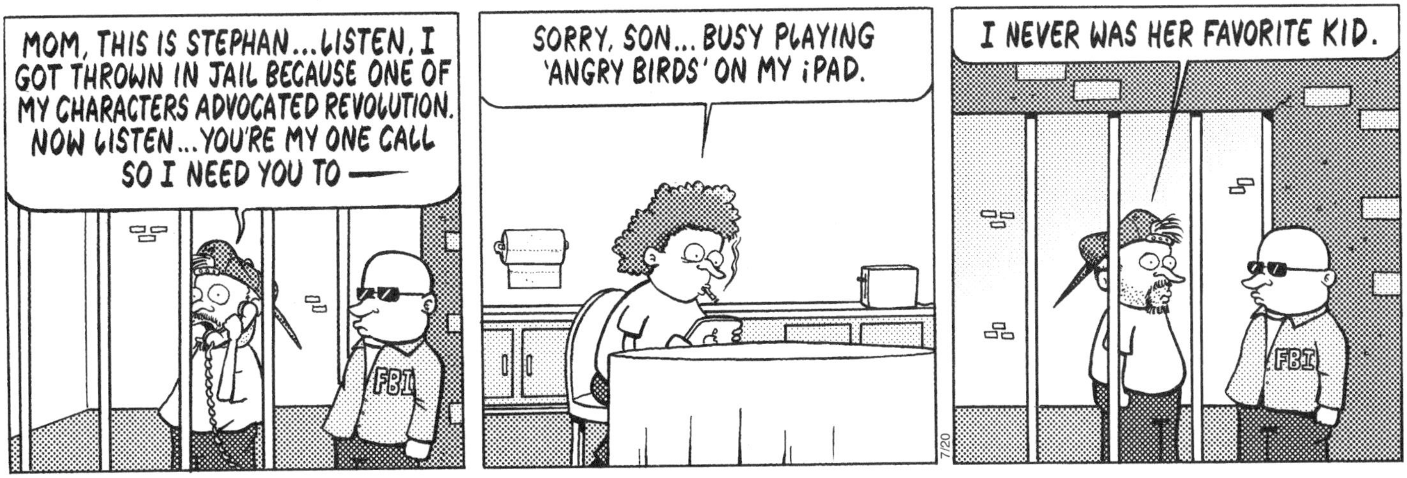
MOM, THIS IS STEPHAN... LISTEN, I GOT THROWN IN JAIL BECAUSE ONE OF MY CHARACTERS ADVOCATED REVOLUTION. NOW LISTEN... YOU'RE MY ONE CALL SO I NEED YOU TO —
FBI
SORRY, SON... BUSY PLAYING 'ANGRY BIRDS' ON MY iPAD.
7/20
I NEVER WAS HER FAVORITE KID.
FBI

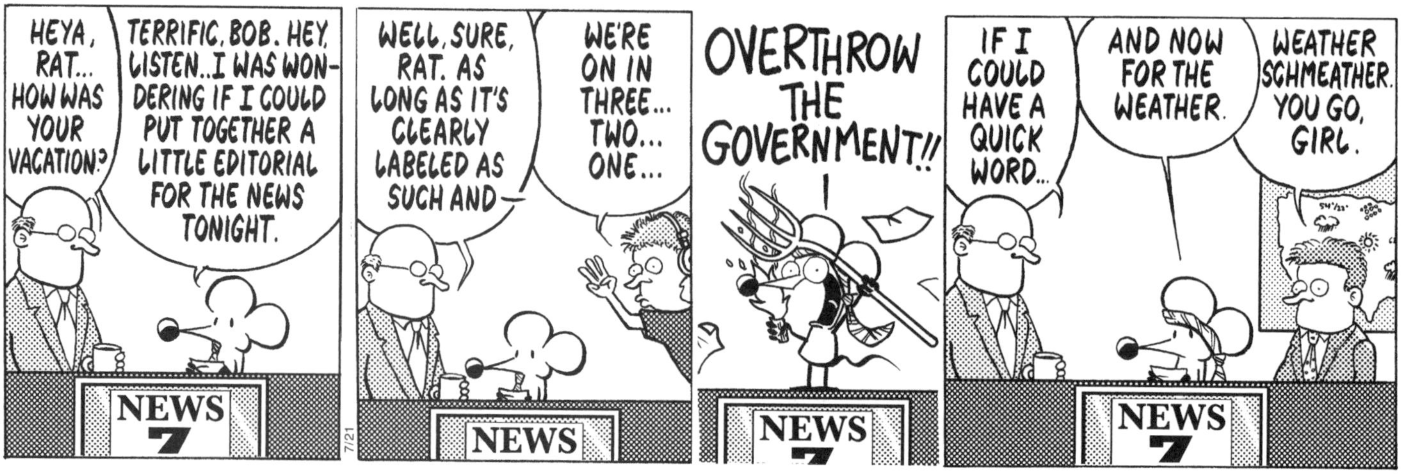
HEYA, RAT... HOW WAS YOUR VACATION?
TERRIFIC, BOB. HEY, LISTEN...I WAS WONDERING IF I COULD PUT TOGETHER A LITTLE EDITORIAL FOR THE NEWS TONIGHT.
NEWS 7
7/21
WELL, SURE, RAT. AS LONG AS IT'S CLEARLY LABELED AS SUCH AND—
WE'RE ON IN THREE... TWO... ONE...
NEWS
OVERTHROW THE GOVERNMENT!!
NEWS 7
IF I COULD HAVE A QUICK WORD...
AND NOW FOR THE WEATHER.
WEATHER SCHMEATHER. YOU GO, GIRL.
NEWS 7

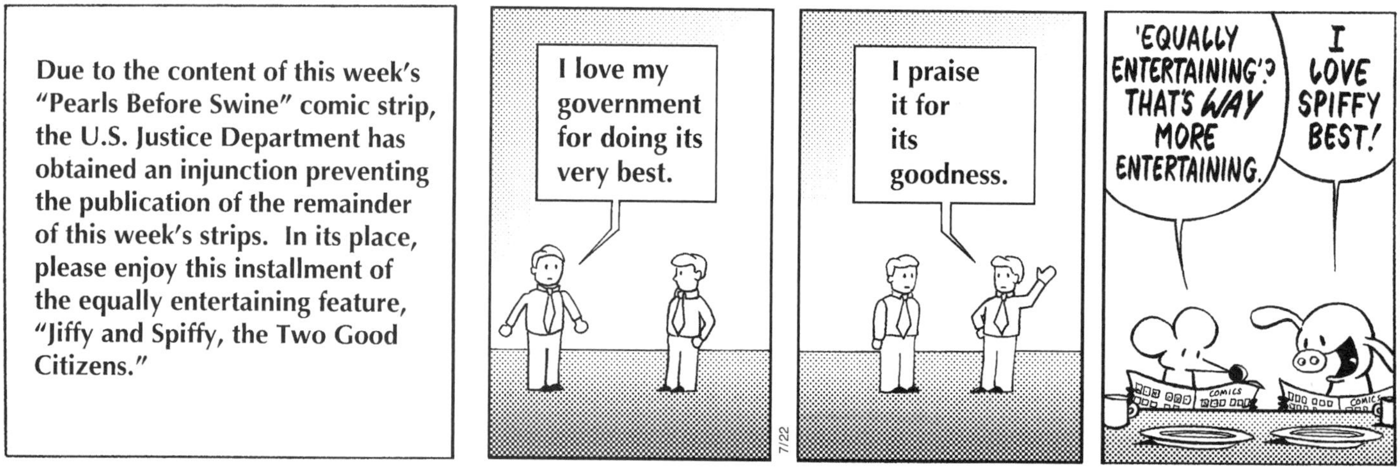
Due to the content of this week's "Pearls Before Swine" comic strip, the U.S. Justice Department has obtained an injunction preventing the publication of the remainder of this week's strips. In its place, please enjoy this installment of the equally entertaining feature, "Jiffy and Spiffy, the Two Good Citizens."
I love my government for doing its very best.
7/22
I praise it for its goodness.
'EQUALLY ENTERTAINING'? THAT'S WAY MORE ENTERTAINING.
I LOVE SPIFFY BEST!

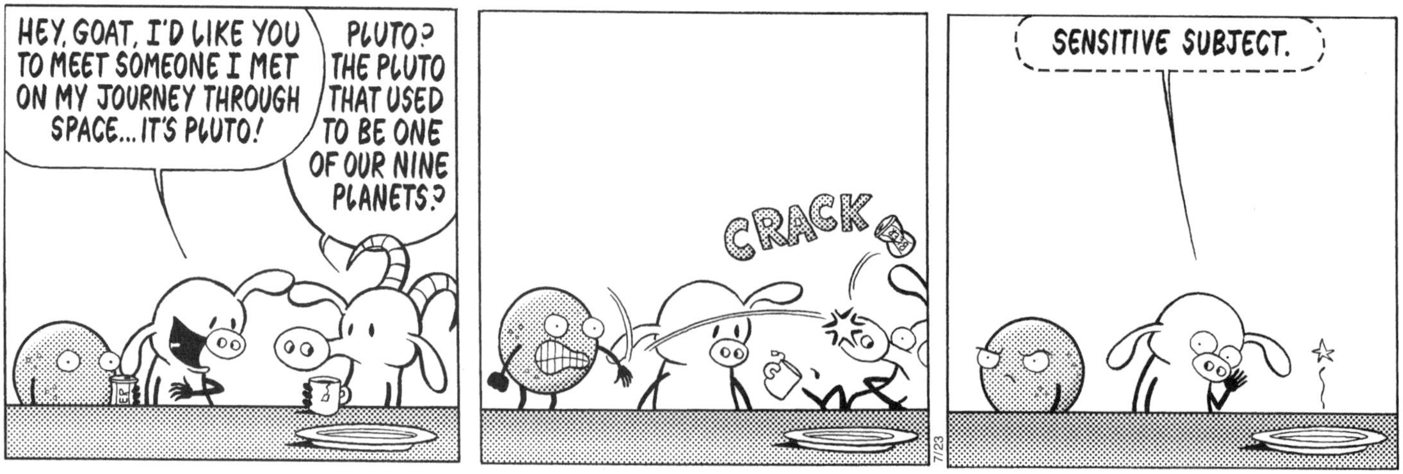
HEY, GOAT, I'D LIKE YOU TO MEET SOMEONE I MET ON MY JOURNEY THROUGH SPACE...IT'S PLUTO!
PLUTO? THE PLUTO THAT USED TO BE ONE OF OUR NINE PLANETS?
CRACK
7/23
SENSITIVE SUBJECT.

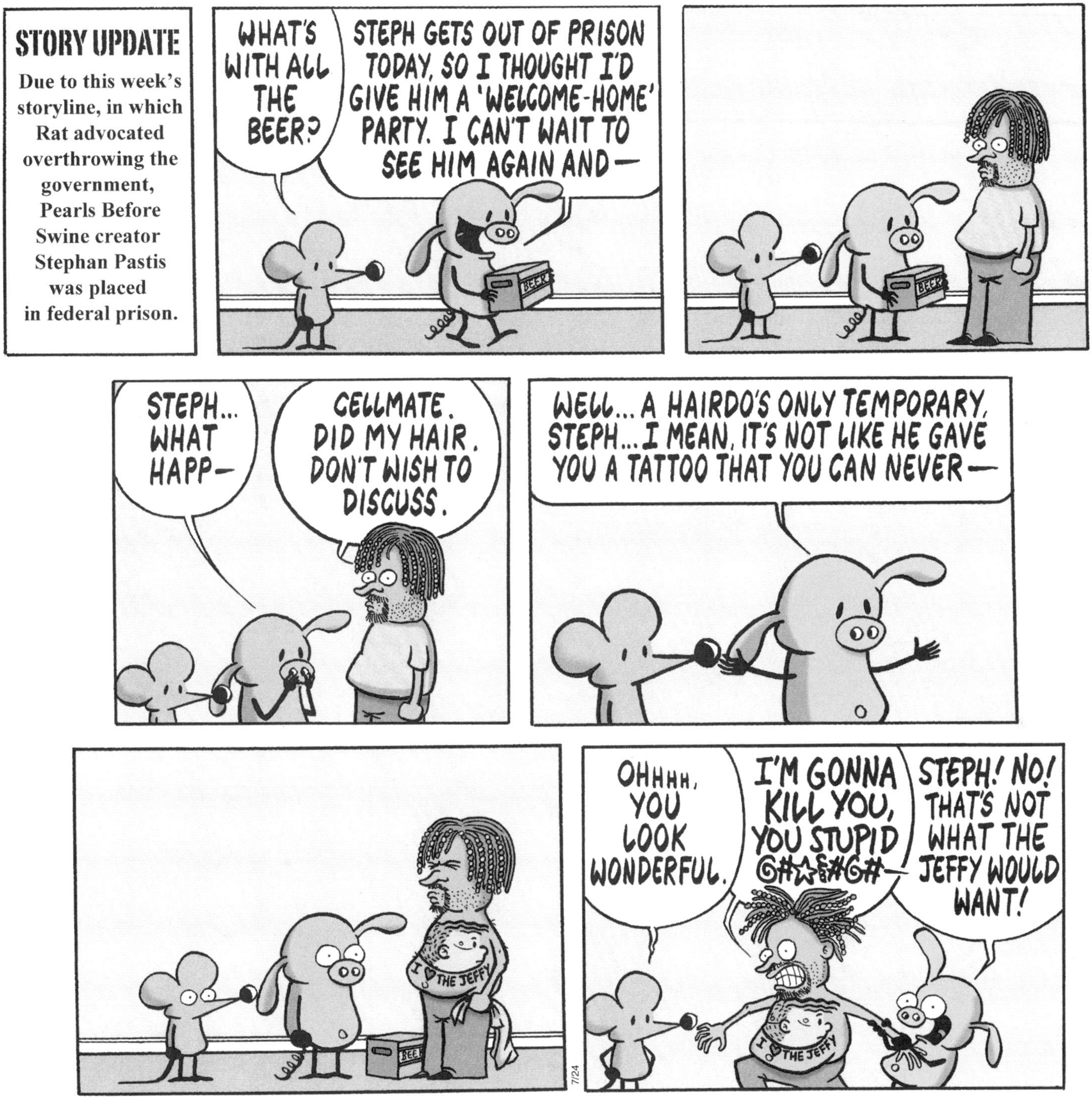
STORY UPDATE
Due to this week's storyline, in which Rat advocated overthrowing the government, Pearls Before Swine creator Stephan Pastis was placed in federal prison.
WHAT'S WITH ALL THE BEER?
STEPH GETS OUT OF PRISON TODAY, SO I THOUGHT I'D GIVE HIM A 'WELCOME-HOME' PARTY. I CAN'T WAIT TO SEE HIM AGAIN AND—
BEER
STEPH... WHAT HAPP—
CELLMATE. DID MY HAIR. DON'T WISH TO DISCUSS.
WELL... A HAIRDO'S ONLY TEMPORARY, STEPH... I MEAN, IT'S NOT LIKE HE GAVE YOU A TATTOO THAT YOU CAN NEVER—
I ♡ THE JEFFY
7/24
OHHHH, YOU LOOK WONDERFUL.
I'M GONNA KILL YOU, YOU STUPID @#☆$#@#—
STEPH! NO! THAT'S NOT WHAT THE JEFFY WOULD WANT!

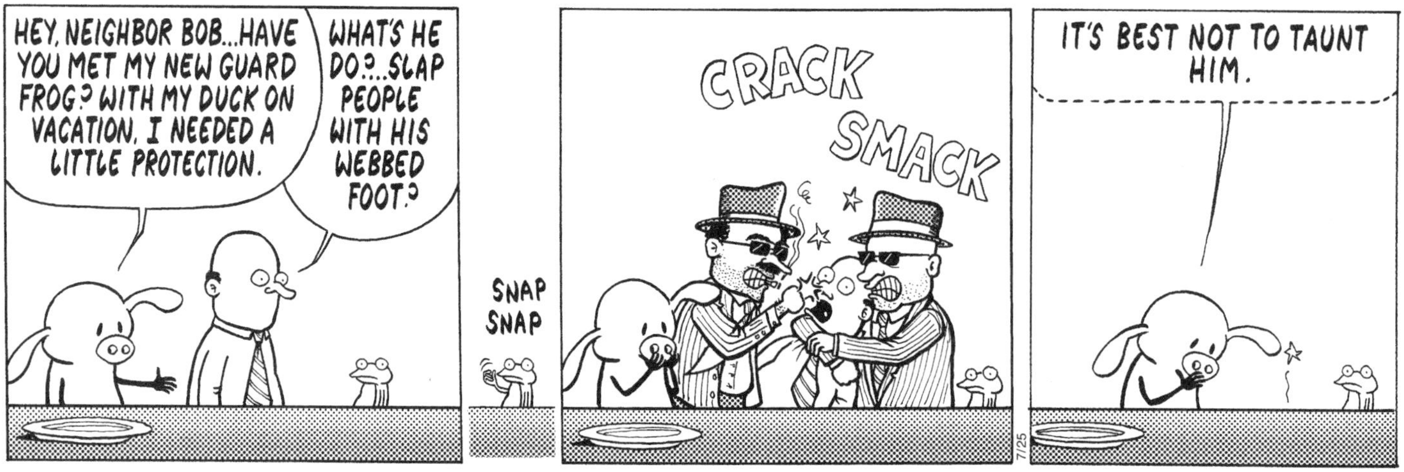
HEY, NEIGHBOR BOB...HAVE YOU MET MY NEW GUARD FROG? WITH MY DUCK ON VACATION, I NEEDED A LITTLE PROTECTION.
WHAT'S HE DO?...SLAP PEOPLE WITH HIS WEBBED FOOT?
SNAP SNAP
CRACK
SMACK
IT'S BEST NOT TO TAUNT HIM.
7/25

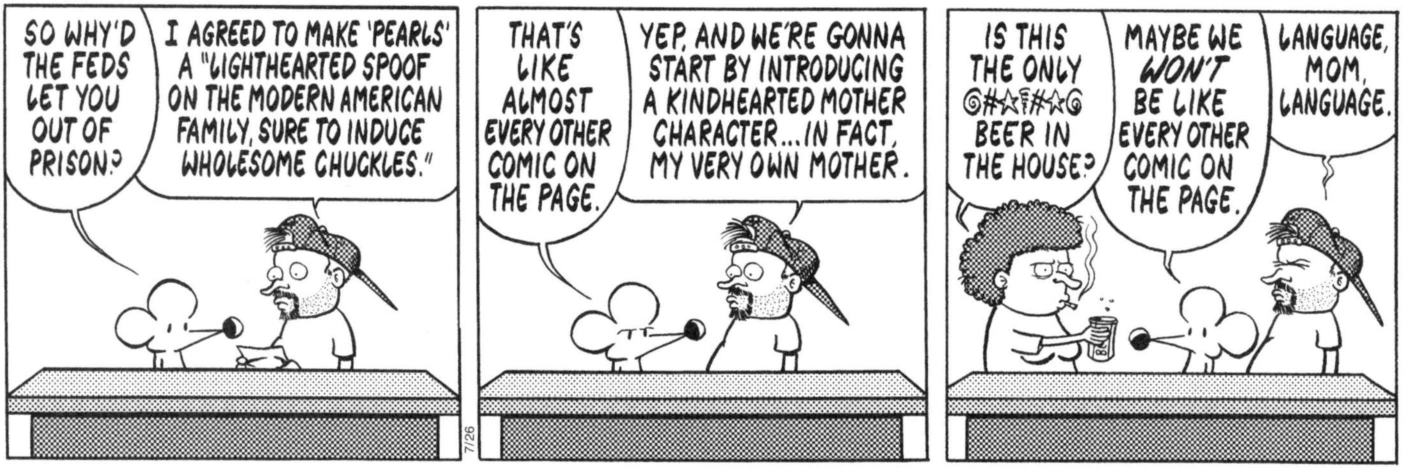
SO WHY'D THE FEDS LET YOU OUT OF PRISON?
I AGREED TO MAKE 'PEARLS' A "LIGHTHEARTED SPOOF ON THE MODERN AMERICAN FAMILY, SURE TO INDUCE WHOLESOME CHUCKLES."
7/26
THAT'S LIKE ALMOST EVERY OTHER COMIC ON THE PAGE.
YEP, AND WE'RE GONNA START BY INTRODUCING A KINDHEARTED MOTHER CHARACTER... IN FACT, MY VERY OWN MOTHER.
IS THIS THE ONLY @#☆!#☆@ BEER IN THE HOUSE?
MAYBE WE WON'T BE LIKE EVERY OTHER COMIC ON THE PAGE.
LANGUAGE, MOM, LANGUAGE.

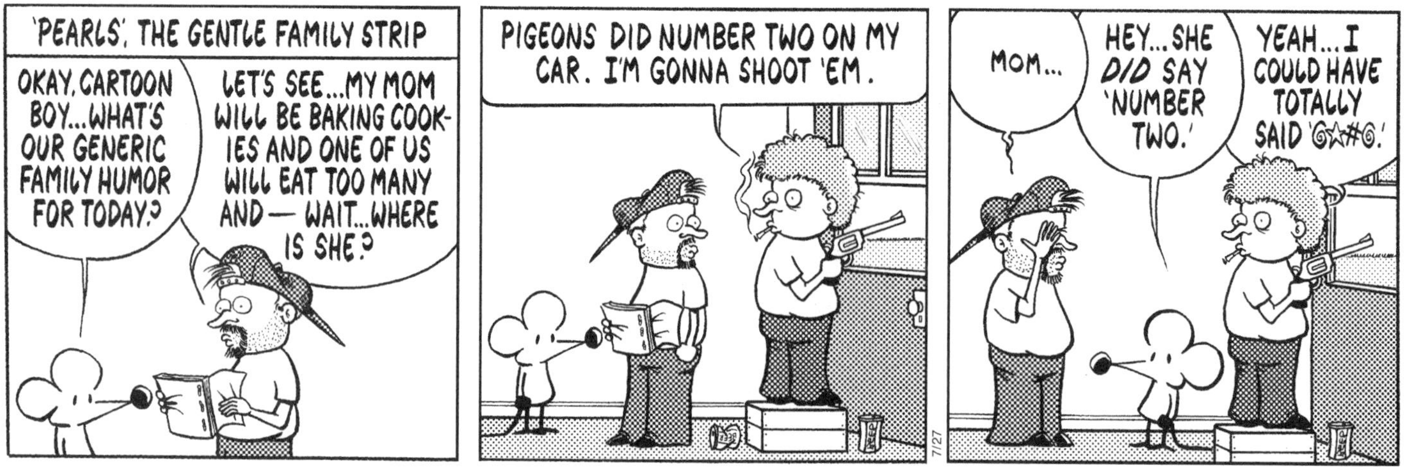
'PEARLS', THE GENTLE FAMILY STRIP
OKAY, CARTOON BOY...WHAT'S OUR GENERIC FAMILY HUMOR FOR TODAY?
LET'S SEE...MY MOM WILL BE BAKING COOKIES AND ONE OF US WILL EAT TOO MANY AND— WAIT...WHERE IS SHE?
PIGEONS DID NUMBER TWO ON MY CAR. I'M GONNA SHOOT 'EM.
7/27
MOM...
HEY...SHE DID SAY 'NUMBER TWO.'
YEAH...I COULD HAVE TOTALLY SAID '@☆#@.'

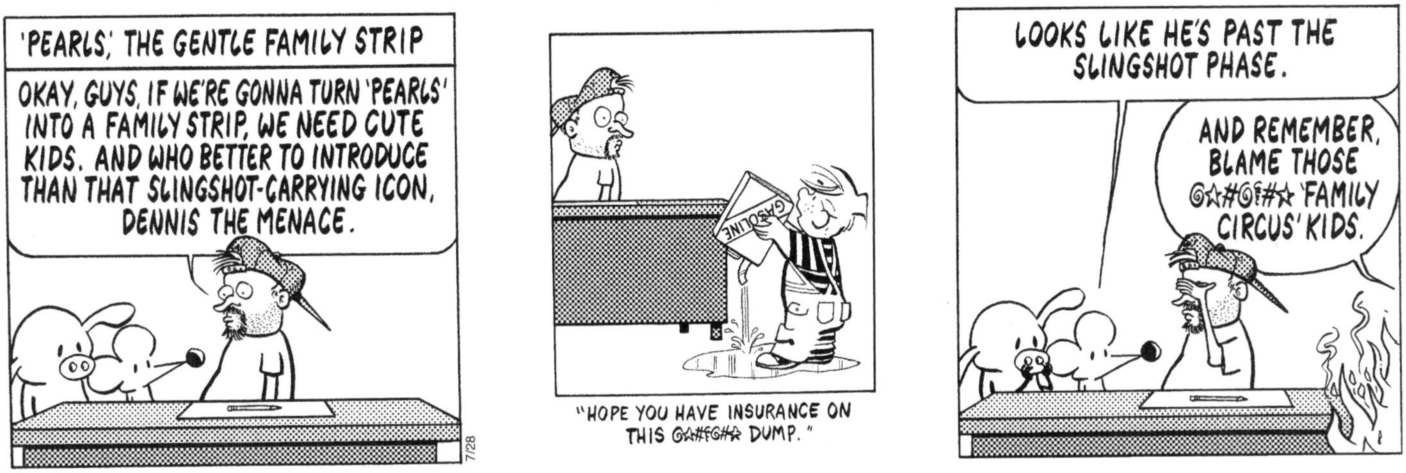
'PEARLS,' THE GENTLE FAMILY STRIP
OKAY, GUYS, IF WE'RE GONNA TURN 'PEARLS' INTO A FAMILY STRIP, WE NEED CUTE KIDS. AND WHO BETTER TO INTRODUCE THAN THAT SLINGSHOT-CARRYING ICON, DENNIS THE MENACE.
7/28
GASOLINE
"HOPE YOU HAVE INSURANCE ON THIS @☆#‡@#☆ DUMP."
LOOKS LIKE HE'S PAST THE SLINGSHOT PHASE.
AND REMEMBER, BLAME THOSE @☆#@‡#☆ 'FAMILY CIRCUS' KIDS.

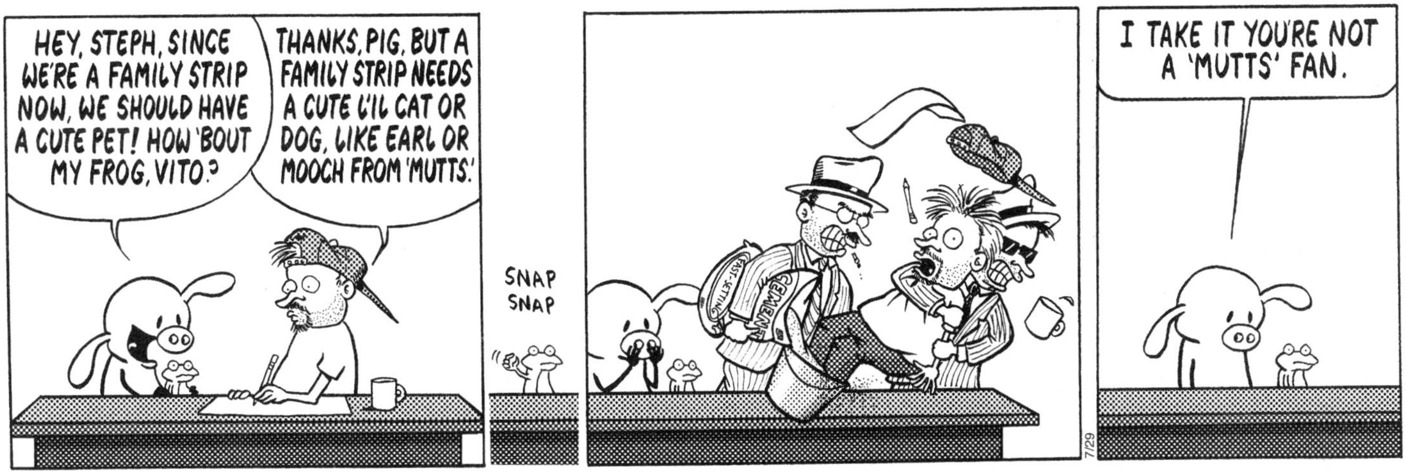
HEY, STEPH, SINCE WE'RE A FAMILY STRIP NOW, WE SHOULD HAVE A CUTE PET! HOW 'BOUT MY FROG, VITO?
THANKS, PIG, BUT A FAMILY STRIP NEEDS A CUTE L'IL CAT OR DOG, LIKE EARL OR MOOCH FROM 'MUTTS.'
SNAP
SNAP
CEMENT
FAST-SETTING
7/29
I TAKE IT YOU'RE NOT A 'MUTTS' FAN.

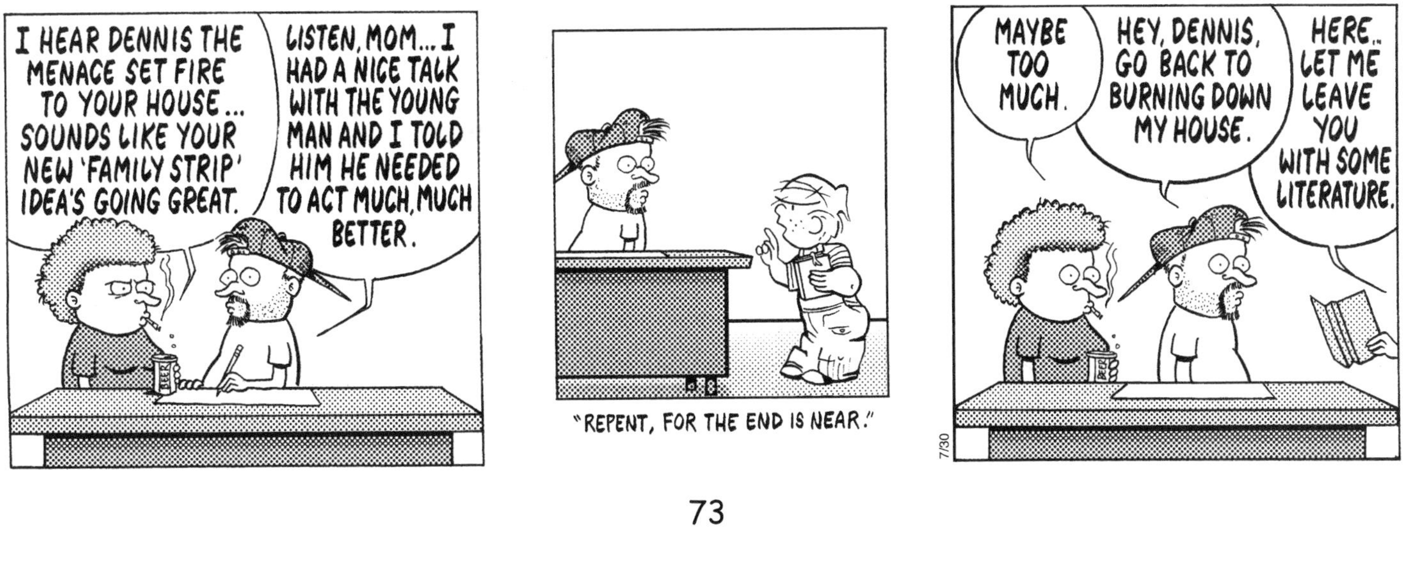
I HEAR DENNIS THE MENACE SET FIRE TO YOUR HOUSE... SOUNDS LIKE YOUR NEW 'FAMILY STRIP' IDEA'S GOING GREAT.
LISTEN, MOM... I HAD A NICE TALK WITH THE YOUNG MAN AND I TOLD HIM HE NEEDED TO ACT MUCH, MUCH BETTER.
BEER
"REPENT, FOR THE END IS NEAR."
7/30
MAYBE TOO MUCH.
HEY, DENNIS, GO BACK TO BURNING DOWN MY HOUSE.
HERE.. LET ME LEAVE YOU WITH SOME LITERATURE.

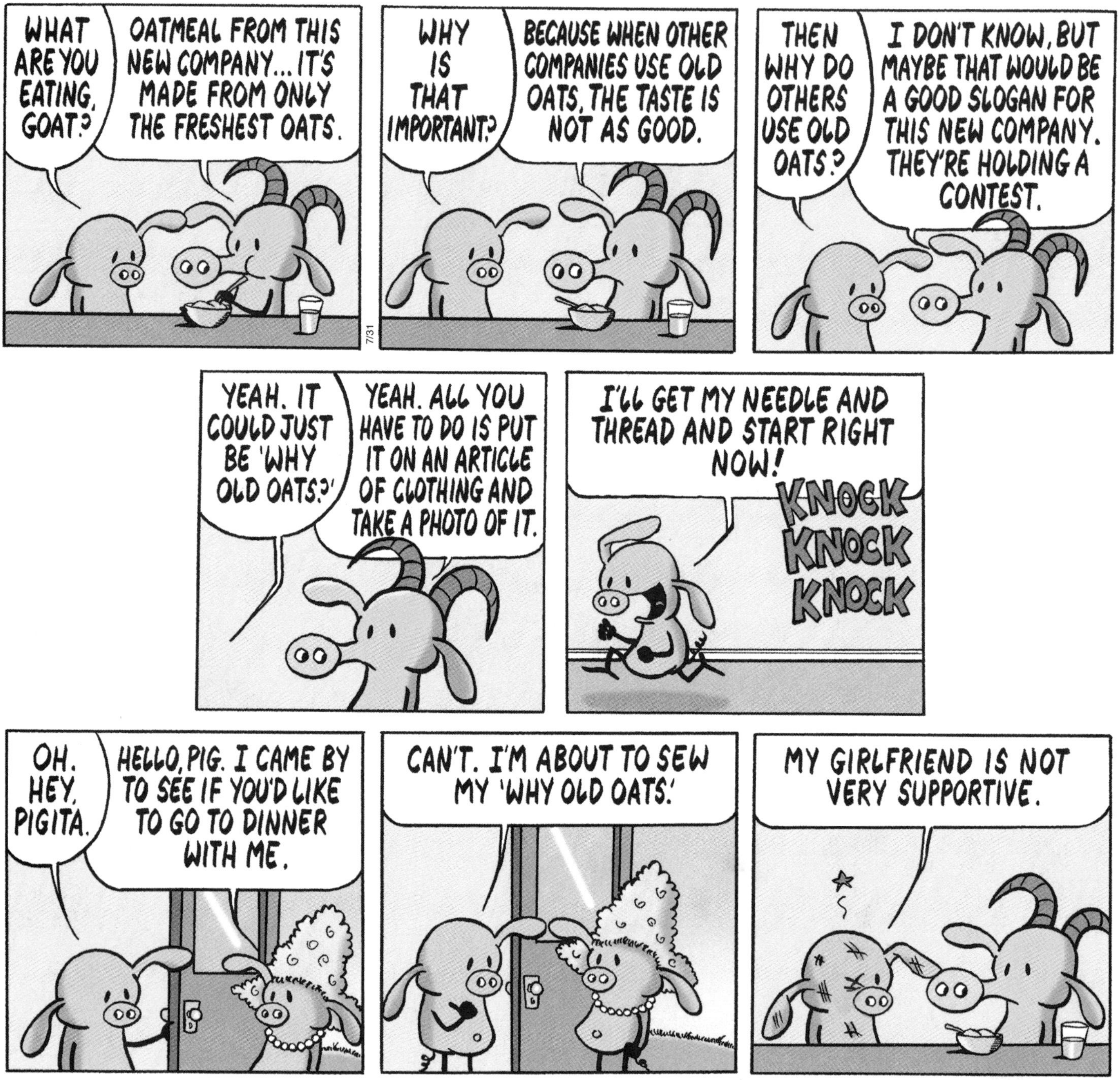
WHAT ARE YOU EATING, GOAT?
OATMEAL FROM THIS NEW COMPANY... IT'S MADE FROM ONLY THE FRESHEST OATS.
7/31
WHY IS THAT IMPORTANT?
BECAUSE WHEN OTHER COMPANIES USE OLD OATS, THE TASTE IS NOT AS GOOD.
THEN WHY DO OTHERS USE OLD OATS?
I DON'T KNOW, BUT MAYBE THAT WOULD BE A GOOD SLOGAN FOR THIS NEW COMPANY. THEY'RE HOLDING A CONTEST.
YEAH. IT COULD JUST BE 'WHY OLD OATS?'
YEAH. ALL YOU HAVE TO DO IS PUT IT ON AN ARTICLE OF CLOTHING AND TAKE A PHOTO OF IT.
I'LL GET MY NEEDLE AND THREAD AND START RIGHT NOW!
KNOCK KNOCK KNOCK
OH. HEY, PIGITA.
HELLO, PIG. I CAME BY TO SEE IF YOU'D LIKE TO GO TO DINNER WITH ME.
CAN'T. I'M ABOUT TO SEW MY 'WHY OLD OATS.'
MY GIRLFRIEND IS NOT VERY SUPPORTIVE.

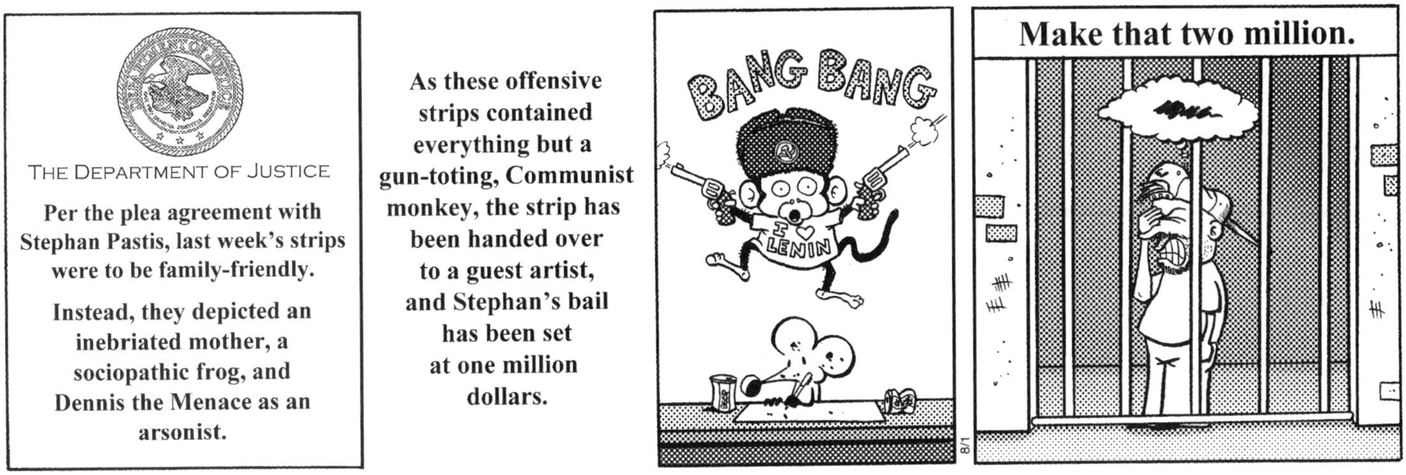
THE DEPARTMENT OF JUSTICE
Per the plea agreement with Stephan Pastis, last week's strips were to be family-friendly.
Instead, they depicted an inebriated mother, a sociopathic frog, and Dennis the Menace as an arsonist.
As these offensive strips contained everything but a gun-toting, Communist monkey, the strip has been handed over to a guest artist, and Stephan's bail has been set at one million dollars.
BANG BANG
I ♥ LENIN
8/1
Make that two million.

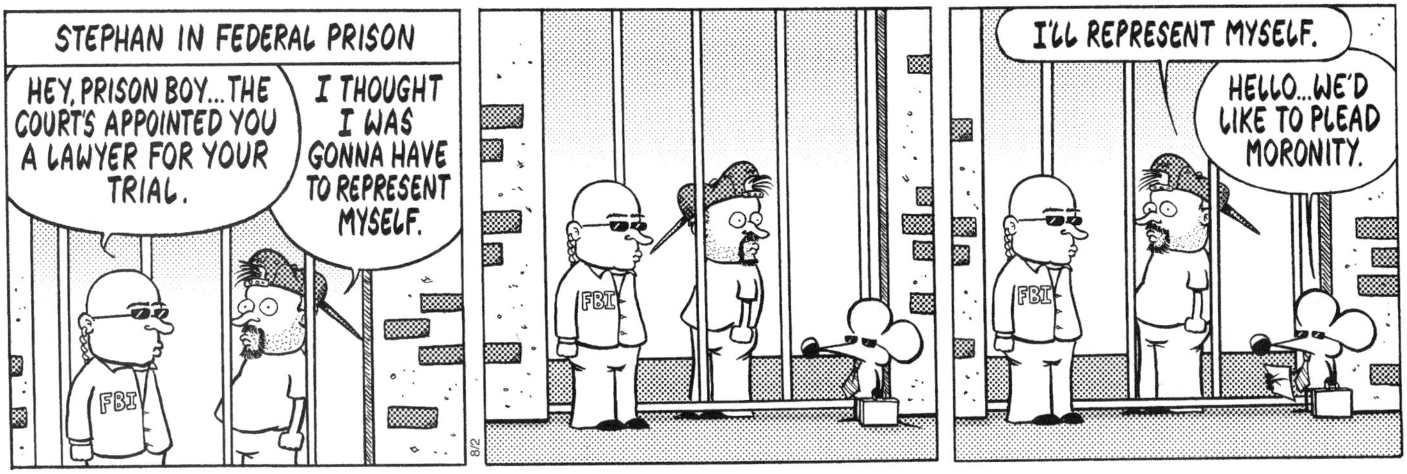
STEPHAN IN FEDERAL PRISON
HEY, PRISON BOY... THE COURT'S APPOINTED YOU A LAWYER FOR YOUR TRIAL.
I THOUGHT I WAS GONNA HAVE TO REPRESENT MYSELF.
FBI
8/2
I'LL REPRESENT MYSELF.
HELLO... WE'D LIKE TO PLEAD MORONITY.

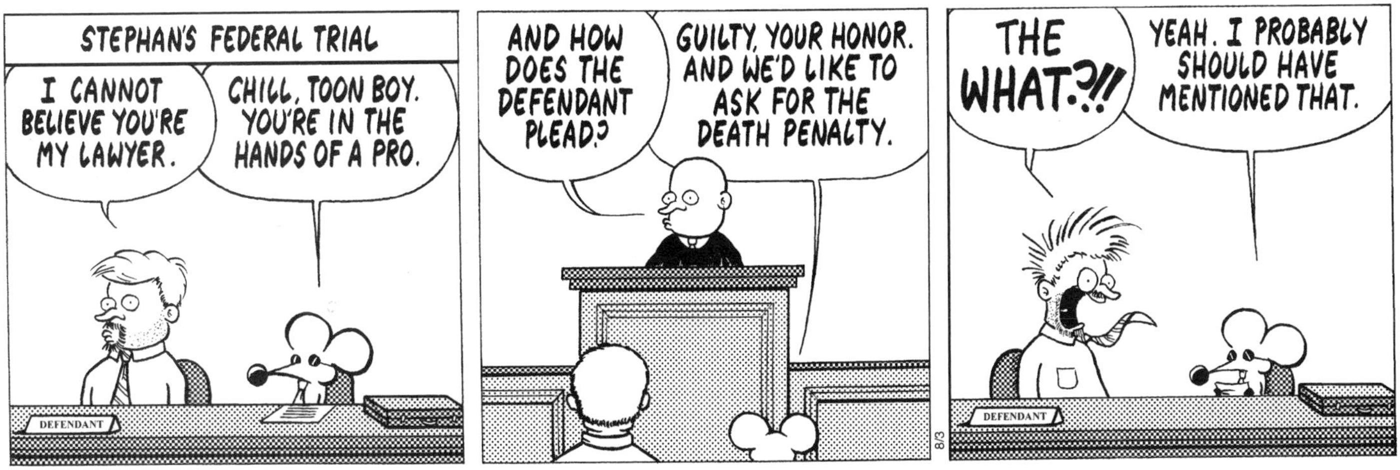
STEPHAN'S FEDERAL TRIAL
I CANNOT BELIEVE YOU'RE MY LAWYER.
CHILL, TOON BOY. YOU'RE IN THE HANDS OF A PRO.
DEFENDANT
AND HOW DOES THE DEFENDANT PLEAD?
GUILTY, YOUR HONOR. AND WE'D LIKE TO ASK FOR THE DEATH PENALTY.
8/3
THE WHAT?!!
YEAH. I PROBABLY SHOULD HAVE MENTIONED THAT.
DEFENDANT

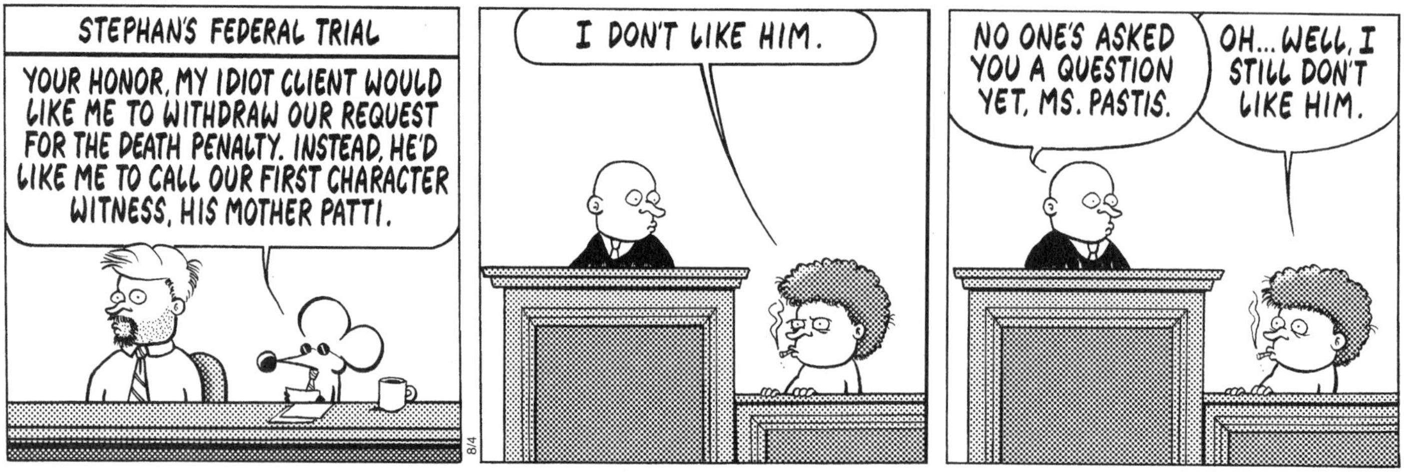
STEPHAN'S FEDERAL TRIAL
YOUR HONOR, MY IDIOT CLIENT WOULD LIKE ME TO WITHDRAW OUR REQUEST FOR THE DEATH PENALTY. INSTEAD, HE'D LIKE ME TO CALL OUR FIRST CHARACTER WITNESS, HIS MOTHER PATTI.
I DON'T LIKE HIM.
8/4
NO ONE'S ASKED YOU A QUESTION YET, MS. PASTIS.
OH... WELL, I STILL DON'T LIKE HIM.

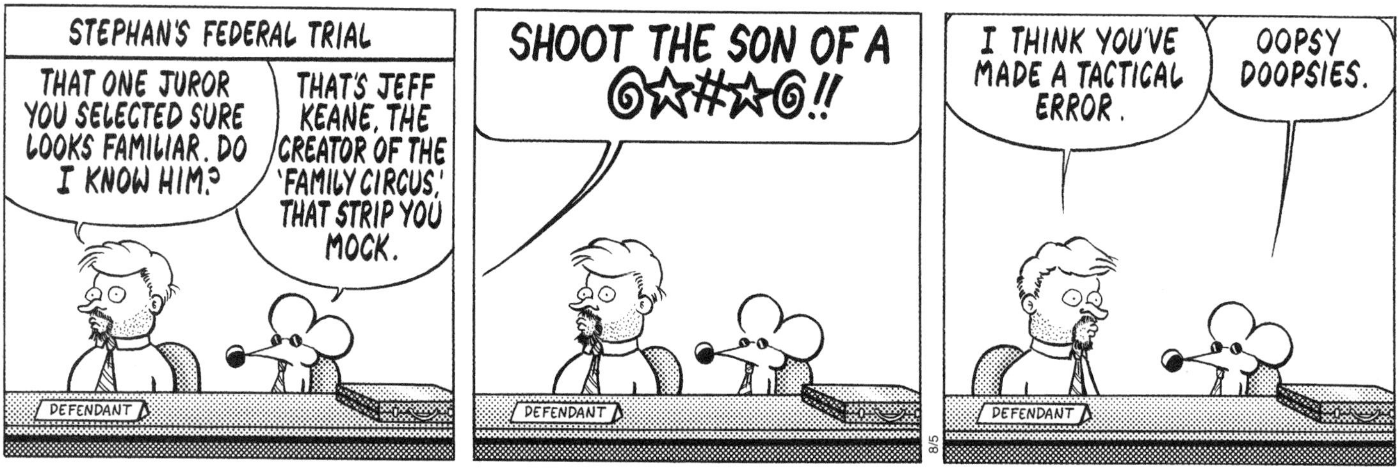
STEPHAN'S FEDERAL TRIAL
THAT ONE JUROR YOU SELECTED SURE LOOKS FAMILIAR. DO I KNOW HIM?
THAT'S JEFF KEANE, THE CREATOR OF THE 'FAMILY CIRCUS,' THAT STRIP YOU MOCK.
DEFENDANT
SHOOT THE SON OF A @☆#☆@!!
DEFENDANT
I THINK YOU'VE MADE A TACTICAL ERROR.
OOPSY DOOPSIES.
DEFENDANT
8/5

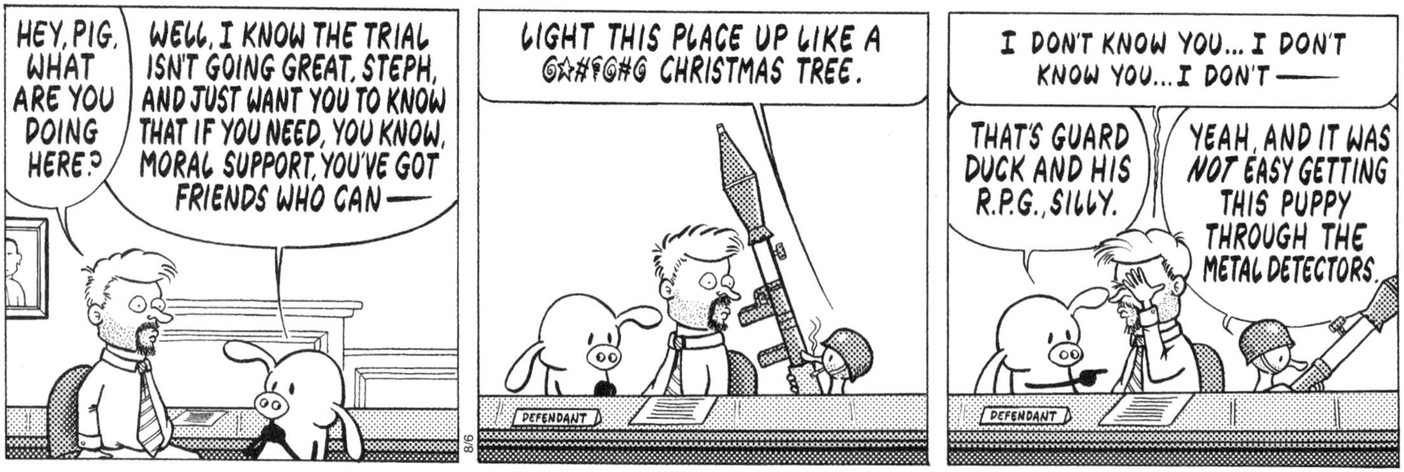
HEY, PIG. WHAT ARE YOU DOING HERE?
WELL, I KNOW THE TRIAL ISN'T GOING GREAT, STEPH, AND JUST WANT YOU TO KNOW THAT IF YOU NEED, YOU KNOW, MORAL SUPPORT, YOU'VE GOT FRIENDS WHO CAN—
8/6
LIGHT THIS PLACE UP LIKE A @☆#?@#@ CHRISTMAS TREE.
DEFENDANT
I DON'T KNOW YOU... I DON'T KNOW YOU... I DON'T—
THAT'S GUARD DUCK AND HIS R.P.G., SILLY.
YEAH, AND IT WAS *NOT* EASY GETTING THIS PUPPY THROUGH THE METAL DETECTORS.
DEFENDANT

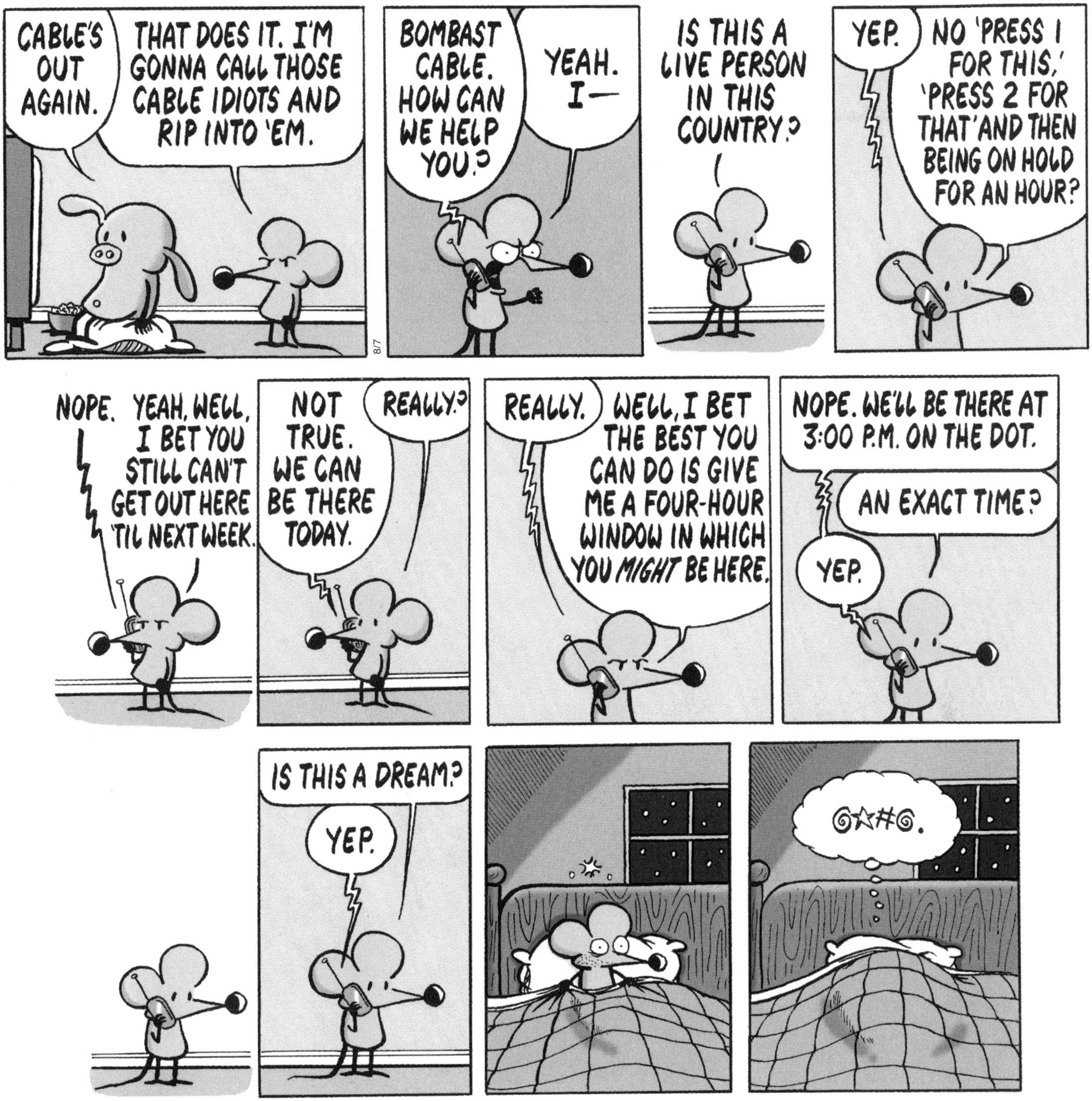
CABLE'S OUT AGAIN.
THAT DOES IT. I'M GONNA CALL THOSE CABLE IDIOTS AND RIP INTO 'EM.
8/7
BOMBAST CABLE. HOW CAN WE HELP YOU?
YEAH. I—
IS THIS A LIVE PERSON IN THIS COUNTRY?
YEP.
NO 'PRESS 1 FOR THIS,' 'PRESS 2 FOR THAT' AND THEN BEING ON HOLD FOR AN HOUR?
NOPE.
YEAH, WELL, I BET YOU STILL CAN'T GET OUT HERE 'TIL NEXT WEEK.
NOT TRUE. WE CAN BE THERE TODAY.
REALLY?
REALLY.
WELL, I BET THE BEST YOU CAN DO IS GIVE ME A FOUR-HOUR WINDOW IN WHICH YOU *MIGHT* BE HERE.
NOPE. WE'LL BE THERE AT 3:00 P.M. ON THE DOT.
AN EXACT TIME?
YEP.
IS THIS A DREAM?
YEP.

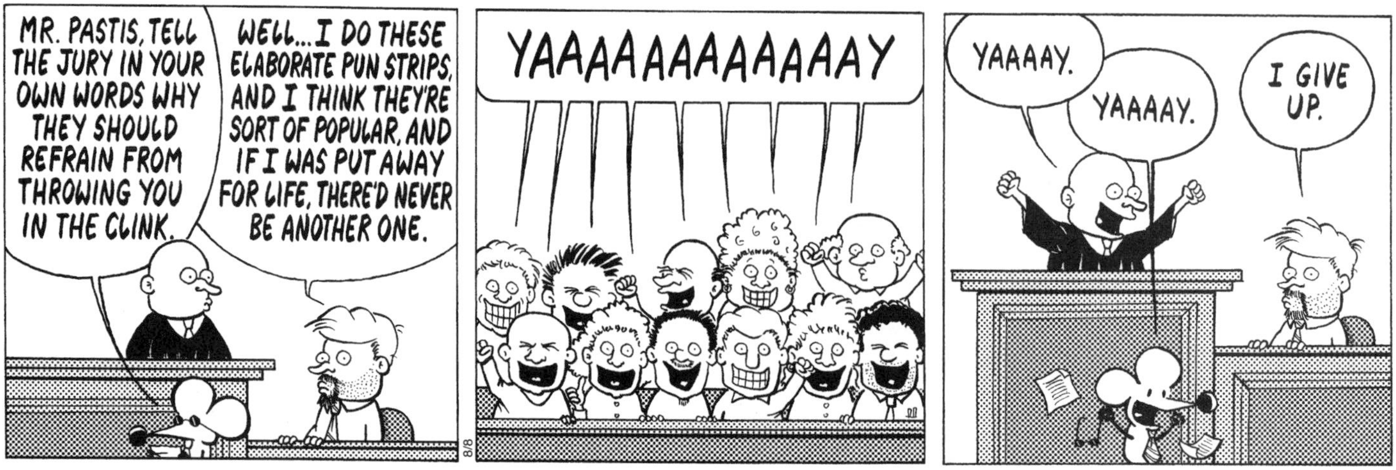
MR. PASTIS, TELL THE JURY IN YOUR OWN WORDS WHY THEY SHOULD REFRAIN FROM THROWING YOU IN THE CLINK.
WELL... I DO THESE ELABORATE PUN STRIPS, AND I THINK THEY'RE SORT OF POPULAR, AND IF I WAS PUT AWAY FOR LIFE, THERE'D NEVER BE ANOTHER ONE.
8/8
YAAAAAAAAAAAAY
YAAAAY.
YAAAAY.
I GIVE UP.

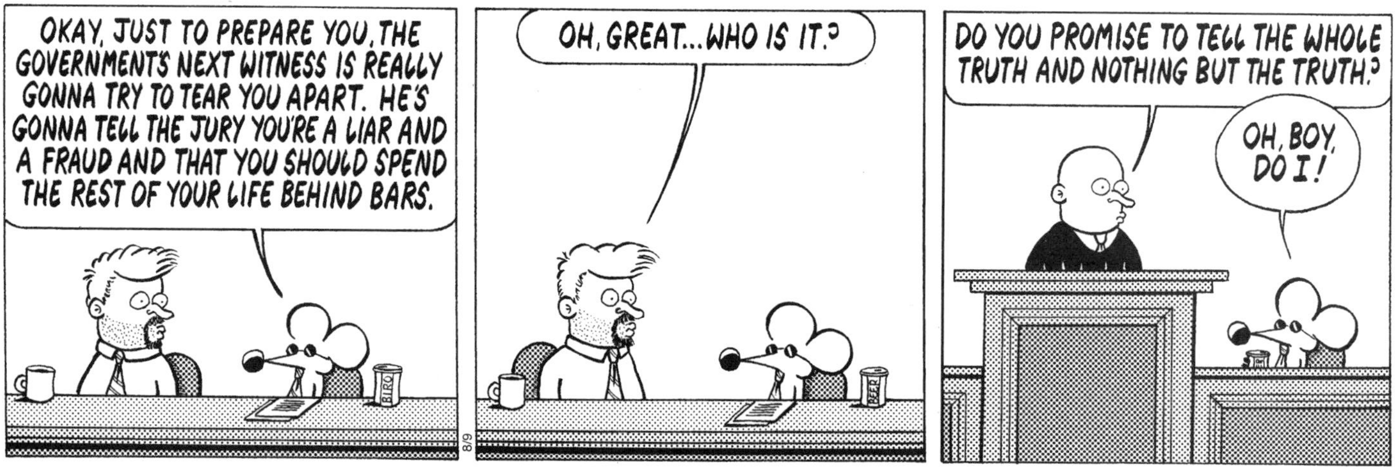
OKAY, JUST TO PREPARE YOU, THE GOVERNMENT'S NEXT WITNESS IS REALLY GONNA TRY TO TEAR YOU APART. HE'S GONNA TELL THE JURY YOU'RE A LIAR AND A FRAUD AND THAT YOU SHOULD SPEND THE REST OF YOUR LIFE BEHIND BARS.
8/9
OH, GREAT... WHO IS IT?
DO YOU PROMISE TO TELL THE WHOLE TRUTH AND NOTHING BUT THE TRUTH?
OH, BOY, DO I!

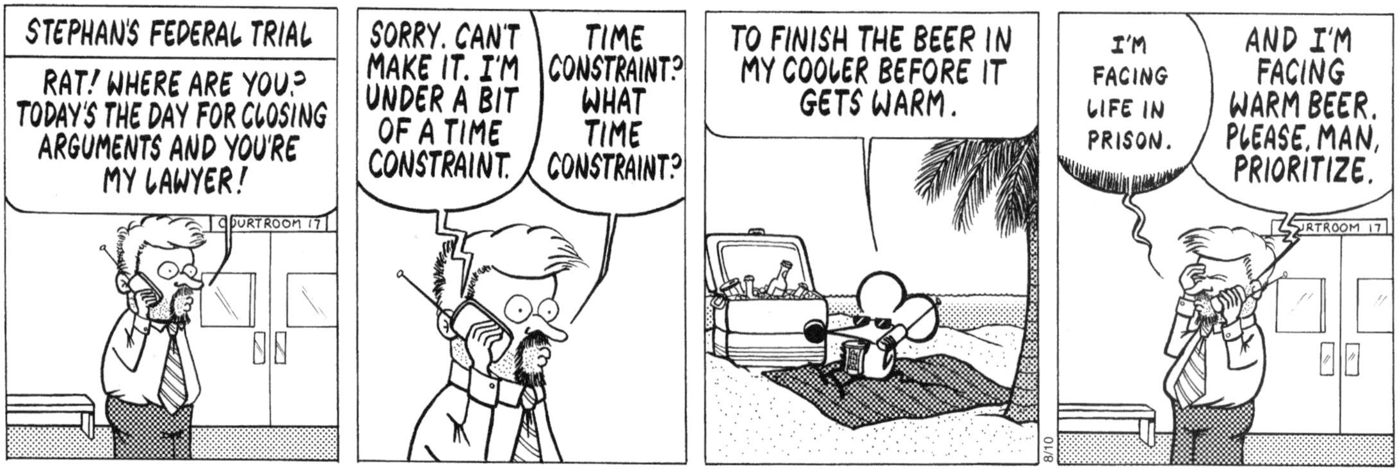
STEPHAN'S FEDERAL TRIAL
RAT! WHERE ARE YOU? TODAY'S THE DAY FOR CLOSING ARGUMENTS AND YOU'RE MY LAWYER!
COURTROOM 17
SORRY. CAN'T MAKE IT. I'M UNDER A BIT OF A TIME CONSTRAINT.
TIME CONSTRAINT? WHAT TIME CONSTRAINT?
TO FINISH THE BEER IN MY COOLER BEFORE IT GETS WARM.
8/10
I'M FACING LIFE IN PRISON.
AND I'M FACING WARM BEER. PLEASE, MAN, PRIORITIZE.

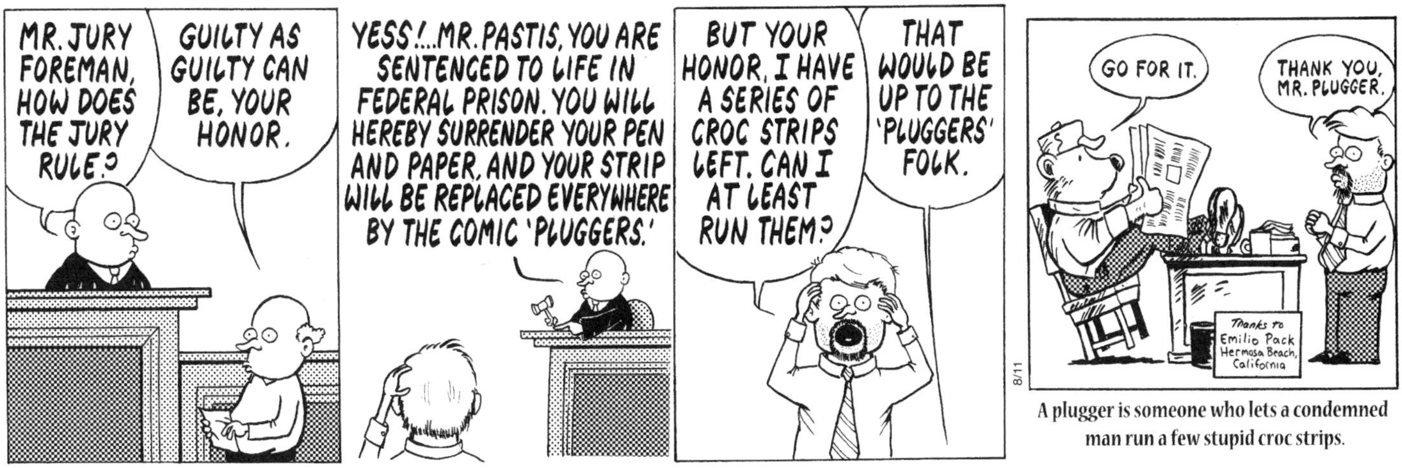
MR. JURY FOREMAN, HOW DOES THE JURY RULE?
GUILTY AS GUILTY CAN BE, YOUR HONOR.
YESS!...MR. PASTIS, YOU ARE SENTENCED TO LIFE IN FEDERAL PRISON. YOU WILL HEREBY SURRENDER YOUR PEN AND PAPER, AND YOUR STRIP WILL BE REPLACED EVERYWHERE BY THE COMIC 'PLUGGERS.'
BUT YOUR HONOR, I HAVE A SERIES OF CROC STRIPS LEFT. CAN I AT LEAST RUN THEM?
THAT WOULD BE UP TO THE 'PLUGGERS' FOLK.
GO FOR IT.
THANK YOU, MR. PLUGGER.
Thanks to Emilio Pack Hermosa Beach, California
8/11

A plugger is someone who lets a condemned man run a few stupid croc strips.

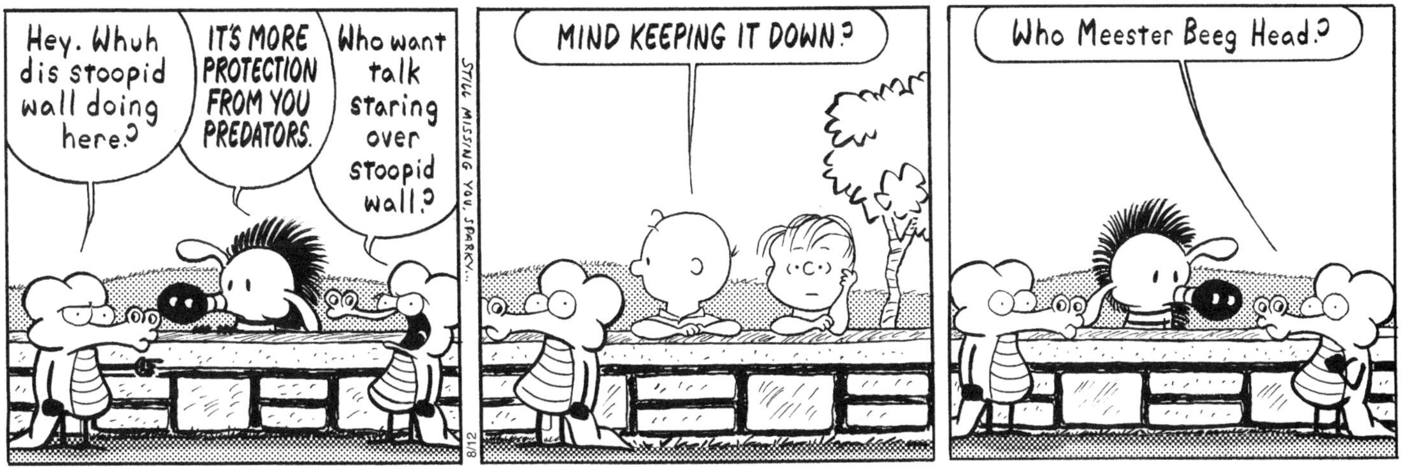
Hey. Whuh dis stoopid wall doing here?
IT'S MORE PROTECTION FROM YOU PREDATORS.
Who want talk staring over stoopid wall?
STILL MISSING YOU, SPARKY...
8/12
MIND KEEPING IT DOWN?
Who Meester Beeg Head?

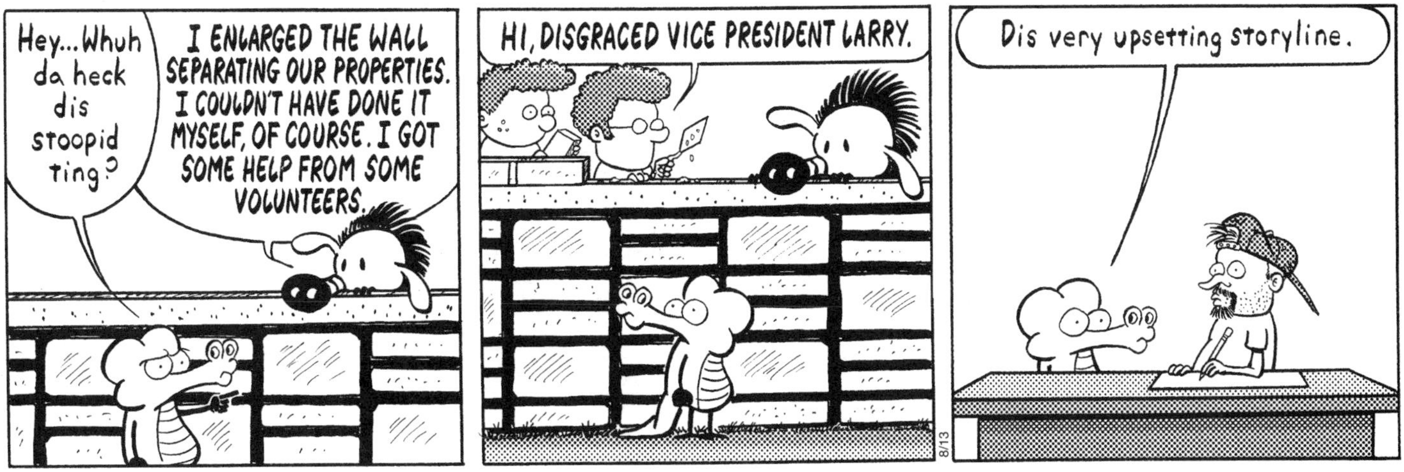
Hey...Whuh da heck dis stoopid ting?
I ENLARGED THE WALL SEPARATING OUR PROPERTIES. I COULDN'T HAVE DONE IT MYSELF, OF COURSE. I GOT SOME HELP FROM SOME VOLUNTEERS.
HI, DISGRACED VICE PRESIDENT LARRY.
8/13
Dis very upsetting storyline.

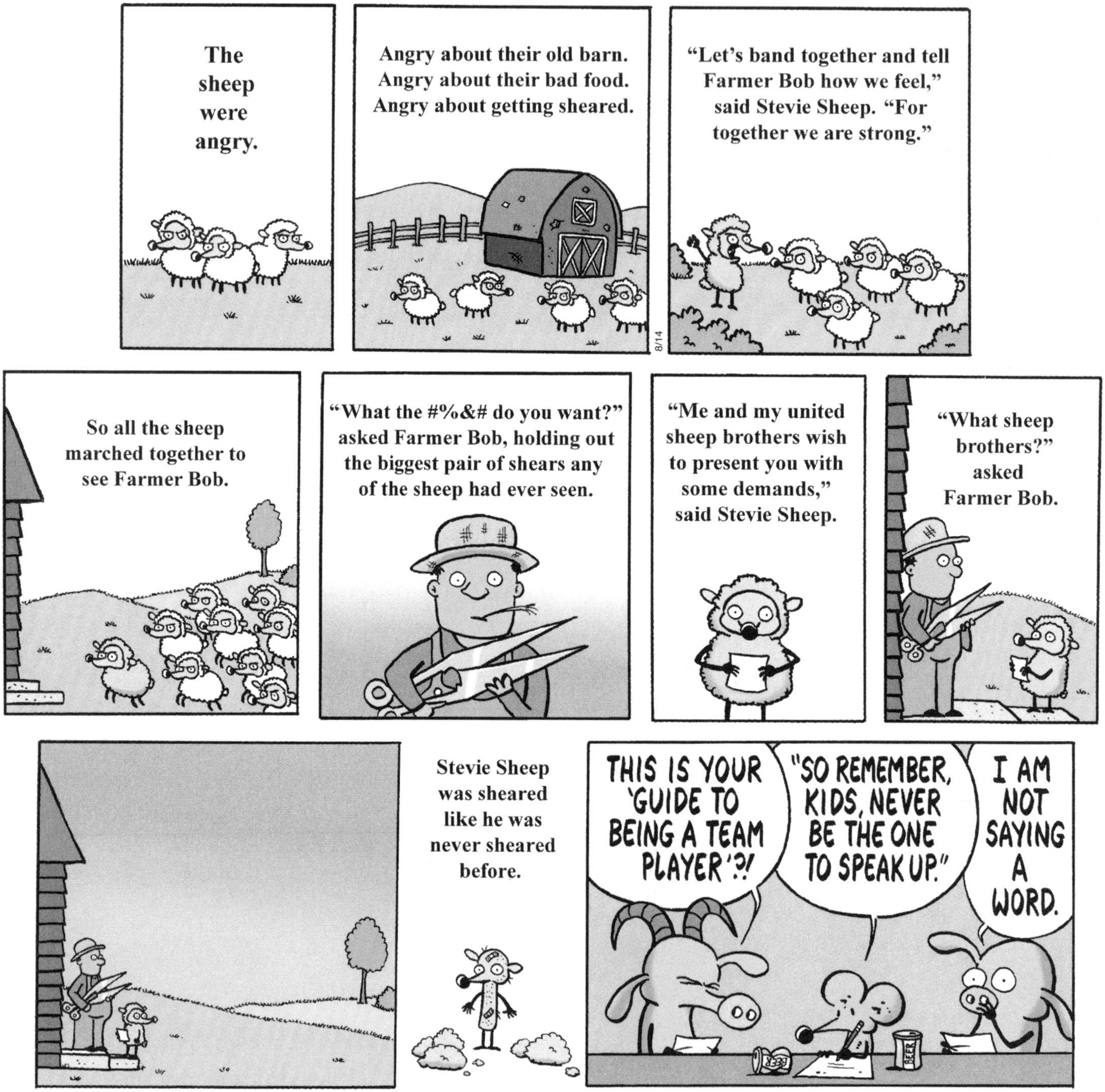
The sheep were angry.
Angry about their old barn. Angry about their bad food. Angry about getting sheared.
8/14
"Let's band together and tell Farmer Bob how we feel," said Stevie Sheep. "For together we are strong."
So all the sheep marched together to see Farmer Bob.
"What the #%&# do you want?" asked Farmer Bob, holding out the biggest pair of shears any of the sheep had ever seen.
"Me and my united sheep brothers wish to present you with some demands," said Stevie Sheep.
"What sheep brothers?" asked Farmer Bob.
Stevie Sheep was sheared like he was never sheared before.
THIS IS YOUR 'GUIDE TO BEING A TEAM PLAYER'?!
"SO REMEMBER, KIDS, NEVER BE THE ONE TO SPEAK UP."
I AM NOT SAYING A WORD.
BEER
BEER

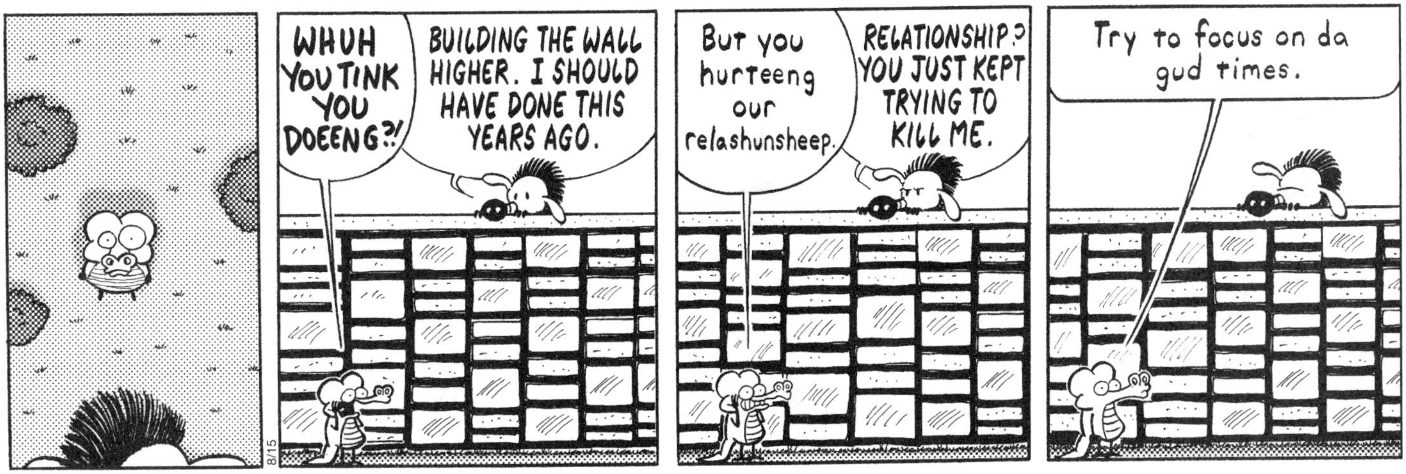
8/15
WHUH YOU TINK YOU DOEENG?!
BUILDING THE WALL HIGHER. I SHOULD HAVE DONE THIS YEARS AGO.
But you hurteeng our relashunsheep.
RELATIONSHIP? YOU JUST KEPT TRYING TO KILL ME.
Try to focus on da gud times.

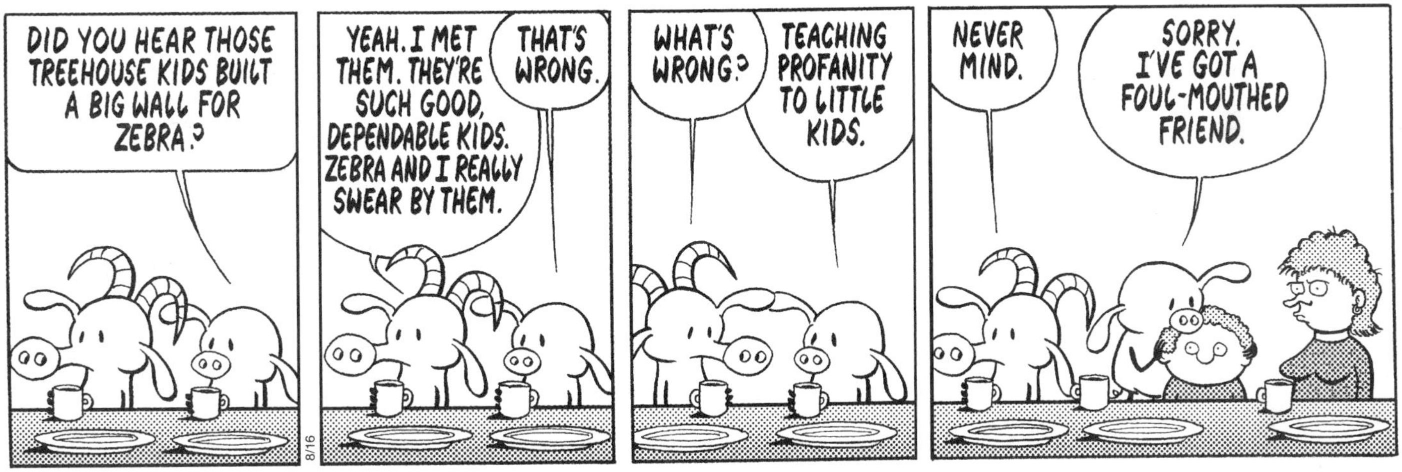
DID YOU HEAR THOSE TREEHOUSE KIDS BUILT A BIG WALL FOR ZEBRA?
8/16
YEAH. I MET THEM. THEY'RE SUCH GOOD, DEPENDABLE KIDS. ZEBRA AND I REALLY SWEAR BY THEM.
THAT'S WRONG.
WHAT'S WRONG?
TEACHING PROFANITY TO LITTLE KIDS.
NEVER MIND.
SORRY. I'VE GOT A FOUL-MOUTHED FRIEND.

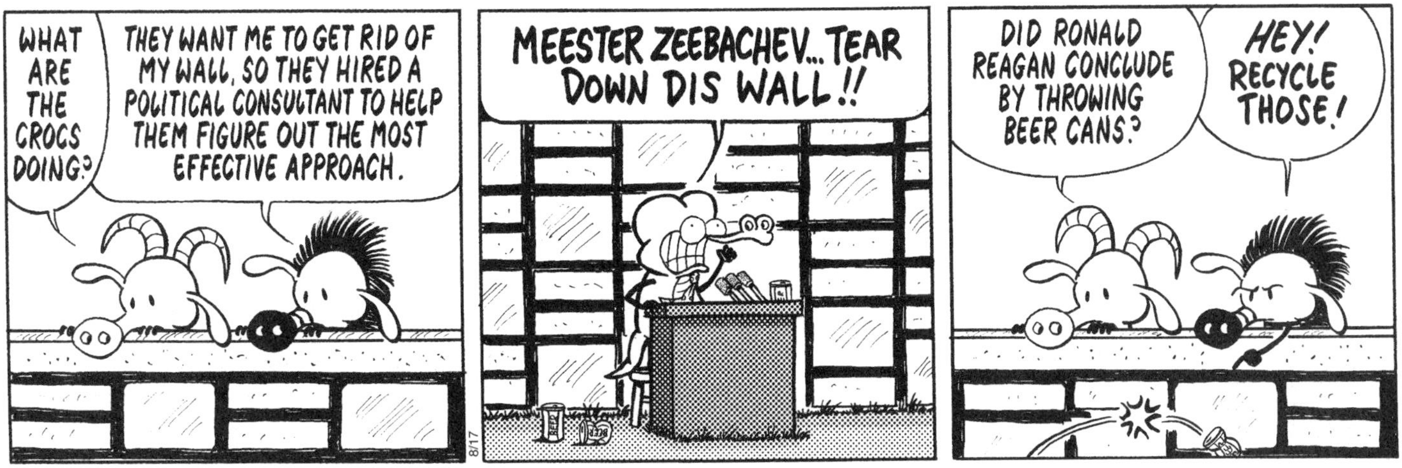
WHAT ARE THE CROCS DOING?
THEY WANT ME TO GET RID OF MY WALL, SO THEY HIRED A POLITICAL CONSULTANT TO HELP THEM FIGURE OUT THE MOST EFFECTIVE APPROACH.
8/17
MEESTER ZEEBACHEV... TEAR DOWN DIS WALL!!
DID RONALD REAGAN CONCLUDE BY THROWING BEER CANS?
HEY! RECYCLE THOSE!

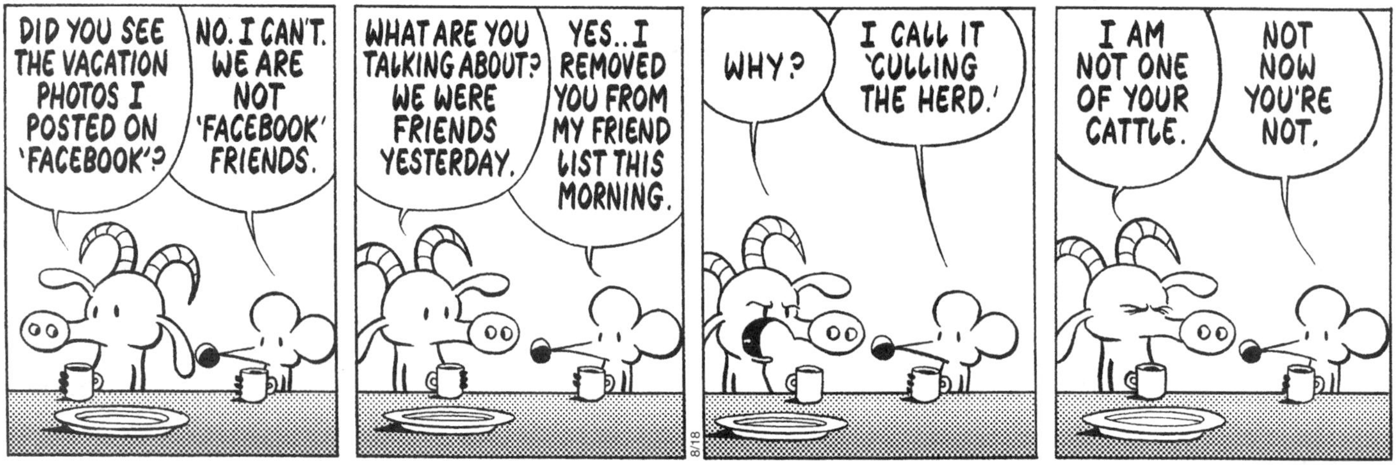
DID YOU SEE THE VACATION PHOTOS I POSTED ON 'FACEBOOK'?
NO. I CAN'T. WE ARE NOT 'FACEBOOK' FRIENDS.
WHAT ARE YOU TALKING ABOUT? WE WERE FRIENDS YESTERDAY.
YES.. I REMOVED YOU FROM MY FRIEND LIST THIS MORNING.
WHY?
I CALL IT 'CULLING THE HERD.'
8/18
I AM NOT ONE OF YOUR CATTLE.
NOT NOW YOU'RE NOT.

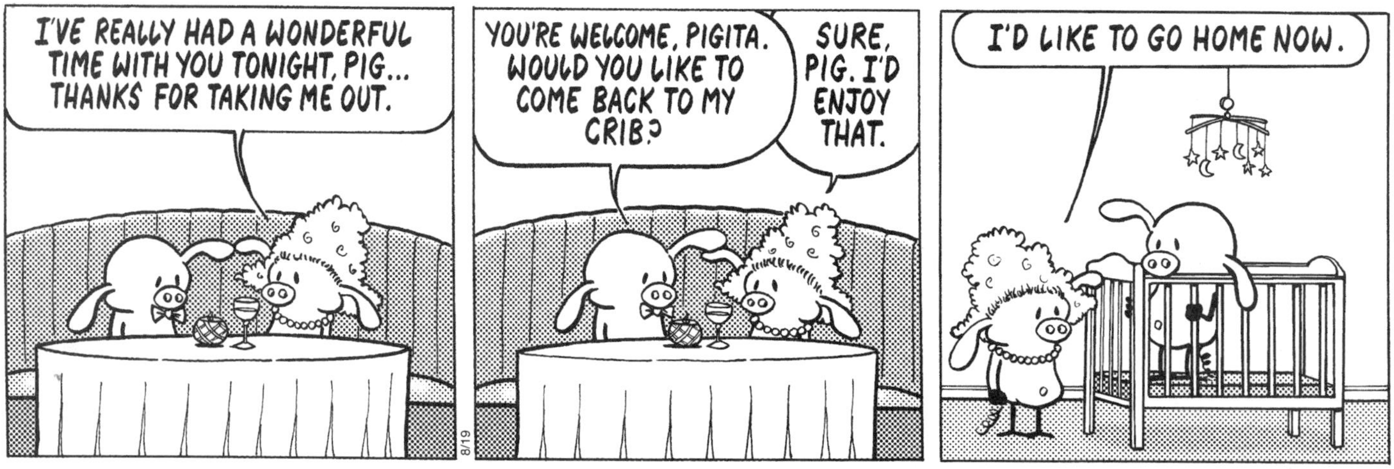
I'VE REALLY HAD A WONDERFUL TIME WITH YOU TONIGHT, PIG... THANKS FOR TAKING ME OUT.
8/19
YOU'RE WELCOME, PIGITA. WOULD YOU LIKE TO COME BACK TO MY CRIB?
SURE, PIG. I'D ENJOY THAT.
I'D LIKE TO GO HOME NOW.

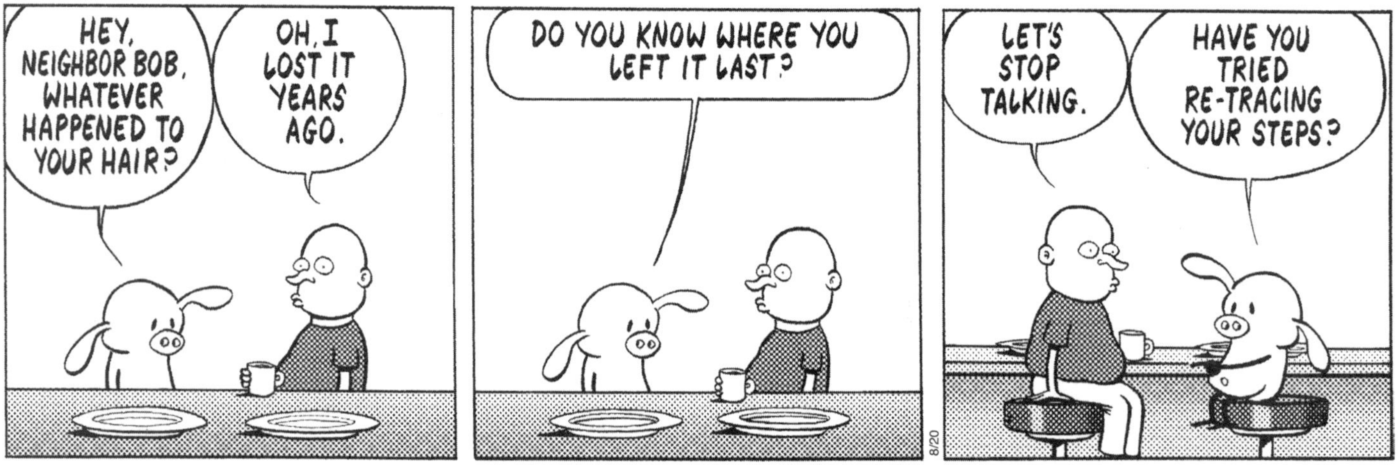
HEY, NEIGHBOR BOB, WHATEVER HAPPENED TO YOUR HAIR?
OH, I LOST IT YEARS AGO.
DO YOU KNOW WHERE YOU LEFT IT LAST?
8/20
LET'S STOP TALKING.
HAVE YOU TRIED RE-TRACING YOUR STEPS?

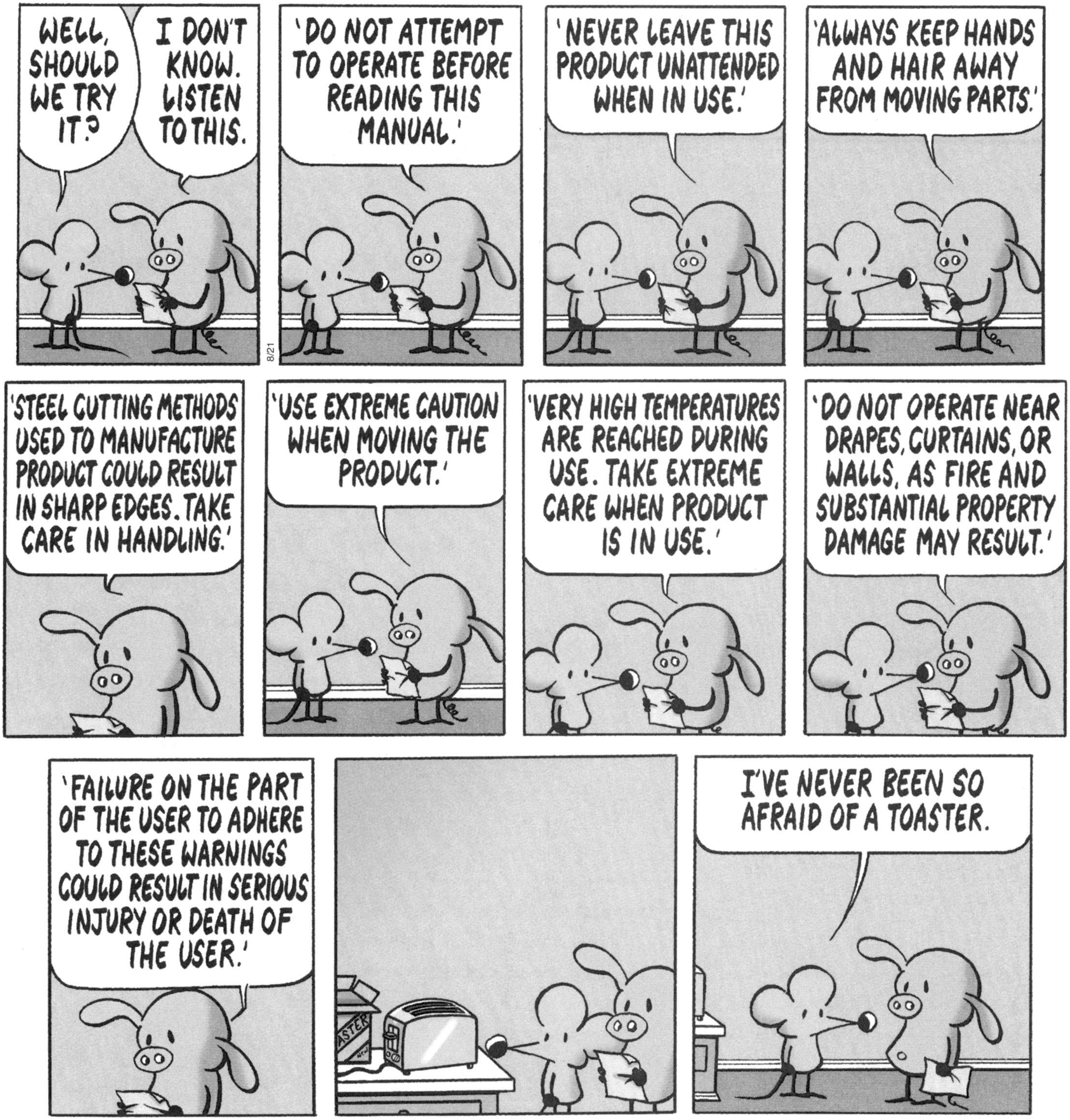
WELL, SHOULD WE TRY IT?
I DON'T KNOW. LISTEN TO THIS.
8/21
'DO NOT ATTEMPT TO OPERATE BEFORE READING THIS MANUAL.'
'NEVER LEAVE THIS PRODUCT UNATTENDED WHEN IN USE.'
'ALWAYS KEEP HANDS AND HAIR AWAY FROM MOVING PARTS.'
'STEEL CUTTING METHODS USED TO MANUFACTURE PRODUCT COULD RESULT IN SHARP EDGES. TAKE CARE IN HANDLING.'
'USE EXTREME CAUTION WHEN MOVING THE PRODUCT.'
'VERY HIGH TEMPERATURES ARE REACHED DURING USE. TAKE EXTREME CARE WHEN PRODUCT IS IN USE.'
'DO NOT OPERATE NEAR DRAPES, CURTAINS, OR WALLS, AS FIRE AND SUBSTANTIAL PROPERTY DAMAGE MAY RESULT.'
'FAILURE ON THE PART OF THE USER TO ADHERE TO THESE WARNINGS COULD RESULT IN SERIOUS INJURY OR DEATH OF THE USER.'
TOASTER
I'VE NEVER BEEN SO AFRAID OF A TOASTER.

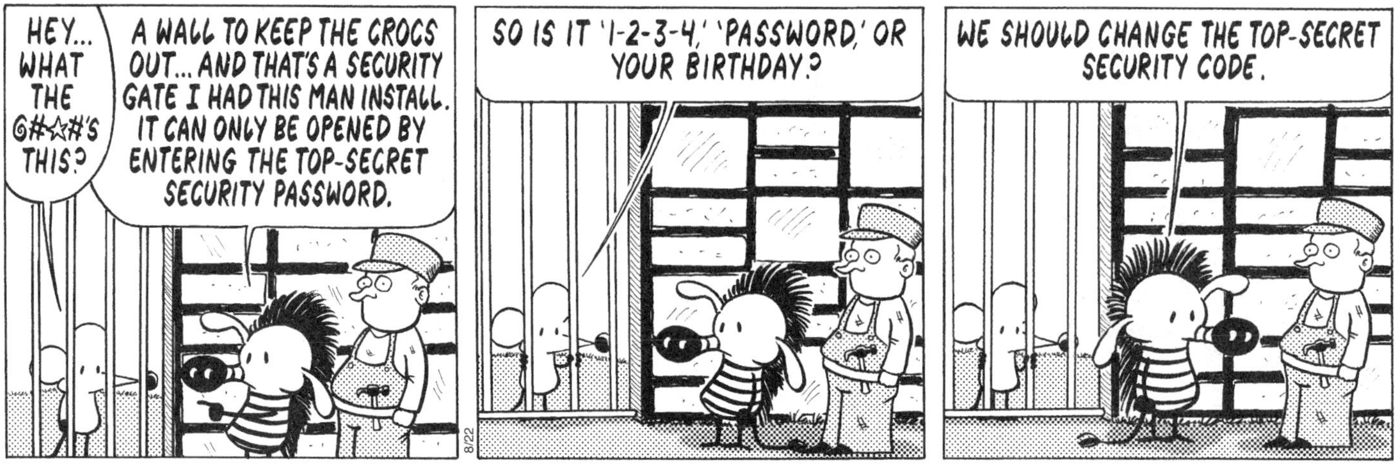
HEY... WHAT THE @#☆#'S THIS?
A WALL TO KEEP THE CROCS OUT... AND THAT'S A SECURITY GATE I HAD THIS MAN INSTALL. IT CAN ONLY BE OPENED BY ENTERING THE TOP-SECRET SECURITY PASSWORD.
8/22
SO IS IT '1-2-3-4,' 'PASSWORD,' OR YOUR BIRTHDAY?
WE SHOULD CHANGE THE TOP-SECRET SECURITY CODE.

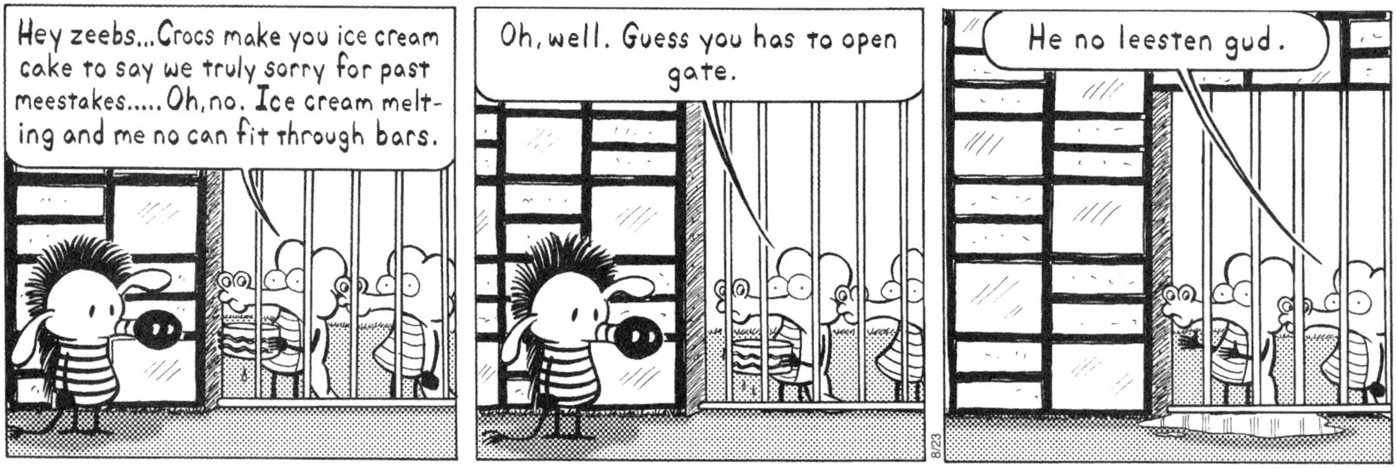
Hey zeebs...Crocs make you ice cream cake to say we truly sorry for past meestakes..... Oh, no. Ice cream melting and me no can fit through bars.
Oh, well. Guess you has to open gate.
8/23
He no leesten gud.

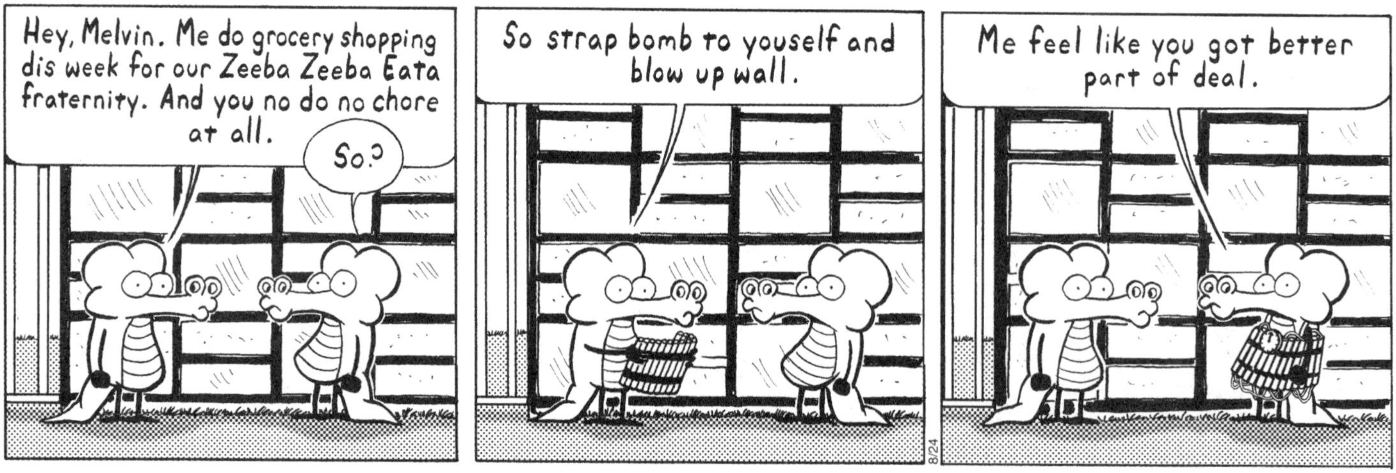
Hey, Melvin. Me do grocery shopping dis week for our Zeeba Zeeba Eata fraternity. And you no do no chore at all.
So?
So strap bomb to youself and blow up wall.
8/24
Me feel like you got better part of deal.

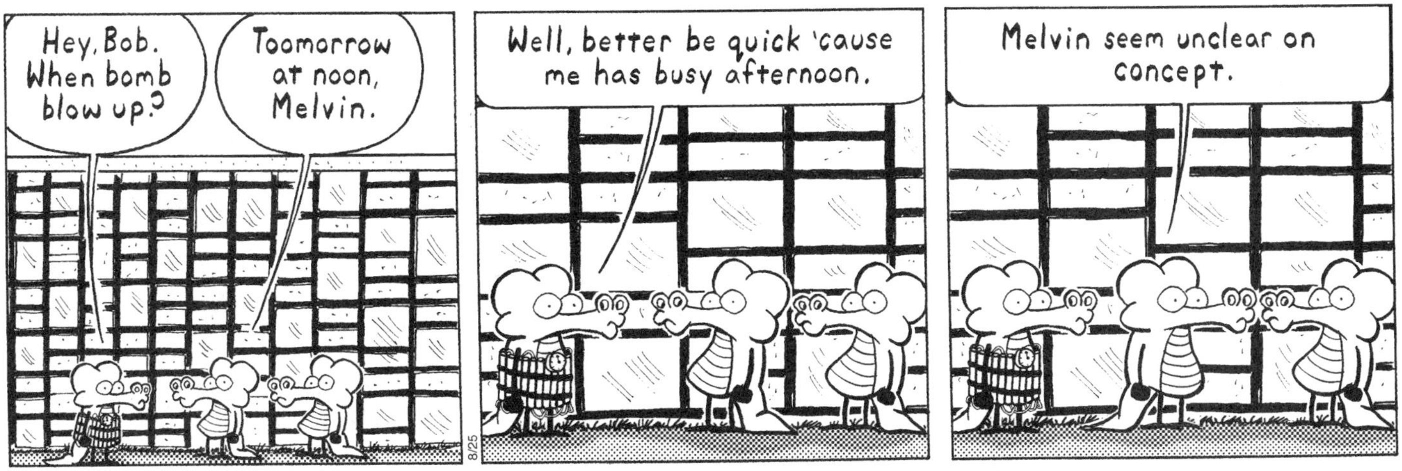
Hey, Bob. When bomb blow up?
Toomorrow at noon, Melvin.
8/25
Well, better be quick 'cause me has busy afternoon.
Melvin seem unclear on concept.

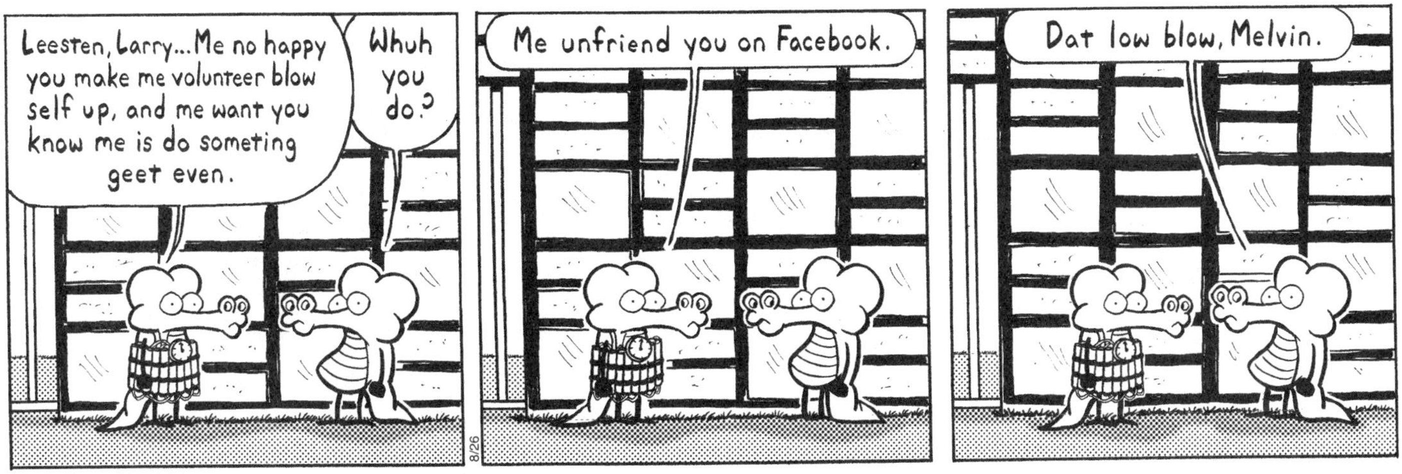
Leesten, Larry... Me no happy you make me volunteer blow self up, and me want you know me is do someting geet even.
Whuh you do?
8/26
Me unfriend you on Facebook.
Dat low blow, Melvin.

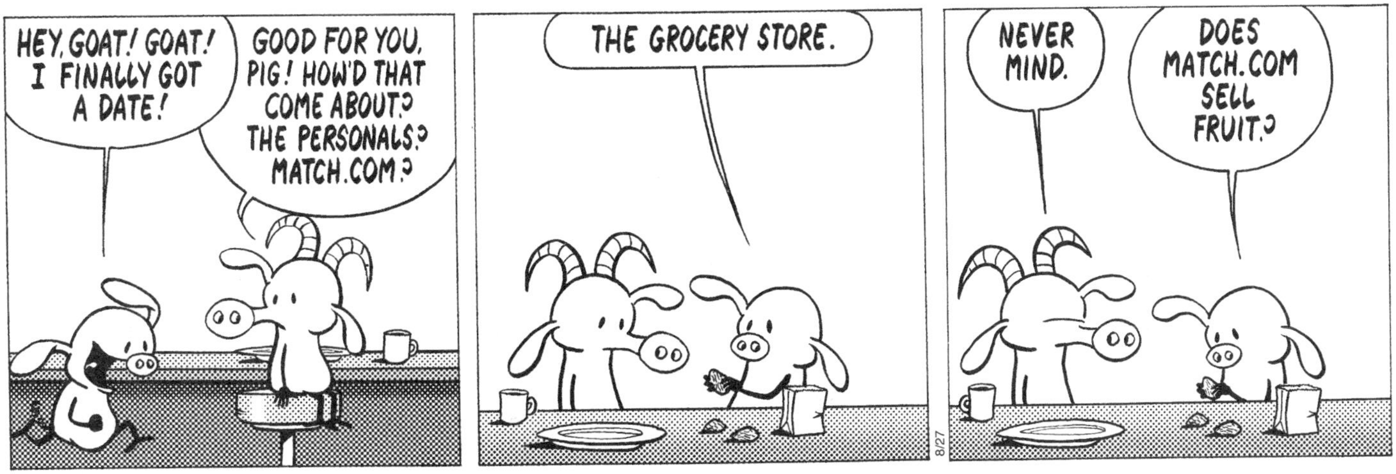
HEY, GOAT! GOAT! I FINALLY GOT A DATE!
GOOD FOR YOU, PIG! HOW'D THAT COME ABOUT? THE PERSONALS? MATCH.COM?
THE GROCERY STORE.
8/27
NEVER MIND.
DOES MATCH.COM SELL FRUIT?

HI, MS. JONES. HAVE YOU MET MY NEIGHBOR BOB'S SON, JOJO? HE'S LEARNING KAZOO. HE'S HOPING IT WILL ONE DAY BE A NICE EXTRACURRICULAR ACTIVITY THAT COULD BEEF UP HIS COLLEGE APPLICATION.

SHOW HER, JOJO.

TOOT.

THAT'S NICE. THIS IS MY SON, PHILLIP. HE PLAYS VIOLIN.

HE'S ALSO PRESIDENT OF THE STUDENT BODY, THE DEBATE TEAM, AND THE DRAMA CLUB.

WHICH HASN'T STOPPED HIM FROM GETTING A 4.6 G.P.A. AND THE HIGHEST S.A.T. SCORE IN HIS SCHOOL'S HISTORY.

NOT BAD CONSIDERING HE SPENT THE SUMMER SAVING AN ENTIRE AFRICAN NATION FROM STARVATION.

TOOOOOT

8/28

HE IS SUCH A SHOW-OFF.

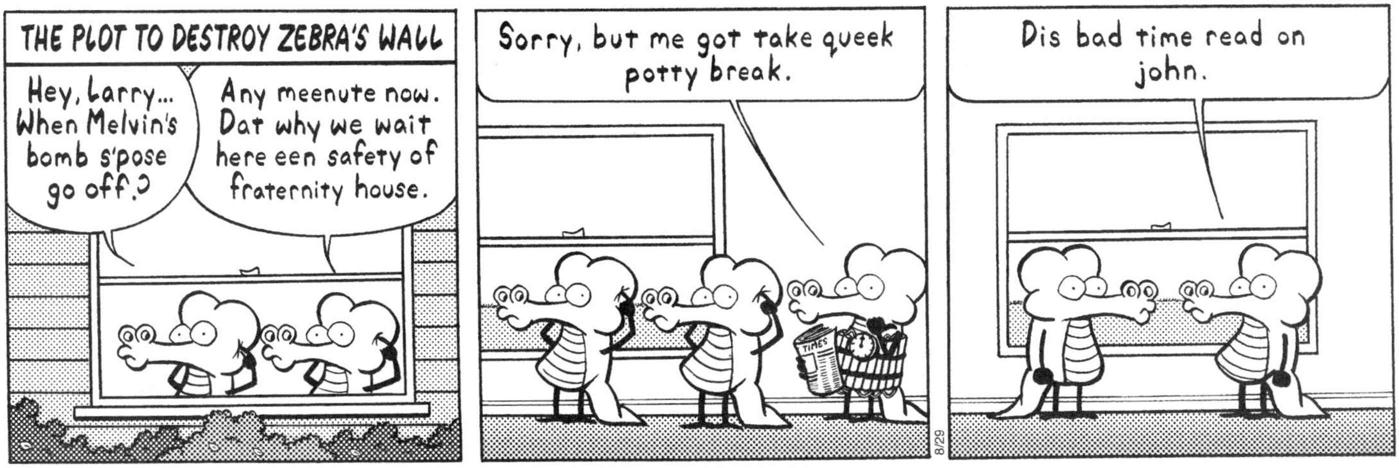
THE PLOT TO DESTROY ZEBRA'S WALL
Hey, Larry... When Melvin's bomb s'pose go off?
Any meenute now. Dat why we wait here een safety of fraternity house.
Sorry, but me got take queek potty break.
TIMES
Dis bad time read on john.
8/29

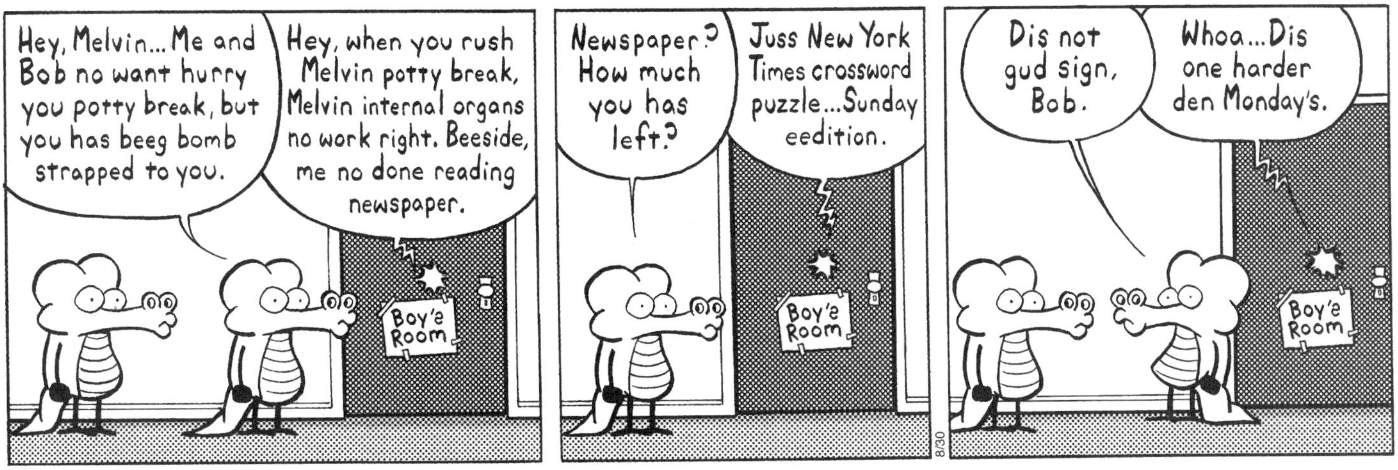
Hey, Melvin... Me and Bob no want hurry you potty break, but you has beeg bomb strapped to you.
Hey, when you rush Melvin potty break, Melvin internal organs no work right. Beeside, me no done reading newspaper.
Boy'e Room
Newspaper? How much you has left?
Juss New York Times crossword puzzle... Sunday eedition.
Boy'e Room
Dis not gud sign, Bob.
Whoa... Dis one harder den Monday's.
Boy'e Room
8/30

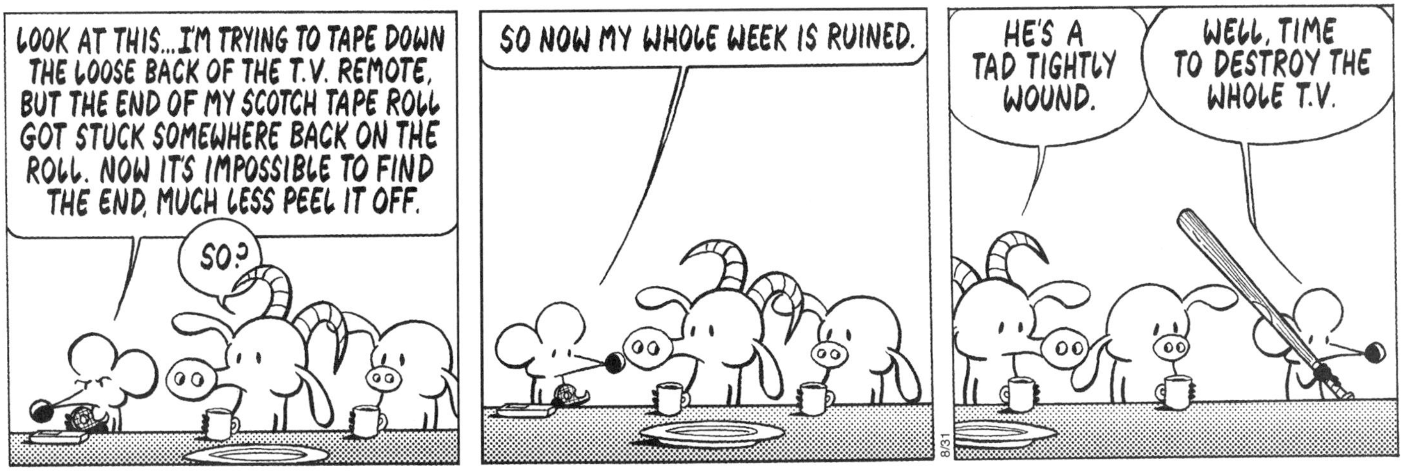
LOOK AT THIS...I'M TRYING TO TAPE DOWN THE LOOSE BACK OF THE T.V. REMOTE, BUT THE END OF MY SCOTCH TAPE ROLL GOT STUCK SOMEWHERE BACK ON THE ROLL. NOW IT'S IMPOSSIBLE TO FIND THE END, MUCH LESS PEEL IT OFF.
SO?
SO NOW MY WHOLE WEEK IS RUINED.
HE'S A TAD TIGHTLY WOUND.
WELL, TIME TO DESTROY THE WHOLE T.V.
8/31

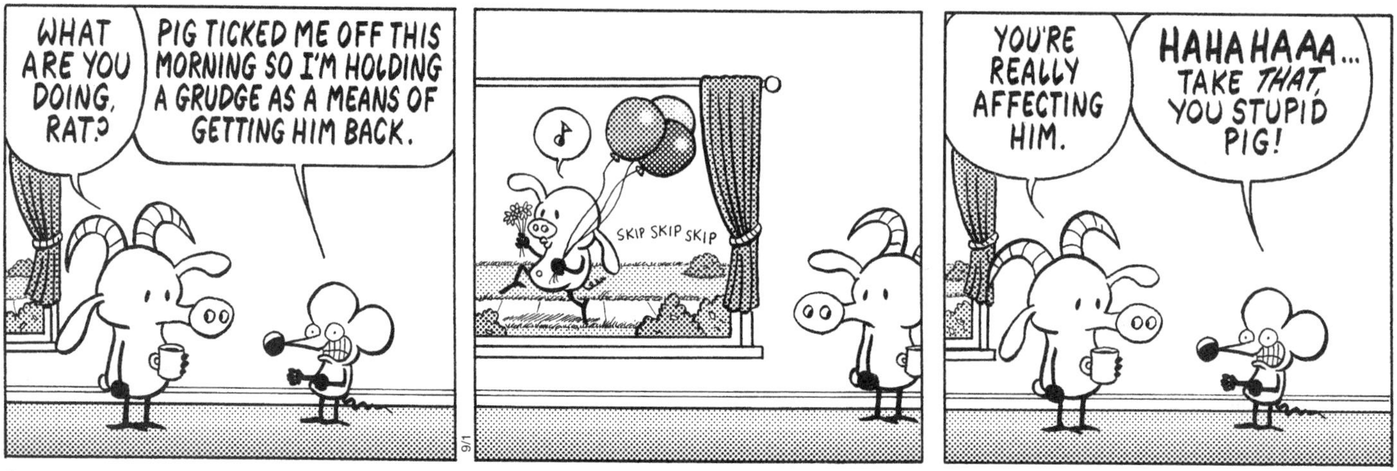
WHAT ARE YOU DOING, RAT?
PIG TICKED ME OFF THIS MORNING SO I'M HOLDING A GRUDGE AS A MEANS OF GETTING HIM BACK.
SKIP SKIP SKIP
YOU'RE REALLY AFFECTING HIM.
HAHAHAAA... TAKE *THAT,* YOU STUPID PIG!
9/1

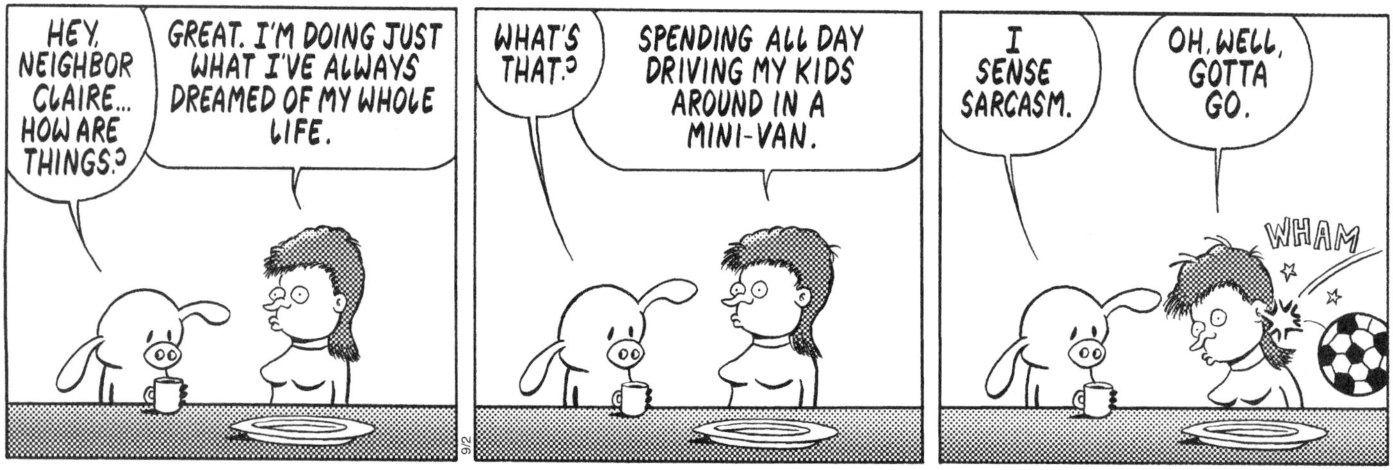
HEY, NEIGHBOR CLAIRE... HOW ARE THINGS?
GREAT. I'M DOING JUST WHAT I'VE ALWAYS DREAMED OF MY WHOLE LIFE.
WHAT'S THAT?
SPENDING ALL DAY DRIVING MY KIDS AROUND IN A MINI-VAN.
I SENSE SARCASM.
OH, WELL, GOTTA GO.
WHAM
9/2

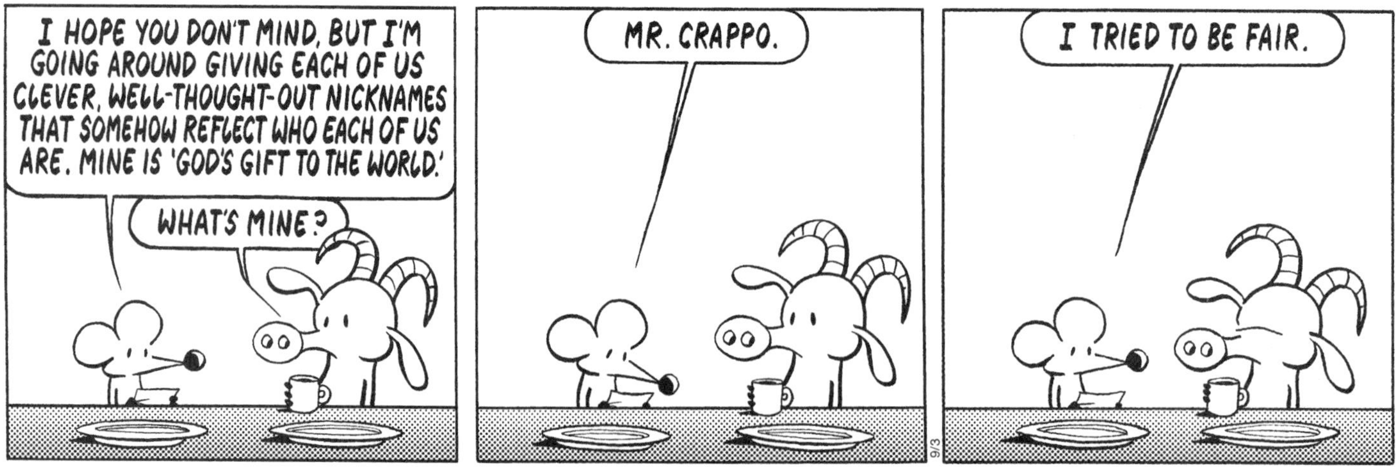
I HOPE YOU DON'T MIND, BUT I'M GOING AROUND GIVING EACH OF US CLEVER, WELL-THOUGHT-OUT NICKNAMES THAT SOMEHOW REFLECT WHO EACH OF US ARE. MINE IS 'GOD'S GIFT TO THE WORLD.'
WHAT'S MINE?
MR. CRAPPO.
I TRIED TO BE FAIR.
9/3

STORY UPDATE

Melvin the crocodile has been selected by the other crocs to have a bomb strapped to his chest, in order that he might blow up a large wall built by Zebra to protect his property. With the bomb set to explode, Melvin walks back inside the crocs' house to take a potty break, and will not come out until he has finished the New York Times Sunday crossword.

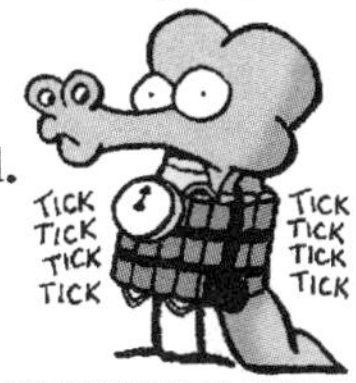
TICK TICK TICK TICK
TICK TICK TICK TICK

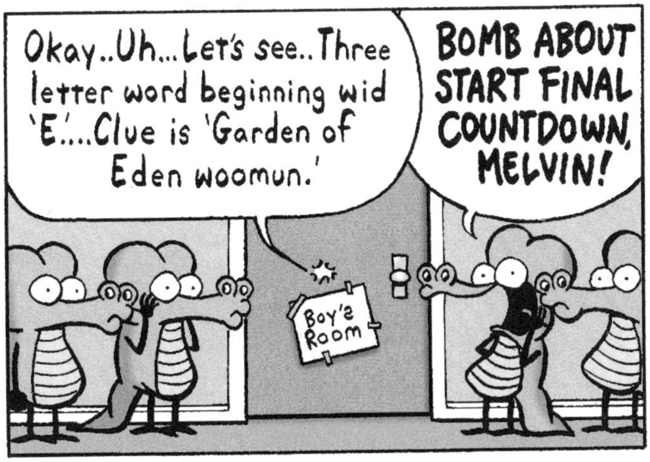
Okay..Uh...Let's see..Three letter word beginning wid 'E.'....Clue is 'Garden of Eden woomun.'
BOMB ABOUT START FINAL COUNTDOWN, MELVIN!
Boy'z Room

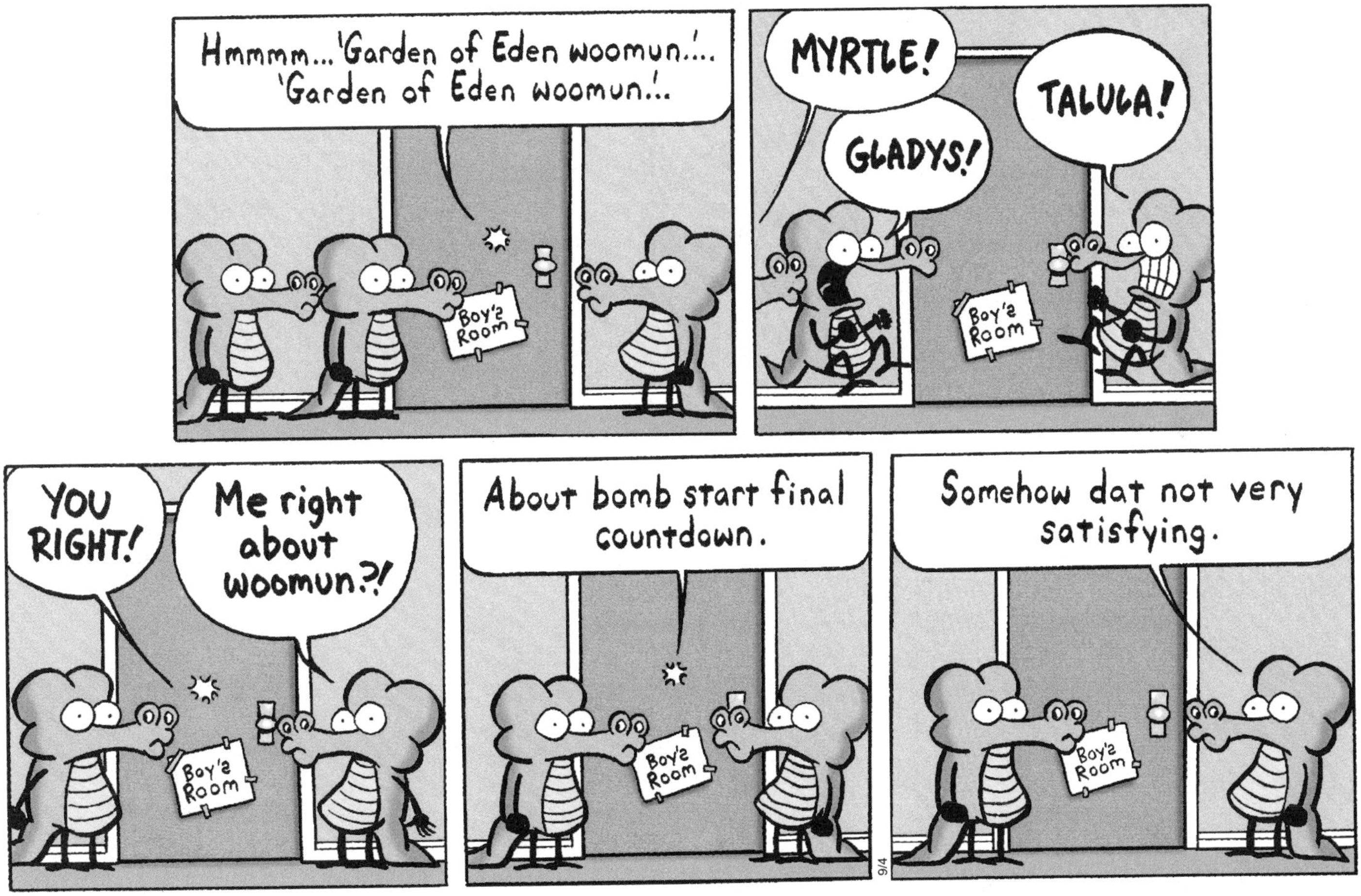
Hmmmm...'Garden of Eden woomun.'... 'Garden of Eden woomun.'..
Boy'z Room
MYRTLE!
GLADYS!
TALULA!
Boy'z Room
YOU RIGHT!
Me right about woomun?!
Boy'z Room
About bomb start final countdown.
Boy'z Room
9/4
Somehow dat not very satisfying.
Boy'z Room

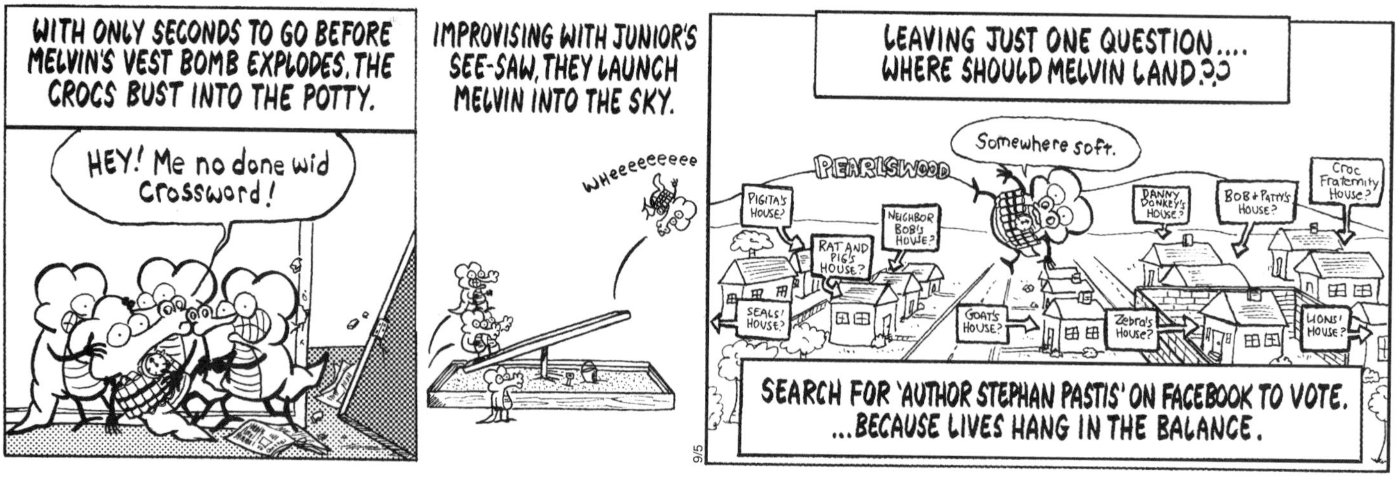
WITH ONLY SECONDS TO GO BEFORE MELVIN'S VEST BOMB EXPLODES, THE CROCS BUST INTO THE POTTY.
HEY! Me no done wid crossword!
IMPROVISING WITH JUNIOR'S SEE-SAW, THEY LAUNCH MELVIN INTO THE SKY.
Wheeeeeeeee
LEAVING JUST ONE QUESTION.... WHERE SHOULD MELVIN LAND???
Somewhere soft.
PEARLSWOOD
PIGITA'S HOUSE?
RAT AND PIG'S HOUSE?
NEIGHBOR BOB'S HOUSE?
SEALS' HOUSE?
GOAT'S HOUSE?
DANNY DONKEY'S HOUSE?
BOB + PATTY'S HOUSE?
Croc Fraternity House?
Zebra's House?
LIONS' HOUSE?
SEARCH FOR 'AUTHOR STEPHAN PASTIS' ON FACEBOOK TO VOTE. ...BECAUSE LIVES HANG IN THE BALANCE.
9/5

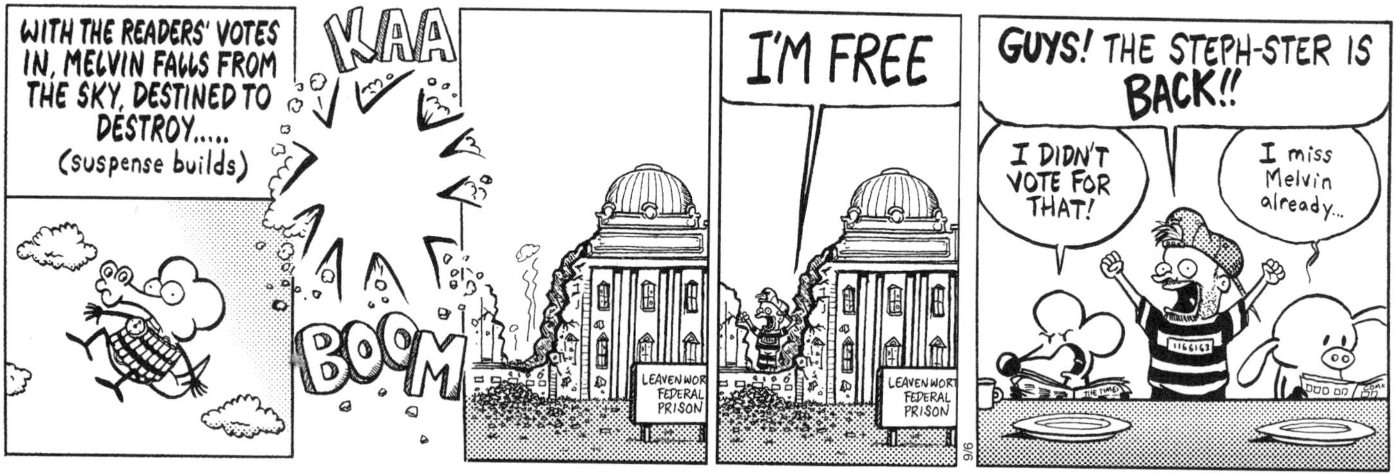
WITH THE READERS' VOTES IN, MELVIN FALLS FROM THE SKY, DESTINED TO DESTROY..... (suspense builds)
KAA
BOOM
LEAVENWORTH FEDERAL PRISON
I'M FREE
GUYS! THE STEPH-STER IS BACK!!
I DIDN'T VOTE FOR THAT!
I miss Melvin already...
9/6

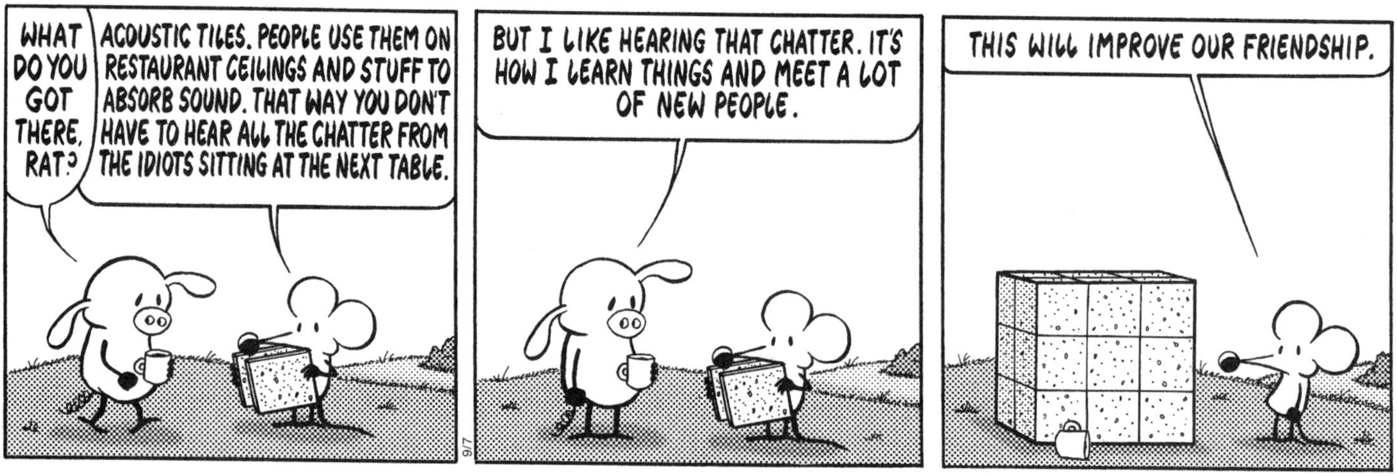
WHAT DO YOU GOT THERE, RAT?
ACOUSTIC TILES. PEOPLE USE THEM ON RESTAURANT CEILINGS AND STUFF TO ABSORB SOUND. THAT WAY YOU DON'T HAVE TO HEAR ALL THE CHATTER FROM THE IDIOTS SITTING AT THE NEXT TABLE.
BUT I LIKE HEARING THAT CHATTER. IT'S HOW I LEARN THINGS AND MEET A LOT OF NEW PEOPLE.
THIS WILL IMPROVE OUR FRIENDSHIP.
9/7

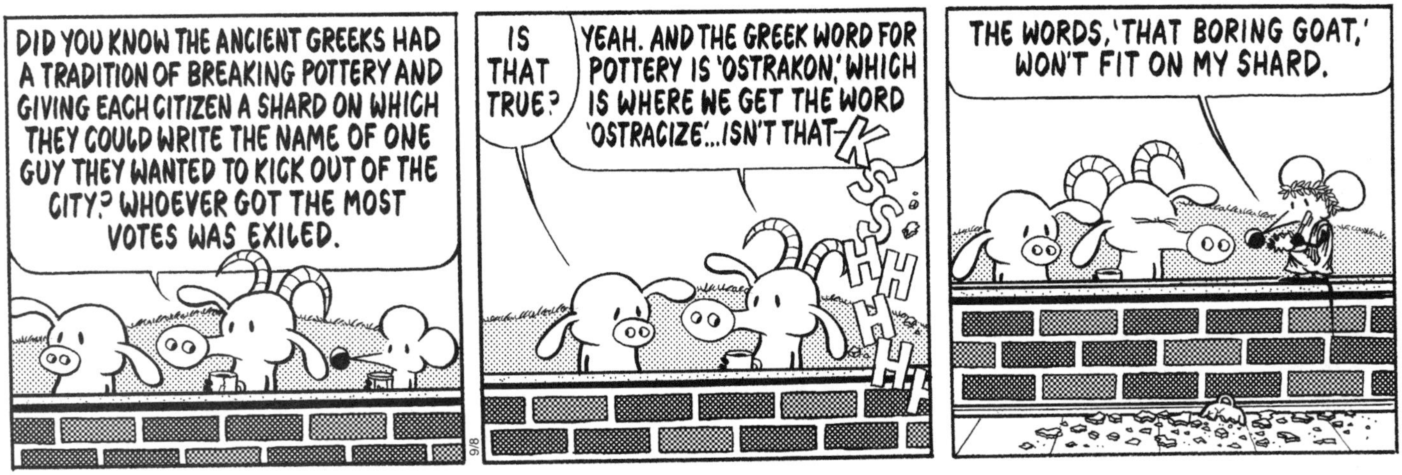
DID YOU KNOW THE ANCIENT GREEKS HAD A TRADITION OF BREAKING POTTERY AND GIVING EACH CITIZEN A SHARD ON WHICH THEY COULD WRITE THE NAME OF ONE GUY THEY WANTED TO KICK OUT OF THE CITY? WHOEVER GOT THE MOST VOTES WAS EXILED.
9/8
IS THAT TRUE?
YEAH. AND THE GREEK WORD FOR POTTERY IS 'OSTRAKON,' WHICH IS WHERE WE GET THE WORD 'OSTRACIZE'...ISN'T THAT—
KSSHHHH
THE WORDS, 'THAT BORING GOAT,' WON'T FIT ON MY SHARD.

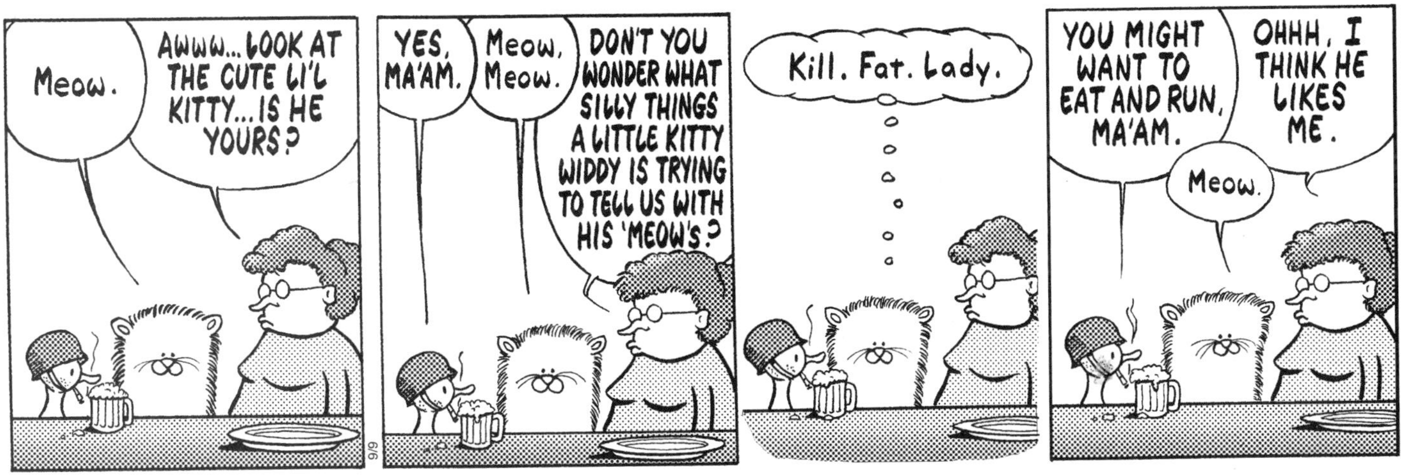
Meow.
AWWW...LOOK AT THE CUTE LI'L KITTY...IS HE YOURS?
9/9
YES, MA'AM.
Meow, Meow.
DON'T YOU WONDER WHAT SILLY THINGS A LITTLE KITTY WIDDY IS TRYING TO TELL US WITH HIS 'MEOW'S?
Kill. Fat. Lady.
YOU MIGHT WANT TO EAT AND RUN, MA'AM.
OHHH, I THINK HE LIKES ME.
Meow.

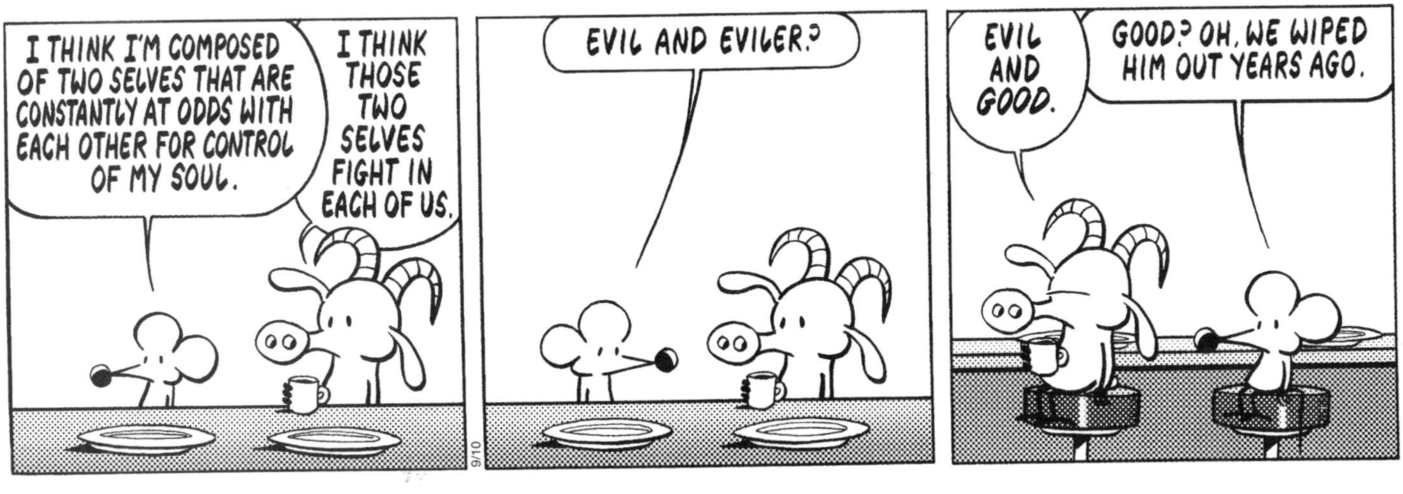
I THINK I'M COMPOSED OF TWO SELVES THAT ARE CONSTANTLY AT ODDS WITH EACH OTHER FOR CONTROL OF MY SOUL.
I THINK THOSE TWO SELVES FIGHT IN EACH OF US.
9/10
EVIL AND EVILER?
EVIL AND GOOD.
GOOD? OH, WE WIPED HIM OUT YEARS AGO.

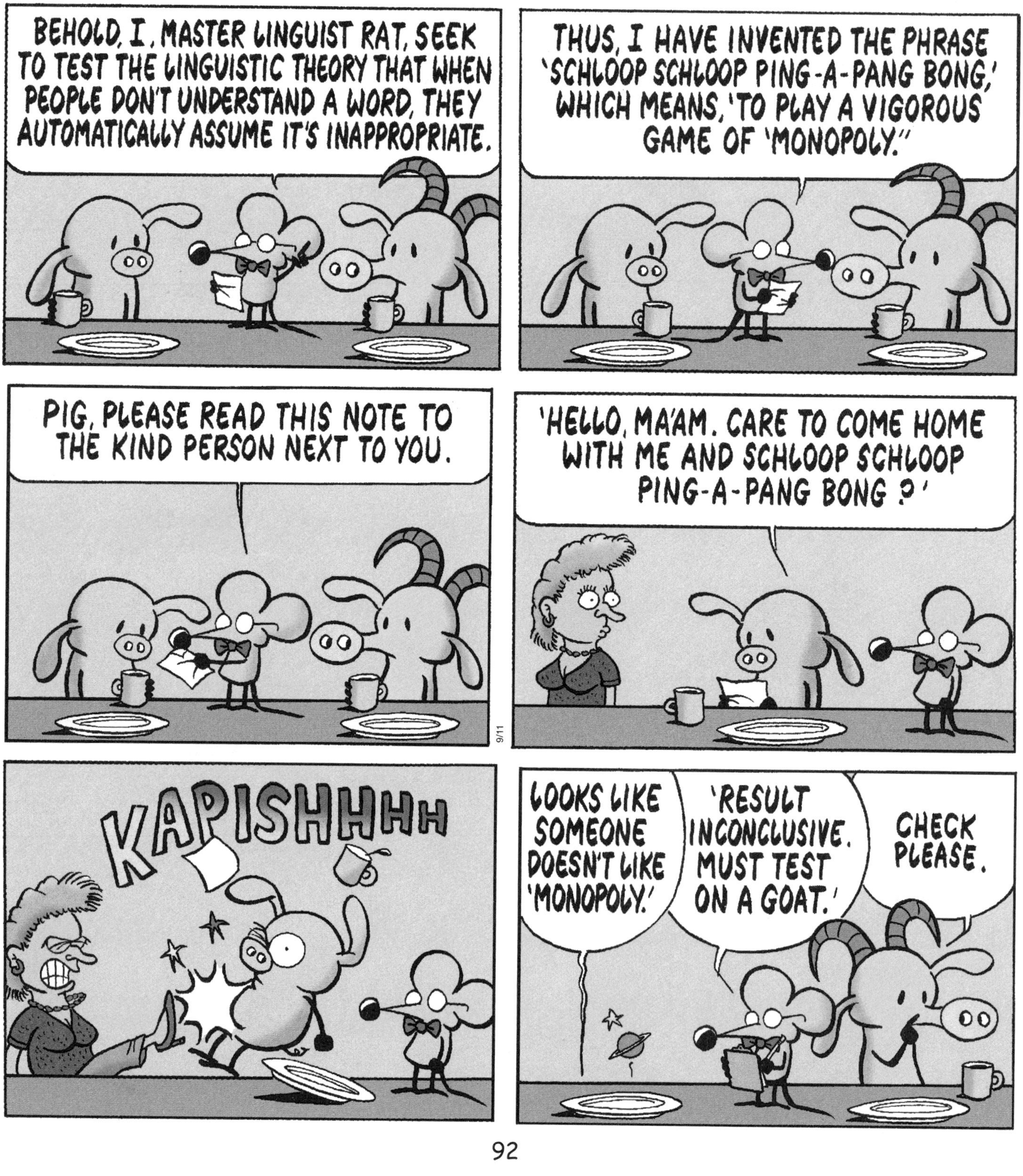
BEHOLD, I, MASTER LINGUIST RAT, SEEK TO TEST THE LINGUISTIC THEORY THAT WHEN PEOPLE DON'T UNDERSTAND A WORD, THEY AUTOMATICALLY ASSUME IT'S INAPPROPRIATE.
THUS, I HAVE INVENTED THE PHRASE 'SCHLOOP SCHLOOP PING-A-PANG BONG,' WHICH MEANS, 'TO PLAY A VIGOROUS GAME OF 'MONOPOLY.''
PIG, PLEASE READ THIS NOTE TO THE KIND PERSON NEXT TO YOU.
'HELLO, MA'AM. CARE TO COME HOME WITH ME AND SCHLOOP SCHLOOP PING-A-PANG BONG?'
9/11
KAPISHHHHH
LOOKS LIKE SOMEONE DOESN'T LIKE 'MONOPOLY.'
'RESULT INCONCLUSIVE. MUST TEST ON A GOAT.'
CHECK PLEASE.

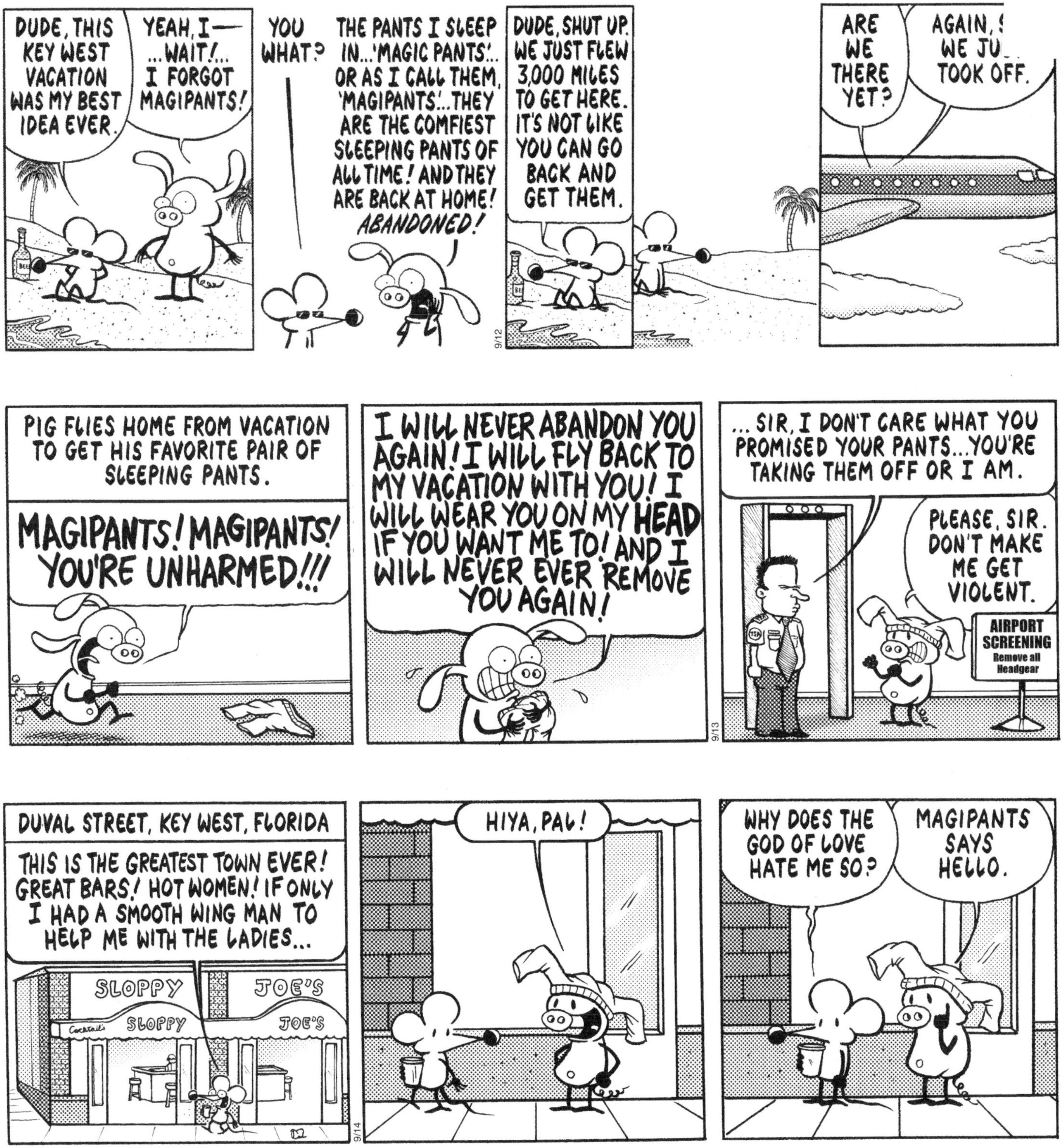
DUDE, THIS KEY WEST VACATION WAS MY BEST IDEA EVER.
YEAH, I— ...WAIT!... I FORGOT MAGIPANTS!
YOU WHAT?
THE PANTS I SLEEP IN...'MAGIC PANTS'... OR AS I CALL THEM, 'MAGIPANTS'...THEY ARE THE COMFIEST SLEEPING PANTS OF ALL TIME! AND THEY ARE BACK AT HOME! ABANDONED!
9/12
DUDE, SHUT UP. WE JUST FLEW 3,000 MILES TO GET HERE. IT'S NOT LIKE YOU CAN GO BACK AND GET THEM.
ARE WE THERE YET?
AGAIN, WE JU TOOK OFF.
PIG FLIES HOME FROM VACATION TO GET HIS FAVORITE PAIR OF SLEEPING PANTS.
MAGIPANTS! MAGIPANTS! YOU'RE UNHARMED!!!
I WILL NEVER ABANDON YOU AGAIN! I WILL FLY BACK TO MY VACATION WITH YOU! I WILL WEAR YOU ON MY HEAD IF YOU WANT ME TO! AND I WILL NEVER EVER REMOVE YOU AGAIN!
9/13
...SIR, I DON'T CARE WHAT YOU PROMISED YOUR PANTS...YOU'RE TAKING THEM OFF OR I AM.
PLEASE, SIR. DON'T MAKE ME GET VIOLENT.
AIRPORT SCREENING
Remove all Headgear
DUVAL STREET, KEY WEST, FLORIDA
THIS IS THE GREATEST TOWN EVER! GREAT BARS! HOT WOMEN! IF ONLY I HAD A SMOOTH WING MAN TO HELP ME WITH THE LADIES...
SLOPPY JOE'S
Cocktails SLOPPY JOE'S
9/14
HIYA, PAL!
WHY DOES THE GOD OF LOVE HATE ME SO?
MAGIPANTS SAYS HELLO.

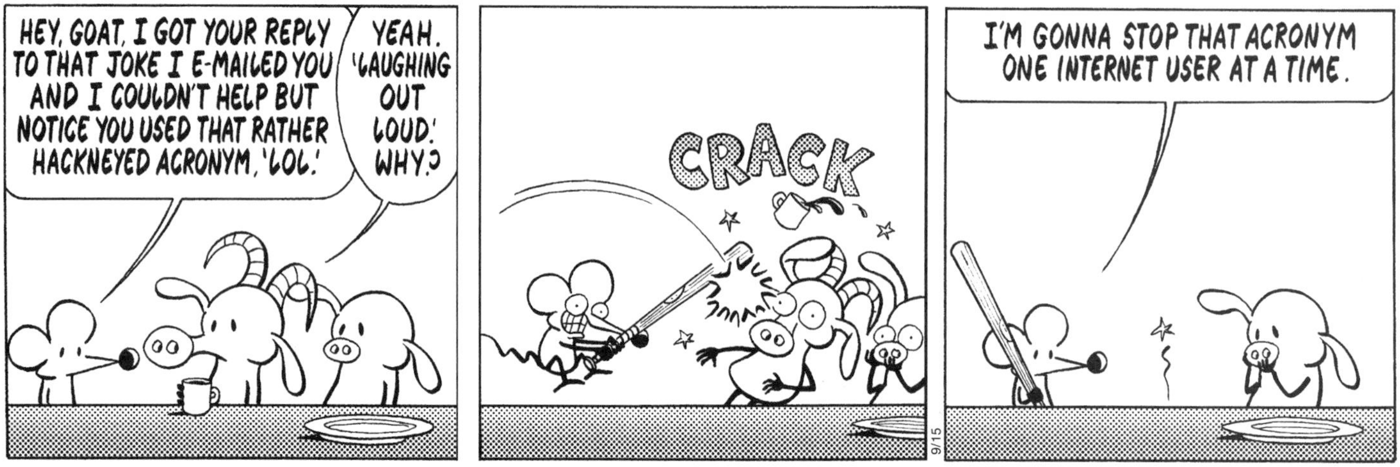
HEY, GOAT, I GOT YOUR REPLY TO THAT JOKE I E-MAILED YOU AND I COULDN'T HELP BUT NOTICE YOU USED THAT RATHER HACKNEYED ACRONYM, 'LOL.'
YEAH. 'LAUGHING OUT LOUD.' WHY?
CRACK
9/15
I'M GONNA STOP THAT ACRONYM ONE INTERNET USER AT A TIME.

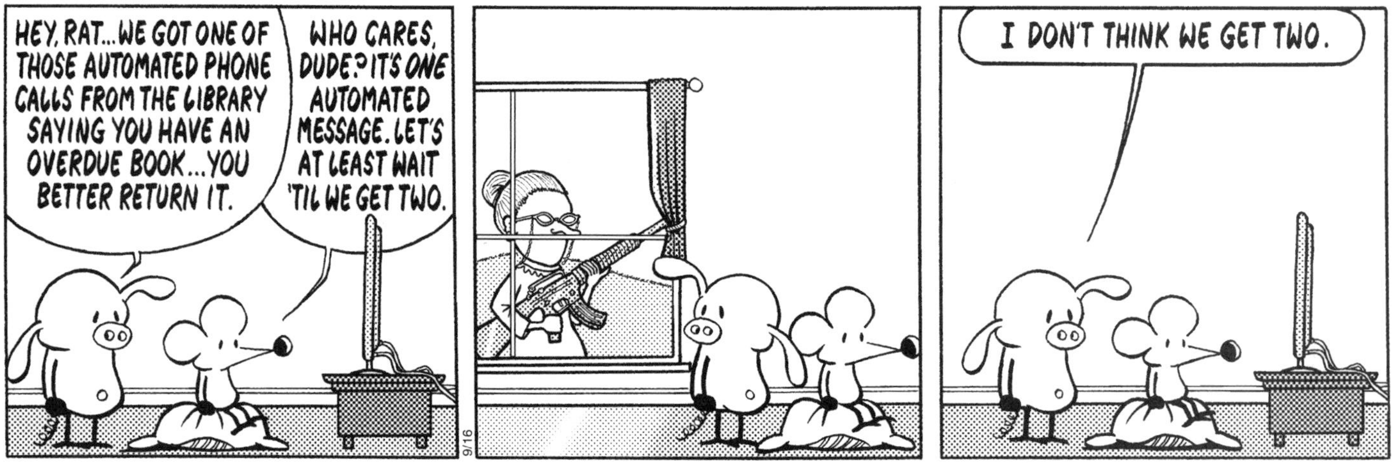
HEY, RAT... WE GOT ONE OF THOSE AUTOMATED PHONE CALLS FROM THE LIBRARY SAYING YOU HAVE AN OVERDUE BOOK... YOU BETTER RETURN IT.
WHO CARES, DUDE? IT'S ONE AUTOMATED MESSAGE. LET'S AT LEAST WAIT 'TIL WE GET TWO.
9/16
I DON'T THINK WE GET TWO.

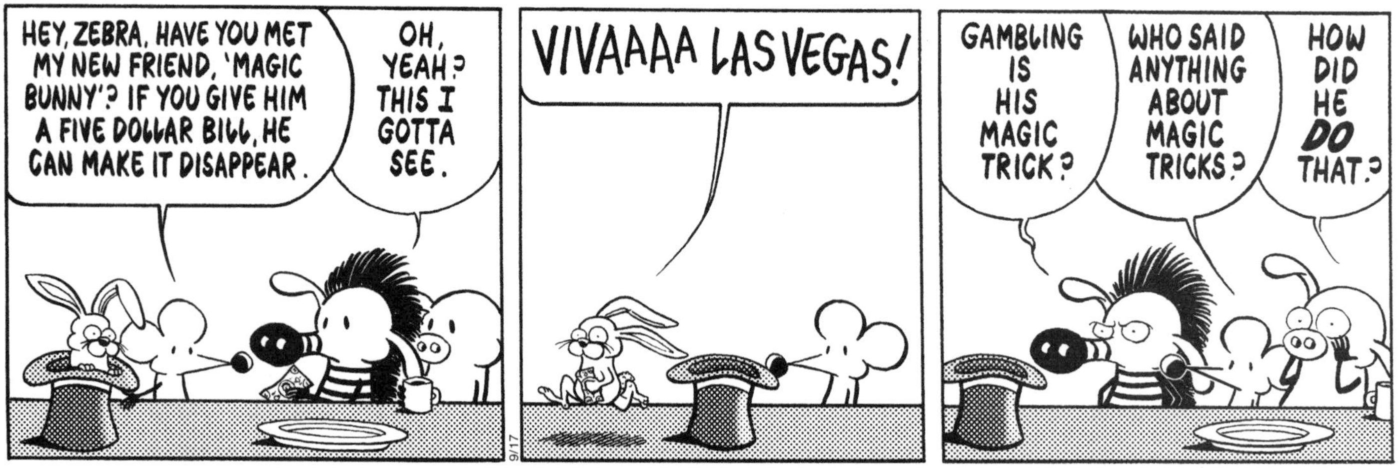
HEY, ZEBRA, HAVE YOU MET MY NEW FRIEND, 'MAGIC BUNNY'? IF YOU GIVE HIM A FIVE DOLLAR BILL, HE CAN MAKE IT DISAPPEAR.
OH, YEAH? THIS I GOTTA SEE.
9/17
VIVAAAA LAS VEGAS!
GAMBLING IS HIS MAGIC TRICK?
WHO SAID ANYTHING ABOUT MAGIC TRICKS?
HOW DID HE DO THAT?

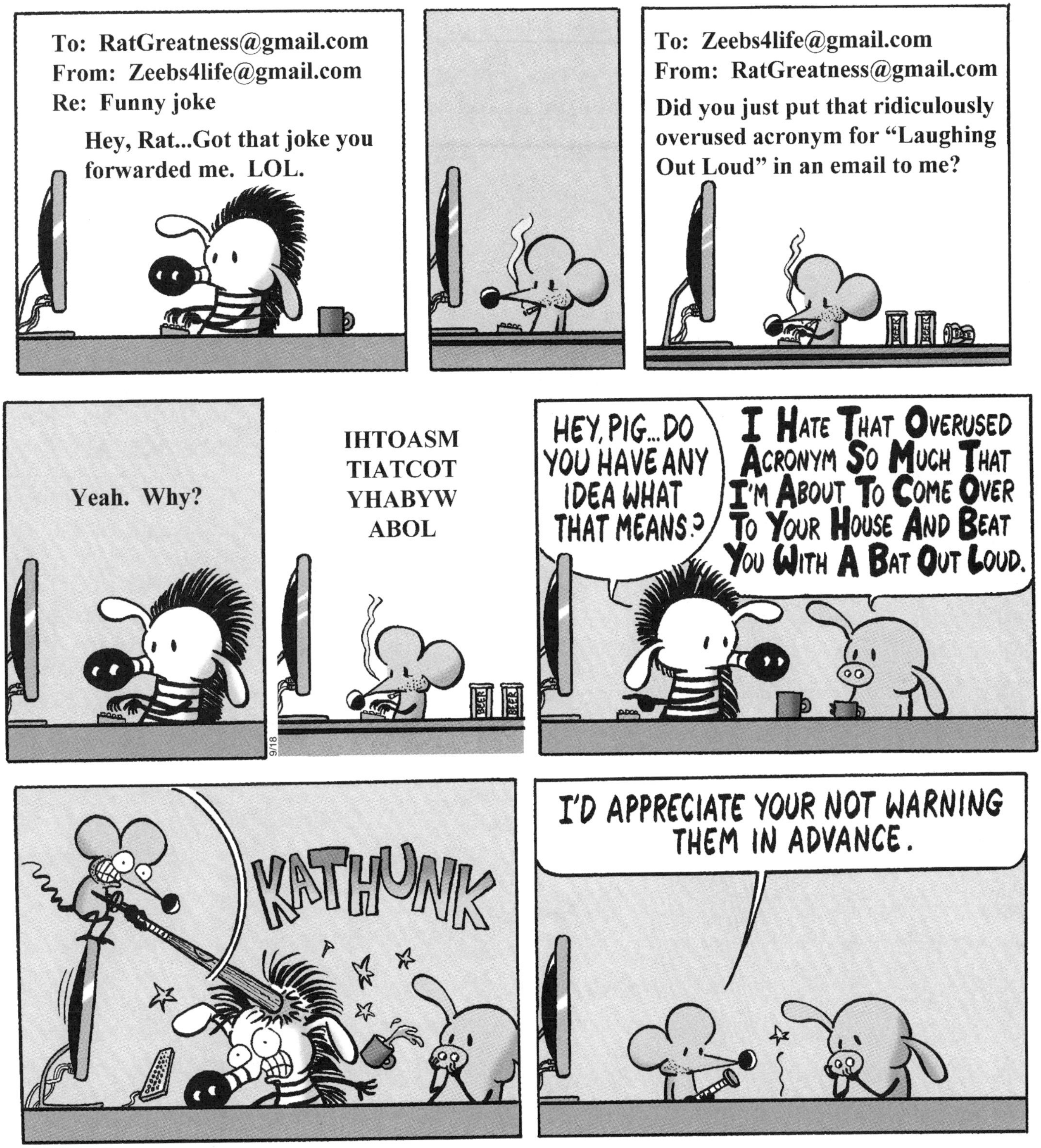
To: RatGreatness@gmail.com
From: Zeebs4life@gmail.com
Re: Funny joke
Hey, Rat...Got that joke you forwarded me. LOL.
To: Zeebs4life@gmail.com
From: RatGreatness@gmail.com
Did you just put that ridiculously overused acronym for "Laughing Out Loud" in an email to me?
Yeah. Why?
IHTOASM
TIATCOT
YHABYW
ABOL
HEY, PIG... DO YOU HAVE ANY IDEA WHAT THAT MEANS?
I HATE THAT OVERUSED ACRONYM SO MUCH THAT I'M ABOUT TO COME OVER TO YOUR HOUSE AND BEAT YOU WITH A BAT OUT LOUD.
KATHUNK
I'D APPRECIATE YOUR NOT WARNING THEM IN ADVANCE.

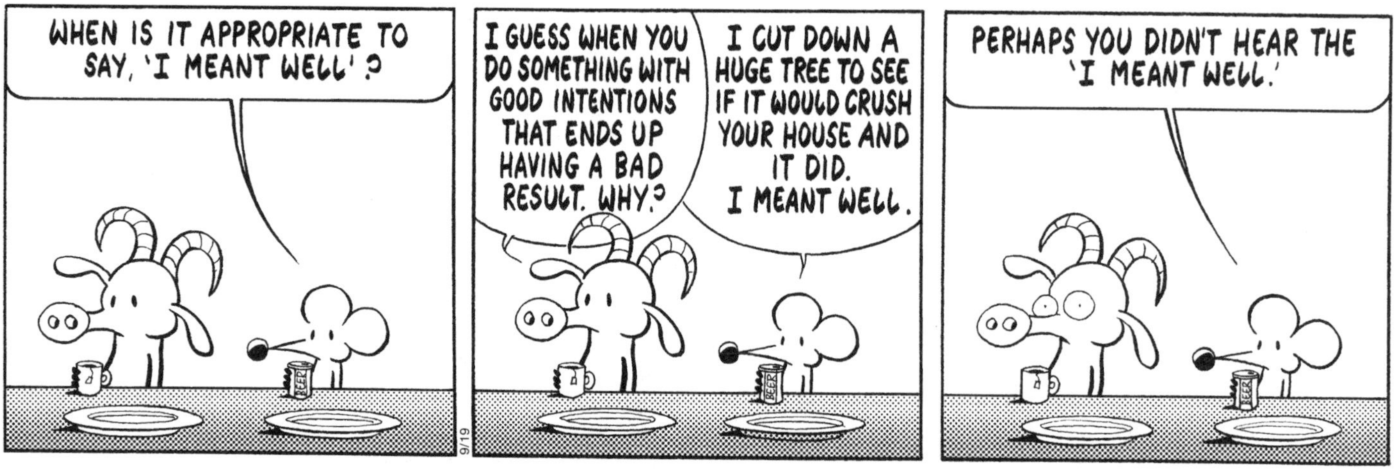
WHEN IS IT APPROPRIATE TO SAY, 'I MEANT WELL'?
I GUESS WHEN YOU DO SOMETHING WITH GOOD INTENTIONS THAT ENDS UP HAVING A BAD RESULT. WHY?
I CUT DOWN A HUGE TREE TO SEE IF IT WOULD CRUSH YOUR HOUSE AND IT DID. I MEANT WELL.
PERHAPS YOU DIDN'T HEAR THE 'I MEANT WELL.'
9/19

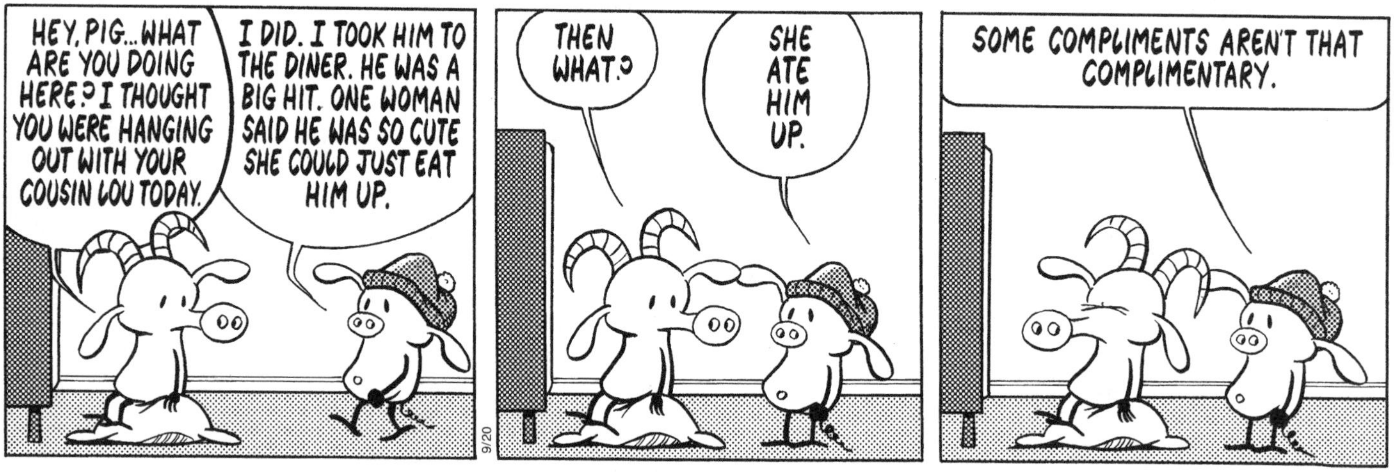
HEY, PIG...WHAT ARE YOU DOING HERE? I THOUGHT YOU WERE HANGING OUT WITH YOUR COUSIN LOU TODAY.
I DID. I TOOK HIM TO THE DINER. HE WAS A BIG HIT. ONE WOMAN SAID HE WAS SO CUTE SHE COULD JUST EAT HIM UP.
THEN WHAT?
SHE ATE HIM UP.
SOME COMPLIMENTS AREN'T THAT COMPLIMENTARY.
9/20

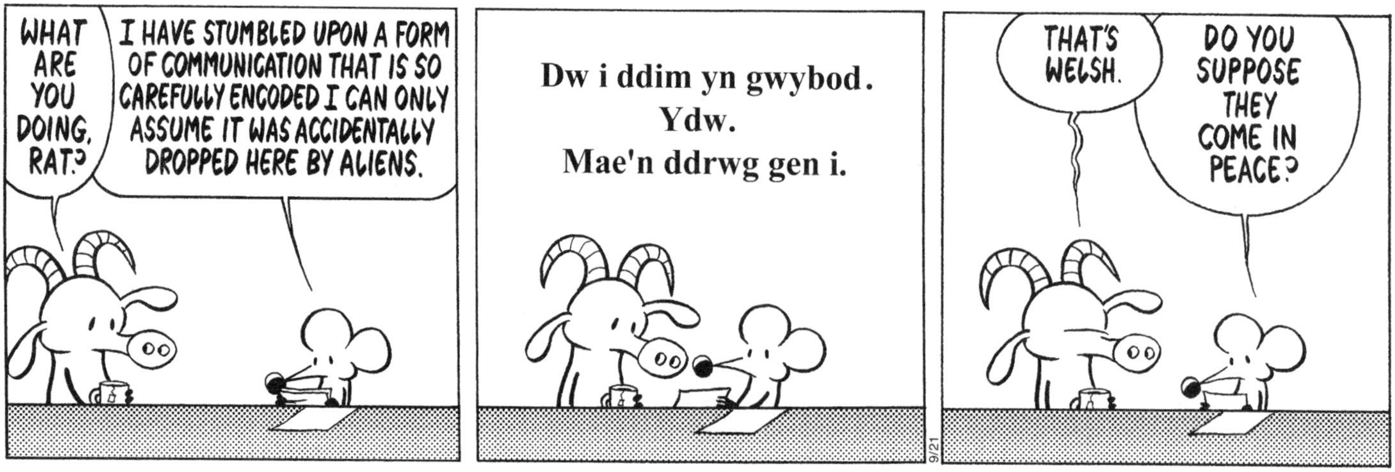
WHAT ARE YOU DOING, RAT?
I HAVE STUMBLED UPON A FORM OF COMMUNICATION THAT IS SO CAREFULLY ENCODED I CAN ONLY ASSUME IT WAS ACCIDENTALLY DROPPED HERE BY ALIENS.
Dw i ddim yn gwybod.
Ydw.
Mae'n ddrwg gen i.
THAT'S WELSH.
DO YOU SUPPOSE THEY COME IN PEACE?
9/21

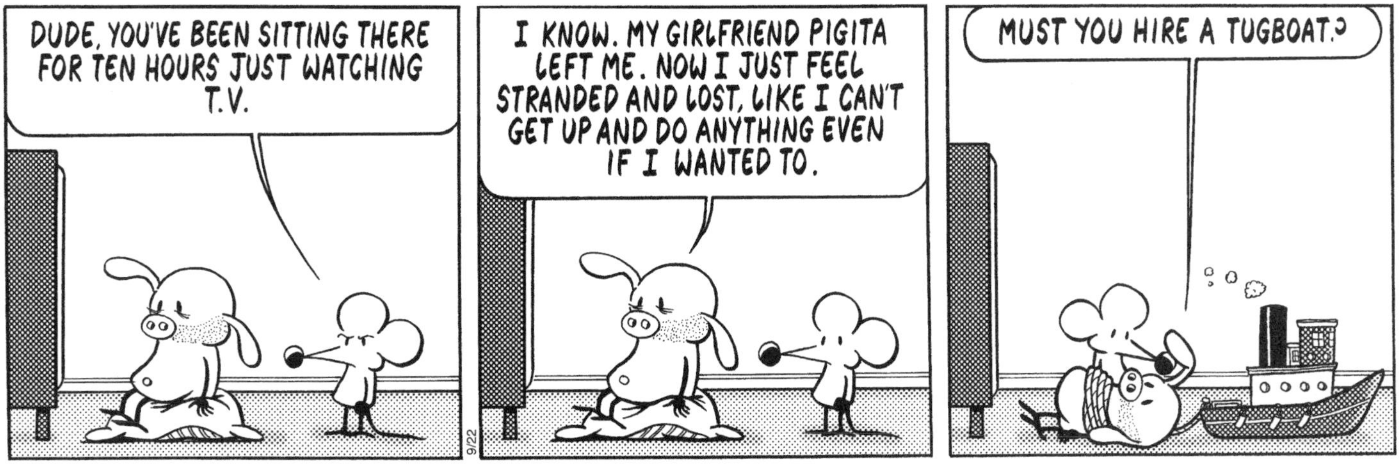
DUDE, YOU'VE BEEN SITTING THERE FOR TEN HOURS JUST WATCHING T.V.
I KNOW. MY GIRLFRIEND PIGITA LEFT ME. NOW I JUST FEEL STRANDED AND LOST, LIKE I CAN'T GET UP AND DO ANYTHING EVEN IF I WANTED TO.
MUST YOU HIRE A TUGBOAT?
9/22

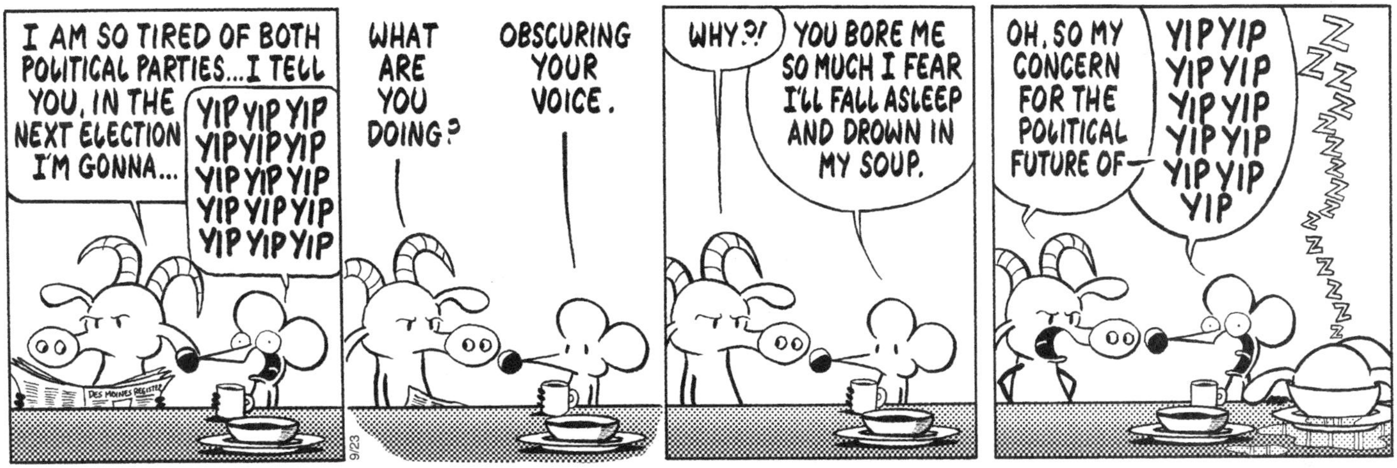
I AM SO TIRED OF BOTH POLITICAL PARTIES...I TELL YOU, IN THE NEXT ELECTION I'M GONNA...
YIP YIP YIP YIP YIP YIP YIP YIP YIP YIP YIP YIP YIP YIP YIP
DES MOINES REGISTER
WHAT ARE YOU DOING?
OBSCURING YOUR VOICE.
WHY?!
YOU BORE ME SO MUCH I FEAR I'LL FALL ASLEEP AND DROWN IN MY SOUP.
OH, SO MY CONCERN FOR THE POLITICAL FUTURE OF—
YIP YIP YIP YIP YIP YIP YIP YIP YIP YIP YIP
9/23

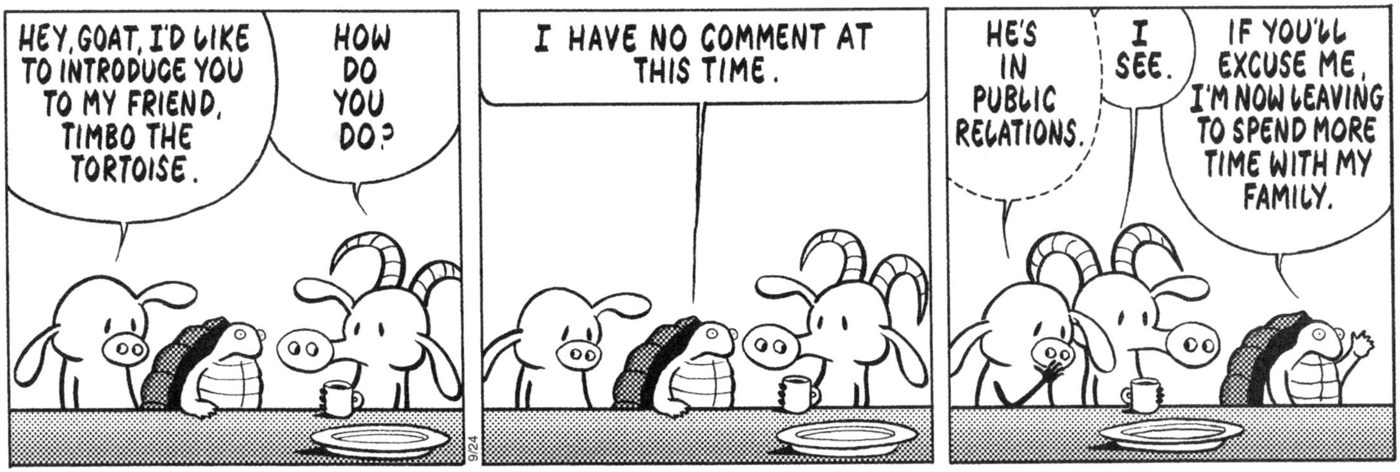
HEY, GOAT, I'D LIKE TO INTRODUCE YOU TO MY FRIEND, TIMBO THE TORTOISE.
HOW DO YOU DO?
I HAVE NO COMMENT AT THIS TIME.
HE'S IN PUBLIC RELATIONS.
I SEE.
IF YOU'LL EXCUSE ME, I'M NOW LEAVING TO SPEND MORE TIME WITH MY FAMILY.
9/24

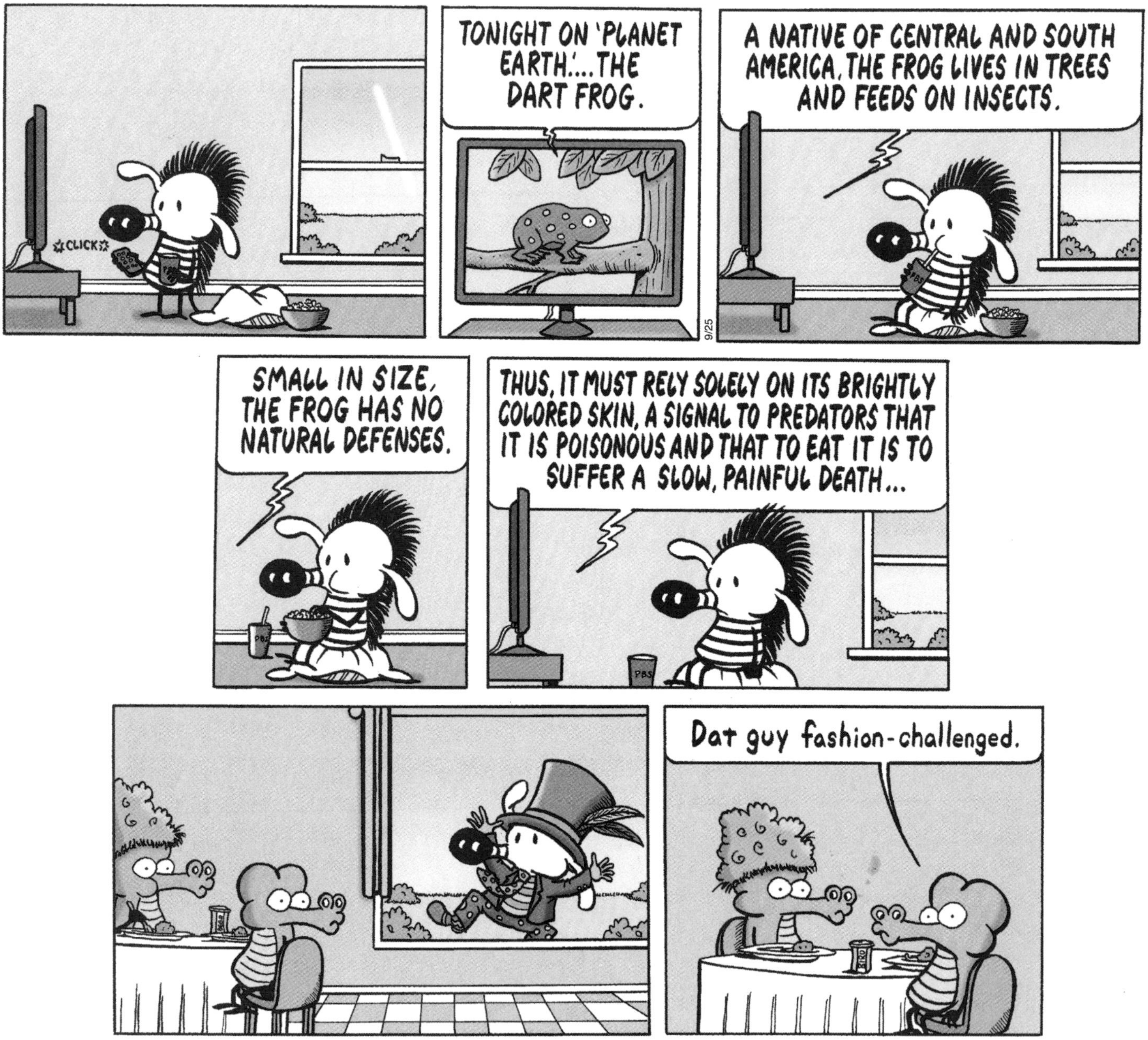
☆CLICK☆
TONIGHT ON 'PLANET EARTH.'...THE DART FROG.
9/25
A NATIVE OF CENTRAL AND SOUTH AMERICA, THE FROG LIVES IN TREES AND FEEDS ON INSECTS.
PBS
SMALL IN SIZE, THE FROG HAS NO NATURAL DEFENSES.
THUS, IT MUST RELY SOLELY ON ITS BRIGHTLY COLORED SKIN, A SIGNAL TO PREDATORS THAT IT IS POISONOUS AND THAT TO EAT IT IS TO SUFFER A SLOW, PAINFUL DEATH...
Dat guy fashion-challenged.

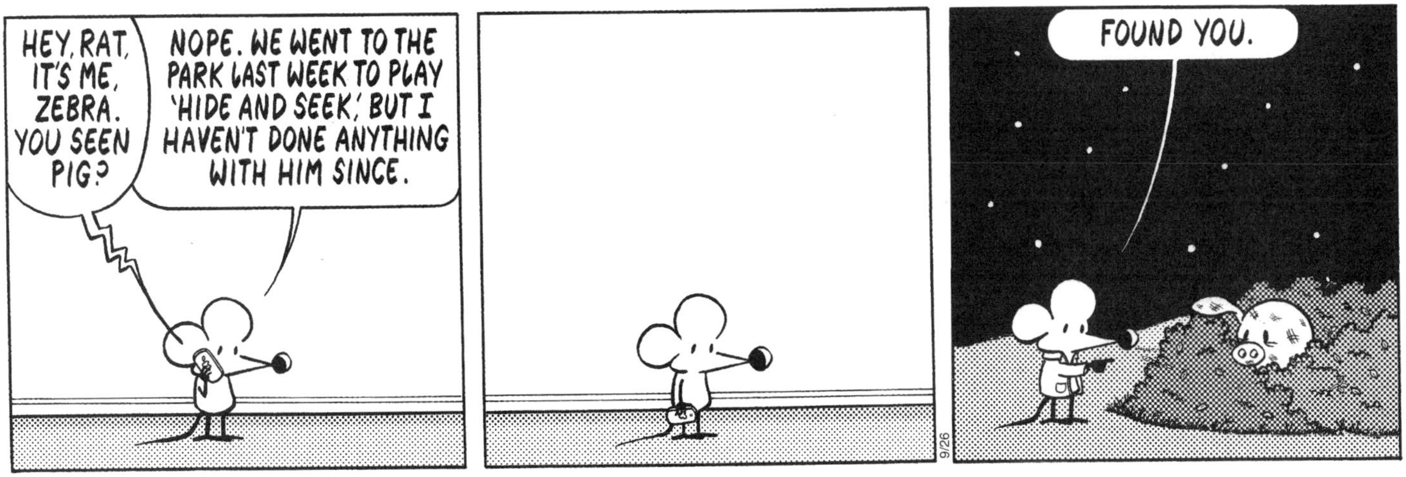

HEY, RAT, IT'S ME, ZEBRA. YOU SEEN PIG?
NOPE. WE WENT TO THE PARK LAST WEEK TO PLAY 'HIDE AND SEEK,' BUT I HAVEN'T DONE ANYTHING WITH HIM SINCE.
FOUND YOU.
9/26

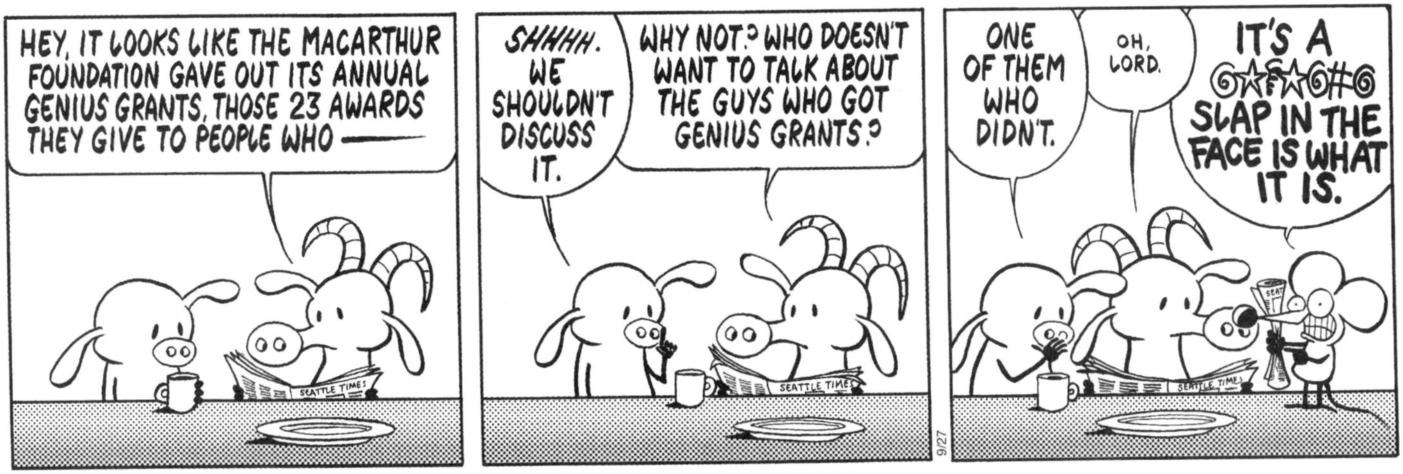

HEY, IT LOOKS LIKE THE MACARTHUR FOUNDATION GAVE OUT ITS ANNUAL GENIUS GRANTS, THOSE 23 AWARDS THEY GIVE TO PEOPLE WHO —
SHHHH. WE SHOULDN'T DISCUSS IT.
WHY NOT? WHO DOESN'T WANT TO TALK ABOUT THE GUYS WHO GOT GENIUS GRANTS?
ONE OF THEM WHO DIDN'T.
OH, LORD.
IT'S A
SLAP IN THE FACE IS WHAT IT IS.
SEATTLE TIMES
9/27

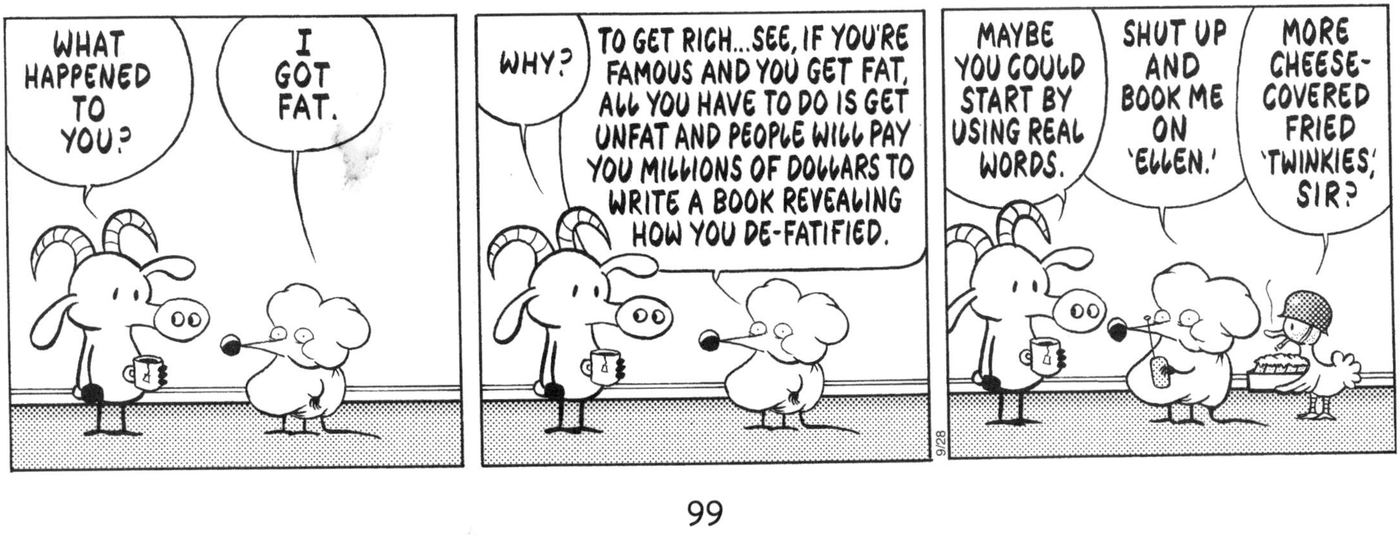

WHAT HAPPENED TO YOU?
I GOT FAT.
WHY?
TO GET RICH... SEE, IF YOU'RE FAMOUS AND YOU GET FAT, ALL YOU HAVE TO DO IS GET UNFAT AND PEOPLE WILL PAY YOU MILLIONS OF DOLLARS TO WRITE A BOOK REVEALING HOW YOU DE-FATIFIED.
MAYBE YOU COULD START BY USING REAL WORDS.
SHUT UP AND BOOK ME ON 'ELLEN.'
MORE CHEESE-COVERED FRIED 'TWINKIES,' SIR?
9/28

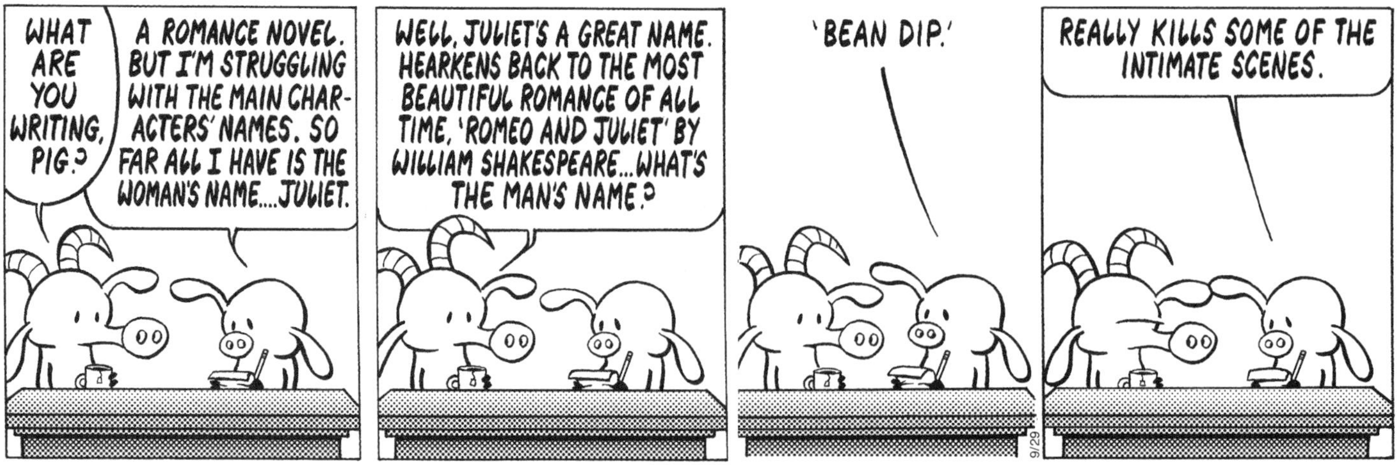
WHAT ARE YOU WRITING, PIG?
A ROMANCE NOVEL. BUT I'M STRUGGLING WITH THE MAIN CHARACTERS' NAMES. SO FAR ALL I HAVE IS THE WOMAN'S NAME....JULIET.
WELL, JULIET'S A GREAT NAME. HEARKENS BACK TO THE MOST BEAUTIFUL ROMANCE OF ALL TIME, 'ROMEO AND JULIET' BY WILLIAM SHAKESPEARE...WHAT'S THE MAN'S NAME?
'BEAN DIP.'
REALLY KILLS SOME OF THE INTIMATE SCENES.
9/29

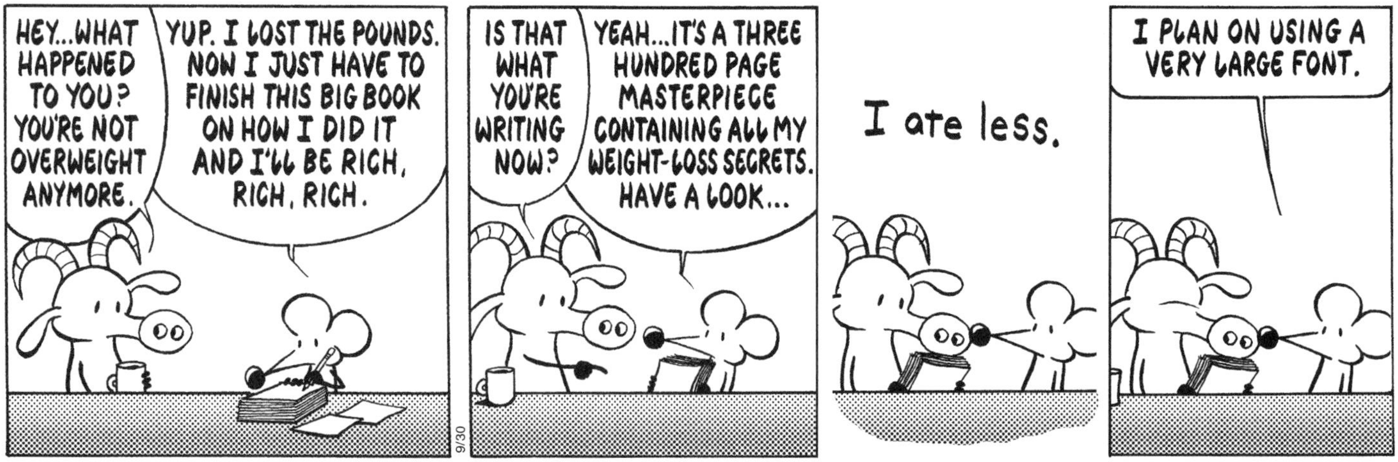
HEY...WHAT HAPPENED TO YOU? YOU'RE NOT OVERWEIGHT ANYMORE.
YUP. I LOST THE POUNDS. NOW I JUST HAVE TO FINISH THIS BIG BOOK ON HOW I DID IT AND I'LL BE RICH, RICH, RICH.
IS THAT WHAT YOU'RE WRITING NOW?
YEAH...IT'S A THREE HUNDRED PAGE MASTERPIECE CONTAINING ALL MY WEIGHT-LOSS SECRETS. HAVE A LOOK...
I ate less.
I PLAN ON USING A VERY LARGE FONT.
9/30

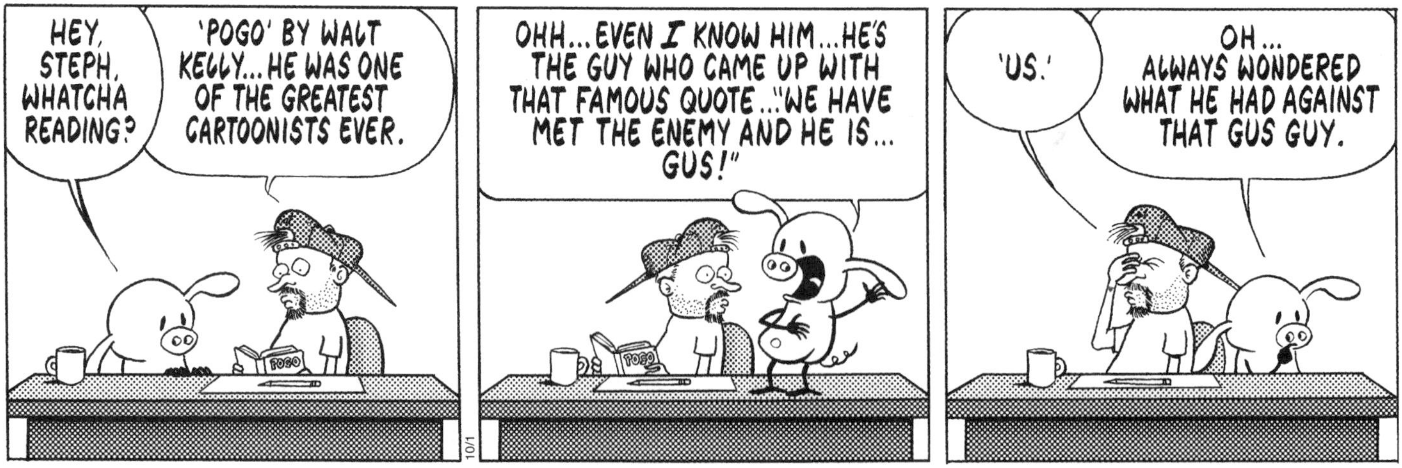
HEY, STEPH, WHATCHA READING?
'POGO' BY WALT KELLY...HE WAS ONE OF THE GREATEST CARTOONISTS EVER.
POGO
OHH...EVEN I KNOW HIM...HE'S THE GUY WHO CAME UP WITH THAT FAMOUS QUOTE..."WE HAVE MET THE ENEMY AND HE IS... GUS!"
'US.'
OH... ALWAYS WONDERED WHAT HE HAD AGAINST THAT GUS GUY.
10/1

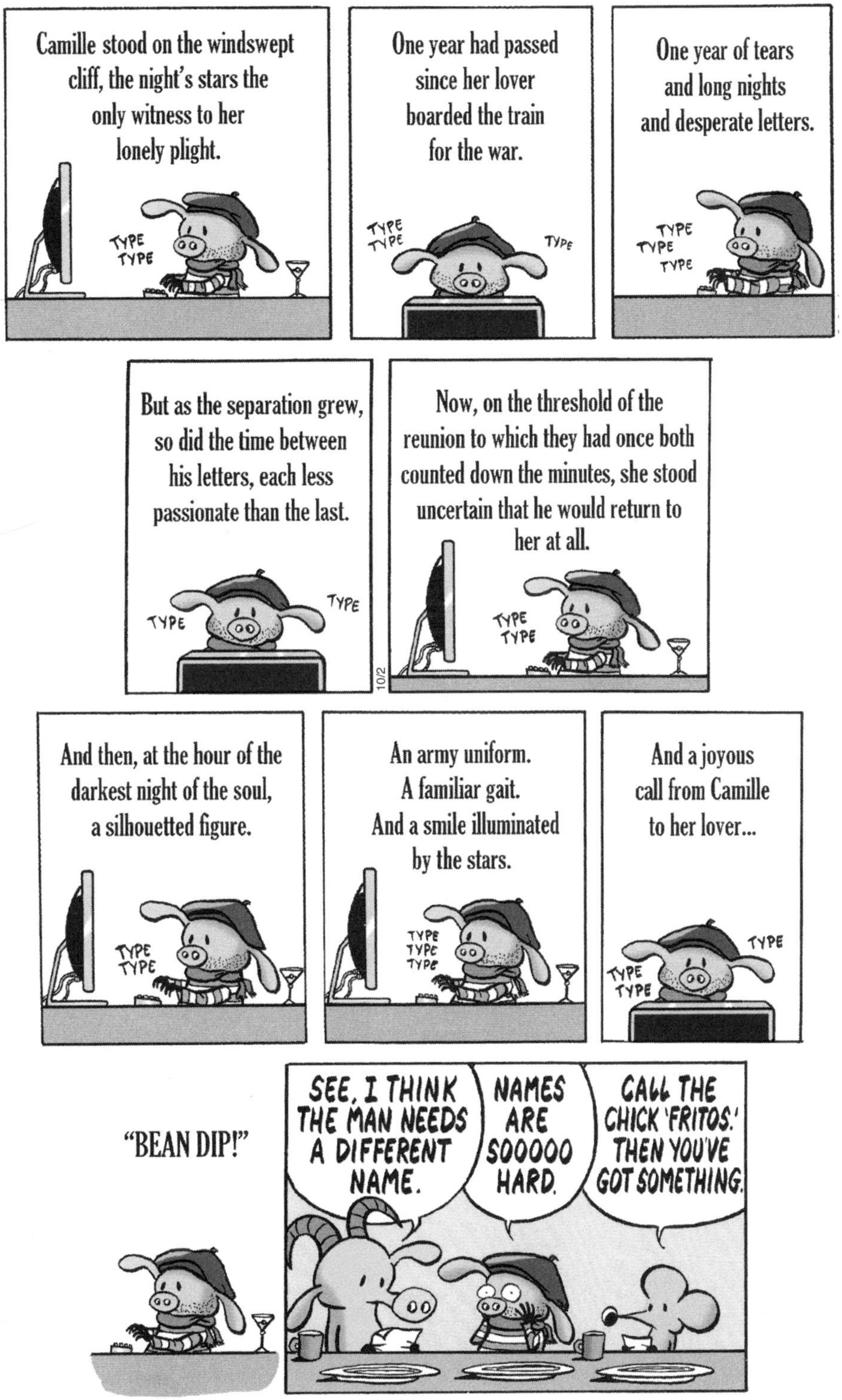

Camille stood on the windswept cliff, the night's stars the only witness to her lonely plight.
TYPE TYPE
One year had passed since her lover boarded the train for the war.
TYPE TYPE
TYPE
One year of tears and long nights and desperate letters.
TYPE TYPE TYPE
But as the separation grew, so did the time between his letters, each less passionate than the last.
TYPE
TYPE
Now, on the threshold of the reunion to which they had once both counted down the minutes, she stood uncertain that he would return to her at all.
TYPE TYPE
10/2
And then, at the hour of the darkest night of the soul, a silhouetted figure.
TYPE TYPE
An army uniform. A familiar gait. And a smile illuminated by the stars.
TYPE TYPE TYPE
And a joyous call from Camille to her lover...
TYPE
TYPE TYPE
"BEAN DIP!"
SEE, I THINK THE MAN NEEDS A DIFFERENT NAME.
NAMES ARE SOOOOO HARD.
CALL THE CHICK 'FRITOS.' THEN YOU'VE GOT SOMETHING.

Panel 1: OKAY, WE'VE GOT MOTHER'S DAY, FATHER'S DAY, BLACK HISTORY MONTH, GRANDMOTHER'S DAY, EARTH DAY, HISPANIC HERITAGE MONTH, SECRETARY'S DAY AND WOMEN'S HISTORY MONTH.

SO?

Panel 2: SO IS THERE ONE PERSON, THING OR GROUP THAT DOESN'T YET HAVE ITS OWN SPECIAL DAY ON THE CALENDAR?

I DON'T KNOW. IS THERE?

Panel 3: GARBANZO BEANS.

Panel 4: GOODBYE.

FRIDAY, OCTOBER 7TH IS GARBANZO BEAN DAY!!

ONLY FOUR DAYS TO BUY A CARD!

10/3

Panel 5: HEY, BOSS MAN...DO WE GET OFF THURSDAY AND FRIDAY THIS WEEK, OR JUST FRIDAY?

YOU GET OFF NEITHER.

JOE'S ROASTERY

10/4

Panel 6: I QUIT.

JOE'S ROASTERY

Panel 7: NO ONE DISRESPECTS GARBANZO BEAN FRIDAY.

Panel 8: HEY, ABOUT YOUR CELEBRATION OF THE GARBANZO BEAN ON FRIDAY, YOU MIGHT WANT TO KNOW THAT HALF THE COUNTRY DOESN'T EVEN CALL THEM THAT. THEY CALL THEM 'CHICKPEAS.'

Panel 9:

Panel 10: CRACK

10/5

Panel 11: IT'S BEST TO DESTROY THESE SPLINTER MOVEMENTS EARLY.

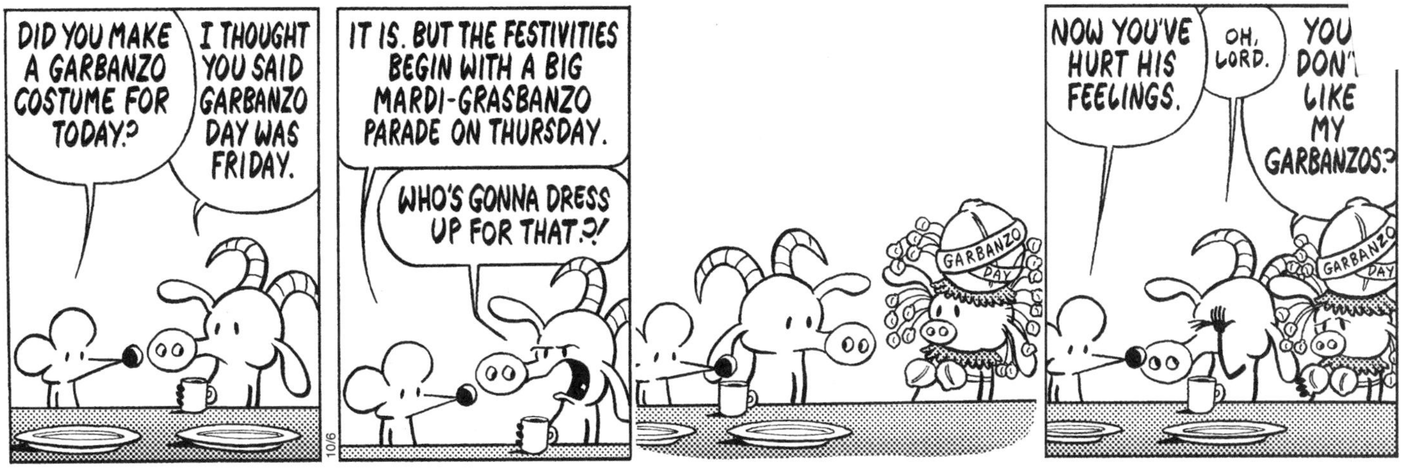
DID YOU MAKE A GARBANZO COSTUME FOR TODAY?
I THOUGHT YOU SAID GARBANZO DAY WAS FRIDAY.
IT IS. BUT THE FESTIVITIES BEGIN WITH A BIG MARDI-GRASBANZO PARADE ON THURSDAY.
WHO'S GONNA DRESS UP FOR THAT?!
10/6
GARBANZO DAY
NOW YOU'VE HURT HIS FEELINGS.
OH, LORD.
YOU DON'T LIKE MY GARBANZOS?

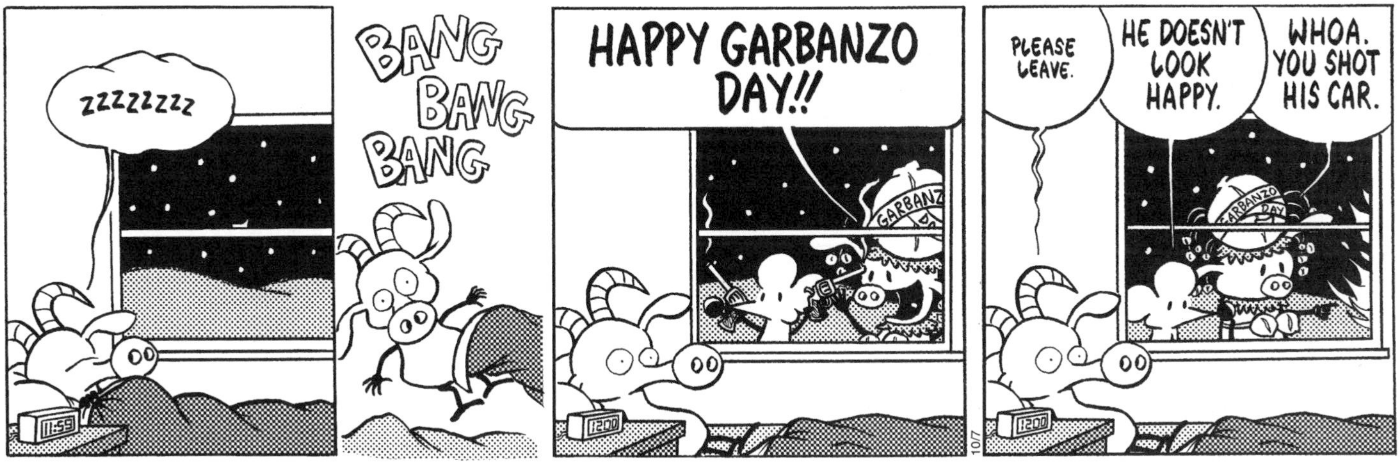
ZZZZZZZZ
11:59
BANG BANG BANG
HAPPY GARBANZO DAY!!
12:00
PLEASE LEAVE.
HE DOESN'T LOOK HAPPY.
WHOA. YOU SHOT HIS CAR.
10/7

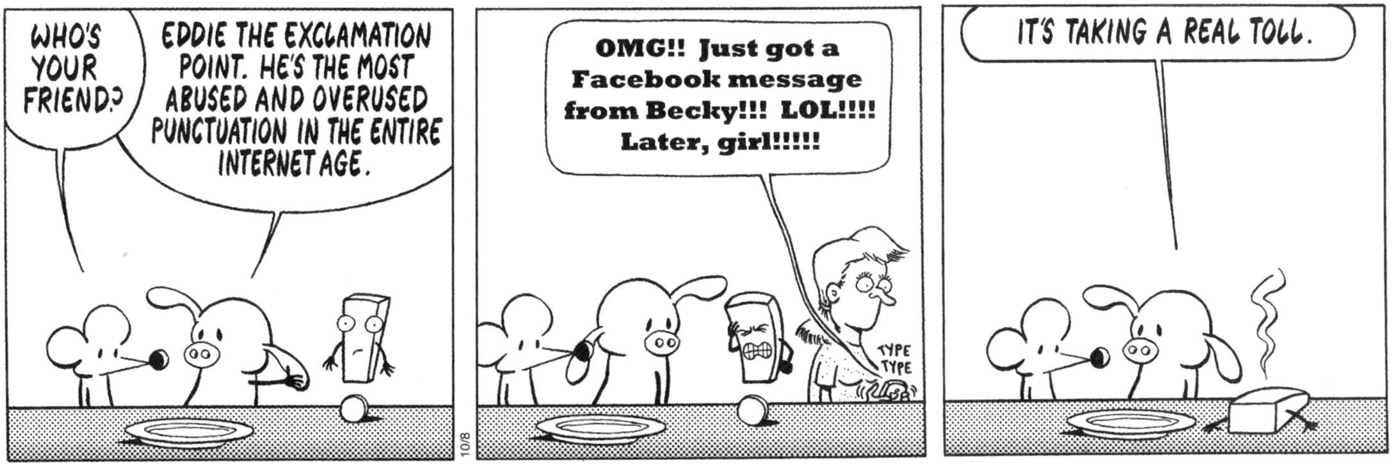
WHO'S YOUR FRIEND?
EDDIE THE EXCLAMATION POINT. HE'S THE MOST ABUSED AND OVERUSED PUNCTUATION IN THE ENTIRE INTERNET AGE.
10/8
OMG!! Just got a Facebook message from Becky!!! LOL!!!! Later, girl!!!!!
TYPE TYPE
IT'S TAKING A REAL TOLL.

RIIIIIIIIIIING...
10/9
HELLO, RAT...THIS IS YOUR MOTHER.
HiMom WhaddyaWant?
WELL, I'M JUST CALLING TO GIVE YOU SOME SAD NEWS...YOUR AUNT CLAIRE PASSED AWAY LAST—
That'sBad IsThatIt?
WELL, I JUST THOUGHT YOU MIGHT WANT THE ADDRESS WHERE YOU CAN SEND FLOWERS AND—
Nope I'llGoogleIt.
YOU WHAT?
GottaGo
YOU DON'T WANT THE—
ByeNow!
CLICK
WHEN YOU'RE OVER YOUR CELL PHONE MINUTES, YOU'RE OVER YOUR CELL PHONE MINUTES.

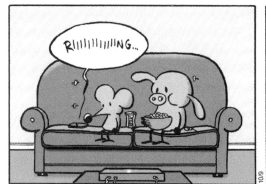

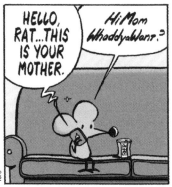

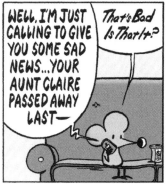

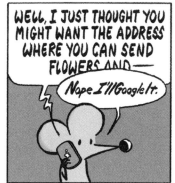

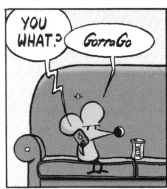

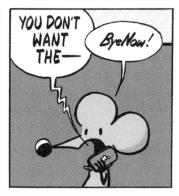

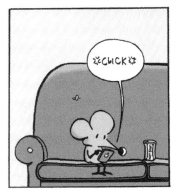

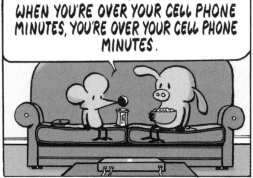

Panel 1: I THINK IT'S TIME TO MOVE TO A DIFFERENT PART OF THE COMICS PAGE.

Panel 2: WHY DO YOU SAY THAT? / THIRD PANEL.

Panel 3:

Panel 4: AND IT USED TO BE SUCH A NICE NEIGHBORHOOD.

Panel 5: WHERE WERE YOU THIS MORNING? / I GOT A JOB ENTERTAINING LITTLE KIDS AS A BIRTHDAY PARTY CLOWN. HERE, LOOK AT THE COSTUME I MADE...

Panel 6:

Panel 7: YOU ARE NOT WEARING THAT TO CHILDREN'S BIRTHDAY PARTIES. / I CALL MYSELF 'DISTURBO, THE CLOWN YOU DON'T HIRE TWICE.'

Panel 8: OKAY, PIG, WE NEED TO START DIVIDING UP ALL THE HOUSEHOLD CHORES, SO I TOOK THE TIME TO MAKE THIS LIST.

Panel 9: YOU HAVE ME DOING ALL THE CHORES. / NO I DON'T.

Panel 10: THEN WHICH ONES ARE YOURS? / I MAKE THE LIST.

Panel 11: IT DOES TAKE A LOT OF WORK TO WRITE 'PIG' FIFTY TIMES. / YEAH. PUT 'MASSAGE RAT'S WRITING HAND' ON THERE, WILL YOU?

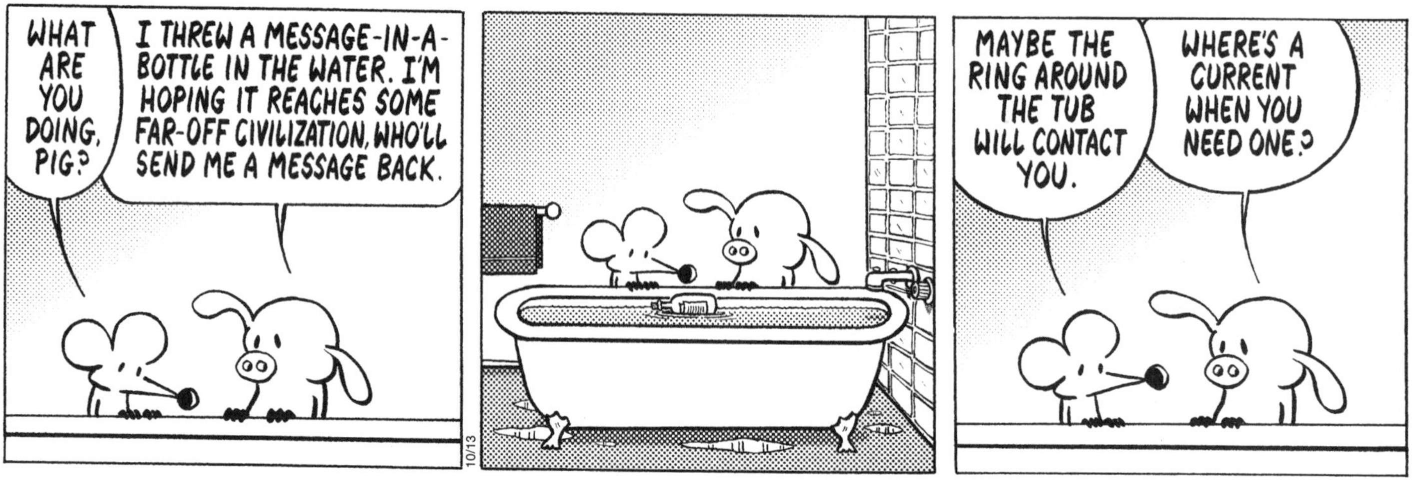
WHAT ARE YOU DOING, PIG?
I THREW A MESSAGE-IN-A-BOTTLE IN THE WATER. I'M HOPING IT REACHES SOME FAR-OFF CIVILIZATION, WHO'LL SEND ME A MESSAGE BACK.
10/13
MAYBE THE RING AROUND THE TUB WILL CONTACT YOU.
WHERE'S A CURRENT WHEN YOU NEED ONE?

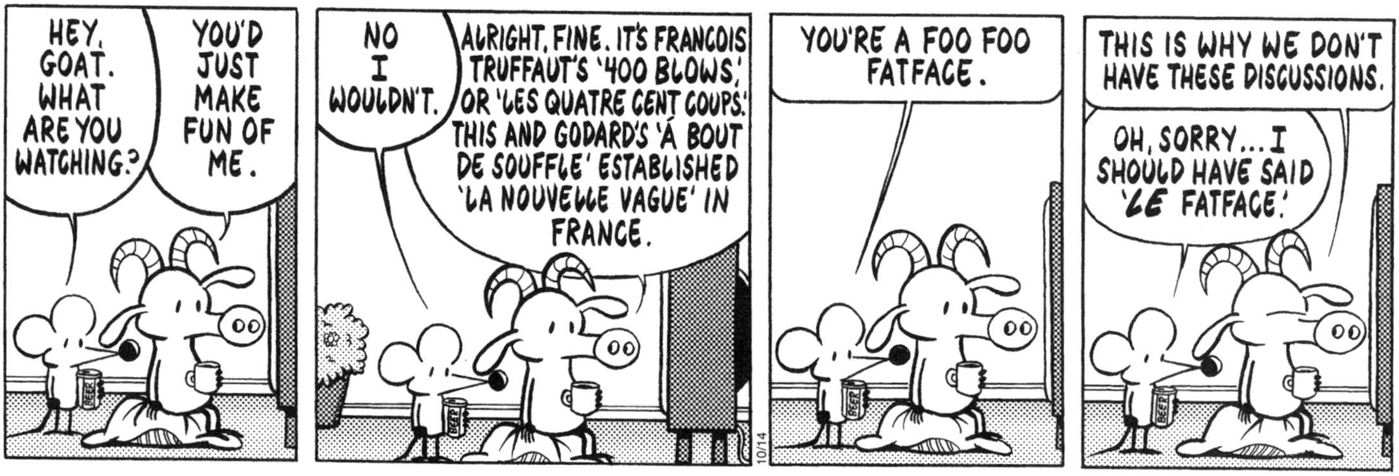
HEY, GOAT. WHAT ARE YOU WATCHING?
YOU'D JUST MAKE FUN OF ME.
NO I WOULDN'T.
ALRIGHT, FINE. IT'S FRANCOIS TRUFFAUT'S '400 BLOWS,' OR 'LES QUATRE CENT COUPS.' THIS AND GODARD'S 'Á BOUT DE SOUFFLE' ESTABLISHED 'LA NOUVELLE VAGUE' IN FRANCE.
10/14
YOU'RE A FOO FOO FATFACE.
THIS IS WHY WE DON'T HAVE THESE DISCUSSIONS.
OH, SORRY... I SHOULD HAVE SAID 'LE FATFACE.'

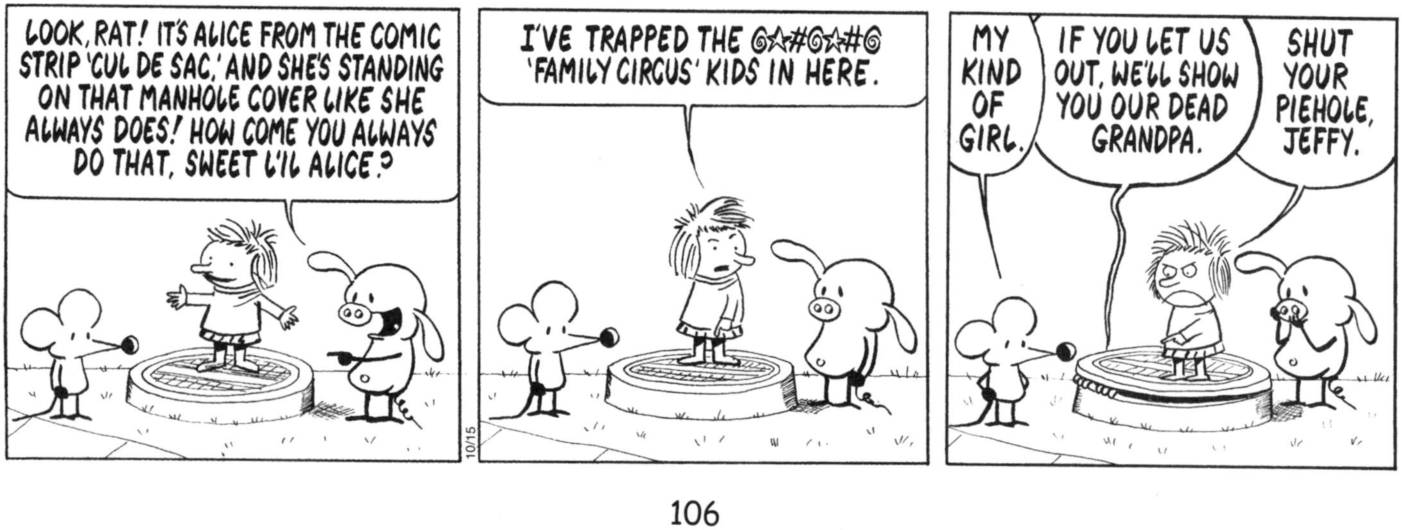
LOOK, RAT! IT'S ALICE FROM THE COMIC STRIP 'CUL DE SAC,' AND SHE'S STANDING ON THAT MANHOLE COVER LIKE SHE ALWAYS DOES! HOW COME YOU ALWAYS DO THAT, SWEET L'IL ALICE?
10/15
I'VE TRAPPED THE @☆#@☆#@ 'FAMILY CIRCUS' KIDS IN HERE.
MY KIND OF GIRL.
IF YOU LET US OUT, WE'LL SHOW YOU OUR DEAD GRANDPA.
SHUT YOUR PIEHOLE, JEFFY.

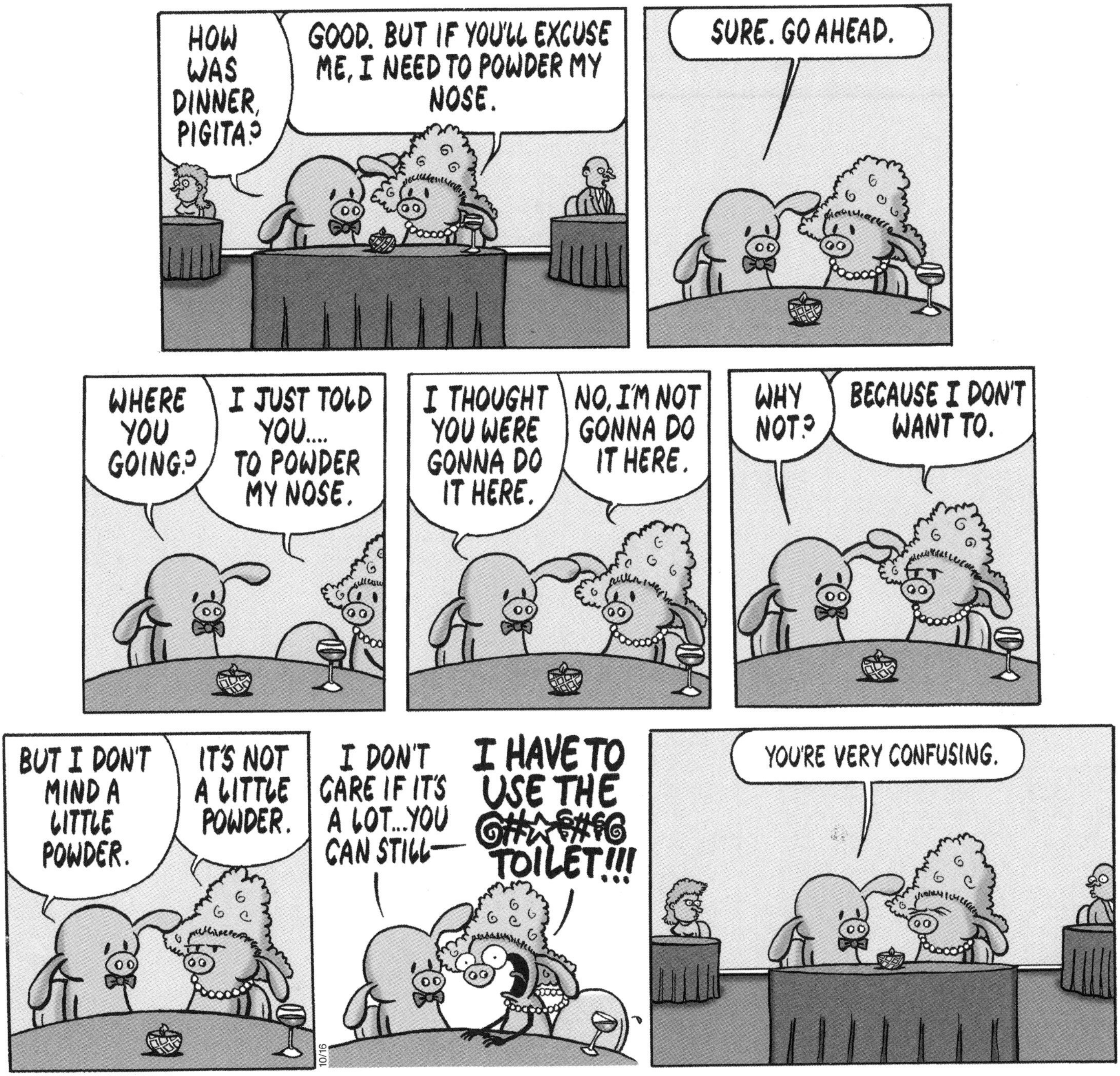
HOW WAS DINNER, PIGITA?
GOOD. BUT IF YOU'LL EXCUSE ME, I NEED TO POWDER MY NOSE.
SURE. GO AHEAD.
WHERE YOU GOING?
I JUST TOLD YOU.... TO POWDER MY NOSE.
I THOUGHT YOU WERE GONNA DO IT HERE.
NO, I'M NOT GONNA DO IT HERE.
WHY NOT?
BECAUSE I DON'T WANT TO.
BUT I DON'T MIND A LITTLE POWDER.
IT'S NOT A LITTLE POWDER.
I DON'T CARE IF IT'S A LOT...YOU CAN STILL—
I HAVE TO USE THE @#☆$#@ TOILET!!!
10/16
YOU'RE VERY CONFUSING.

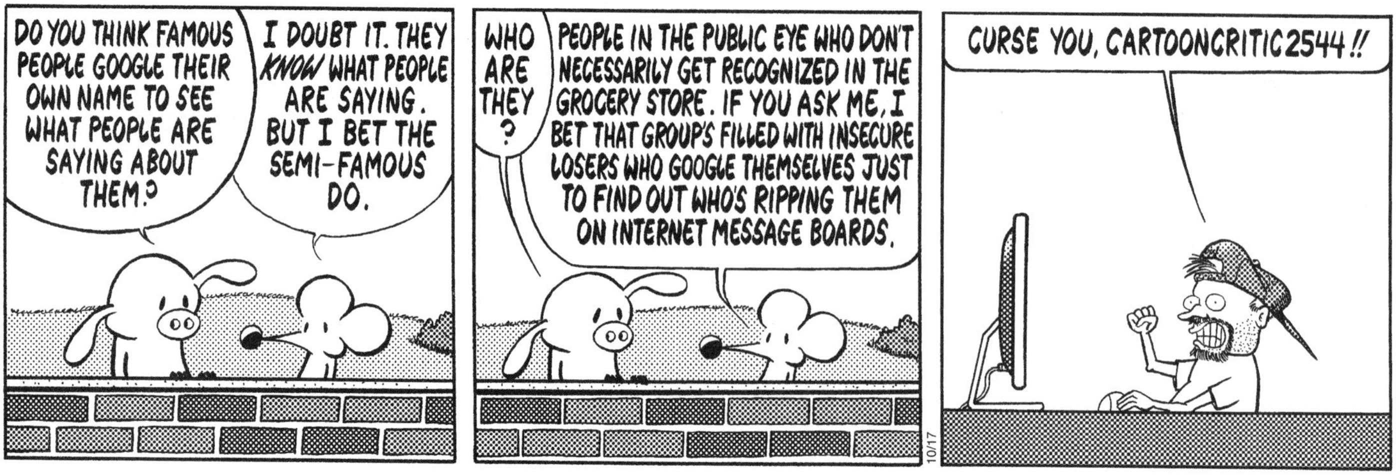
DO YOU THINK FAMOUS PEOPLE GOOGLE THEIR OWN NAME TO SEE WHAT PEOPLE ARE SAYING ABOUT THEM?
I DOUBT IT. THEY *KNOW* WHAT PEOPLE ARE SAYING. BUT I BET THE SEMI-FAMOUS DO.
WHO ARE THEY?
PEOPLE IN THE PUBLIC EYE WHO DON'T NECESSARILY GET RECOGNIZED IN THE GROCERY STORE. IF YOU ASK ME, I BET THAT GROUP'S FILLED WITH INSECURE LOSERS WHO GOOGLE THEMSELVES JUST TO FIND OUT WHO'S RIPPING THEM ON INTERNET MESSAGE BOARDS.
CURSE YOU, CARTOONCRITIC2544!!
10/17

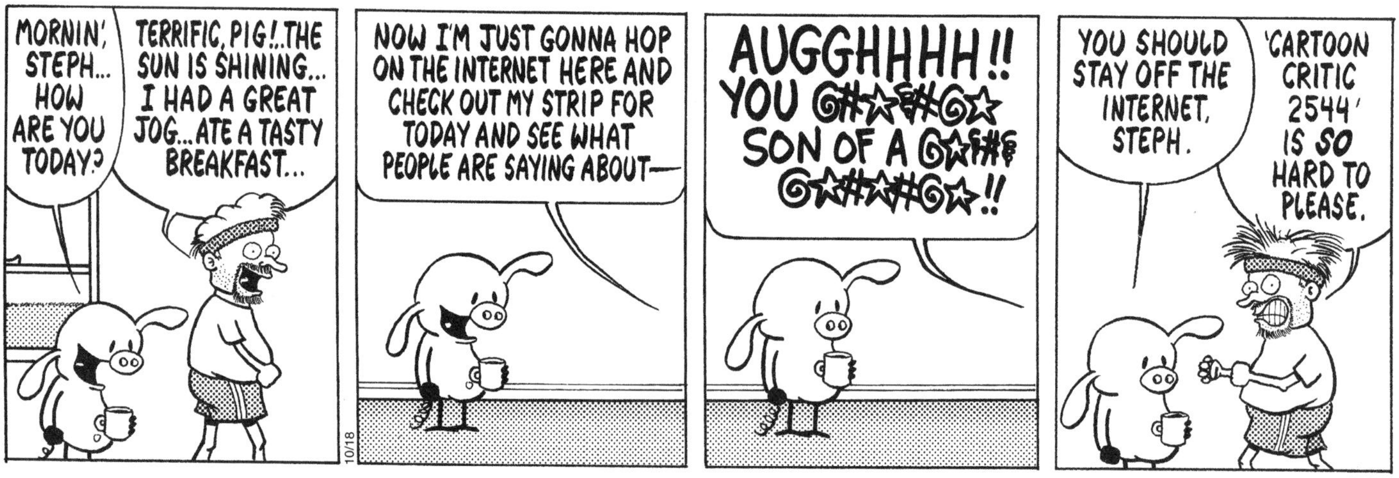
MORNIN', STEPH... HOW ARE YOU TODAY?
TERRIFIC, PIG!..THE SUN IS SHINING... I HAD A GREAT JOG...ATE A TASTY BREAKFAST...
NOW I'M JUST GONNA HOP ON THE INTERNET HERE AND CHECK OUT MY STRIP FOR TODAY AND SEE WHAT PEOPLE ARE SAYING ABOUT—
AUGGHHHH!!
YOU
SON OF A
!!
YOU SHOULD STAY OFF THE INTERNET, STEPH.
'CARTOON CRITIC 2544' IS *SO* HARD TO PLEASE.
10/18

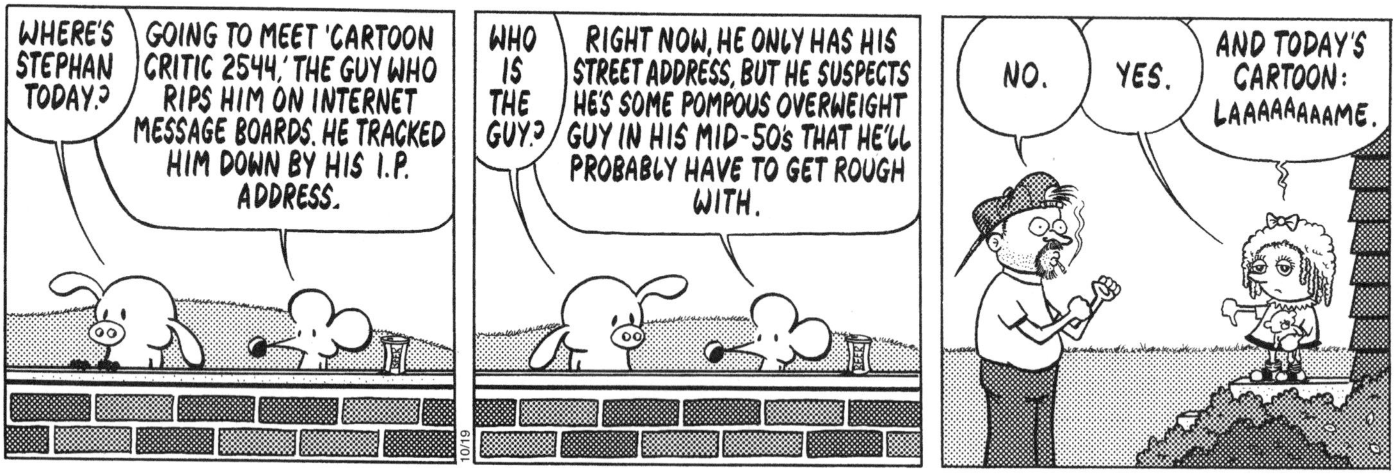
WHERE'S STEPHAN TODAY?
GOING TO MEET 'CARTOON CRITIC 2544,' THE GUY WHO RIPS HIM ON INTERNET MESSAGE BOARDS. HE TRACKED HIM DOWN BY HIS I.P. ADDRESS.
WHO IS THE GUY?
RIGHT NOW, HE ONLY HAS HIS STREET ADDRESS, BUT HE SUSPECTS HE'S SOME POMPOUS OVERWEIGHT GUY IN HIS MID-50'S THAT HE'LL PROBABLY HAVE TO GET ROUGH WITH.
NO.
YES.
AND TODAY'S CARTOON: LAAAAAAAAME.
10/19

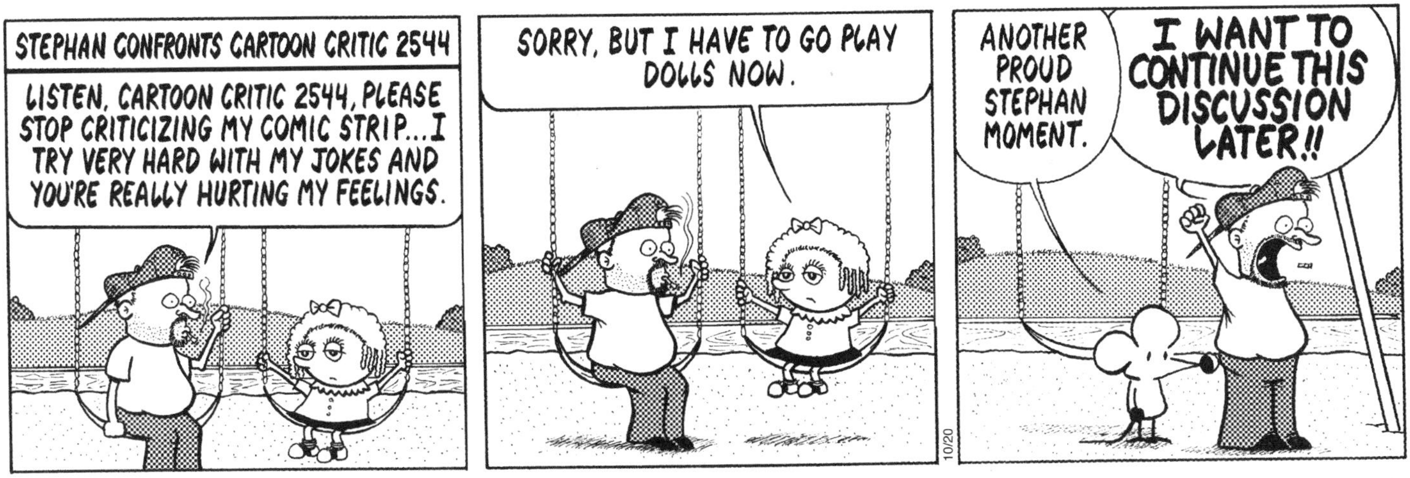
STEPHAN CONFRONTS CARTOON CRITIC 2544
LISTEN, CARTOON CRITIC 2544, PLEASE STOP CRITICIZING MY COMIC STRIP...I TRY VERY HARD WITH MY JOKES AND YOU'RE REALLY HURTING MY FEELINGS.
SORRY, BUT I HAVE TO GO PLAY DOLLS NOW.
10/20
ANOTHER PROUD STEPHAN MOMENT.
I WANT TO CONTINUE THIS DISCUSSION LATER!!

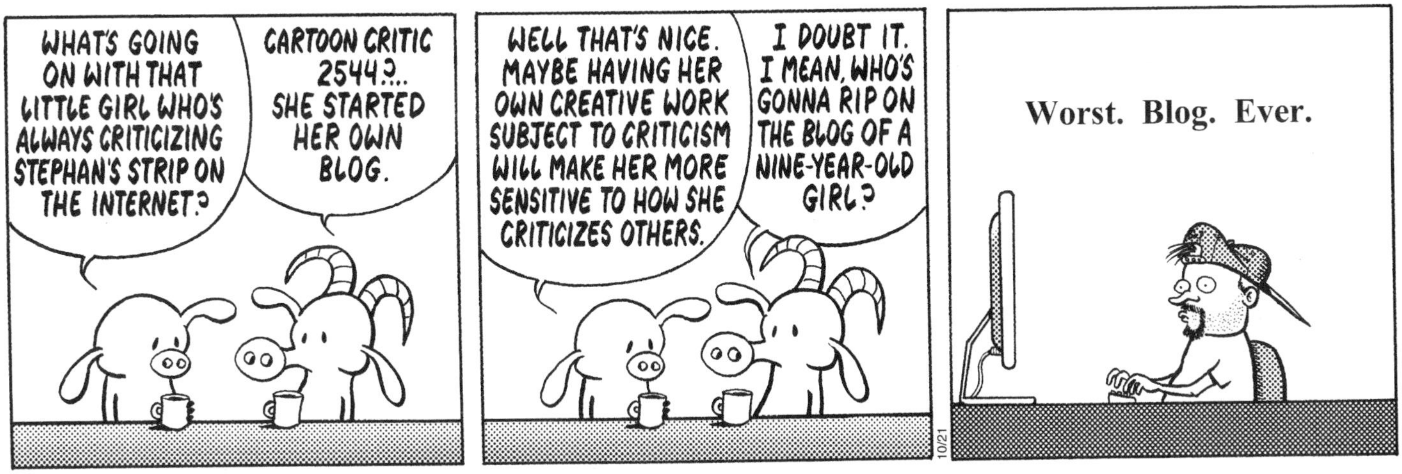
WHAT'S GOING ON WITH THAT LITTLE GIRL WHO'S ALWAYS CRITICIZING STEPHAN'S STRIP ON THE INTERNET?
CARTOON CRITIC 2544?... SHE STARTED HER OWN BLOG.
WELL THAT'S NICE. MAYBE HAVING HER OWN CREATIVE WORK SUBJECT TO CRITICISM WILL MAKE HER MORE SENSITIVE TO HOW SHE CRITICIZES OTHERS.
I DOUBT IT. I MEAN, WHO'S GONNA RIP ON THE BLOG OF A NINE-YEAR-OLD GIRL?
10/21
Worst. Blog. Ever.

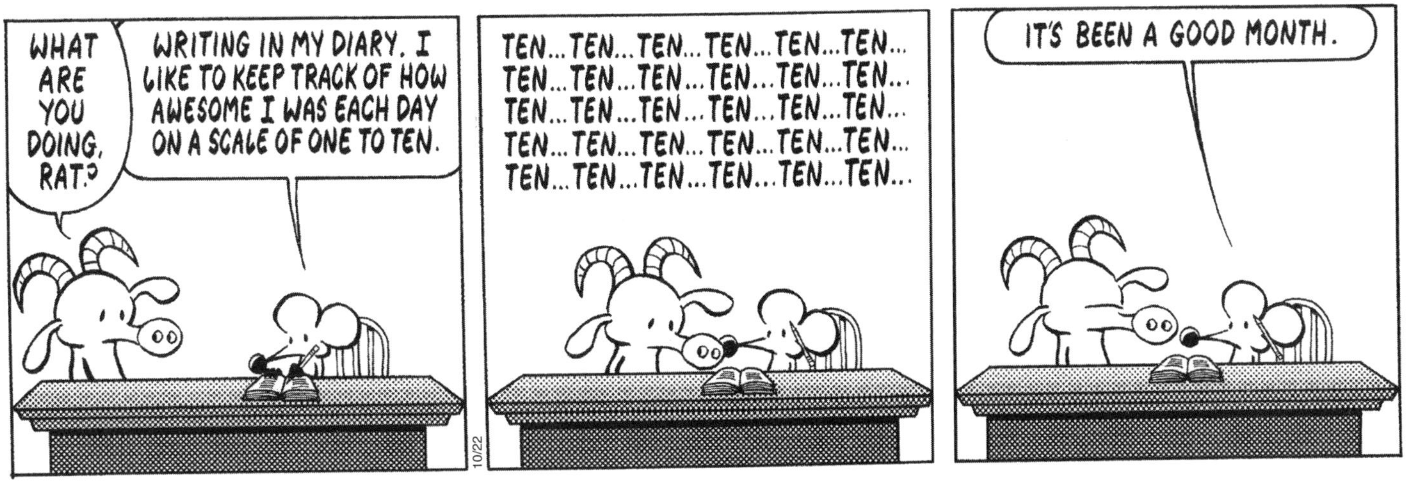
WHAT ARE YOU DOING, RAT?
WRITING IN MY DIARY. I LIKE TO KEEP TRACK OF HOW AWESOME I WAS EACH DAY ON A SCALE OF ONE TO TEN.
10/22
TEN...TEN...TEN...TEN...TEN...TEN... TEN...TEN...TEN...TEN...TEN...TEN... TEN...TEN...TEN...TEN...TEN...TEN... TEN...TEN...TEN...TEN...TEN...TEN... TEN...TEN...TEN...TEN...TEN...TEN...
IT'S BEEN A GOOD MONTH.

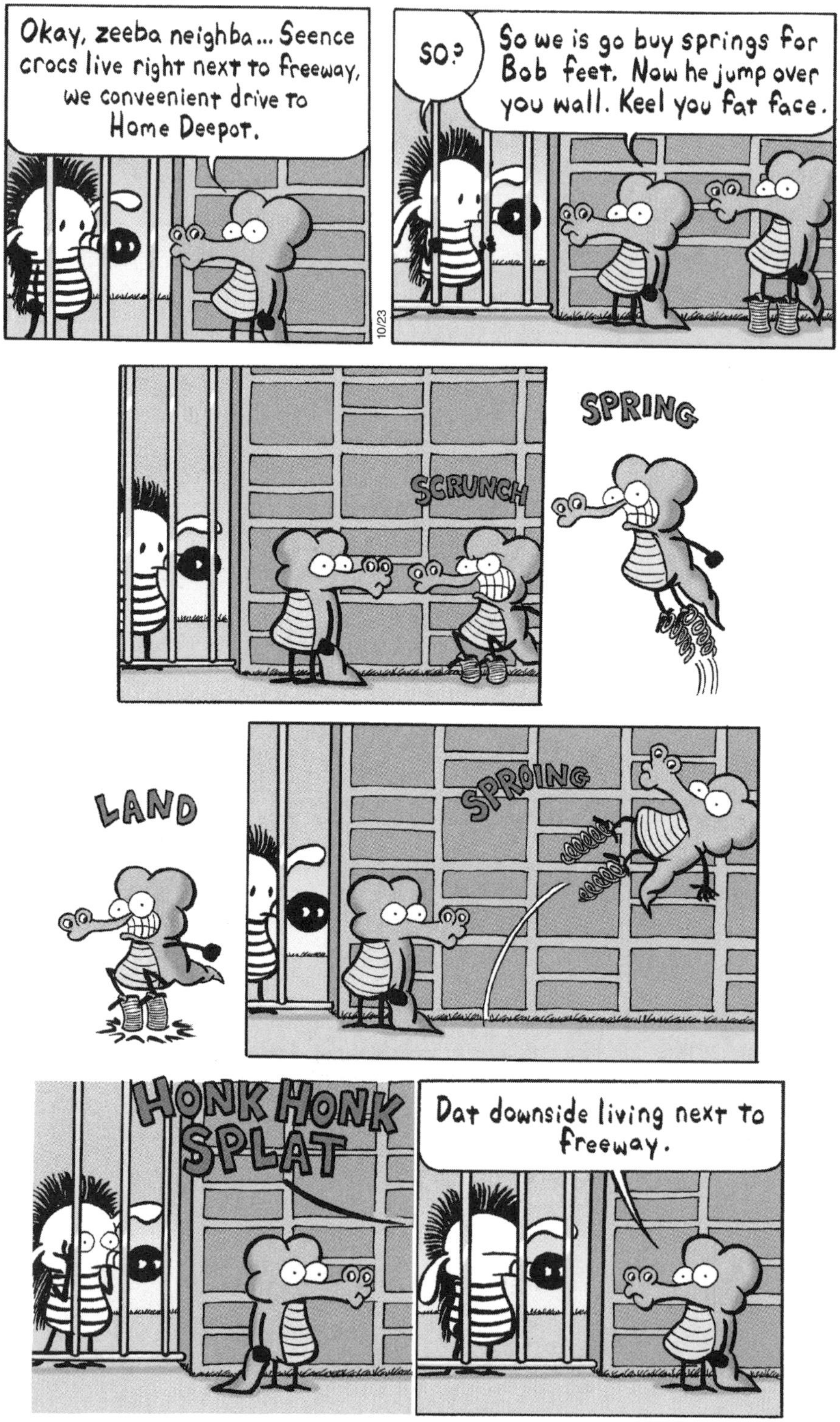
Okay, zeeba neighba... Seence crocs live right next to freeway, we conveenient drive to Home Deepot.
10/23
SO?
So we is go buy springs for Bob feet. Now he jump over you wall. Keel you fat face.
SCRUNCH
SPRING
LAND
SPROING
HONK HONK SPLAT
Dat downside living next to freeway.

Panel 1:
WELL, GOAT, I'VE FINALLY DECIDED... I'M QUITTING COLD TURKEY.

OH, YEAH? WHAT ARE YOU QUITTING? COFFEE? TELEVISION?

Panel 2:
COLD TURKEY.

Panel 3:
NEVER MIND.

YOU DON'T LISTEN WELL.

Panel 4:
I DATED THE CUTEST GIRL LAST NIGHT. SHE WAS SMART, INTERESTING, SWEET, EVERYTHING. BUT THEN I TOLD A JOKE.

Panel 5:
AND WHAT, SHE DIDN'T LIKE IT?

SHE DID.

Panel 6:
HAHA SNOOOOORT CACKLE CACKLE HOOO HAWW COUGH COUGH GUFFAWWWEEE HOOHOO SNOOOOORTT CACKLE CACKLE GUFFAAAAW

Panel 7:
BAD LAUGHS: THE GREAT DEAL-BREAKER.

Panel 8:
LOOKS LIKE THEY FINALLY CAUGHT THAT GUY WHO'S BEEN ROBBING BANKS... IT'S THE BIG HOUSE FOR HIM.

OOOOH...DO YOU SUPPOSE IT HAS A NICE STUDY AND PRETTY CURTAINS?

Panel 9:
BOOOOOOOOOO THAT'S ABOUT AS FUNNY AS A 'FAMILY CIRCUS' COMIC

Panel 10:
IT'S NOT EVERY DAY YOU SEE A COMIC STRIP HECKLED.

HEY...WHY IS THAT AN INSULT?

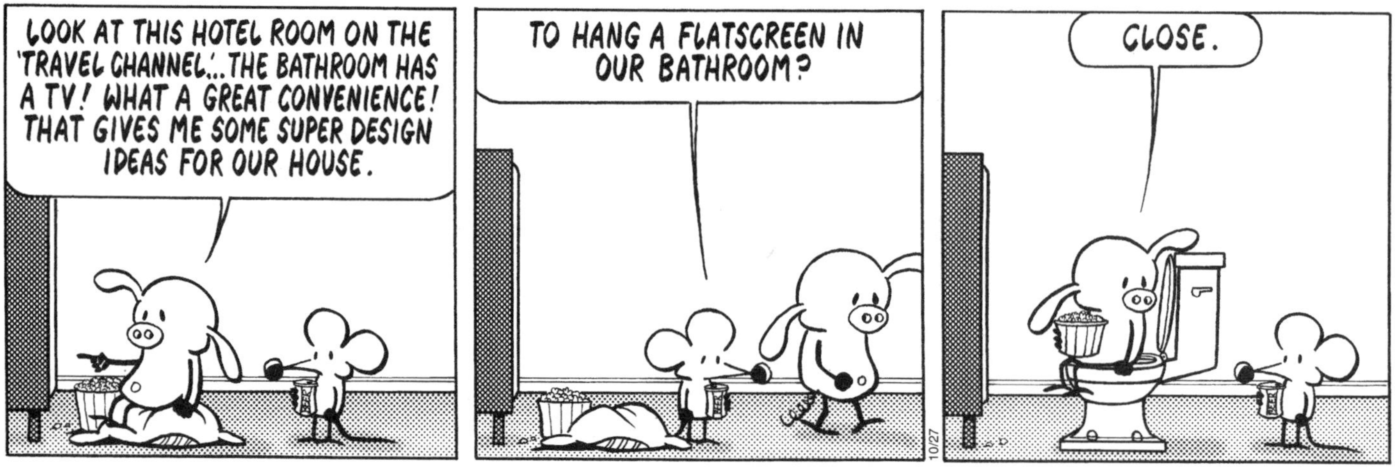
LOOK AT THIS HOTEL ROOM ON THE 'TRAVEL CHANNEL'... THE BATHROOM HAS A TV! WHAT A GREAT CONVENIENCE! THAT GIVES ME SOME SUPER DESIGN IDEAS FOR OUR HOUSE.
TO HANG A FLATSCREEN IN OUR BATHROOM?
CLOSE.

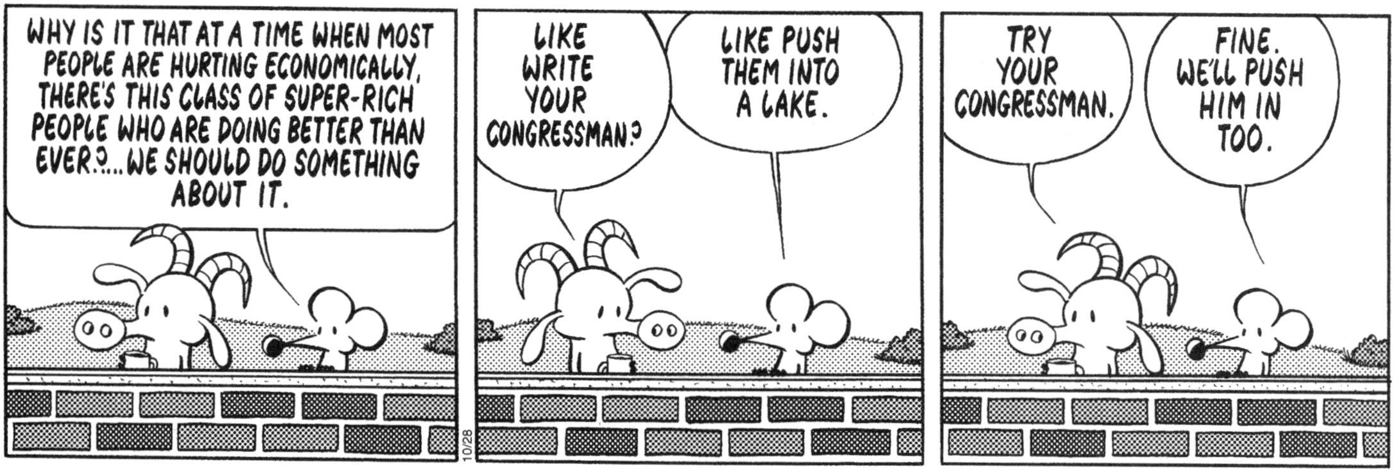
WHY IS IT THAT AT A TIME WHEN MOST PEOPLE ARE HURTING ECONOMICALLY, THERE'S THIS CLASS OF SUPER-RICH PEOPLE WHO ARE DOING BETTER THAN EVER?... WE SHOULD DO SOMETHING ABOUT IT.
LIKE WRITE YOUR CONGRESSMAN?
LIKE PUSH THEM INTO A LAKE.
TRY YOUR CONGRESSMAN.
FINE. WE'LL PUSH HIM IN TOO.

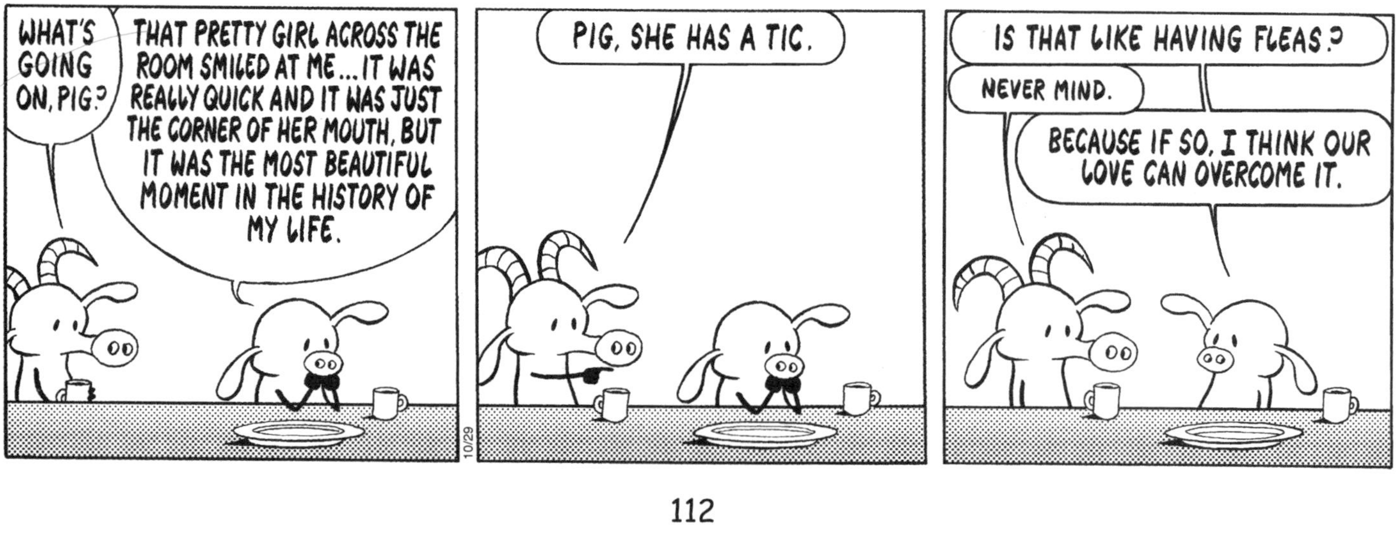
WHAT'S GOING ON, PIG?
THAT PRETTY GIRL ACROSS THE ROOM SMILED AT ME... IT WAS REALLY QUICK AND IT WAS JUST THE CORNER OF HER MOUTH, BUT IT WAS THE MOST BEAUTIFUL MOMENT IN THE HISTORY OF MY LIFE.
PIG, SHE HAS A TIC.
IS THAT LIKE HAVING FLEAS?
NEVER MIND.
BECAUSE IF SO, I THINK OUR LOVE CAN OVERCOME IT.

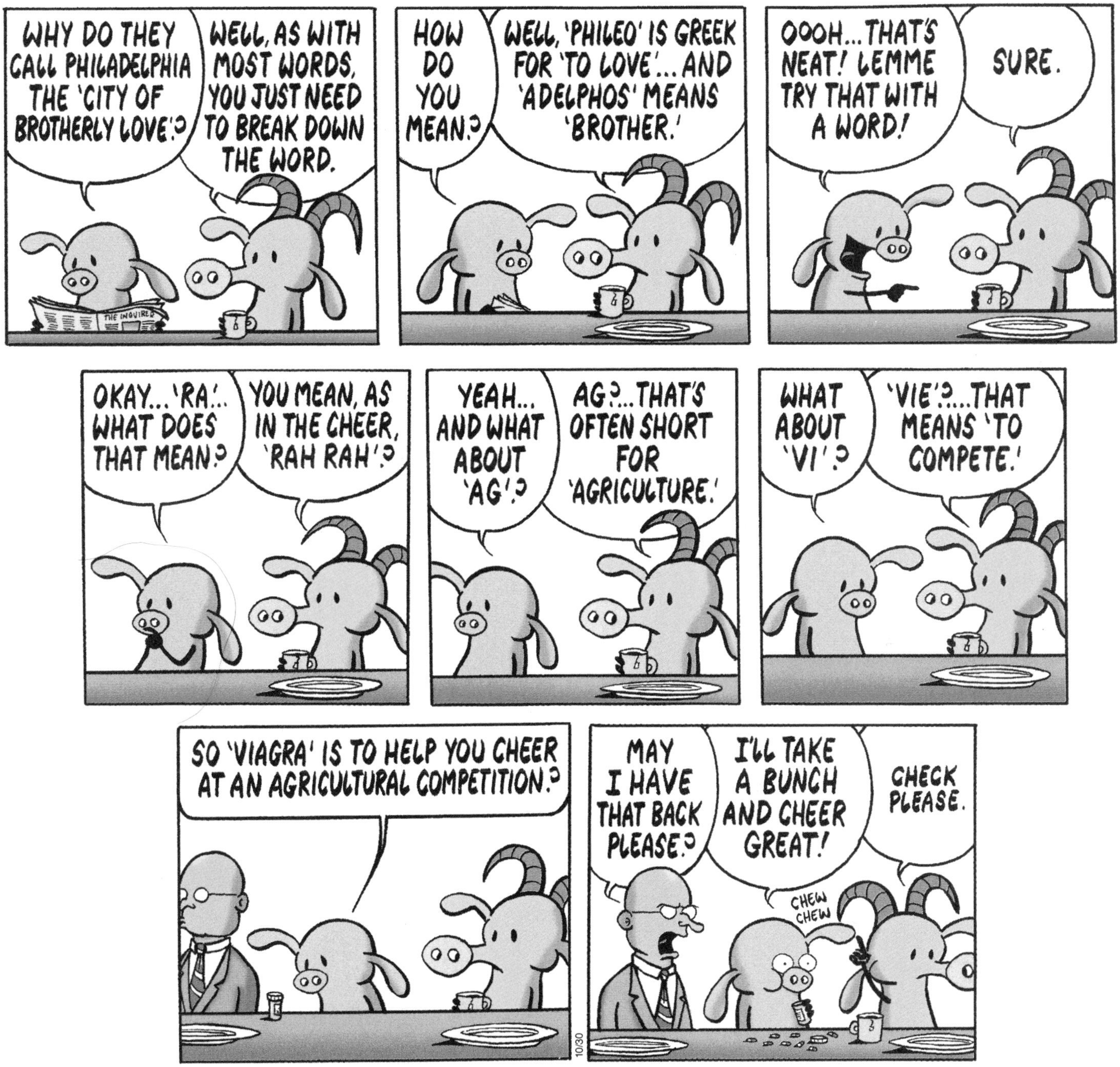
WHY DO THEY CALL PHILADELPHIA THE 'CITY OF BROTHERLY LOVE'?
WELL, AS WITH MOST WORDS, YOU JUST NEED TO BREAK DOWN THE WORD.
HOW DO YOU MEAN?
WELL, 'PHILEO' IS GREEK FOR 'TO LOVE'... AND 'ADELPHOS' MEANS 'BROTHER.'
OOOH... THAT'S NEAT! LEMME TRY THAT WITH A WORD!
SURE.
OKAY... 'RA'... WHAT DOES THAT MEAN?
YOU MEAN, AS IN THE CHEER, 'RAH RAH'?
YEAH... AND WHAT ABOUT 'AG'?
AG?... THAT'S OFTEN SHORT FOR 'AGRICULTURE.'
WHAT ABOUT 'VI'?
'VIE'?... THAT MEANS 'TO COMPETE.'
SO 'VIAGRA' IS TO HELP YOU CHEER AT AN AGRICULTURAL COMPETITION?
MAY I HAVE THAT BACK PLEASE?
I'LL TAKE A BUNCH AND CHEER GREAT!
CHECK PLEASE.
CHEW CHEW
10/30

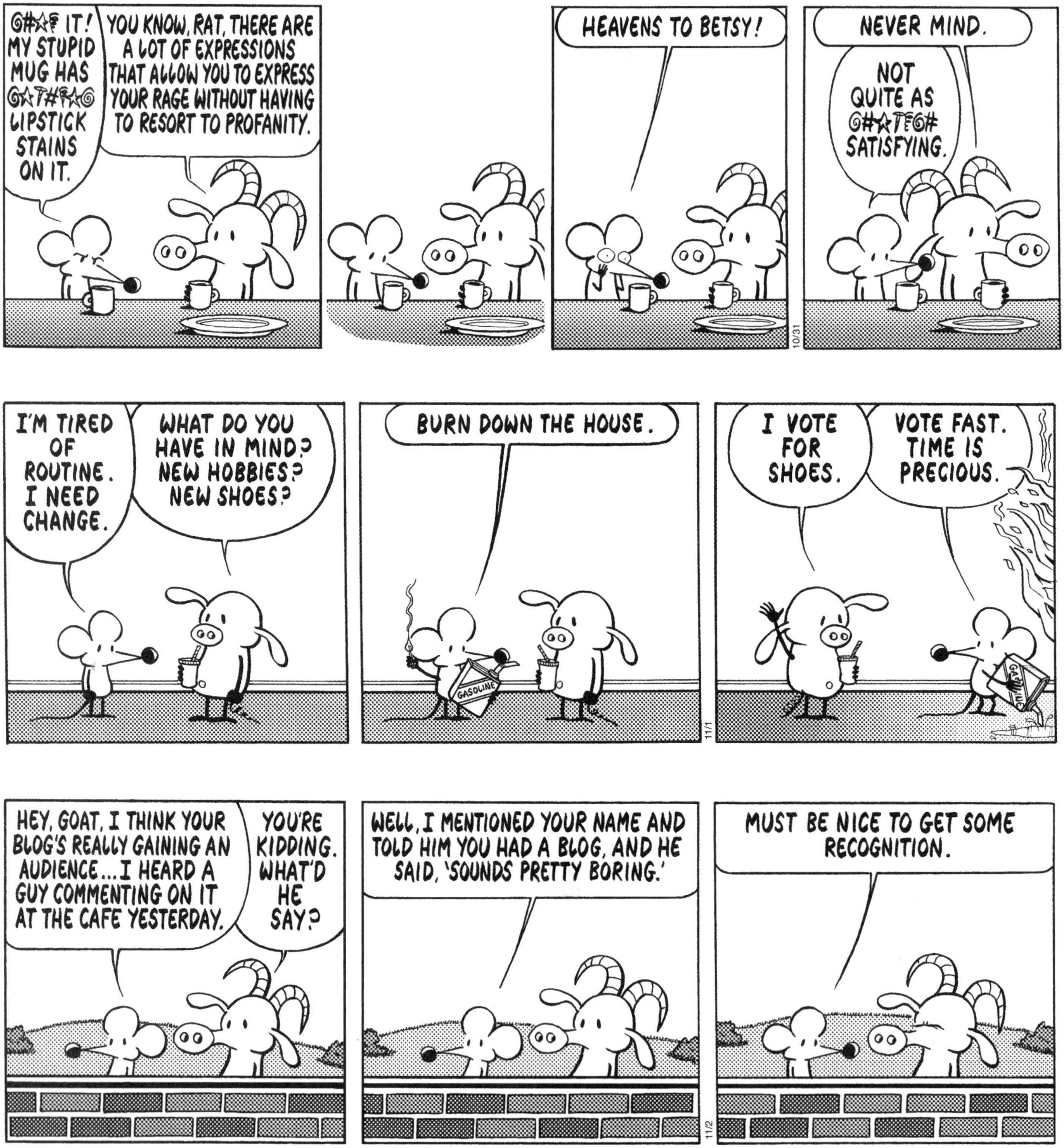
G#☆F IT! MY STUPID MUG HAS G☆T#F☆G LIPSTICK STAINS ON IT.
YOU KNOW, RAT, THERE ARE A LOT OF EXPRESSIONS THAT ALLOW YOU TO EXPRESS YOUR RAGE WITHOUT HAVING TO RESORT TO PROFANITY.
HEAVENS TO BETSY!
NEVER MIND.
NOT QUITE AS G#☆T F G# SATISFYING.
10/31
I'M TIRED OF ROUTINE. I NEED CHANGE.
WHAT DO YOU HAVE IN MIND? NEW HOBBIES? NEW SHOES?
BURN DOWN THE HOUSE.
GASOLINE
I VOTE FOR SHOES.
VOTE FAST. TIME IS PRECIOUS.
11/1
HEY, GOAT, I THINK YOUR BLOG'S REALLY GAINING AN AUDIENCE...I HEARD A GUY COMMENTING ON IT AT THE CAFE YESTERDAY.
YOU'RE KIDDING. WHAT'D HE SAY?
WELL, I MENTIONED YOUR NAME AND TOLD HIM YOU HAD A BLOG, AND HE SAID, 'SOUNDS PRETTY BORING.'
MUST BE NICE TO GET SOME RECOGNITION.
11/2

Panel 1: MY BUDDY BOB GOT KICKED OUT YESTERDAY FOR TWEETING FROM HERE IN THE DINER.

Panel 2: YEAH, A LOT OF RESTAURANTS NOW ASK YOU TO TURN OFF ALL CELL PHONES AND OTHER DIGITAL DEVICES BECAUSE OF THE NOISE THEY MAKE. AND I HAVE TO AGREE. IT'S RUDE TO YOUR FELLOW DINERS.

Panel 3: WHAT'S THAT HAVE TO DO WITH BOB? / FORGET IT. / MIND IF I POST YOUR HUMILIATED FACE ON MY TWITTER PAGE?

Panel 4: HEY, RAT... WHY YOU WEARING AN 'EVEL KNIEVEL' SUIT? / BECAUSE THE CITY INSTALLED LITTLE JUMP RAMPS ON OUR STREET. IF I DRIVE OVER 'EM REALLY FAST, MY CAR ACTUALLY GETS AIR...SO I'M A DAREDEVIL NOW!

Panel 5: THOSE ARE SPEED BUMPS. THEY'RE THERE TO SLOW YOU DOWN.

Panel 6: THEN WHY CALL 'EM SPEED BUMPS? / PLEASE STOP TALKING. / PERHAPS GOAT'S THINKING OF SLOW BUMPS.

Panel 7: HOW COME SOMETIMES WHEN I TRY TO DO THE RIGHT THING, EVERYTHING TURNS OUT BADLY FOR ME?

Panel 8: WELL, YOU KNOW, PIG, ACTING WITH HONOR IS ITS OWN REWARD. AFTER ALL, WHAT'S LIFE WITHOUT PRINCIPLES?

Panel 9: FUN. / DON'T LISTEN TO— / I WANT THAT!!

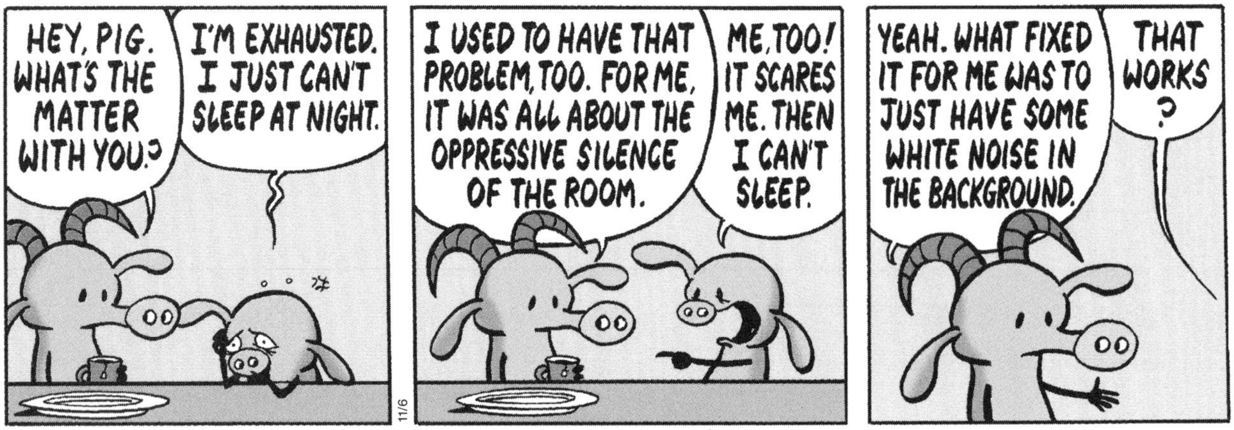
HEY, PIG. WHAT'S THE MATTER WITH YOU?
I'M EXHAUSTED. I JUST CAN'T SLEEP AT NIGHT.
11/6
I USED TO HAVE THAT PROBLEM, TOO. FOR ME, IT WAS ALL ABOUT THE OPPRESSIVE SILENCE OF THE ROOM.
ME, TOO! IT SCARES ME. THEN I CAN'T SLEEP.
YEAH. WHAT FIXED IT FOR ME WAS TO JUST HAVE SOME WHITE NOISE IN THE BACKGROUND.
THAT WORKS?

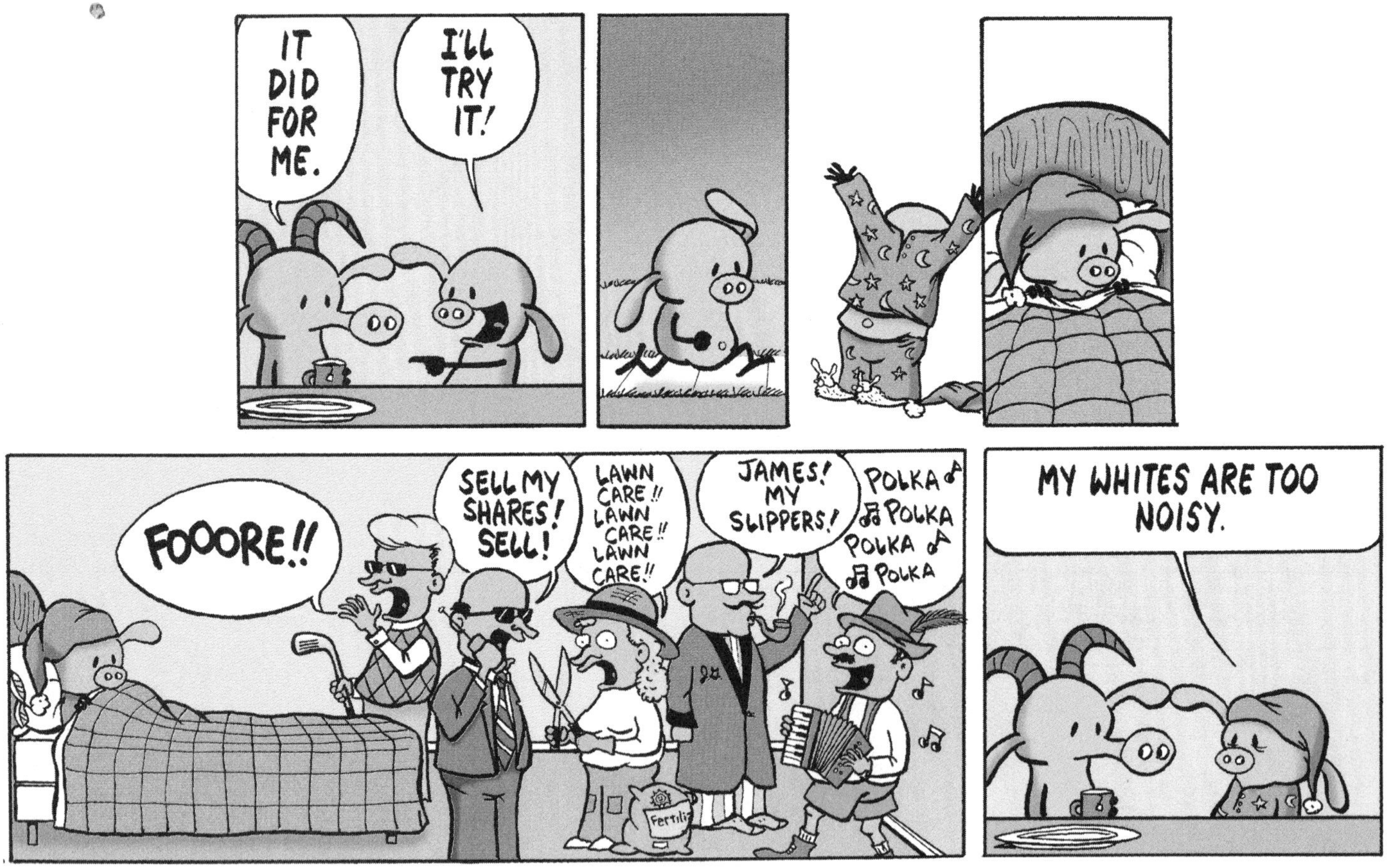
IT DID FOR ME.
I'LL TRY IT!
FOOORE!!
SELL MY SHARES! SELL!
LAWN CARE!! LAWN CARE!! LAWN CARE!!
JAMES! MY SLIPPERS!
POLKA POLKA POLKA POLKA
Fertiliz
MY WHITES ARE TOO NOISY.

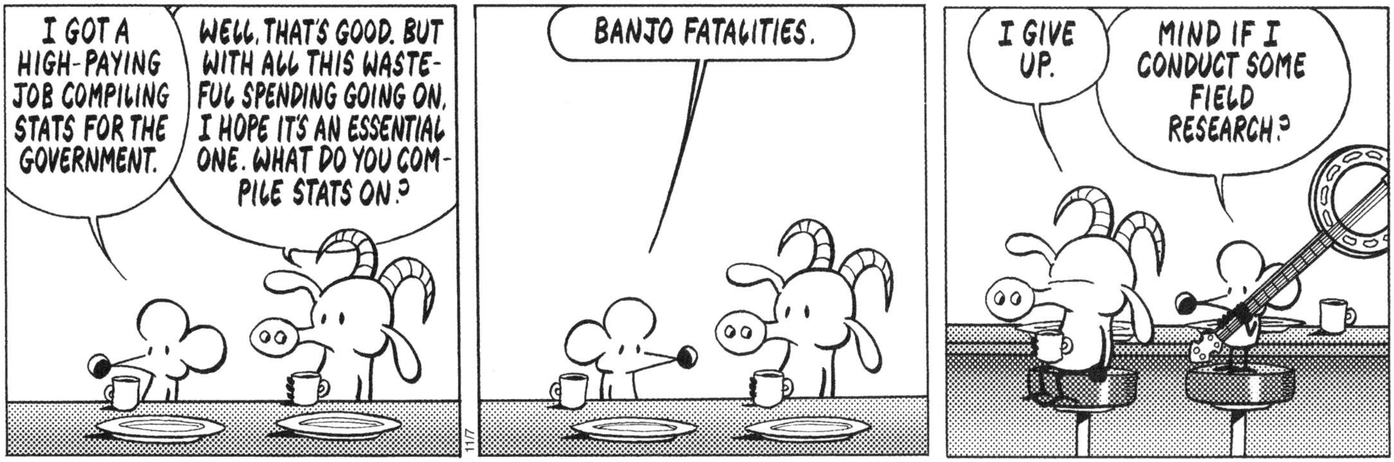
I GOT A HIGH-PAYING JOB COMPILING STATS FOR THE GOVERNMENT.
WELL, THAT'S GOOD. BUT WITH ALL THIS WASTEFUL SPENDING GOING ON, I HOPE IT'S AN ESSENTIAL ONE. WHAT DO YOU COMPILE STATS ON?
11/7
BANJO FATALITIES.
I GIVE UP.
MIND IF I CONDUCT SOME FIELD RESEARCH?

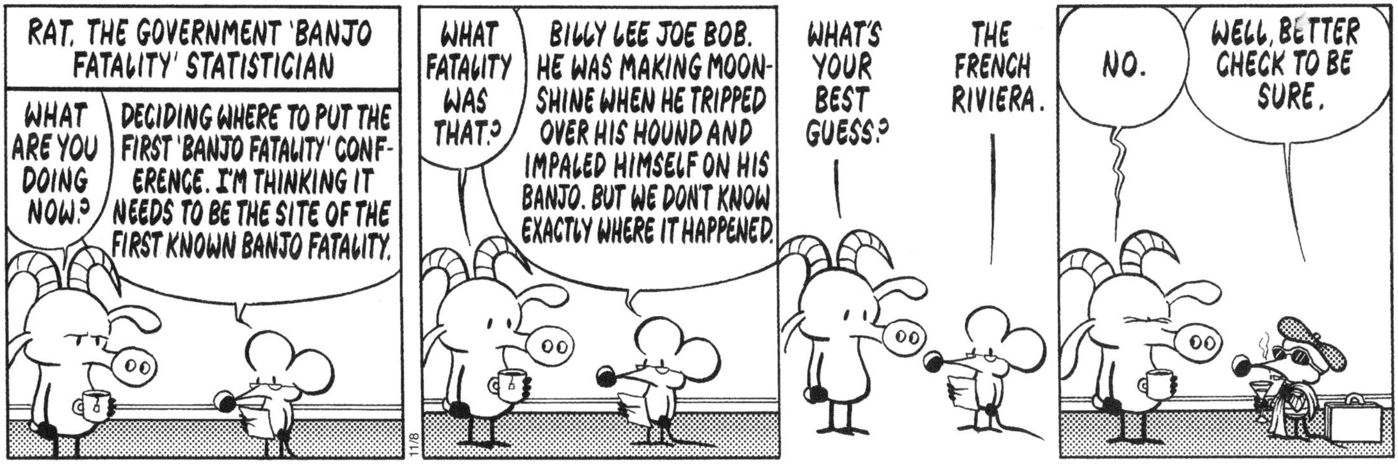
RAT, THE GOVERNMENT 'BANJO FATALITY' STATISTICIAN
WHAT ARE YOU DOING NOW?
DECIDING WHERE TO PUT THE FIRST 'BANJO FATALITY' CONFERENCE. I'M THINKING IT NEEDS TO BE THE SITE OF THE FIRST KNOWN BANJO FATALITY.
11/8
WHAT FATALITY WAS THAT?
BILLY LEE JOE BOB. HE WAS MAKING MOONSHINE WHEN HE TRIPPED OVER HIS HOUND AND IMPALED HIMSELF ON HIS BANJO. BUT WE DON'T KNOW EXACTLY WHERE IT HAPPENED.
WHAT'S YOUR BEST GUESS?
THE FRENCH RIVIERA.
NO.
WELL, BETTER CHECK TO BE SURE.

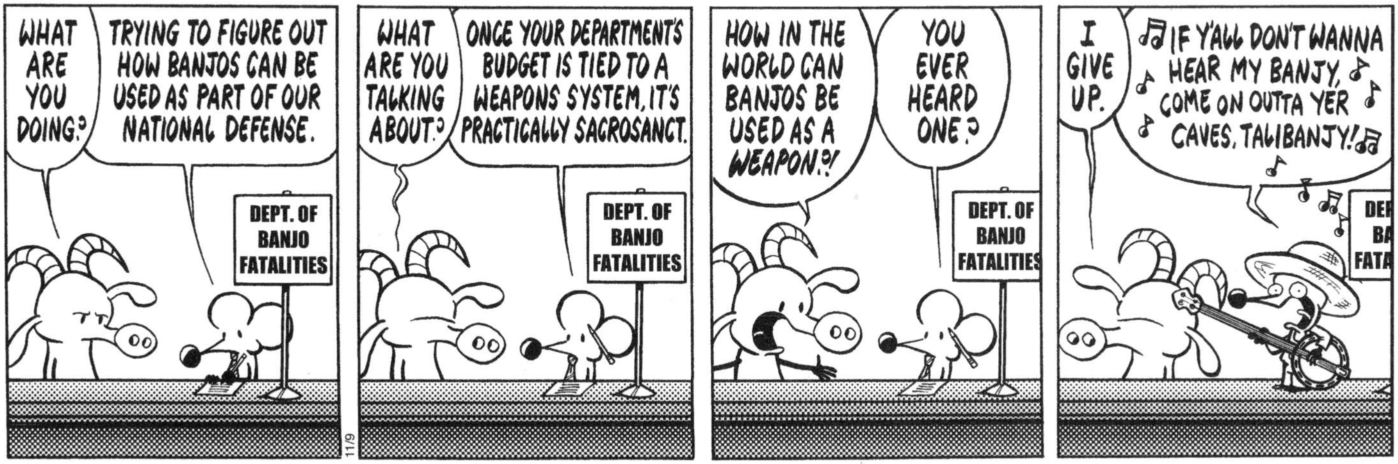
WHAT ARE YOU DOING?
TRYING TO FIGURE OUT HOW BANJOS CAN BE USED AS PART OF OUR NATIONAL DEFENSE.
DEPT. OF BANJO FATALITIES
11/9
WHAT ARE YOU TALKING ABOUT?
ONCE YOUR DEPARTMENT'S BUDGET IS TIED TO A WEAPONS SYSTEM, IT'S PRACTICALLY SACROSANCT.
DEPT. OF BANJO FATALITIES
HOW IN THE WORLD CAN BANJOS BE USED AS A WEAPON?!
YOU EVER HEARD ONE?
DEPT. OF BANJO FATALITIES
I GIVE UP.
IF Y'ALL DON'T WANNA HEAR MY BANJY, COME ON OUTTA YER CAVES, TALIBANJY!

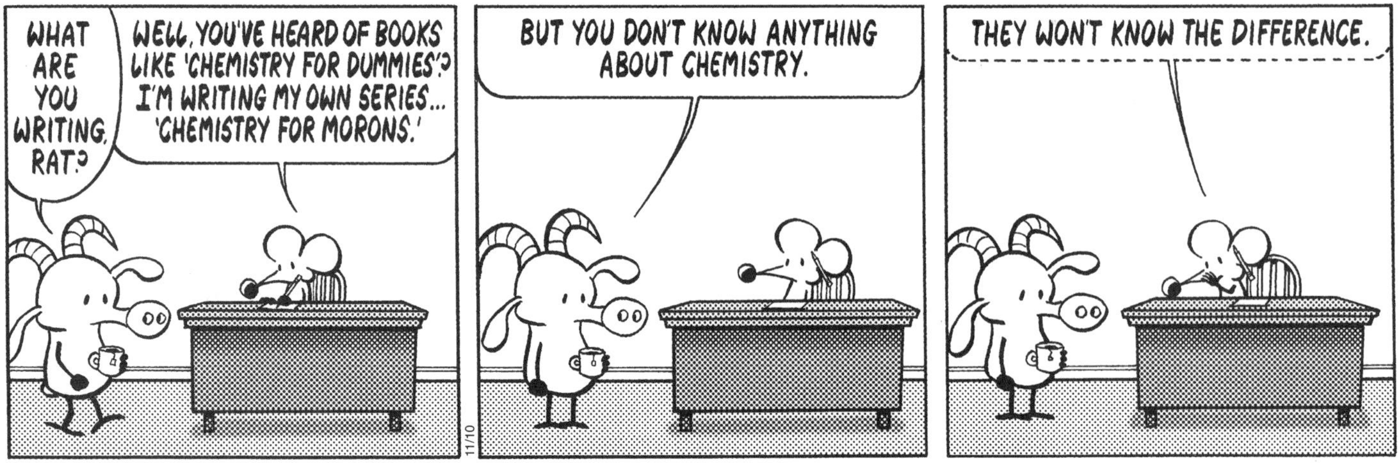
WHAT ARE YOU WRITING, RAT?
WELL, YOU'VE HEARD OF BOOKS LIKE 'CHEMISTRY FOR DUMMIES'? I'M WRITING MY OWN SERIES... 'CHEMISTRY FOR MORONS.'
BUT YOU DON'T KNOW ANYTHING ABOUT CHEMISTRY.
THEY WON'T KNOW THE DIFFERENCE.
11/10

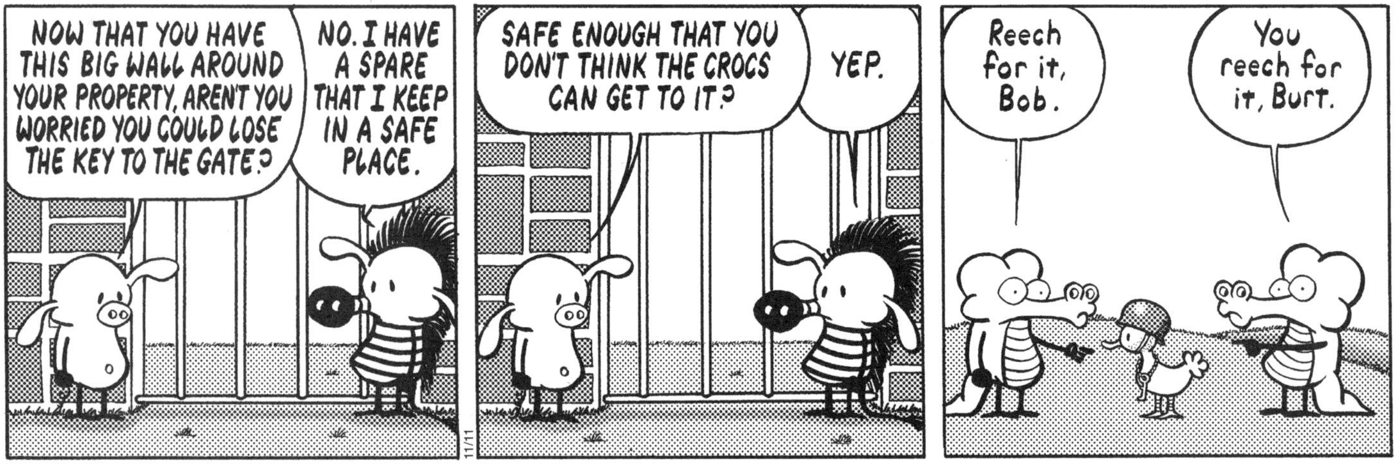
NOW THAT YOU HAVE THIS BIG WALL AROUND YOUR PROPERTY, AREN'T YOU WORRIED YOU COULD LOSE THE KEY TO THE GATE?
NO. I HAVE A SPARE THAT I KEEP IN A SAFE PLACE.
SAFE ENOUGH THAT YOU DON'T THINK THE CROCS CAN GET TO IT?
YEP.
Reech for it, Bob.
You reech for it, Burt.
11/11

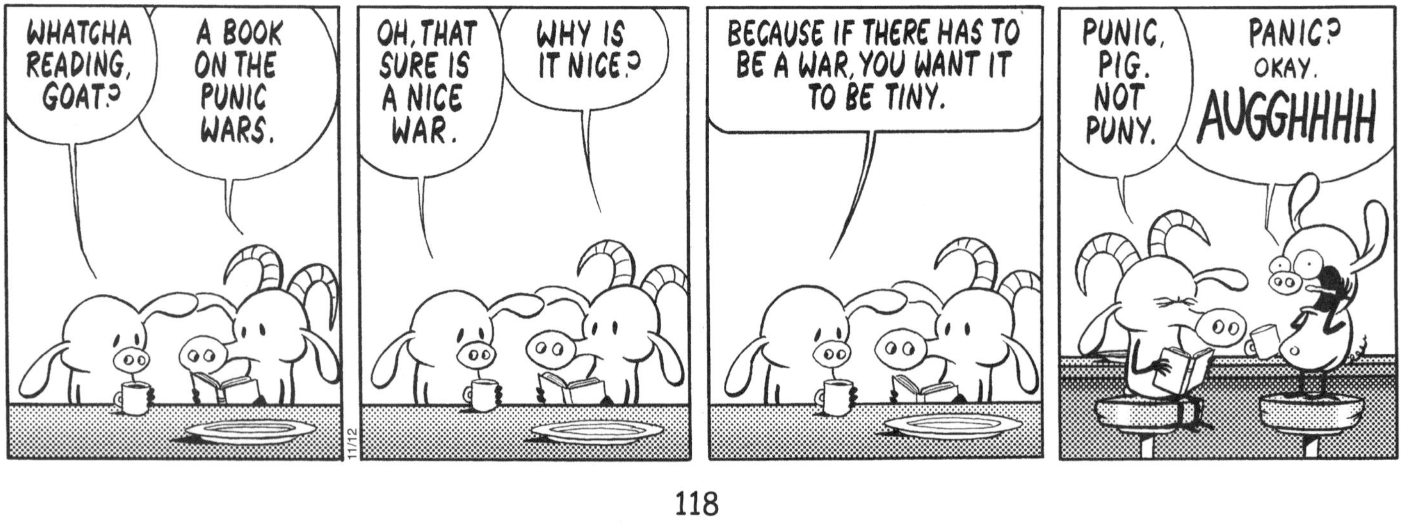
WHATCHA READING, GOAT?
A BOOK ON THE PUNIC WARS.
OH, THAT SURE IS A NICE WAR.
WHY IS IT NICE?
BECAUSE IF THERE HAS TO BE A WAR, YOU WANT IT TO BE TINY.
PUNIC, PIG. NOT PUNY.
PANIC? OKAY. AUGGHHHH
11/12

**A dance for Steve
(from a Rat who doesn't
even *like* to dance).**

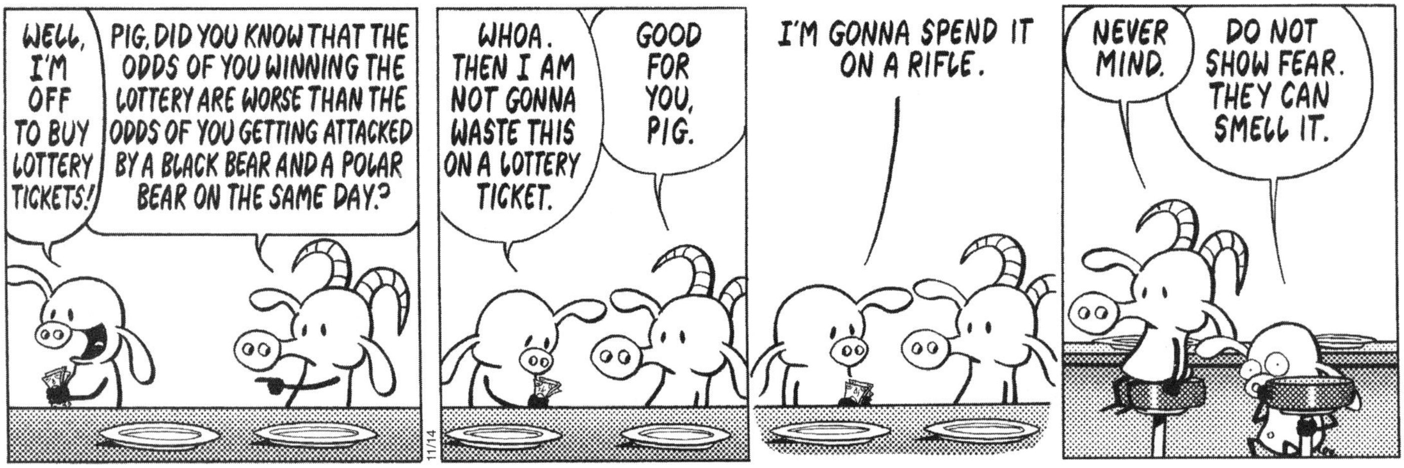
WELL, I'M OFF TO BUY LOTTERY TICKETS!
PIG, DID YOU KNOW THAT THE ODDS OF YOU WINNING THE LOTTERY ARE WORSE THAN THE ODDS OF YOU GETTING ATTACKED BY A BLACK BEAR AND A POLAR BEAR ON THE SAME DAY?
WHOA. THEN I AM NOT GONNA WASTE THIS ON A LOTTERY TICKET.
GOOD FOR YOU, PIG.
I'M GONNA SPEND IT ON A RIFLE.
NEVER MIND.
DO NOT SHOW FEAR. THEY CAN SMELL IT.
11/14

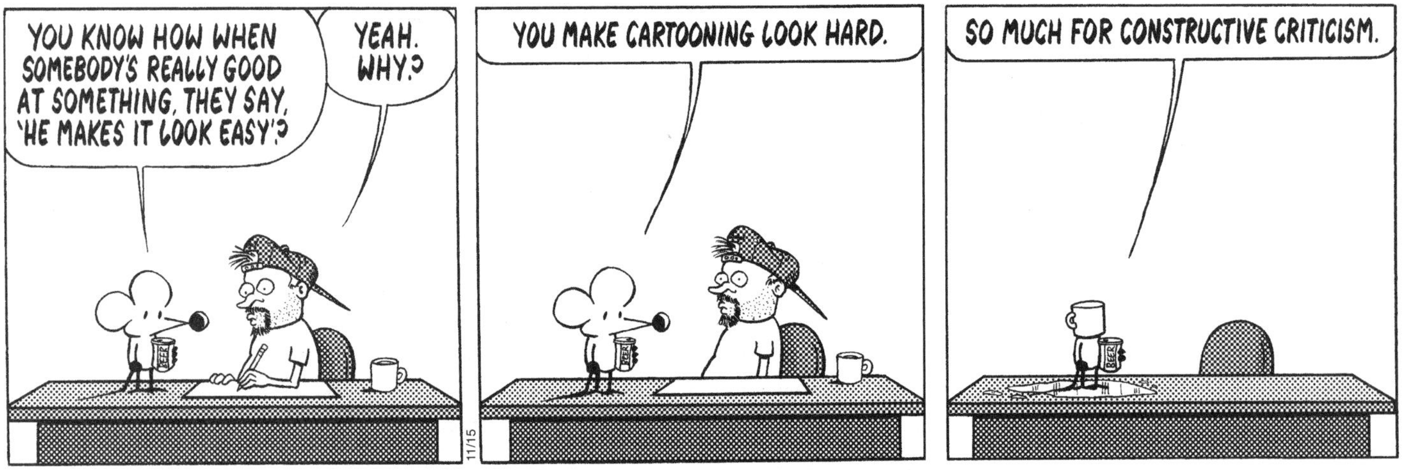
YOU KNOW HOW WHEN SOMEBODY'S REALLY GOOD AT SOMETHING, THEY SAY, 'HE MAKES IT LOOK EASY'?
YEAH. WHY?
YOU MAKE CARTOONING LOOK HARD.
SO MUCH FOR CONSTRUCTIVE CRITICISM.
BEER
11/15

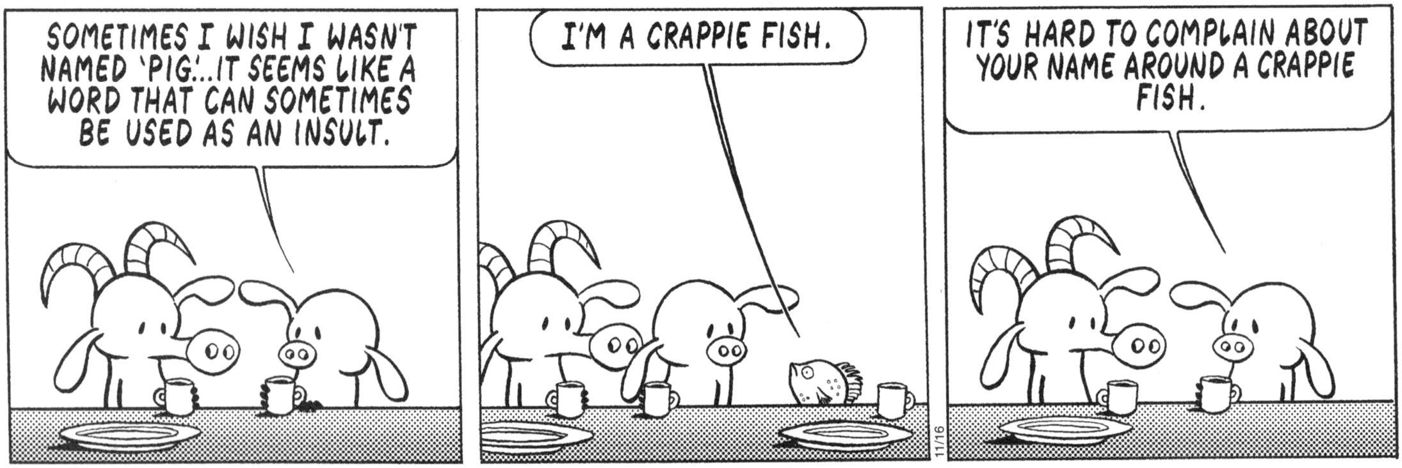
SOMETIMES I WISH I WASN'T NAMED 'PIG'...IT SEEMS LIKE A WORD THAT CAN SOMETIMES BE USED AS AN INSULT.
I'M A CRAPPIE FISH.
IT'S HARD TO COMPLAIN ABOUT YOUR NAME AROUND A CRAPPIE FISH.
11/16

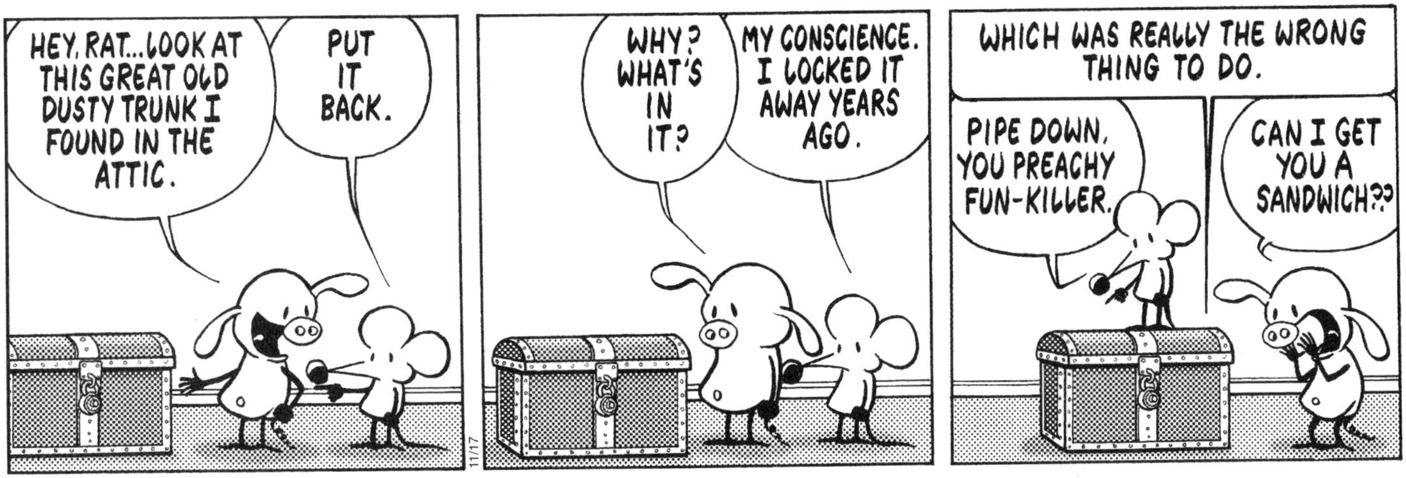
HEY, RAT...LOOK AT THIS GREAT OLD DUSTY TRUNK I FOUND IN THE ATTIC.
PUT IT BACK.
11/17
WHY? WHAT'S IN IT?
MY CONSCIENCE. I LOCKED IT AWAY YEARS AGO.
WHICH WAS REALLY THE WRONG THING TO DO.
PIPE DOWN, YOU PREACHY FUN-KILLER.
CAN I GET YOU A SANDWICH??

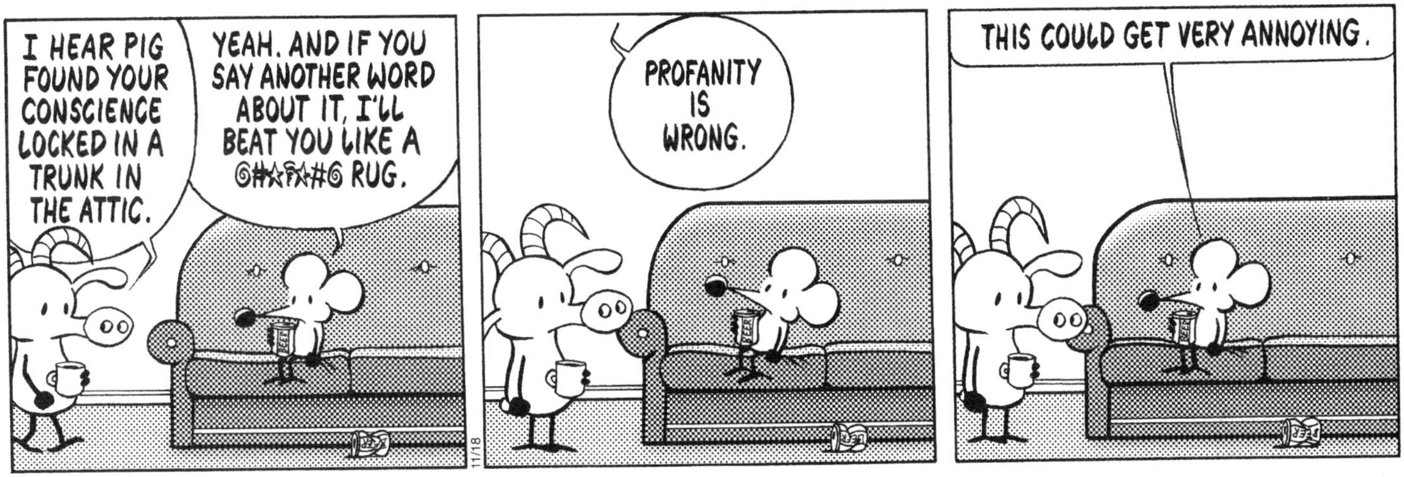
I HEAR PIG FOUND YOUR CONSCIENCE LOCKED IN A TRUNK IN THE ATTIC.
YEAH. AND IF YOU SAY ANOTHER WORD ABOUT IT, I'LL BEAT YOU LIKE A @#☆F☆#@ RUG.
BEER
11/18
PROFANITY IS WRONG.
THIS COULD GET VERY ANNOYING.

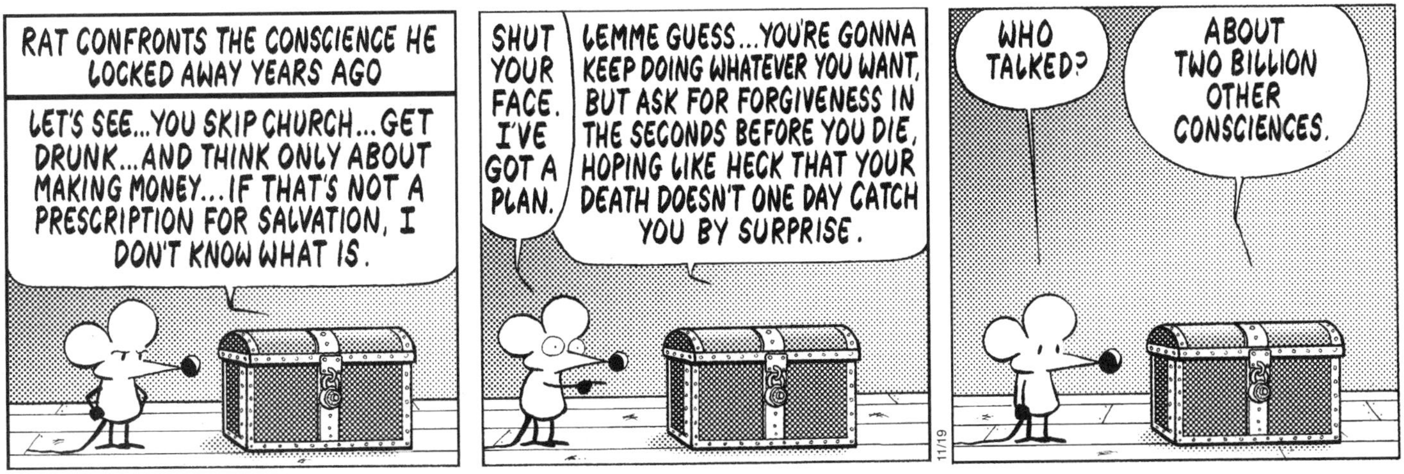
RAT CONFRONTS THE CONSCIENCE HE LOCKED AWAY YEARS AGO
LET'S SEE...YOU SKIP CHURCH...GET DRUNK...AND THINK ONLY ABOUT MAKING MONEY...IF THAT'S NOT A PRESCRIPTION FOR SALVATION, I DON'T KNOW WHAT IS.
SHUT YOUR FACE. I'VE GOT A PLAN.
LEMME GUESS...YOU'RE GONNA KEEP DOING WHATEVER YOU WANT, BUT ASK FOR FORGIVENESS IN THE SECONDS BEFORE YOU DIE, HOPING LIKE HECK THAT YOUR DEATH DOESN'T ONE DAY CATCH YOU BY SURPRISE.
11/19
WHO TALKED?
ABOUT TWO BILLION OTHER CONSCIENCES.

STORY UPDATE:
Rat has obtained a government job compiling stats on banjo fatalities.

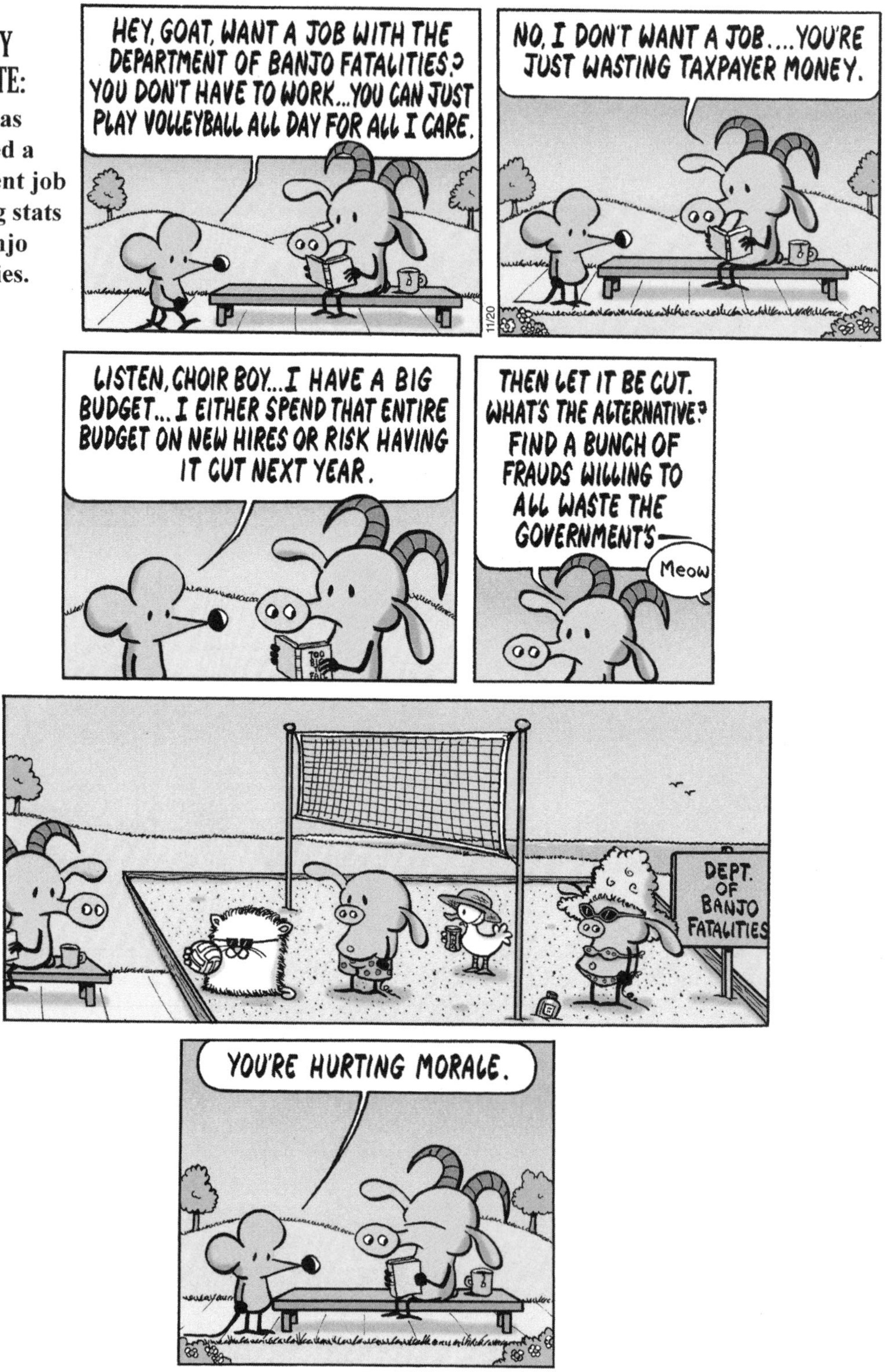
HEY, GOAT, WANT A JOB WITH THE DEPARTMENT OF BANJO FATALITIES? YOU DON'T HAVE TO WORK...YOU CAN JUST PLAY VOLLEYBALL ALL DAY FOR ALL I CARE.
11/20
NO, I DON'T WANT A JOB....YOU'RE JUST WASTING TAXPAYER MONEY.
LISTEN, CHOIR BOY...I HAVE A BIG BUDGET...I EITHER SPEND THAT ENTIRE BUDGET ON NEW HIRES OR RISK HAVING IT CUT NEXT YEAR.
THEN LET IT BE CUT. WHAT'S THE ALTERNATIVE? FIND A BUNCH OF FRAUDS WILLING TO ALL WASTE THE GOVERNMENT'S—
Meow
DEPT. OF BANJO FATALITIES
YOU'RE HURTING MORALE.

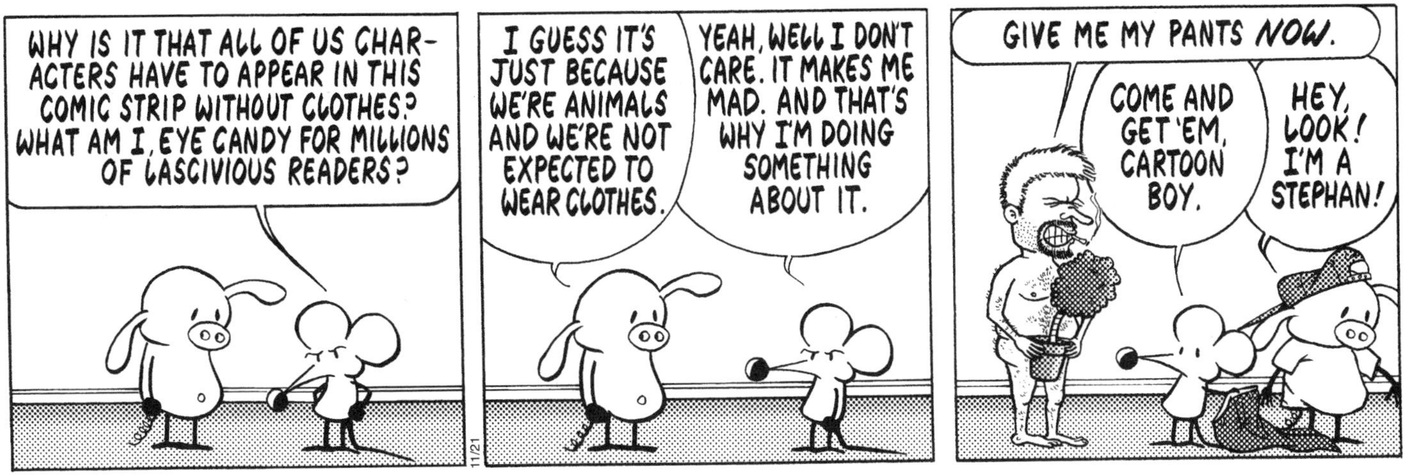
WHY IS IT THAT ALL OF US CHARACTERS HAVE TO APPEAR IN THIS COMIC STRIP WITHOUT CLOTHES? WHAT AM I, EYE CANDY FOR MILLIONS OF LASCIVIOUS READERS?
I GUESS IT'S JUST BECAUSE WE'RE ANIMALS AND WE'RE NOT EXPECTED TO WEAR CLOTHES.
YEAH, WELL I DON'T CARE. IT MAKES ME MAD. AND THAT'S WHY I'M DOING SOMETHING ABOUT IT.
11/21
GIVE ME MY PANTS *NOW*.
COME AND GET 'EM, CARTOON BOY.
HEY, LOOK! I'M A STEPHAN!

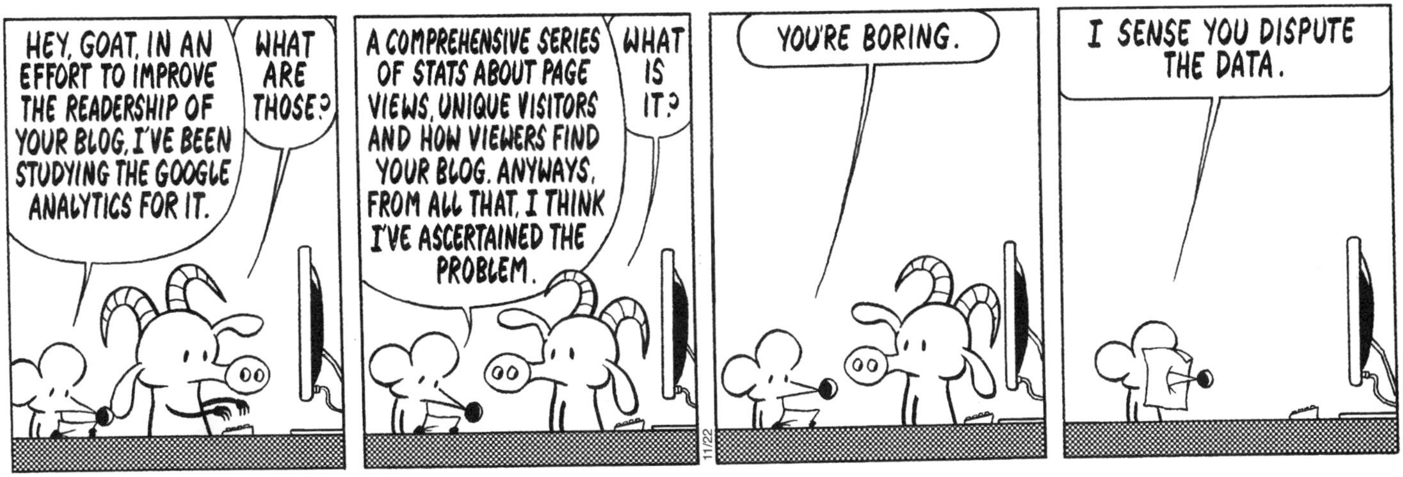
HEY, GOAT, IN AN EFFORT TO IMPROVE THE READERSHIP OF YOUR BLOG, I'VE BEEN STUDYING THE GOOGLE ANALYTICS FOR IT.
WHAT ARE THOSE?
A COMPREHENSIVE SERIES OF STATS ABOUT PAGE VIEWS, UNIQUE VISITORS AND HOW VIEWERS FIND YOUR BLOG. ANYWAYS, FROM ALL THAT, I THINK I'VE ASCERTAINED THE PROBLEM.
WHAT IS IT?
11/22
YOU'RE BORING.
I SENSE YOU DISPUTE THE DATA.

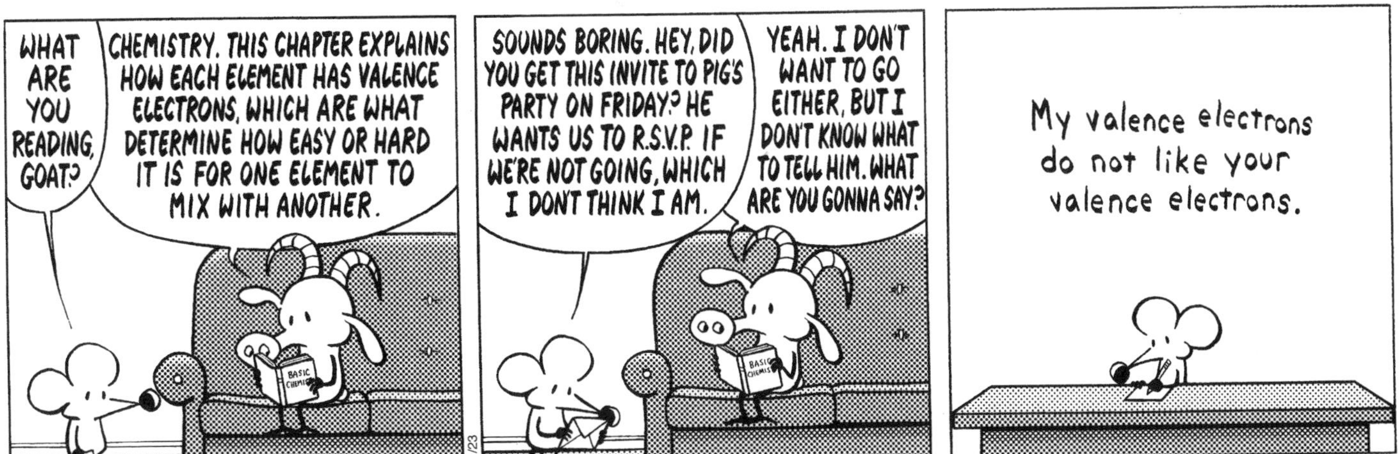
WHAT ARE YOU READING, GOAT?
CHEMISTRY. THIS CHAPTER EXPLAINS HOW EACH ELEMENT HAS VALENCE ELECTRONS, WHICH ARE WHAT DETERMINE HOW EASY OR HARD IT IS FOR ONE ELEMENT TO MIX WITH ANOTHER.
BASIC CHEMIS
11/23
SOUNDS BORING. HEY, DID YOU GET THIS INVITE TO PIG'S PARTY ON FRIDAY? HE WANTS US TO R.S.V.P. IF WE'RE NOT GOING, WHICH I DON'T THINK I AM.
YEAH. I DON'T WANT TO GO EITHER, BUT I DON'T KNOW WHAT TO TELL HIM. WHAT ARE YOU GONNA SAY?
My valence electrons do not like your valence electrons.

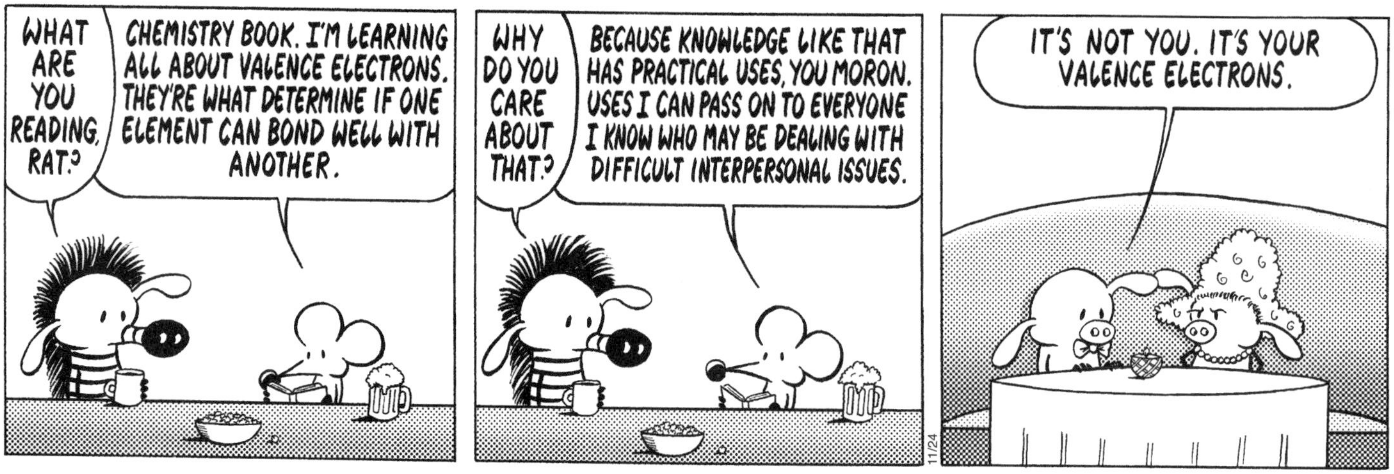
WHAT ARE YOU READING, RAT?
CHEMISTRY BOOK. I'M LEARNING ALL ABOUT VALENCE ELECTRONS. THEY'RE WHAT DETERMINE IF ONE ELEMENT CAN BOND WELL WITH ANOTHER.
WHY DO YOU CARE ABOUT THAT?
BECAUSE KNOWLEDGE LIKE THAT HAS PRACTICAL USES, YOU MORON. USES I CAN PASS ON TO EVERYONE I KNOW WHO MAY BE DEALING WITH DIFFICULT INTERPERSONAL ISSUES.
IT'S NOT YOU. IT'S YOUR VALENCE ELECTRONS.
11/24

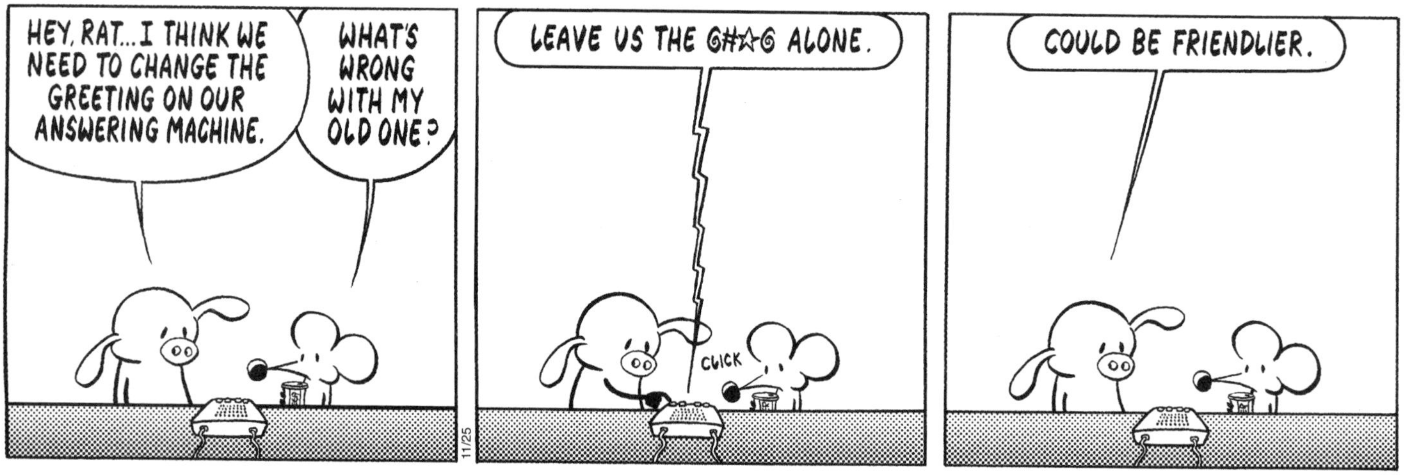
HEY, RAT...I THINK WE NEED TO CHANGE THE GREETING ON OUR ANSWERING MACHINE.
WHAT'S WRONG WITH MY OLD ONE?
LEAVE US THE G#☆G ALONE.
CLICK
COULD BE FRIENDLIER.
11/25

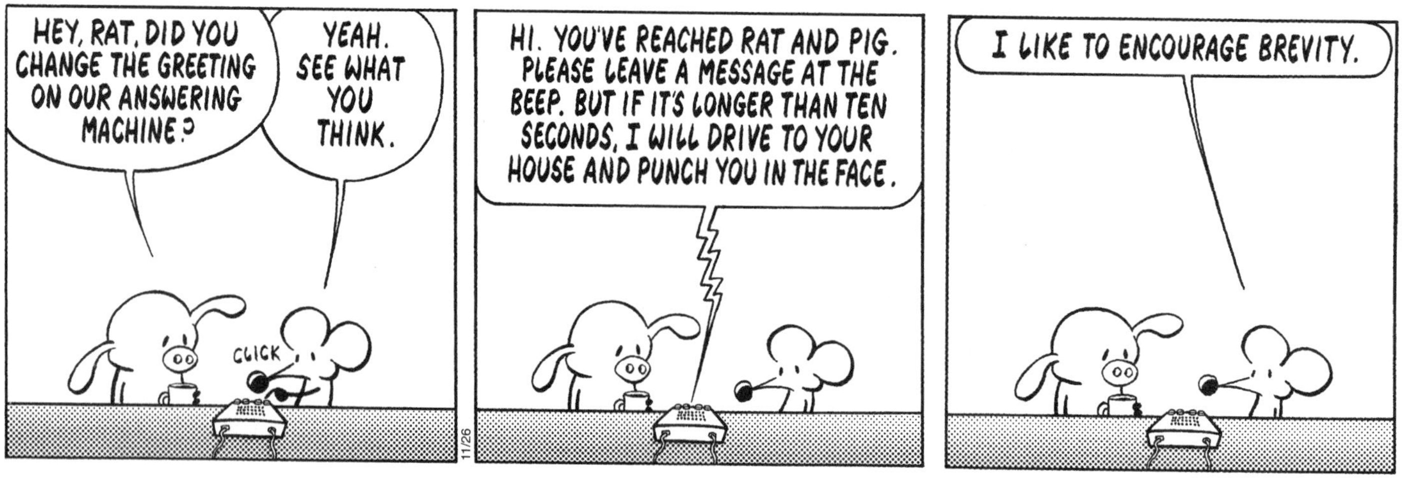
HEY, RAT, DID YOU CHANGE THE GREETING ON OUR ANSWERING MACHINE?
YEAH. SEE WHAT YOU THINK.
CLICK
HI. YOU'VE REACHED RAT AND PIG. PLEASE LEAVE A MESSAGE AT THE BEEP. BUT IF IT'S LONGER THAN TEN SECONDS, I WILL DRIVE TO YOUR HOUSE AND PUNCH YOU IN THE FACE.
I LIKE TO ENCOURAGE BREVITY.
11/26

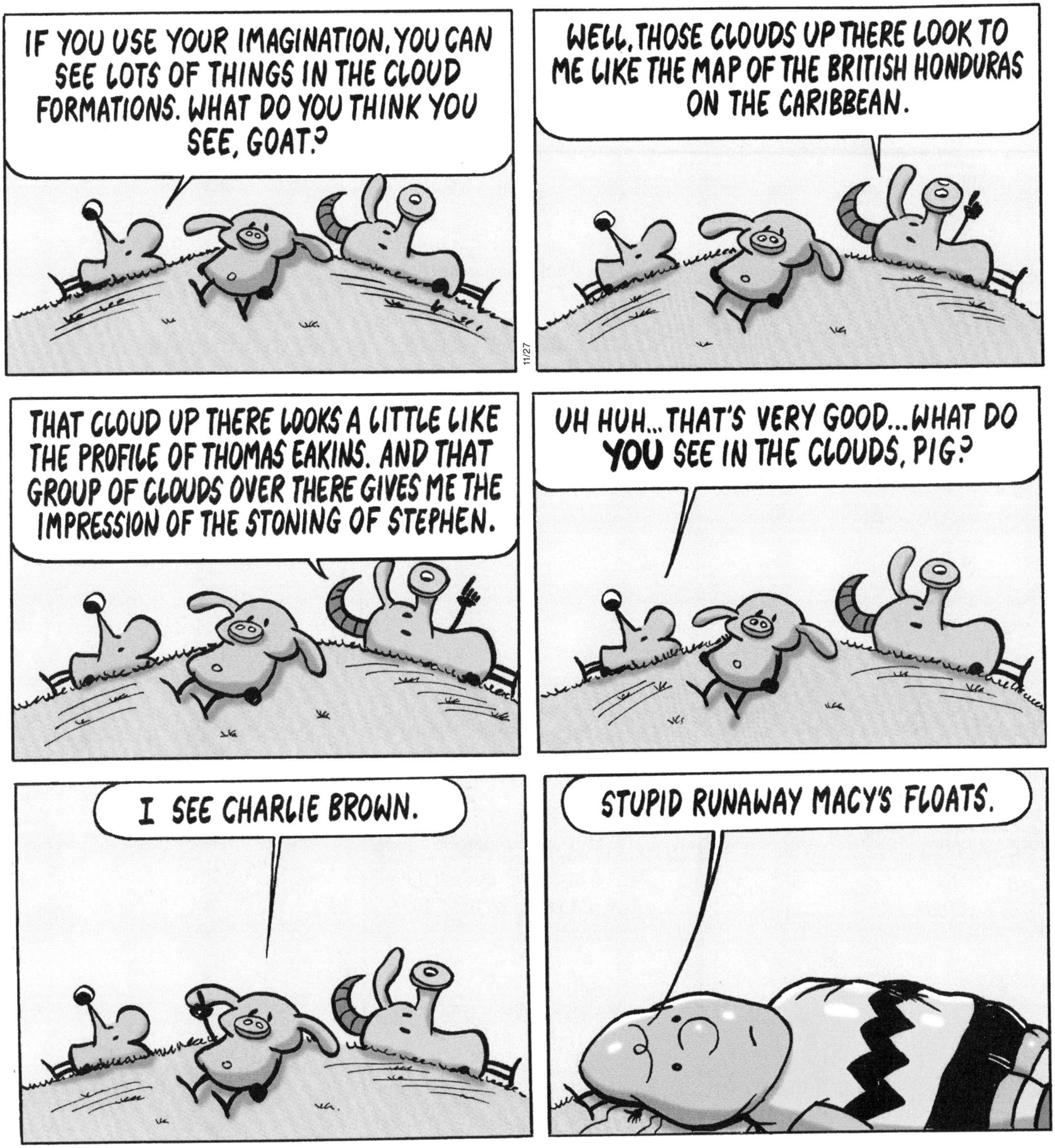
IF YOU USE YOUR IMAGINATION, YOU CAN SEE LOTS OF THINGS IN THE CLOUD FORMATIONS. WHAT DO YOU THINK YOU SEE, GOAT?
WELL, THOSE CLOUDS UP THERE LOOK TO ME LIKE THE MAP OF THE BRITISH HONDURAS ON THE CARIBBEAN.
11/27
THAT CLOUD UP THERE LOOKS A LITTLE LIKE THE PROFILE OF THOMAS EAKINS. AND THAT GROUP OF CLOUDS OVER THERE GIVES ME THE IMPRESSION OF THE STONING OF STEPHEN.
UH HUH... THAT'S VERY GOOD... WHAT DO YOU SEE IN THE CLOUDS, PIG?
I SEE CHARLIE BROWN.
STUPID RUNAWAY MACY'S FLOATS.

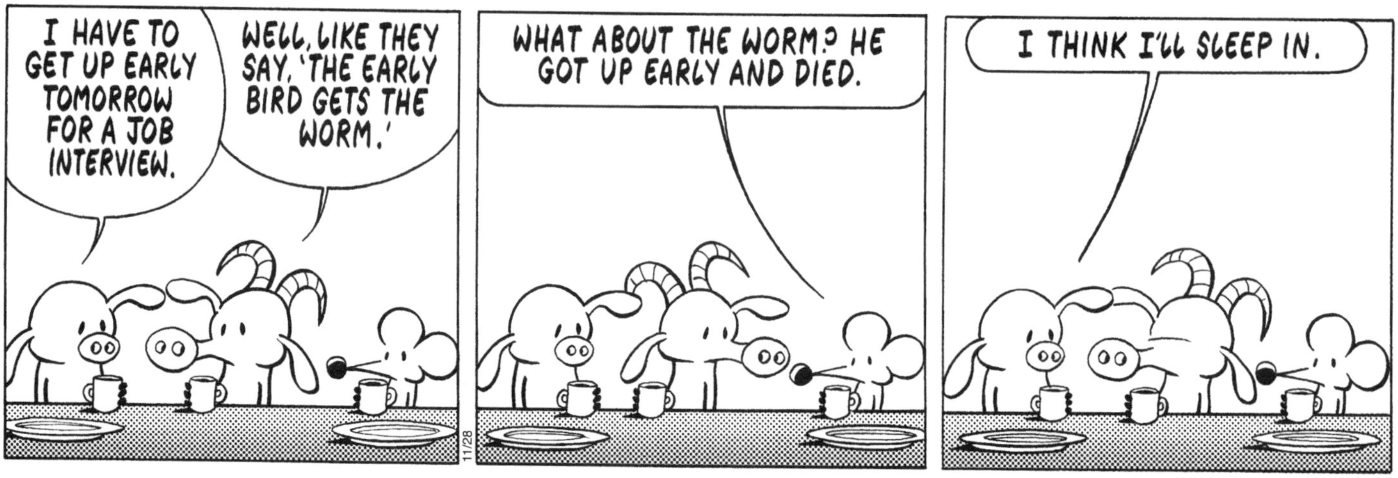

I HAVE TO GET UP EARLY TOMORROW FOR A JOB INTERVIEW.
WELL, LIKE THEY SAY, 'THE EARLY BIRD GETS THE WORM.'
WHAT ABOUT THE WORM? HE GOT UP EARLY AND DIED.
I THINK I'LL SLEEP IN.
11/28

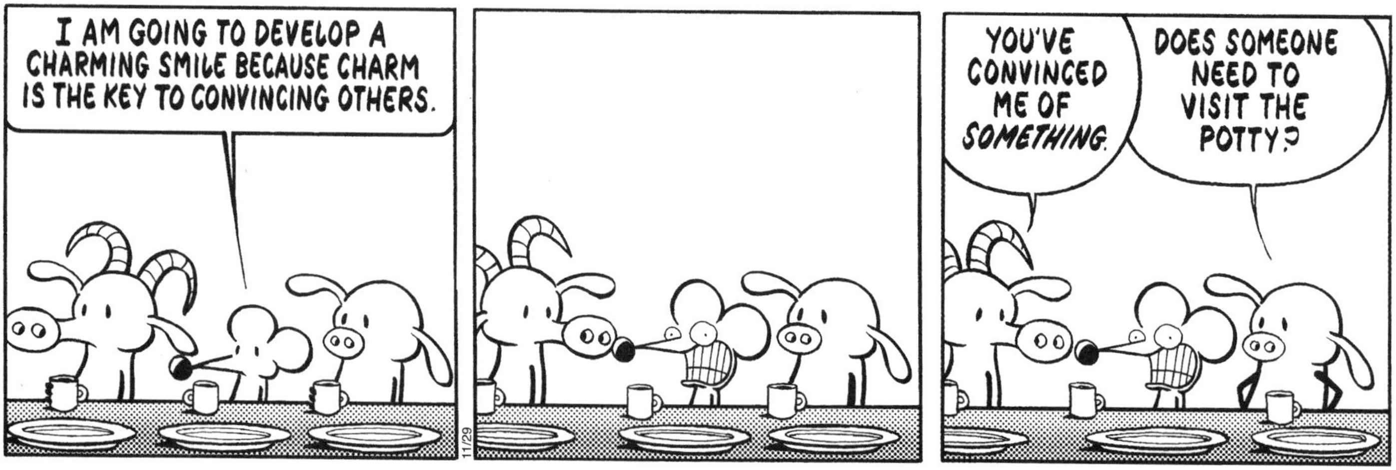

I AM GOING TO DEVELOP A CHARMING SMILE BECAUSE CHARM IS THE KEY TO CONVINCING OTHERS.
YOU'VE CONVINCED ME OF *SOMETHING*.
DOES SOMEONE NEED TO VISIT THE POTTY?
11/29

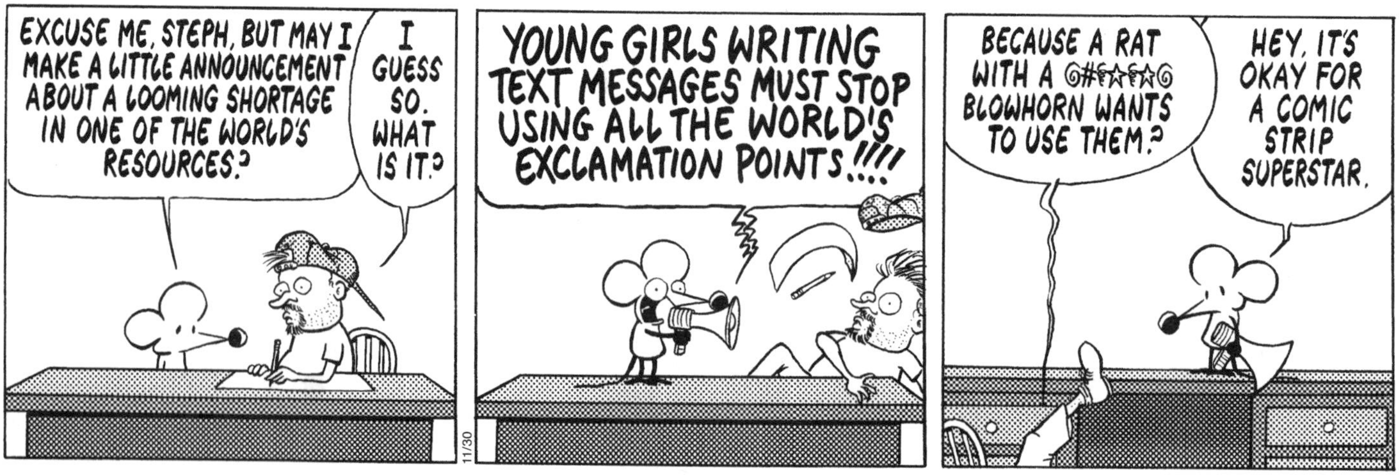

EXCUSE ME, STEPH, BUT MAY I MAKE A LITTLE ANNOUNCEMENT ABOUT A LOOMING SHORTAGE IN ONE OF THE WORLD'S RESOURCES?
I GUESS SO. WHAT IS IT?
YOUNG GIRLS WRITING TEXT MESSAGES MUST STOP USING ALL THE WORLD'S EXCLAMATION POINTS!!!!
BECAUSE A RAT WITH A @#$☆$☆@ BLOWHORN WANTS TO USE THEM?
HEY, IT'S OKAY FOR A COMIC STRIP SUPERSTAR.
11/30

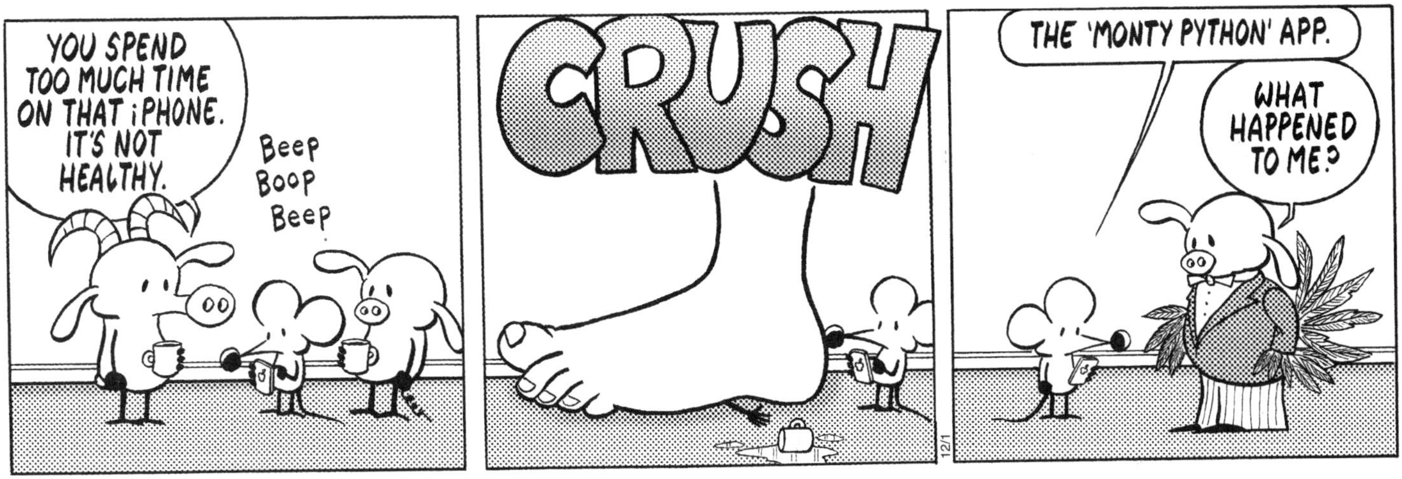
YOU SPEND TOO MUCH TIME ON THAT iPHONE. IT'S NOT HEALTHY.
Beep Boop Beep
CRUSH
THE 'MONTY PYTHON' APP.
WHAT HAPPENED TO ME?
12/1

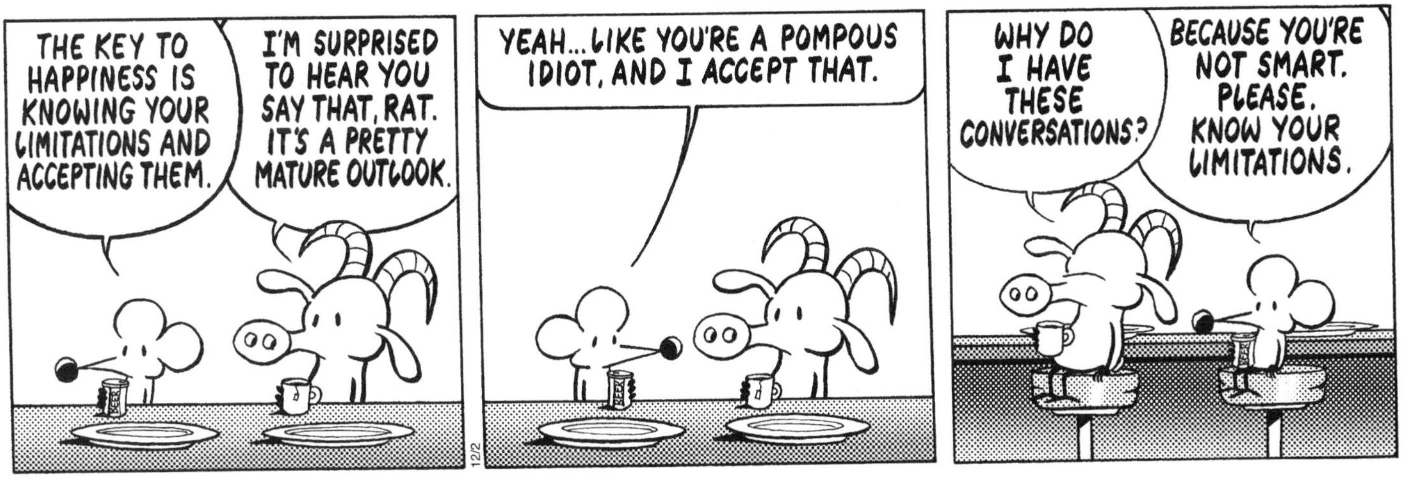
THE KEY TO HAPPINESS IS KNOWING YOUR LIMITATIONS AND ACCEPTING THEM.
I'M SURPRISED TO HEAR YOU SAY THAT, RAT. IT'S A PRETTY MATURE OUTLOOK.
YEAH... LIKE YOU'RE A POMPOUS IDIOT, AND I ACCEPT THAT.
WHY DO I HAVE THESE CONVERSATIONS?
BECAUSE YOU'RE NOT SMART. PLEASE. KNOW YOUR LIMITATIONS.
12/2

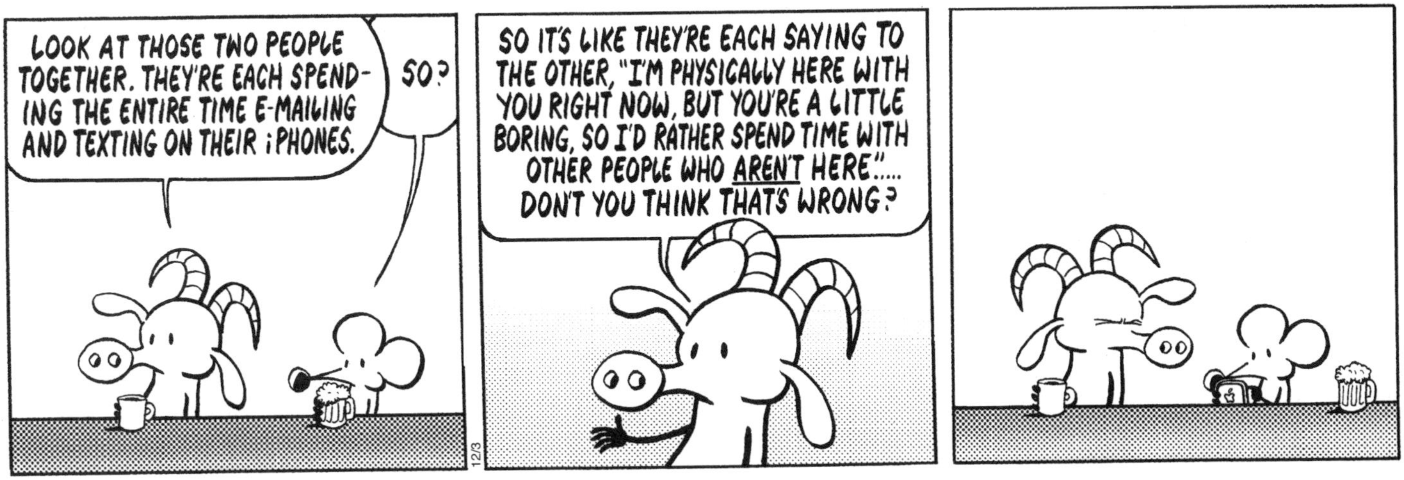
LOOK AT THOSE TWO PEOPLE TOGETHER. THEY'RE EACH SPENDING THE ENTIRE TIME E-MAILING AND TEXTING ON THEIR iPHONES.
SO?
SO IT'S LIKE THEY'RE EACH SAYING TO THE OTHER, "I'M PHYSICALLY HERE WITH YOU RIGHT NOW, BUT YOU'RE A LITTLE BORING, SO I'D RATHER SPEND TIME WITH OTHER PEOPLE WHO AREN'T HERE."..... DON'T YOU THINK THAT'S WRONG?
12/3

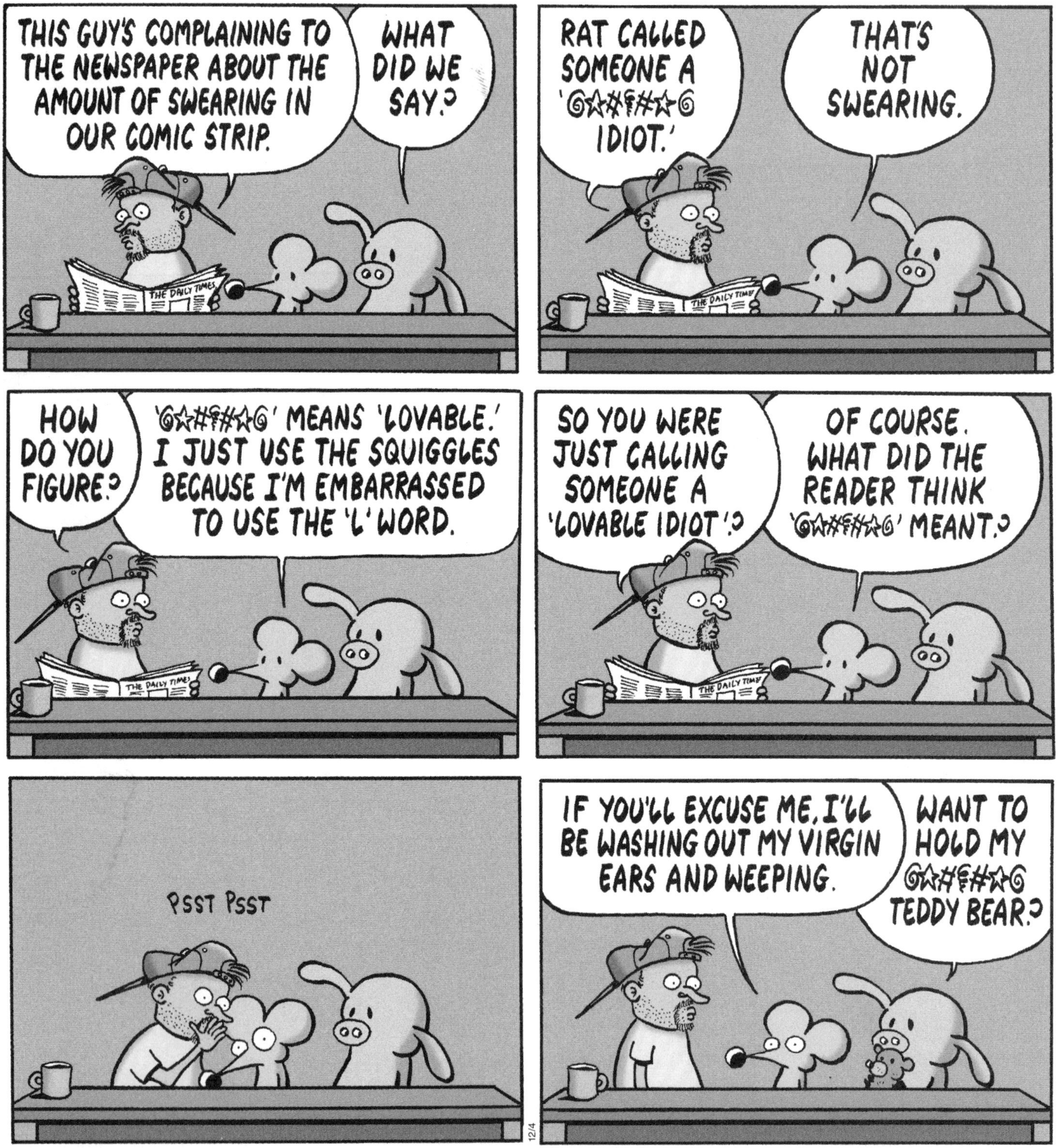
THIS GUY'S COMPLAINING TO THE NEWSPAPER ABOUT THE AMOUNT OF SWEARING IN OUR COMIC STRIP.
WHAT DID WE SAY?
RAT CALLED SOMEONE A '@☆#$#☆@ IDIOT.'
THAT'S NOT SWEARING.
HOW DO YOU FIGURE?
'@☆#$#☆@' MEANS 'LOVABLE.' I JUST USE THE SQUIGGLES BECAUSE I'M EMBARRASSED TO USE THE 'L' WORD.
SO YOU WERE JUST CALLING SOMEONE A 'LOVABLE IDIOT'?
OF COURSE. WHAT DID THE READER THINK '@☆#$#☆@' MEANT?
PSST PSST
IF YOU'LL EXCUSE ME, I'LL BE WASHING OUT MY VIRGIN EARS AND WEEPING.
WANT TO HOLD MY @☆#$#☆@ TEDDY BEAR?